A BRIEF HISTORY OF IRELAND

PAUL F. STATE

An imprint of Infobase Publishing

A Brief History of Ireland

Copyright © 2009 by Paul F. State

Facts On File, Inc.
An imprint of Infobase Publishing
132 West 31st Street
New York NY 10001

Library of Congress Cataloging-in-Publication Data
State, Paul F.
   A brief history of Ireland / Paul F. State.
      p. cm.
   Includes bibliographical references and index.
   ISBN-13: 978-0-8160-7516-4 (acid-free paper)
   ISBN-10: 0-8160-7516-6 (acid-free paper) 1. Ireland—History. I. Title.
   DA910.S73 2009
   941.5—dc22   2008029243

Text design by Lina Farinella
Cover design by Semadar Megged / Takeshi Takahashi
Maps by Jeremy Eagle

Printed in the United States of America

Bang Hermitage 10 9 8 7 6 5 4 3 2 1

This book is printed on acid-free paper.

This book is dedicated to
Thomas James Quinlivan (1954–1999),
an American heir of Erin's heritage and
a wonderful friend of enduring memory.

CONTENTS

LIST OF ILLUSTRATIONS

LIST OF MAPS

ACKNOWLEDGMENTS

I would like to express my sincere appreciation to the staffs of the National Museum of Ireland, Trinity College Dublin, the New York Public Library, and the National Library of Ireland for their kind assistance with my research. A special thank-you to Justin Furlong and Sandra McDermott of the National Library of Ireland for permission to use prints from the library collection. My thanks to my editor at Facts On File, Claudia Schaab, for her always insightful input. Thanks are also due to Michael G. Laraque, chief copy editor at Facts On File, whose attention to detail is without equal.

INTRODUCTION

The history of Ireland (in Irish, Éire) is rooted in the central fact of its geography. A windswept island located on the very western fringe of the European continent, Ireland remained relatively remote from cultural, economic, and political currents emanating from the east. At times, Ireland found itself only tangentially touched by events (the Roman Empire). At other times, it was one of the last places in Europe to be affected by developments (Celtic settlements). On very rare occasions, Ireland served as either a guardian or a source of happenings of profound importance to general European history (post-Roman cultural preservation, spread of Christianity). Its close geographical proximity to the larger island of Great Britain just to the east has proved of paramount significance. Since the Middle Ages interaction and confrontation between the peoples and cultures of the two islands have shaped Ireland's story line. Beginning in the 16th century, the political and cultural colonization of Ireland, introduced by fits and starts centuries before, intensified, culminating in 1801 in the absorption of Ireland into Great Britain.

The Irish fought back. In doing so, they drew on an impressive history that predated the English conquest. Ireland possessed a complex indigenous social system, which had evolved since ancient times, replete with a vibrant native culture, distinguished by the oldest vernacular literature in Europe north of the Alps. In the fifth century the Irish took readily to Christianity, incorporating the new faith into the fabric of their society. Although the island lay outside the mainstream of ancient Western civilization—Ireland had never been a part of the Roman Empire—in a reversal of roles, Irish monastic settlements played a major part in preserving classical learning during Europe's "Dark Ages" while, at the same time, scholarly Irish clerics set out across the Continent on missions of conversion.

The Irish struggled, first, to retain their separate ethnic identity, defined by a distinctive language and cultural traditions and by the Roman Catholic religion, and, later, beginning in the late 18th century with the rise of political nationalism, to win varying degrees of autonomy and then actual independence. Religious discord, social and political instability, and outbreaks of armed rebellion mark the historical record. Long the inveterate losers, the Irish managed to survive and, in the end, they succeeded in securing their cherished goal of national self-identity.

In place of the starkly contrasting black-and-white coloring that can be applied to so much of Ireland's past history in which successive English victories always meant Irish defeats, the modern country is set in tones of gray. A democratic, prosperous nation open to the world, Ireland today comprises a synthesis of both Irish and English heritages, and the Irish people seem increasingly at ease with that reality. English became and remains the dominant tongue, but the Irish Gaelic language is a living presence. Ireland is the world's only Celtic independent nation. As heirs of this rich bicultural heritage, the Irish are renowned for their ability to craft remarkable works in literature, song, and dance. And as a country that is at once an ex-colony and a Western nation with a political system modeled partly on that of its former ruler, Ireland offers a unique guide for developing countries worldwide.

The island's partition between North and South—the outstanding surviving legacy of the past—grows ever more muted as an issue of contention. Substantial progress has been made toward resolution of the violent struggle in Northern Ireland, which, with its sectarian hatreds, terrorism, and state repression, has served for 30 years as a playback of all that has been most tragic in Ireland's history. Reconciliation and cooperation increasingly characterize Northern Ireland's social and political scene.

Even one of Ireland's major historical misfortunes has become a source of pride and strength. Religious persecution, famine, and economic destitution forced generations of Irish to emigrate, leading, for over a century, to steady demographic declines. But the loss of so many is counted as a gain by those living in Ireland today. This small island boasts a globe-girdling presence thanks to Irish emigrants who settled in many lands—their legacy on display in the social and political achievements of their descendants—and the cultural symbols that they took with them make Ireland identifiable virtually everywhere.

Recent economic and social progress have brought booming prosperity and broadening outlooks that serve to dim the power of age-old memories in Ireland today—memories that forged the mental armor and primed the weapons that drove so much of the country's conflicted history. Time, for so long Ireland's curse in tolling back to remembered hurts and defeats, now marches ahead to an uplifting beat.

The Land

Ireland is an island situated in the North Atlantic Ocean. Located at 51.5° and 55.5° north latitude and 5.5° and 10.5° west longitude, it occupies the westernmost fringe of the Eurasian continental shelf. The third-largest island in Europe after Great Britain and Iceland, Ireland is shadowed from the east by Great Britain, from which it is separated by narrow, easily navigable seas—from the northeast coast of Ireland, Scotland is easily seen. Britain in turn not only separates it from, but also links it with, the European landmass. Its westerly location puts

Provinces and Counties of Ireland

SCOTLAND (U.K.)

North Channel

ATLANTIC OCEAN

Aran I.

Gwecbarra Bay

Donegal

Londonderry
Londonderry
Antrim

NORTHERN IRELAND (U.K.)

Tyrone

Ulster

Lough Neagh

Belfast

Lisburn

Down

Donegal Bay

Innisfree I.

Sligo Bay

Fermanagh

Armagh

Monaghan

Carlingford Lough

Blacksod Bay

Lough Conn

Achill I.

Clare I.

Clew Bay

Mayo

Lough Mask

Lough Corrib

Connacht

Sligo

Leitrim

Cavan

Louth

Roscommon

Longford

Meath

Dough Ree

Westmeath

Leinster

Dublin
Dublin

Galway

Galway

Galway Bay

Aran Is.

REPUBLIC OF IRELAND

Offaly

Lough Derg

Kildare

Laois

Wicklow

Irish Sea

Clare

Kilkenny

Carlow

Limerick

Tipperary

Kilkenny

Limerick

Wexford

Blasket Is.

Munster

Cork

Waterford
Waterford

Saltee Is.

St. George's Channel

Valentia I.

Kerry

Cork

Cork

Bear I.

Clear I.

N

National border
Province border
County border
Ulster Province
Cork County

0   50 miles
0   50 km

© Infobase Publishing

Ireland closer to the North American continent than any part of Europe except Iceland.

Ireland totals 32,052 square miles (83,015 sq. km). Its geography consists largely, but not uniformly, of a flat central plain ringed by gradually rising highlands and steep-sided glens around the coastal perimeter. The geology reflects the physical legacy of the lengthy ice ages. The mountains of the northwest comprise the western extension of a tectonic system that runs through the highlands of Scotland to Scandinavia, while those of the south constitute a parallel connection to southern England and Brittany in France. The oldest hills, composed of Caledonian quartzites and granites, are found in counties Donegal and Mayo and in the Connemara region of western County Galway. Higher mountains are not high by European standards, most rising above 1,000 feet (300 m) with many peaks of 3,000 feet (900 m). Ireland's highest summit is Carrantuohill in County Kerry at 3,414 feet (1,040 m). Altogether, hills make up about one-eighth of the land surface.

Central areas consist primarily of a Carboniferous limestone lowland, which gives rise to the relatively fertile, lush landscape of lasting fame, together with a cover of glacial drift that, in places, accounts for an undulating terrain. Bare peat bog and bog pastureland lace the land running north from County Laois through counties Offaly, Westmeath, Longford, and Roscommon. The limestone is exposed most prominently in the Burren region of northern County Clare, where it slopes down to the sea in a series of terraces. Much of County Antrim in the northeast is unique in that it consists of a plateau of basalt of volcanic origin, while a major portion of the southern province of Munster is made up of a sandstone base. During the Pleistocene period, the ice advanced and retreated from the northeast, altering the shape of many valleys and producing, in the north, a maze of many small hills called drumlins and eskers, packed tightly together, low but very steep, and interspersed with patches of bog and lakes. Where drainage was poor, they proved difficult to traverse.

Rocky wasteland, covered with bogs and coarse grass and heather, make up about a third of the terrain in the Republic of Ireland. Forests, once abundant but long since cut down for fuel, account for less than 3 percent of the area despite vigorous reforestation efforts, chiefly in conifers. Nearly half of the country consists of pastureland, while in areas that are cultivable, soils vary in fertility, with a tendency toward acidity, and they are markedly more shallow in the west.

The long Irish coastline (1,988 miles; 3,200 km) features deep bays formed by submerged former river valleys that can extend far inland; rock cliffs, most famously those of Moher in County Clare; and many sandy beaches, especially along the south coast of County Wicklow and in counties Wexford and Waterford. The coasts are sprinkled with tiny offshore islands, found primarily in the west, notably the Skellig Islands of historical repute and the Aran Islands of cultural import.

The clinging hills that characterize the coastal pattern are broken in the area between Dundalk and Dublin, a gap that, because it features fewer mountains and bog, facilitated settlement of the interior from this region.

The many rivers that intersect the landscape also aided settlement. On a small island, they are nowhere long, although the Shannon (An tSionna, "the old one," named for the ancient goddess Sinann) is the longest river in the British Isles, running 224 miles (360.4 km). Lakes are numerous. They range from small ones of glacial origin in the mountains and among the drumlins—the lakes and mountains of Killarney are major tourist draws—to larger bodies that form part of the river systems, the most extensive of which are the Shannon, Corrib, and Erne groups. Lough Neagh in Northern Ireland, at 153 square miles (396 sq. km), is the largest lake in the British Isles.

Climate extremes are muted by the warm waters of the North Atlantic drift flowing offshore. The mean temperature is 39–46°F (4–8°C) in January and 59–63°F (15–17°C) in July. Maritime conditions predominate year-round with prevailing northwesterly winds blowing from the Atlantic, which, along with cyclonic depressions, bring frequent rain. The mean annual rainfall is between 28 inches

The Ladies' View, Lake District, County Kerry. The panorama takes its name from the pleasure expressed by Queen Victoria's ladies-in-waiting on their visit in September 1861. (Archive Timothy McCarthy/Art Resource, NY)

and 142 inches (700 and 3,600 mm), decreasing from west to east and from higher to lower regions. Rainfall is the outstanding feature of the climate. Mild, moist conditions produce a long growing season for grass, and livestock are able to graze out of doors throughout the year. High winds near the north and west coasts limit tree growth here. Inland areas are warmer in summer and colder in winter. The mildest climate featuring the most sunshine and the lowest average rainfall is found in the southeast.

Because Ireland was isolated by rising sea levels after the ice ages, the island is host to only a small number of native plant and animal species. Only 26 land animals are native to Ireland. The red fox, hedgehog, and badger are very common, while the red deer and Irish hare are less so. The great Irish elk, great auk, and wolf, once found in abundance, are extinct, while the golden eagle, also formerly found in Ireland, is being reintroduced. There are no snakes, and only one reptile—the common lizard—is native to Ireland.

The People

The Irish population stands at approximately 6 million (2007 est.). The number includes 4.25 million in the Republic of Ireland and 1.75 million in Northern Ireland. The population has shown steady increases since the 1980s.

Inhabited for at least 9,000 years, Ireland was a place of immigration from its earliest beginnings. Little factual information is available on the earliest peoples, the historical and mythological records inextricably mixed. The Celts began to arrive around 500 B.C.E., and they came to dominate, laying the foundations for Ireland's modern-day ethnic identity. Celtic society survived for 1,000 years, resisting challenges from newcomers, many of whom adopted Celtic customs. Later arrivals included, in succession, Vikings, Normans, Scots, and English. The latter two began to settle in significant numbers in the late 1500s, and their presence today is most pronounced in Northern Ireland.

Beginning in the 17th century, Ireland experienced growing levels of emigration, although its population increased steadily, reaching 8.17 million in 1841. The Great Famine of the mid 19th century, through heavy mortality, delayed marriage, and external migration, launched a steady decline that, propelled in succeeding decades by persistent high levels of poverty, continued into the mid 20th century. The country's population plummeted, falling to 4.2 million islandwide by 1971.

Growing prosperity in the mid 1980s started a slow upward trend that continues to accelerate. Accompanying its growing wealth, the Republic of Ireland is today again a country of immigration. A member of the European Union, Ireland has witnessed increasing numbers of arrivals from Poland, the Czech Republic, Latvia, and Lithuania since admission of these and other eastern European countries to the union in 2004. But people from outside Europe, notably from mainland China and Nigeria, have also come to Ireland during the past decade.

Ireland's largest religious faith is Roman Catholicism, professed by about 70 percent of the population islandwide and 80 percent in the republic. Protestant denominations predominate among the rest of the inhabitants, including the Anglican Church of Ireland—the largest islandwide—as well as Presbyterianism and Methodism. A tiny Jewish community (about 1,800) and a small, though growing, Muslim population (32,539, 2006 est.) also exist.

In Northern Ireland approximately 53.1 percent of the population identify themselves as Protestants and 43.8 percent as Roman Catholics. The demographic balance between the two grows increasingly delicate given that Catholic numbers show steady gains over Protestant. While they continue to constitute a majority, the Protestants are themselves divided into several denominations, including, in descending order of size, the Presbyterians, Anglicans, Methodists, and several others. Since the political violence that began in 1969, many Protestants have moved away from border areas; thus, the counties of Londonderry, Fermanagh, and Tyrone have large Catholic majorities, while eastern areas have increased their proportions of Protestants, except for the city of Belfast, where Catholics dominate.

The Republic of Ireland's official first language is Gaelic (*Gaeilge*), colloquially known as Irish, although English is spoken as the first language by the vast majority of the population. Irish features a number of regional dialects, and although it is spoken as a first language by only about 260,000 inhabitants, approximately 1.8 million claim some degree of linguistic facility. It is the oldest among the Goidelic (or Gaelic) subfamily of Indo-European languages, which includes, in addition to Irish, Scottish Gaelic (or Erse) and Manx, spoken on the Isle of Man. Until the early 19th century, Irish was widely spoken throughout the country, but it is now largely confined to extreme western coastal areas known as the Gaeltacht (Gaeltachtaí). In Northern Ireland, approximately 2 percent of the population claim to speak Ulster Scots, a dialect of Scottish Gaelic spoken by descendants of settlers from Scotland.

The Government

Ireland is divided politically between the Republic of Ireland (in Irish, Poblacht na hÉireann), which occupies five-sixths of the island's territory and comprises 26 counties in the south, east, and west, and Northern Ireland, which is composed of six counties in the remaining one-sixth in the extreme northeastern corner.

The Republic of Ireland is an independent, democratic state with a presidential, cabinet-style government. It became a republic in 1949 when Commonwealth ties with the United Kingdom were severed.

The president of Ireland is the head of state and is elected by direct popular vote for a seven-year term. Largely a ceremonial office, the president is responsible for appointing the government, convening and dissolving the lower house of parliament, signing bills into law, and representing the state in foreign affairs. The president's official residence is Áras an Uachteráin, located in Phoenix Park, Dublin.

Lawmaking powers are vested in a bicameral legislature, known as the Oireachtas. The lower house, or the Dáil Éireann, is elected directly by the public. Totaling 166 members, who are each known as a Teachta Dála (TD), or deputy, the Dáil has the power to pass virtually any law it wishes. The upper house, or Seanad Éireann, has 60 members, 11 appointed by the prime minister, six elected by the universities, and 43 chosen by an electoral college made up of five panels—Cultural and Educational, Agricultural, Labour, Industrial and Commercial, and Administrative—of some 900 representatives with knowledge of, and expertise in, the subjects represented by each panel. The upper house can initiate bills, other than money bills, and annul statutory instruments. It has complementary powers with the Dáil in broad areas, including the declaration and termination of a state of emergency and the removal from office of the president or a judge. However, its powers are more limited in that, while it can delay, it can never prevent passage of legislation. Since 1922, the Oireachtas has met in Leinster House in Dublin.

Members of the Dáil are elected from various political parties through a system of proportional representation by means of the Single Transferable Vote system. Under the system, an individual's vote is first allocated to the most preferred candidate and, after candidates have been either elected or eliminated, any unneeded or unused votes are transferred according to the voter's stated preference. Elections must be held at least once every five years. The most important political parties are Fianna Fáil and Fine Gael, in existence since the 1920s and the 1930s, respectively, which have remained consistently the two largest parties. Others include the Progressive Democratic Party, Labour Party,

Green Party, and Sinn Féin. Voting is open to men and women 18 years of age and older.

The lower house has the power to sustain or bring down governments in the parliamentary tradition. Executive power rests with a cabinet, which forms a government of some 15 ministers. The cabinet is responsible to the Dáil. The head of the government is the Taoiseach (prime minister), who is appointed by the president after nomination by the lower house and who can be removed by the same body. Members of the government head the administrative departments, or ministries. They are chosen by the Taoiseach, approved by the Dáil, and appointed by the president.

Ireland is a common law jurisdiction in which trial by jury is customary for serious offenses. Judicial authority is vested in superior courts and lower courts. Superior courts include the Supreme Court and the High Court. The Supreme Court is the court of final appeal. Both courts hold the power of judicial review to determine the constitutionality of all laws. The High Court holds additional powers to try the most serious criminal and civil cases and to hear certain appeals from lower courts. When it sits as a criminal court it is called the Central Criminal Court. Lower courts include circuit courts and district courts. Circuit courts deal with matters that require a jury trial, while district courts handle minor matters. Judges are appointed by the president on the recommendation of the government.

Counties are governed by county councils, which include 29 councils following the split of County Dublin into Dun Laoghaire–Rathdown, Fingal, and South Dublin in 1994 and the division of County Tipperary into North Tipperary and South Tipperary in 2002. The five cities of Dublin, Cork, Limerick, Galway, and Waterford are governed by city councils (formerly known as corporations). Services administered at the local level include health and sanitation, housing, water supply, and libraries. Local officials are popularly elected, usually for five-year terms.

Ireland is divided into four traditional provinces: Connacht, Leinster, Munster, and Ulster. They derive from ancient Celtic kingdoms, but today they designate only geographic regions.

Northern Ireland comprises six of the nine counties of the ancient province of Ulster. It constitutes one of the four "home nations"—the constituent countries—that make up the United Kingdom of Great Britain and Northern Ireland, namely, England, Scotland, Wales, and Northern Ireland. The British government's Northern Ireland Office, headed by the secretary of state for Northern Ireland, oversees constitutional, police, and justice affairs. The head of state is the British monarch.

The Northern Ireland Assembly is the legislature of Northern Ireland. The assembly is a unicameral body comprising 108 members elected by universal adult suffrage (18 years and older) from 18 six-member constituencies under the Single Transferable Vote form of proportional representation. Elections must take place at least once every five years, set for the first Thursday in May unless the assembly is dissolved earlier.

The assembly elects the first minister, who also serves as head of the Northern Ireland Executive, and the deputy first minister, his second in command. Remaining ministers on the executive are not elected but rather are chosen by nominating officers of each political party, and each party is entitled to a share of ministerial positions roughly proportional to its share of seats in the assembly. Political parties, among others, include unionist parties—the Ulster Unionist Party and the Democratic Unionist Party—that support union with Great Britain; nationalist parties—Sinn Féin and the Social Democratic Labour Party—that support union with the Republic of Ireland; and nonaligned parties, the Alliance Party and the Green Party, which transcend the two communities in appealing to voters on both sides. Every member of the assembly (MLA) is designated officially as "unionist," "nationalist," or "nonaligned." The election of the heads of the Northern Ireland Executive, the assembly's speaker and deputy speakers, any changes to the assembly's standing orders, and certain money bills must obtain cross-community support.

The assembly is chaired by the Speaker and three deputy Speakers. Powers have been devolved to it to legislate in fields known as "transferred matters," which include education, social development, trade and investment, and culture, arts, and leisure. "Excepted matters," such as criminal law, police, and telecommunications, and "reserved matters," such as royal succession, international relations, defense, and currency, are retained by the British parliament in London. All bills passed by the assembly must receive the royal assent, and all laws are subject to judicial review. The assembly meets at the parliament buildings at Stormont in Belfast.

The head of the judiciary is the lord chief justice of Northern Ireland, who presides over the courts. The British House of Lords is the highest court of appeal, but it will be replaced in that role by the Supreme Court of the United Kingdom, which was statutorily approved in 2005 and will become operative in 2009. Other courts include the Court of Appeal, High Court, and various lower courts.

Northern Ireland is divided into 26 local districts each with elected councils. Local governments are responsible for licensing, economic development, sanitation, and arts and cultural events, and they have an advisory role in provision of regional services such as planning, education, housing, and health and social welfare.

The Economy

The Republic of Ireland's economy is small but modern, robust, and prosperous. Growth since 1995 has proven among the most rapid anywhere on the globe, transforming a once poor nation into one of the world's wealthiest. Measurements of national income and output rank among the highest both globally and among the member states of the European Union, which Ireland joined in 1973.

A country with an economy rooted from its origins in farming and fishing activities is today a pacesetter in the production of high-tech products. Major multinationals manufacture computers, computer parts, and software, much of it for the European market. Machinery, chemicals, steel, transportation equipment, clothing, and textiles make up parts of the manufacturing mix. The construction industry, a consequence of the economic boom, has become a major component of the economy. The nation boasts few major, indigenous multinational companies (AIB, Kerry Group, Ryanair), although the Guinness Brewing Company, universally recognized for its trademark Irish product, has long been marketed worldwide.

Services account for about half of Irish economic activity today, employing about two-thirds of workers. Customer and legal service firms as well as finance and stock-broking companies, most U.S.-based, avail themselves of the country's youthful, educated workforce whose fluency in English makes them attractive in the global economy. Tourism earns major revenues in drawing visitors—many descendants of Ireland's millions of emigrants—and they help to sustain specialty industries, including high-quality glass and crystal ware, linen and lace, and wearable woolens.

The lush green pasturage that once supported Ireland's agriculture-based economy now accounts for only about 5 percent of economic activity and less than 10 percent of exports. Cattle, beef, and dairy products are the principal agricultural products, and they are exported mainly to the traditional U.K. market. The main crops are barley, wheat, oats, sugar beets, potatoes, and mushrooms. Ocean fishing, especially in cod, and freshwater catches of salmon and trout have suffered from

A man and a woman dig and collect peat in a bog, ca. 1915. (Library of Congress LC- USZ62-123763)

overexploitation. Ireland is a major exporter of zinc to the European Union, and significant deposits of lead, gypsum, and limestone exist together with small amounts of copper, silver, gold, and bauxite.

The Irish Republic possesses a mixed public/private ownership economy. The government controls much of the market in electricity generation, and it owns most of the bus and all of the railway networks. In addition, the government holds financial and regulatory control of the radio and television broadcasting sector. Aer Lingus, the government-owned airline, was privatized in 2006, and reforms to open up other public industries to private competition are under way.

All of Ireland is heavily dependent on imports for energy supplies, primarily fossil fuels that include oil and coal, though the governments are actively encouraging and assisting alternative sources. Peat, for centuries the traditional fuel, remains in abundance though ecologically deleterious.

Hydroelectric power has been available since the 1930s. Natural gas was first found in the mid 1970s at the Kinsale Head off County Cork. In 1999, Enterprise Oil announced the discovery of the Corrib Field off County Mayo. Fields off the west coast are exploited, and exploratory drilling is ongoing there and in the Irish Sea and St. Georges Channel. Large wind farms are under construction in coastal counties. The facility under development at Arklow Bank off the coast of County Wicklow is expected to be the world's largest offshore wind farm, and it is forecast to supply 10 percent of Ireland's energy needs when finished.

The traditional economic activities of Northern Ireland include textiles and shipbuilding, but these have declined while high-tech, capital-intensive industries have grown. Machinery and equipment making, chemicals, food processing, and electronics manufacturing are the leading industries, and aerospace production and paper and furniture making are also important. Heavy industry is centered in and around Belfast and Londonderry. Livestock and dairy production account for the majority of agricultural output. Potatoes, barley, and wheat are the chief crops.

1

BEGINNINGS TO THE END OF PAGAN IRELAND (PREHISTORY–431)

Ireland did not emerge on the earth's geographic map until the great ice sheets that had covered the Northern Hemisphere for countless millennia melted and the rising waters they left in their wake encircled the higher land that now lay exposed, creating an island off the westernmost fringe of the immense Eurasian landmass. The place that would become Ireland remained barren and forbidding until climatic changes made possible a profusion of life forms. The greenery that carpeted the island emerged eventually as dense forest, interlaced everywhere by networks of streams, rivers, and lakes.

Drawn by the wealth of resources found in the woods and waters here, the first hunters and gatherers appeared. Successive waves of people crossing the seas brought technological abilities, progressively more skilled, based on rendering earthy or mineral matter into usable tools and weapons—starting with stone and advancing to bronze. Massive stone burial tombs attest to a search by the prehistoric Irish for spiritual sustenance and give evidence that Ireland had an impressive culture in the Neolithic period and the Bronze Age. Iron—the last of the ores to arrive—constituted the strongest of all the metals worked, and the Celts, the people who brought the iron, proved the most powerful of all the newcomers. They settled across the island and ruled a myriad of kingdoms, bringing patterns of social organization that survived for a thousand years and a language that endures today. Celtic society remained intact when the Roman Empire, which had swept across much of Europe, stopped at the shores of the Irish Sea. Ireland was left undisturbed, to be conquered in time by a force of another kind. The Irish would succumb not to the might of imperial arms but to the spiritual power of a new religious faith nurtured in the very same empire that never ruled here.

In time slightly cooler temperatures prevailed and rainfall increased, creating boglands—areas of muck and mire—whose ideal conditions for preservation have allowed researchers to uncover physical evidence of how the early Irish lived, worked, and dressed during a period of time for which the only other sources are orally transmitted legends and tales written down many centuries later. The boglands still blotch the terrain, and searchers find much material heritage—tools, weapons, and adornments—in their watery confines. And the monuments in stone also remain. These are the sources that tell us something of the lives of Ireland's earliest inhabitants.

The Land Takes Shape

Ireland emerged in conjunction with the rest of the northwestern European continent from the great ice sheets that covered most of the land for millions of years. From approximately 1.7 million to 13,000 years ago, the ground lay frozen, crushed under a thick, heavy blanket of ice that stretched from Ireland to Britain and across northern and central Europe.

The ice cover, however, did not remain constant. Warm periods would alternate with cold spells, causing the glaciers to periodically retreat and expand. About 75,000 years ago a cold period began, called the Midlothian because its glacial deposits are evident today in the midlands of Ireland. At this time, ice completely covered northern and central parts of the country but only for comparatively short periods of time. The landscape resembled tundra of the kind found today in extreme northern latitudes with the ground supporting a meager plant life. The extreme south of Ireland would have been entirely free of ice. Here rich grasslands interspersed with groves of willow or birch and mottled with marshes would have sustained a varied animal population, which included the woolly mammoth, brown bear, arctic fox, reindeer, and the giant Irish elk.

Cold millennia followed warm. The ice thrust south from the northeast in a final expansionist drive some 15,000 years ago, which lasted until about 11,000 B.C.E. The snow and ice then melted, to be succeeded yet again, a scant 2,000 years later, by a return of frigid temperatures. Finally, in about 8000 B.C.E., a warm phase set in known as the Littletonian, named for a bog in County Tipperary where its history has been calculated by counting plant and tree pollen. Unlike before, higher temperatures did not subsequently abate, and the ice that began to melt everywhere caused sea levels to rise. By about 6000 B.C.E. water flooded the land bridges that until this time connected Ireland in one or more places to Britain. The submersion of the dry ground created the island that Ireland would remain.

While higher elevations—basalt cliffs in Antrim, granite and quartzite mountains in Donegal, Mayo, and Galway—remained barren and forbidding places, the richer midland soils, under a warming sun, sprouted a carpet of meadows and, in succession soon after, groves of juniper, willow, and birch trees. These varied woods flourished especially in upland areas, and by about 3500 B.C.E., they were joined in the lowlands by alder, hazel, elm, and oak. The climate now became slightly wetter, providing conditions for the development of bogs as the land in places turned swampy. A topography of dense forest, bogs, and scrub cover, intersprinkled only by lakes and river-channels left by the melting ice, emerged. Temperate times saw the return of a profusion of warmth-loving plant and animal life, and, endowed with an abundant flora and fauna, the rich landscape drew the first people to Ireland's shores.

The Earliest Settlers
Mesolithic Hunter-Gatherers

No firm proof has been found of human populations in Ireland during the Paleolithic or Old Stone Age period—approximately 20,000 to 15,000 years ago. The first settlers arrived in Ireland during the Mesolithic or Middle Stone Age (about 7500 to 3300 B.C.E.). Traveling along the coastlines and forest edges, fishermen, hunters, and food-gatherers in postglacial Europe would have reached the western shores of Scotland, England, and Wales. How they came to Ireland remains an open question. Scholars debate the date when the land link between Ireland and Britain was severed, and some acknowledge it is possible humans arrived in Ireland on dry land. It is more likely, however, that they sailed across the strait that forms the North Channel to the coast of Antrim, which they could see from the Scottish shore, in small, hide-covered boats called coracles, variants of which remained in use on Irish rivers down to modern times. Others may have reached the island by boat from coastal locations in Wales and northwestern England. New arrivals sheltered along the coast, where they survived by killing game, catching fish, and gathering berries. Soon they ventured inland, following the river-channels and settling on the banks of these sole highways through the dense forests.

Little is known about these earliest inhabitants, but a clearer picture of life during Irish Mesolithic times emerged following excavations at Mount Sandel in County Derry. On a 98.4-foot (30-m)-high bluff overlooking the river Bann, archaeologists, digging in the 1970s, discovered the remnants of a settlement that radiocarbon dating places between approximately 7010 B.C.E. and 6460 B.C.E., which makes it the oldest yet found in Ireland and predates any known site in Britain. Postholes, angled slightly inward, with rounded stains in the ground reveal that dome-shaped dwellings made of saplings bent inward once stood here. These habitations were likely covered with animal skins. Small stakeholes around the remains of a hearth suggest the existence of a primitive structure set up around a fire for cooking purposes, and excavation of duck, grouse, pigeon, and pig bones as well as the remains of eels and both fresh- and saltwater fish such as sea bass and salmon tell us what kinds of food they consumed. Large amounts of waste flint lay scattered around the site together with a few finished tools—choppers, chisels, scrapers, and awls. The flint had been brought probably from the coast of County Antrim, where abundant supplies in the chalk outcroppings may have attracted the first comers to Ireland. Flint finds farther afield—at Lough Boura, near Kilcourne in County Offaly—show that settlement spread to the Irish midlands, discounting the traditional belief that the northeast counties of Antrim and Down dominated among early Mesolithic sites.

Little evidence exists to fill the gap in knowledge of human populations between the early and late Mesolithic periods. Late Mesolithic inhabitants have been distinguished largely on the basis of a change identified in the nature of the stoneware they used. Weightier blades; flint flakes, including the so-called Bann flakes, that show finer trimmings at their ends; larger axes; and heavier bores and picks bearing radiocarbon dates ranging from about 6240 B.C.E. to about 3465 B.C.E. give evidence of the transition to more sophisticated stone tools. Although overseas links had probably ceased, helped by the disappearance between the surging seas of the land bridge with Britain, within Ireland small numbers of people were on the move. Two sites across from each other on Dublin Bay—at Sutton and Dalkey Island—testify to a considerable coastal presence while, at the same time, populations penetrated across Ireland to western sections of Munster, reaching even the very end of the Dingle Peninsula.

Utterly dependent on the bounty of nature, these wandering hunters and fishermen could be found wherever the locale offered the easiest access to both woods and water—on islands and along lakes, rivers, and seashores. They founded no towns, nor even large settlements, and we know nothing of their society, but at some time during the broad span of years after 3000 B.C.E. these last Mesolithic people encountered a new group of settlers. In all probability, they assimilated very gradually with the newcomers, who brought with them a revolutionary way of life first developed more than 3,000 years earlier in the Near East, in the Fertile Crescent of Mesopotamia.

Neolithic Farmers

No change proved more revolutionary between the arrival of the earliest inhabitants and the introduction of Christianity than the coming of agriculture. The start of the Neolithic (or New Stone Age) period during the fourth millennium B.C.E. saw the beginnings of new technologies as the first farmers began to till the soil, thus launching a settled way of life. Just as Neolithic populations had done starting in the Near East and spreading through northwestern Europe, people in Ireland cleared the primeval forest to provide living space and land both to grow crops and to furnish fodder for domesticated animals. Cattle, sheep, and goats—together with cereal crops—appeared in Ireland beginning sometime around 4500 B.C.E., although historians and archaeologists are unsure whether they were brought by a new influx of people who would have arrived gradually in small groups, possibly drawn by the fish along the coast, or whether the population already settled in Ireland acquired agricultural knowledge.

Neolithic farmers occupied the whole of the island, and they possessed a considerable supply of skills and materials. We know something of their way of life thanks to excavations undertaken at Lough Gur in County Limerick. They were observant and innovative, noticing that the richest soils were found where elm trees grew in abundance, and so they settled on light limestone soils in upland areas where forest clearance and construction would have been easier than on the heavier lowland clays. They probably combined crop tillage—growing wheat and barley—with animal pasturage. They learned to move their cattle from lower-lying fertile areas in winter to grassy highlands in the spring, thus freeing up the former for crop cultivation, a practice that would be followed for centuries, which the Irish call booleying (*buailtechas*). Production of butter and cheese began, and wheat was ground for bread.

They built sturdy homes—some round, some rectangular—with walls made of peat on a wooden frame and some with stone foundations.

5

Unlike their Mesolithic predecessors, they cooked indoors by lighting a fire in the center of their dwellings. There would have been several houses in a group, and each settlement would have belonged to a wider group of communities that formed a tribe, the tribes trading with each other.

Pots and potsherds in prolific amounts have been found. Bone tools—borers, needles, and awls—were fashioned, and drum-shaped spindles show that they mastered the art of spinning and weaving. They adorned themselves with beads of stone and bone and bracelets of lignite. Sophisticated stone axes of various sizes for cutting trees and hoeing the ground were crafted. Excavations reveal that stone axes were mass-produced at Rathlin Island and Tievebulliagh in County Antrim in what constituted Ireland's first factories. The axes, made of a distinctive speckled stone, were traded locally and also to the Dublin area, to Lough Gur, and even to southern England, thus initiating Ireland's first export trade.

It is during this period that we learn of the earliest religious beliefs to have played a part in the lives of people in Ireland. The Neolithic Irish were the first in Europe to build in monumental-size stone, constructing not dwellings in which to live but rather burial places for their dead and perhaps temples for their gods. Called megaliths (from the Greek *megos*, "large," and *lithos*, "stone"), these massive tombs contain human remains and sometimes pottery, jewelry, foodstuffs, and weapons, presumably for use in the afterlife. The Irish megaliths can be classified into four main types: portal (dolmen) tombs, the simplest; court tombs, the oldest; wedge tombs, the most abundant; and passage tombs. The bleak and stony Burren (from Irish *bhoireann*, "stony place") in County Clare, which contains western Europe's largest deposits of karstic limestone, is replete with megalithic tomb remnants and relics. Most famously, the portal dolmen at Poulnabrone, which dates to about 2500 B.C.E., features a huge horizontal capstone supported by several upright stone slabs.

Passage tombs are the most impressive type of tombs, representing prehistoric man's earliest great achievement in monumental building in Europe. They are aptly named in consisting of a passage that leads to a burial chamber, both of which are covered by a round mound of stone and earth. Found mostly in the north midlands and especially in the Boyne Valley, they are often grouped together in large cemeteries where one large tomb frequently exists surrounded by smaller satellite burial places.

The best-known and most impressive passage tomb is at Newgrange (Irish, Dún Fhearghusa) in County Meath. It was built about 3200 B.C.E.

Poulnabrone dolmen in the Burren, County Clare (DeA Picture Library/Art Resource, NY)

Newgrange played an important role in early Irish mythology, both as the supposed burial site of the prehistoric kings of Tara and as the home of the Tuatha Dé Danaan ("the people of the goddess Danu"), pre-Celtic inhabitants of Ireland who, in the Irish foundation myth, were a race of tall supernatural beings superbly skilled in building and craftsmanship and who went underground after the sons of Mil Espáine, survivors of the Great Flood through descent from Noah, arrived from Spain and wrested Ireland from them. The myth attests that these Milesians—the final inhabitants of Ireland—were the founding race of the Goidels, the Gaelic Celts. The Tuatha Dé Danaan continued to live and perform deeds beyond the power of mortal human beings, devolving eventually into "the little people," the fairies and leprechauns of later Irish legend.

Passage tombs served an important function in Neolithic Irish life both because of where they were sited and because of the purposeful way they were constructed. Their location on the tops of hills and ridges, which affords a commanding view of the surrounding scene, probably means that they were meant to impress. At Newgrange, the lozenges, spirals, and zigzag designs that adorn the stones must have had a religious significance. Sun worship may have been practiced because some tombs are located with their entrances toward the rising sun. The central line of the passage at Newgrange aligns with a point on the horizon where the sun rises on the winter solstice. Entering the tomb on December 21, the visitor sees a slender thread of light pierce the chamber for a brief 17 minutes. Presumably the builders would not have exerted such a gigantic effort to construct such massive mausoleums, laid out in an obviously ceremonial way, without a strong belief system to inspire them.

These great tombs testify to the existence of tribal groups in Ireland because only highly organized societies could have constructed them. Large quantities of burnt human bone have been found in passage tombs, showing that the bodies of many people were burned and buried there over a considerable length of time.

And then a change set in. Archaeologists have discovered that from about 2000 B.C.E. to 1200 B.C.E. some groups were no longer cremating their dead but burying them each in a single grave, often with an original type of very well made and beautifully decorated pottery vessel. A new group of people with new skills had reached Ireland.

Bronze Age

It is not known whether the switch to single-grave burials that occurred in the second millennium B.C.E. in Ireland derived from changes in religious beliefs, but the pottery and other objects found at tomb sites show that novel developments had taken place. New types of vessels known as beaker pottery, probably used as drinking cups, as well as pots and urns that archaeologists assume were filled with food for the dead have been unearthed. The body of a boy buried on the hill of Tara in a small mound was found with a necklace of beads of bronze, amber, and faience.

The amber and faience were imported from the Baltic and the Near East, respectively, probably exchanged for gold or bronze objects exported from Ireland; the boy's jewelry testifies to the arrival of technological innovations that, like those of the Neolithic era before, had their origins in the Near East. Moving beyond the use of stone, early toolmakers learned to recognize ores and fashion metal objects from them. Drawn first to the glitter of gold, prospectors soon found other metals such as copper, which they reduced to molten form and then cast into shapes in molds.

Around 2500 B.C.E. metalworkers reached Ireland, where they found natural gold in gravels in the Wicklow streams, including a Bronze Age mine on Mount Gabriel that survives, as well as copper, the latter in abundant amounts in County Kerry and County Cork. The Beaker folk are associated with the first use of copper. Identified by their distinctive pottery and their single, stone-lined cist-type cremation burial sites, they probably came to Ireland from Britain around 2000 B.C.E. Metalworkers learned to mix the copper with tin, imported from Cornwall in England where plentiful supplies existed, to produce bronze—a metal that made a stronger, more versatile tool.

For the next 1,500 years Bronze Age craftsmen produced a brilliant array of weapons and ornaments unmatched for their beauty anywhere else in Europe. Highly decorated copper axes—the most ubiquitous early Bronze Age objects—and finely balanced leaf-shaped swords attest to their masters' skills. Late Bronze Age artisans were famed for their exquisitely distinctive gold torques (twisted metal necklaces and bracelets), gold sun discs and earrings, and bronze horse tackle and spearheads, the last introduced around 1500 B.C.E. in marking a new method of warfare.

The intricate patterns and designs on jewelry carried a religious significance, a belief system evident as well in circular concentrations of stones that were built at this time. More than 200 great circles exist today, grouped largely in counties Kerry and Cork, in central and north-western Ulster, and in Limerick. The largest stone circle in Ireland is located at Grange in Limerick, where broken bits of beakers and other containers found at the base of the stones may constitute the remains of some religious ritual feast.

Bronze Age dwellers probably inhabited simple settlements—rude huts made of daub and wattle surrounded by wooden stockades in which cattle could be safely penned or perhaps log cabins in the forest clearings. The *crannóg,* or lake dwelling, appeared also, erected on artificial islands laboriously built in lakes, and this type of home would continue to be constructed until the Middle Ages. Evidence from pollen dating evinces a decline after 2000 B.C.E. in elm and hazel and a corresponding increase in bracken ferns, thus suggesting the spread of both heath and land available for cultivation. At this time it is probable that average temperatures began to fall and a corresponding rise in annual rainfall led to an increase in the amount and size of peat bogs. The first raised trackways, made of wooden planks laid longitudinally and supported by piles, date from 1300 B.C.E. Called *toghers,* from the Irish word *tóchar,* meaning "causeway," these raised paths through the marshlands would be built in Ireland for thousands of years.

About 800 B.C.E. advances in farming, toolmaking, and fighting methods entered Ireland. The introduction of the simple ox-drawn plough eliminated the hard work of breaking up the soil by spade. Sharper, more finely honed knives and cutting tools made possible finely wrought, more refined work in metal and wood. Shields of

Replica of a crannóg *by the lake at Graggaunowen, County Clare* (Werner Forman/Art Resource, NY)

bronze, wood, or leather, along with short, heavy swords, facilitated close fighting in warfare.

Improvements in weaponry made combat more frequent and deadly, making defense more essential. Hillforts emerged in the late Bronze Age. These were settlements ringed by wooden palisades, concentric earthen ramparts (*raths*), or stone facings (*cashels*). Excavations of the settlement at Navan Fort in County Armagh reveal that a round house once stood here adjacent to a circular stockade, both of which are encircled by a ditch. Archaeologists have determined that the house was rebuilt nine times and the stockade six times at the same location during the period from 700 B.C.E. to 100 B.C.E. In addition to a bronze pin, glass beads, pottery, and lignite bracelets that researchers unearthed here, they found some iron fragments. Firmly rooted settlements had come to stay in Ireland and, with them, a new kind of metal stronger and more practical than any before.

The Celtic Iron Age

At Navan Fort archaeologists discovered an amazing edifice, one built over the structure of earlier houses. The large circular building they found was made up of many concentric rows of upright timbers each spaced equally apart, the rows surrounded on the outside by another circle of upright timbers linked together by horizontal planking. A ramp pierces the circle of timbers and leads downward to a large hole at the center, where a wooden stump in the cavity clearly indicates that a large tree pole had been erected here. Built about 100 B.C.E., the wooden structure was covered by a heap of limestone, with an outer covering of topsoil and peat, probably soon after its construction. The entire edifice is encircled by a ditch, running not, as would be expected for defensive purposes, outside it but rather inside, giving rise to the belief that a place so carefully laid out must have been used not for ordinary domestic doings but for some ritual purpose.

Navan Fort is equated in Irish saga tradition with Emain Macha (pronounced Ow-en Mock-a), the royal seat of the Ulaid, the ruling tribe of Ulster. The Ulaid's most illustrious king, Connor, was protected from invaders by Cúchulainn (or Cú Chulainn, Cuchulain; pronounced Coo Hullin), the revered Irish hero in the series of early tales known as the Ulster Cycle, of which the most famous is the *Táin Bó Cuailgne*.

The people who built Navan Fort began arriving in Ireland from Britain and continental Europe about 700 B.C.E., carrying with them superior weapons and sturdy agricultural implements made of a new metal—iron—that, because it did not bend or break like bronze, proved more effective and efficient, both reusable and adaptable. Led by wealthy chiefs, and aided perhaps by their advanced weaponry, these iron-using tribes originated in central Europe and, from there, moved outward in all directions. Called by the Greeks *Keltoi*, or Celts, they comprised differing groups of people linked by a common language and shared characteristics of dress and ways of life.

The Celts may have come to Ireland in successive waves, but there is no clear evidence of invasions. Scatterings seem to have arrived in two movements—that of the Fir Bolg (Belgae) coming to western Ireland directly from Gaul on the Continent and that of the Priteni (Pritani, known as Cruithni to the Irish) coming to northeastern Ireland from northern Britain. Individuals may have arrived also, becoming chiefs of resident local groups by seizing power or gaining control through influence or trade. At first a minority among the non-Celtic majority, by about 150 B.C.E. the Celts were well established in Ireland. Their beliefs and institutions would dominate life on the island for the next 1,000 years, with traces of their ways surviving among the Irish-speaking population today.

The Celts settled in isolated rural homesteads of a type unique to Ireland. The *rath* (also known as a *dun, lios,* or *cathair*) consisted of a

TÁIN BÓ CUAILGNE

The *Táin Bó Cuailgne* (pronounced Thaw-in Bow Koo-il-nj; *The Cattle Raid of Cooley*) is the central tale of the Ulster Cycle (formerly known as the Red Branch Cycle), a saga that constitutes one of the four great cycles that have survived of ancient Irish mythological tales. It was written in Old Irish (ca. 600–900 C.E.) and Middle Irish (ca. 1200–1500), mainly in prose with occasional verse passages, and it draws on multiple sources, writers having incorporated and rejected material over the centuries. The *Táin* can be dated perhaps to the first century C.E., perhaps to a century or so later, but exactly when various episodes were added to the narrative remains unknown.

The Ulster Cycle centers on the reign of Connor (Conchobar) mac Nessa, reputedly the king of Ulster around the time of Christ. The foremost hero of the cycle is Connor's nephew, Cúchulainn. The preeminent Irish folk hero, he is sometimes called Ireland's Achilles. A mythological character who some early scholars affirmed was modeled on an actual historical figure, Cúchulainn returned to prominence during the Irish cultural renaissance of the late 19th century. Nationalists in the early 20th century readily adopted him as the image-perfect warrior champion of Irish independence. The Ulster Cycle contains all the elements that make for engaging storytelling, including love, betrayal, heroism, war, jealousy, and revenge. The *Táin* tells of gods and goddesses and mortal kings and queens. The half-man, half-god Cúchulainn guards Ulster from invasion by King Aillil and Queen Medb (Maeve) of Connacht, who invade because the latter seeks to obtain the phenomenally fertile bull Donn Cuailgne ("brown bull of Cooley") in an effort to best her husband, whom she can match in every material possession save for the bull that he already owns. In the end, she acquires Donn Cuailgne, and the two bulls, which are, in fact, otherworldly beings, do battle. Donn Cuailgne wins, though mortally wounded. He wanders around Ireland creating place-names before returning to Cooley to die of exhaustion. Later tales tell of Medb's return to Ulster, the death of Cúchulainn, who is betrayed by a war goddess whose amorous advances he has rejected, and the ultimate triumph of Medb.

small level area enclosed by a circular earthen bank and ditch. The "fairy forts" of Irish folklore, the *raths*, were typically scattered single-family units with room for houses—usually wooden-framed and frequently circular—and for storage spaces and a pen for animals. Patterned after similar types of enclosed dwellings long present on the island, this continuity indicates that the Celts were heavily influenced by the society they found already in existence. It is possible that the Irish Iron Age and the late Bronze Age may have coexisted for a time, with Bronze Age traditions surviving into the first centuries C.E. Late Iron Age (after the fifth century C.E.) culture is known as La Tène, named for a site in Switzerland, and it is represented in Ireland by objects such as beautifully wrought gold collars and torques—typical adornments of Celtic warriors—and by ornamental sword scabbards.

The Irish language, too, borrowed heavily from the pre-Celtic tongues spoken in Ireland. Both variants of Celtic—the Brittonic (or British) as well as the Goidelic, the ordinary Irish form—were spoken in early Ireland. By the time Irish recorded history begins in the fifth century C.E., the earlier non-Indo-European population had become completely Celticized. They shared a common culture and a common Gaelic language, the Irish dialect called Q-Celtic, having emerged as dominant over Brittonic, or P-Celtic, the language of the Celts of Britain and Gaul and the ancestor of Welsh and Breton.

Although local power structures certainly existed in Ireland in earlier times, the Celts were the first to establish a political and social system of record. From the swirl of invasions and assimilations, greater and lesser kings emerged as rulers, and the patterns and customs of life that came to prevail would remain largely unchanged until the coming of the Normans in the 12th century and, across much of Ireland, for a good deal longer after that.

The Rise of the Irish Kings and the Emergence of Gaelic Society

By the start of the Christian era, different tribal groupings were ruling over territories of varying sizes. Over time, groups of persons, or immediate ancestors, who bore a common surname and inhabited the same territory emerged. In turn, clans (groups united by kinship and descent), subgroups within larger clans (septs), and clusters of clans (tribes or dynasties) gradually took shape. Efforts by one band to expand beyond its borders would inevitably ignite conflict. The society that evolved was led by powerful local chiefs or kings (rí), who ruled small pastoral-agricultural territories (túatha; sing. túath). Within his domain, the king's word was law, but beyond his territory chaotic conditions prevailed with strength reigning supreme in deciding the outcome of incessant raids and wars.

13

Violence suffused society and battling was omnipresent. Human sacrifice was all-important—prisoners of war were sacrificed to war gods and newborns to the harvest god. The soul dwelled in the head, they believed, and so the heads of their enemies could be found prominently on display—stuck on palisades and laid out in temples—and used as ceremonial drinking bowls and ornaments. The famed Irish wolfhound was first bred as a hunting dog and a war dog—used to pull men off horseback—by the early Celts, who called them *Cú Faoil*.

Kingship was sacred in character, the title conferred on a man who, in the early narrative literature, marries the goddess of the land and is free from faults. Each king performed two essential functions: leading his people in war and ensuring good government by exercising *fír flaithemon* (ruler's truth), which included raising taxes, promulgating and enforcing laws, carrying out public works, and presiding over a popular assembly *(oénach)* held regularly at which the whole population of the kingdom would gather to conduct familial and tribal business.

Located usually at an ancient tribal cemetery, the *oénach* would be a festive event. Laws were discussed and defined, marriages celebrated, and deaths recorded. Pleasure followed business. Games would be played and horse races held, an early manifestation of a sport that the Irish would come to love. Horses were prized possessions, and they thrived in Ireland, where the moist climate ensured the growth of lush pastures and the limestone subsoil gave to the grass healthy doses of bone-building calcium. Horse races on flat terrain emerged in ancient times, and by the early centuries C.E. they had become a central part of social gatherings.

Greater kings built royal headquarters whose splendor reflected their wealth and power, at Navan Fort in County Armagh, at Dún Ailinne in County Kildare, and, most memorable of all, at the hill of Tara in County Meath, an important burial site since early prehistoric times that Irish lore transformed into the seat of half-legendary kings and a place of superstitious wonder.

Kingship was hierarchical—most of the petty kings paid tribute under the rule of a greater lord—and Irish law recognized three grades of king: the ruler of a single small kingdom *(rí túaithe)*; the ruler of several small kingdoms (overking; *rúiri* or *rí túath*); and, at the summit, the ruler of many kingdoms (provincial overking; *rí ruirech* or *rí cóicid*). By the end of the Iron Age these last types of rulerships had emerged into five federations, the so-called Five Fifths—Ulaid (Ulster), Connachta (Connacht), Munha (Munster), Laigin (Leinster), and Mide (Meath). With the last two combining, these federations in time became the four provinces of Ireland. The high king of Ireland *(Ard Rí na hÉireann)*

HILL OF TARA

The hill of Tara (Irish, Teamhair na Rí, "Hill of the King") is a low limestone ridge standing at 646 feet (197 m) running near the river Boyne in County Meath, Leinster. Its prominence dates to very ancient times, and it has long held a place of singular significance in Irish legend and lore. In the *Lebor gabála Érenn (The Book of the Taking of Ireland)*, the earliest complete copy of which dates to the 12th century, Tara is named for Téa, wife of Eremon, the first Gaelic ruler of Ireland, in replacing the earlier name of Druim Cain (Cain's ridge).

The remnants of an oval-shaped Iron Age hillfort known as the Fort of the Kings, or the Royal Enclosure (Ráith na Ríg), stand at the summit. Enclosed by an internal ditch and an external bank, two ringforts linked to each other within the fort are known as Cormac's House (Teach Chormaic) and the Royal Seat (Forradh). In the middle of the latter, a standing stone protrudes, believed to be the Stone of Destiny (Lia Fáil) at which the high kings of Ireland were supposedly crowned and which, when touched by the royal hand, after the claimant to the throne had won a series of challenges, would emit a screech heard all over the island.

The importance of Tara predates Celtic times, and a legendary account names Tara as the capital of the Tuatha Dé Danann.

The list of those bearing the title of "high king of Ireland" goes back to the second millennium B.C.E (though the earliest names are mostly mythical), and although no proof has been found that Tara served as the political and spiritual capital of the earliest Celtic people in Ireland, it is known that the site evolved to become the chief center of these high kings from before the sixth century C.E. It retained that status until sometime during the 12th century, although its splendor declined over time.

The hostage's mound at the hill of Tara, County Meath (Werner Forman/Art Resource, NY)

stands at the top of the kingly pyramid. An ancient pagan king of all Ireland had long been a staple of Irish lore, but it is unknown when the title refers to actual historical persons and when these individuals were, in fact, genuine "high kings." Most historians believe the figure to be a pseudohistorical creation dating from the eighth century, the idea of a king ruling the entire island acting as a spur to greater centralization over the fragmented political map of Ireland. Only in the ninth century was the idea of a high king converted into political reality as provincial kings began to seek the title.

Little solid historical material is available with which to chronicle the course of events before the fifth century C.E., and historians must rely on stories, poems, and legendary accounts handed down orally over the centuries. Storytellers (*seanachaidhe*, from *seanachas*, meaning "lore") could often relate more than 300 tales, learned by memorization, as the custodians of an ancient oral tradition, and oral storytelling survives into modern times. Not until the ninth century—many centuries after the purported happenings—did scribes begin to set down narratives in the Old Irish Sagas.

The sagas tell of legendary high kings such as Tuathal, one of the earliest to emerge, who returned from exile with his brother to defeat his enemies in battle at Tara, which he then made his capital, the traditional place of power of all the high kings to come. Perhaps the most famous of the ancient high kings was Cormac mac Airt (Cormac Ua Conn), who may have been an authentic historical figure who ruled during the early or mid third century C.E. from his splendid court at Tara. He maintained power backed by a single armed force (*fianna*), an elite military guard of landless young men, often aristocrats who had not yet come into their inheritance of land. The leader of the *fianna* during mac Airt's reign was Finn MacCool (Fionn mac Cumhaill), and the stories of Finn and his followers form the Fenian Cycle, tales that mix fact and legend reportedly narrated by his son Oisín. Stories of Finn's life include defeating a fire-breathing fairy called Aillen and falling in love and marrying Sadbh, a woman turned into a deer by a druid, then turned woman again by Finn's love, and turned deer once more by an angry druid. The druids in the tale attest to the powerful place these pagan priests, who lived and worshipped in sacred groves, occupied in Celtic society, a world in which superstition, legend, dreams, and rituals were all-important. Druids carried out sacrifices of crops, animals, and, during particular festivals, humans.

The *túath* formed the central political institution of Gaelic society. The central social institution was the kinship group, called *derbfhine* (or *derbfine*, and various other spellings). Land and rights were originally structured in terms of the *derbfhine*, which was not the conjugal family (father, mother, and children) but rather an extended family of a man and his brothers but also including the descendants in the male line only of a common great-grandfather (four generations). The degrees of relationship were defined by lawyers according to a complex scheme. The individual had few or no legal rights since all rights were bound up in membership in the *derbfhine*. Land was the basis of wealth, and it would be redistributed on the death of a member of the *derbfhine* to remaining members. Equally, succession to kingship was based on the *derbfhine*—any male member of a king's extended family, including a brother, son, uncle, or nephew, was eligible to assume a newly vacant throne, his selection based on rituals to test a candidate's fitness. Rituals varied and might include, for example, a royal chariot ride in which the candidate would have to prove a worthy passenger and a royal mantle that would have to be the right size to fit the candidate. Another might entail the bull feast or bull sleep *(tarbfheis)*, in which a bull was killed and a chosen man, who had eaten its flesh, would lay down to sleep while four druids chanted an incantation over him, eliciting a dream in which he would identify the next king.

Land was shared equally by brothers. Women could not inherit, but daughters without brothers might obtain an interest in their father's property during his lifetime. Marriages were not often stable—trial marriages of one year, divorce, and remarriage were common—and polygamy was practiced by the noble class. The head of the most elderly family line in the *derbfhine* was the *cenn fine*, who represented the whole family in affairs public and private.

Responsibility for exacting justice in Gaelic society rested with the *brehon*, an anglicization of the Irish *brithemin*, a plural word identifying legal scholars, who in traditional Gaelic society acted as arbitrators in disputes. Families or clans of lawyers evolved who enjoyed high social status. The brehon law system *(cin comhfhocuis)* was based on negotiated justice, in which families were held responsible for the misdeeds of group members. The worst crime of all was murder of one's own kin *(fingal)*. The *derbfhine* punished members who transgressed the law and, in the event a member was slain, exacted vengeance, either in blood or in money. Money in this entirely rural society meant milk cows, a young heifer *(sét, modern Irish séad)* serving as the basic unit, although female slaves were used as higher units, equal to six *séts*.

Túath-based society was strictly hierarchical, divided into kings, lords, and commons. The brehon lawyers precisely defined divisions

17

and subdivisions of classes because status was the means by which legal rights and powers were measured. The distinction between lords and commons was fluid, depending not only on birth but also wealth, and individuals could rise or fall in status. Commoners could acquire higher rank by amassing riches and dependents. Apart from material possessions, the real distinction between commoner and noble lay in the institution of clientship (célsine). Nobles retained clients, men bound to them in a well-defined relationship of mutual benefit.

Commoners were freemen who owned their own land and possessed full legal rights. Freemen also included the professional classes (áes dána, "men of art")—lawyers, poets, priests, genealogists, musicians, artists, physicians, and certain skilled tradesmen such as blacksmiths. They were allowed the freedom to leave their own túatha and travel anywhere in Ireland. Equality existed across society's upper echelons— a chief poet (ollam) and, later, a Christian bishop held equal status with a king. Complex subdivisions of each class based on property qualifications were maintained by the lawyers.

Landless men; workers; lower grades of entertainers; hereditary serfs, who were bound to the soil as part of the lord's estate; and slaves constituted those who were unfree. Bondage was common in early Ireland, and slaves included prisoners of war, children of the poor sold into servitude, and others brought in from abroad.

In this society, the more prosperous possessed more cattle, sheep, and pigs, more luxurious household furnishings, and perhaps even more than one house. Men and women of the upper classes could be distinguished by the voluminous cloak (brat), often secured by a beautiful brooch, that they wore over a shirt or tunic (léine). The color of the clothes, the degree of embroidery, and the quality and extent of ornamental jewelry indicated relative status. Men sported shoulder-length hair, often with two braids to the front. Those who were poorer may have worn trousers, tight-fitting and usually accompanied by a short jacket, a form of dress derived from prehistoric central Europe, but little is known with certainty about the sartorial habits of the lower classes. The opportunity of the better off to acquire greater material wealth expanded with development of trading links that followed the rise to the fore of the powerful empire that came to rule much of the island next door.

Roman Contacts

Roman fleets under Julius Caesar (100 or 102–44 B.C.E.) landed on the south coast of Britain twice, in 55 and 54 B.C.E., but then withdrew.

When the Romans returned in 43 C.E., this time they came to stay. They proceeded to conquer the island up to the Scottish Highlands, building forts along the Forth-Clyde isthmus. During his campaigns in southern Scotland, the Roman general Gnaeus Julius Agricola (40–93 C.E.) could see the coast of Ireland clearly in the distance, and contacts with the island's inhabitants had undoubtedly been made. The historian Tacitus (ca. 56–ca. 120) recorded: "In regard to soil, climate, and the character and ways of its inhabitants . . . it is not markedly different from Britain: We are better informed, thanks to the trade of merchants, about the approaches to the island and its harbours" (Tacitus 1914, 211). Agricola may have even retained an ambition to conquer the island. Tacitus relates: "I have often heard [Agricola] declare that with one single legion and fair contingent of irregulars Hibernia could be overpowered and held" (Tacitus, 1914: 211). But if any plans were prepared for a campaign, they were not enacted. Rome's reach never stretched to Ireland.

The Alexandrian Greek Ptolemy (second century C.E.) has left us the most detailed account of pre-Christian Ireland. Meant to be a sailors' chart, Ptolemy's map is based on a lost work of Marinus of Tyre, and, because it was drafted in the middle of the second century C.E., it probably describes Ireland as it existed about 100 C.E. The map identifies a number of place-names and tribal names that are surprisingly recognizable. On the island known to the Romans as Hibernia or Scotia, to the Greeks as Ierne (used for Scotland in the Middle Ages), and possibly to the Celts as Ériu (modern Irish Éire), he labels the Boyne (Buvinda) and the Shannon (Senos) rivers. Among the kingdoms delineated, the Voluntii are the Ulaid of Ulster; the Iverni are the Érainn of Munster; the Menapii are the Monnaig, found in northeastern Ireland (giving their name Fir Managh to Fermanagh); and the Robogdu, who are perhaps the Redodii or Dál Riata in extreme northeastern Ulster. In giving a glimpse of Ireland, Ptolemy shows that at this date the island shared languages, aristocracies, and tribal groupings, including the Cruithni whom Latin writers called Picti (Picts), with Scotland.

Though Roman legions never tramped through the Irish countryside, close contacts existed between their empire and the Celts on the island. Over time, these contacts intensified. Roman objects dating from the first and second centuries have been found, perhaps acquired through trade or raids on a Roman base. When Roman might began to wane in the fourth and fifth centuries, opportunities opened up for invaders from Ireland to attack with growing success. Celtic fleets sailed to Roman Britain's coastal areas, notably in 397 when Irish, Picts, and Saxons converged from west, north, and east, respectively, to pillage and plunder. At the same time that Roman rule effectively ended in Britain in the early fifth century, Irish settlers arrived to stay. A large colony originating in southern Ireland was founded in southern Wales, and other colonies were established in northern Wales and southern England on the Cornish Peninsula. But the most successful colony possibly proved to be that of the Dál Riata, which some scholars believe laid the basis for the kingdom of Scotland.

Interactions with Britain and with Roman culture produced dramatic changes in Ireland. The booty brought back by marauding expeditions probably changed the balance of power among tribal dynasties within Ireland, and Irish colonies in Britain may have added resources that aided dynastic expansion at home. Most material finds—Roman coins especially—date to the fifth century, though romanization may have begun in the fourth century. Roman influence had an especially significant impact on language. The earliest form of the written Irish language—Ogham—is clearly based on the Latin alphabet. Consisting of 25 varieties of short lines and notches set at different angles on either side of a central rule, Ogham was originally inscribed in wood and then set in stone. Ogham inscriptions are found across Ireland, especially in the south and southwest, and also in areas of Britain colonized by the Irish. They date to the fifth, sixth, and seventh centuries, and the standing stones on which the words are etched probably served as either territorial markers or memorials to the dead.

In Britain also the Irish came upon Christianity. The intense interisland exchanges of the fourth and fifth centuries would have included not only trade in goods but also exposure to the new faith, which was newly arrived in Britain itself, probably in the fourth century. And contacts would have included the taking of hostages. Hostages were routinely demanded by Irish kings to ensure the loyalty of retainers, being well taken care of if relationships remained tranquil or killed if they did not. Captives were also taken by warring and marauding parties, the prisoners considered to be just like any other spoils seized in successful raids. One such hostage taken in one such raid was a young boy destined to change Ireland forever.

2

CHRISTIANITY ARRIVES AND THRIVES (431–795)

Documented history began in Ireland in the year 431, the first specific date on record, and the topic that it treats—the sending of a bishop to minister to Irish Christians—concerns arguably the most momentous happening to occur in Ireland between the arrival of the first humans and that of the Anglo-Normans in the 12th century.

The importance to Ireland's subsequent history of the coming of Christianity cannot be overstated, and the centrality of the new religion to Irish life is apparent from its very beginnings on the island. Saint Patrick is the sole missionary who has left us his story of having brought the faith to Ireland—and so it is Patrick who has earned the fame that has made his name synonymous with the country where he labored so assiduously.

The new faith proved phenomenally successful, spreading everywhere and without violence, the latter much extolled by Ireland's patron saint. Conversion brought a new institution, a church organization led by bishops, which in turn would be largely supplanted, in the seventh and eighth centuries, by monastic congregations. Monasteries large and small in places remote and not so remote founded by a host of men and women whom the church proclaimed to be saints spread throughout Ireland and, from there, across Europe. On the Continent, Irish monks proselytized among pagans and reintroduced learning and literacy to a post-Roman world that had lost its cultural bearings.

The scholarship promoted and preserved overseas had been nurtured back home. From the sixth to the 12th centuries, Irish monasteries served as leading educational centers in Europe and as places of outstanding artistic creativity. The heritage produced by scribes, metalworkers, and stonecutters in magnificently illuminated manuscripts, gem-encrusted sacred vessels, and ornately etched stone crosses gave to seventh- and eighth-century Ireland a cultural golden age.

21

The larger monastic settlements became important economic centers as well. Society was exclusively rural, ruled by the agricultural seasons, by church-imposed laws, and by a host of kings and petty kings. From among a welter of small kingdoms, dynasties emerged that dominated in the five, and then four, provinces. The contests that had formerly been waged on smaller stages now continued on larger playing fields, rulers competing with each other for territorial rights over wide areas. They fought on until powerful new invaders appeared from offshore to disturb their interdynastic rivalries.

The Beginnings of Christianity
The Mission of St. Patrick

Christianity could certainly be found in Ireland by the early fifth century. Trading links with Roman Britain and Gaul ensured that it was so. Missionaries appeared in the late fourth or early fifth centuries probably from Gaul, where the church had an established organization by the end of the fourth century and within whose ecclesiastical jurisdiction both Ireland and Britain lay. In 431 the writer Prosper Tiro records that Pope Celestine I (r. 422–432) sent Palladius, probably deacon of Auxerre in France, as bishop to the Irish "believers in Christ."

Palladius and other clerics undoubtedly worked among the Irish, but it was Patrick who emerged in Irish consciousness as the central player. That he did so stems in large part because it is Patrick alone who has left us a written record of his exploits. While he did not provide a narrative history of the conversion, Patrick does recount how he penetrated parts of the country where no Christian missionary had ventured before. It is certain that he won many converts.

It is less certain how the early church that he so laboriously helped to found was organized. Patrick would likely have established a bishop-based diocesan organization that he was familiar with in his native Britain and in Gaul. But he also introduced monasticism to Ireland. A number of monasteries in northern and central Ireland would claim links to the saint. Christianity in Ireland probably underwent a lengthy, complex development, including the passage of many years before evangelization was complete.

The new religion supplanted, but also adapted to, customs long characteristic of the country's pagan culture. Life in Celtic Ireland, filled with myths, peopled with spirits, and suffused with superstition, provided fertile ground for a faith that professed trinitarian mysteries and acknowledged divine miracles. Belief in the world as a mystical

22

SAINT PATRICK

The greatest of Ireland's missionaries and its national apostle, Patrick (Latin, Patricius; Irish, Pádraig; ?–ca. 461 or 493), tells us little about his life, but the little he does tell forms the only basis on which to trace a biographical sketch, because no other primary sources exist. He wrote two works: his *Confession (Confessio)*, a spiritual biography and vindication of his mission; and *Letter to the Soldiers of Coroticus (Epistola)*, a letter of protest against enslavement of some of his new converts.

Patrick was born in the village of Bannauem Taberniae in Roman Britain, the son of Calpurnius, a deacon. About the age of 16, he was captured by Irish raiders, enslaved, and put to work as a shepherd. Patrick found religious solace in the lonely hours he spent tending sheep in the woods and on the mountains, where he prayed daily. After six years, he heard a voice telling him he would go home again. He fled his master and journeyed to a port, where a ship manned by pagans stood ready. Upon reaching home, now in his early 20s, he did not linger long. He recounts in his *Confession* the appearance of another vision: "And there I saw in the night the vision of a man whose name was Victoricus, coming as it were from Ireland, with countless letters. And he gave me one of them and I read the opening words of the letter, which were 'The voice of the Irish,' and as I read the beginning of the letter I thought that at the same moment I heard their voice . . . and thus did they cry out as with one mouth: 'We ask thee, boy, come and walk among us once more'" (St. Patrick 1953, 28).

(continues)

A harper kneeling in front of St. Patrick. Engraving by Joseph Hoey (Library of Congress, LC-USZ62-96666)

SAINT PATRICK *(continued)*

Patrick proclaimed himself the most "unlearned of men"; nevertheless, he journeyed to Gaul to receive priestly training. He returned to Ireland a bishop in the year dated traditionally as 432, and he began his mission, preaching wherever he traveled, bestowing gifts on kings, debating with the pagan priests, and baptizing thousands.

It is likely Patrick proselytized in northeastern Ireland because most of the churches that later identified him as their personal founder are located here. Armagh later claimed pride of place as the center of Patrick's missionary activities, and the clergy here zealously promoted his cult, which spread widely. By the eighth century, he had become the patron saint of Ireland.

One of the most famous legends surrounding the life of Patrick recounts how he drove the snakes out of Ireland. However, there were no snakes in postglacial Ireland—unless "snakes" refers to the serpent symbol of the druids. The serpent as the symbol of Satan adopted by Christians, which derives from the Garden of Eden account in the Old Testament, may have served as a metaphor for the conversion of the Irish. Similarly, no firm evidence exists that he taught the doctrine of the Trinity by using a shamrock, a three-leafed clover, to explain the existence of three divine persons in one God. However, these and other popular myths that resound down the centuries point to the profound impact made by St. Patrick.

Little known beyond Ireland in his lifetime, he is linked universally today with the land of his mission, and his pilgrimage site at Croagh Patrick, in County Mayo, where he supposedly fasted for 40 days, battled evil spirits, and built a church, draws visitors by the millions.

Patrick found a people thoroughly pagan in belief and practice, and his debates with the druids, some of which have been preserved, have left us a record of early Irish life, though liberally leavened with legendary lore. Because he sought to convert by persuasion rather than by confrontation, he focused on changing beliefs, not customs, and so helped to keep intact Ireland's social structure.

Because of Patrick, Ireland traces its Christian roots to Britain, and Patrick's voice is the first recorded in Western history to declaim unequivocally against slavery. His notion of Christian truth is one filled with emotion, which he conveys movingly in his writings despite his ignorance of Latin style. A tough man who could be high-tempered, someone who was boundlessly optimistic, Patrick never wavered in his conviction that warring pagans could become peaceful Christians; slave masters, liberators; and even murderers, saints. His feast day is March 17, the traditional date of his death.

place was long accepted here, and missionaries to the Irish, unlike their counterparts in continental Europe, did not overly concern themselves with eliminating pagan influences. They tolerated continued celebration of pagan festivals such as May Day and Halloween.

At the same time, Christianity transformed Ireland. Patrick brought a religion that eradicated human sacrifice, looked disfavorably on slavery, and discouraged warfare, ushering in several centuries that saw a marked decline in intertribal conflict. Although love of combat was too ingrained in the Irish psyche for it to disappear entirely, large-scale battles of the kind extolled in the sagas would not reappear until the 11th century.

Christianity itself came to Ireland peacefully. Unlike in much of western and central Europe then subject to barbarian invasion and conquest, the faith took hold here in a stable society, the only country in western Europe where the work of conversion produced no martyrs.

Monasticism Flourishes

Unable to point to examples of "red martyrdom"—the acclaimed proof of sanctity by death—the Irish of the late fifth and early sixth centuries looked to what they called the "green martyrdom" as an alternative path to sanctity. "Green" martyrs left the world of physical comforts behind and journeyed to remote locales—to nature's wilderness outside tribal jurisdictions—there to pray and study and so to find God.

During the sixth century, monasticism made rapid strides and emerged preeminent, Ireland becoming unique in western Europe in having its most important churches ruled by a hierarchy of monks, including some who were not bishops. The episcopal model of church organization of dioceses ruled by bishops, patterned after Roman urban administrative units established in the fifth century, would be supplanted, within a century later, by monastic foundations. Abbots— heads of monasteries—would rule even at Armagh, the church that came to be seen as Patrick's own. The saint's immediate successors here were bishops, but by the end of the fifth century and for two centuries thereafter, the chief cleric was both bishop and abbot.

The impulse behind the drive to monastic life can be traced possibly to a predilection in the Irish temperament for an ascetic lifestyle, but, more factually, to a number of impressive personalities among the great monastic founders. These new arrivals on the scene displaced many of the older centers that dated from Patrick's days in founding their own places of faith and learning. Like Patrick before them,

25

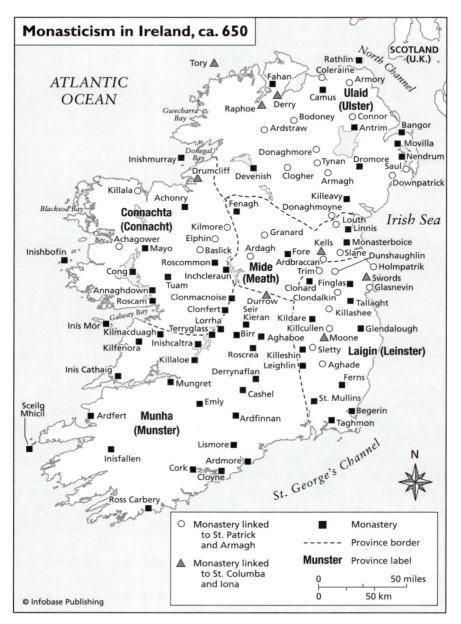

Monasticism in Ireland, ca. 650

SCOTLAND (U.K.)

North Channel

ATLANTIC OCEAN

Tory ▲
Rathlin ■
Coleraine ○
Fahan ○
Armory ○
Camus ○
Ulaid (Ulster)
Derry ▲
Raphoe ▲
Gweebarra Bay
Bodoney ○
Connor ○
Bangor ■
Ardstraw ○
Antrim ■
Movilla ■
Donaghmore ○
Nendrum ■
Inishmurray ■
Donegal Bay
Drumcliff ▲
Devenish ○
Tynan ○
Dromore ■
Saul ○
Downpatrick ○
Clogher ○
Armagh ○
Killala ○
Achonry ■
Killeavy ■
Fenagh ■
Donaghmoyne ○
Irish Sea
Blacksod Bay
Connachta (Connacht)
Kilmore ○
Louth ○
Linnis ■
Clew Bay
Achagower ■
Elphin ○
Granard ○
Kells ▲
Monasterboice ■
Mayo ■
Baslick ○
Ardagh ○
Fore ▲
Slane ▲
Dunshaughlin ■
Inishbofin ○
Roscommon ■
Ardbraccan ○
Holmpatrik ○
Cong ■
Inchcleraun ■
Mide (Meath)
Trim ○
Swords ▲
Annaghdown ■
Tuam ■
Clonard ○
Finglas ■
Glasnevin ○
Roscam ■
Clonmacnoise ■
Durrow ▲
Clondalkin ○
Clonfert ■
Seir Kieran
Kildare ■
Tallaght ○
Inís Mór
Lorrha
Terryglass ■
Killashee ○
Galway Bay
Kilmacduagh ■
Birr ■
Killcullen ○
Glendalough ■
Kilfenora ■
Inishcaltra ■
Aghaboe ■
Moone ▲
Killaloe ■
Roscrea ■
Killeshin ■
Sletty ○
Laigin (Leinster)
Inis Cathaig ■
Derrynaflan ■
Leighlin ■
Aghade ○
Ferns ○
Mungret ■
Cashel ■
St. Mullins ■
Sceilg Mhicíl
Emly ■
Ardfert ■
Munha (Munster)
Ardfinnan ■
Begerin ■
Taghmon ■
Lismore ■
Inisfallen ■
Ardmore ■
Cork ■
Cloyne ■
St. George's Channel
N
Ross Carbery ■

○ Monastery linked to St. Patrick and Armagh

■ Monastery

----- Province border

▲ Monastery linked to St. Columba and Iona

Munster Province label

0   50 miles
0   50 km

© Infobase Publishing

they too came from Britain, now arriving not to convert but rather to instruct the Irish in their regular religious routines. Saint David of Wales (ca. 500–89) taught Scuithin of Slievemargy and Máedóc of Ferns. The monastery of Ninian at Galloway, Scotland, served as the school both of Saint Enda (d. ca. 530), who built churches at Drogheda and later founded Killeaney, the largest monastery on the Aran Islands where many Irish abbots were in turn trained, and of Saint Finnian of Movilla (Moville) (ca. 495–ca. 589), who established the monastery of Movilla in County Down about 550. Both saints are considered founders of Irish monasticism.

Inspired by Welsh reformers Cadoc and Gildas, Saint Finnian of Clonard (ca. 470–ca. 549) brought to his abbey at Clonard in County Meath an innovative emphasis on sacred study, which now joined prayer and manual labor as part of monastic life. In the roll of saints, he is inscribed as early Christian Ireland's preeminent teacher, and his 12 pupils, grouped together as "the twelve apostles of Ireland," shine in Irish history as illustrious founders of their own monastic houses, among them, Brendan at Clonfert, Ciáran at Clonmacnoise, Molaisse at Devenish, Cainneach at Aghaboe, and Mobhi at Glasnevin.

The late fifth and early sixth centuries witnessed a host of houses founded by these and other men—by Jarlath at Tuam, Comgall at Bangor, Fionnbar at Cork, and Kevin at Glendalough. Less numerous but equally noteworthy are those established by women—by Ita at Killeady, Moninne at Killeavy, Safann at Clavin Bronaigh, and Brigid, who established monasteries for both women and men, at Kildare.

Where they were located on the main roads and near native forts, now in decline, such as at Armagh, Clonmacnoise, Glendalough, Kildare, and Monasterboice, settlements served as commercial entrepôts, hostels, and schools as well as religious centers. Others could be found in the most inaccessible places—in deep woods and on mountaintops—wherever hermits could find the isolation they required to practice the severest physical and psychological testing by which to draw nearer to God. Scribes communed with God, copied books, and thrived even on remote rocky islands such as Inishmurray, Inishbofin, and, most famously, Skellig Michael (Sceilg Mhichíl)—the latter a jagged dagger of a rock rising 700 feet from the sea off the coast of County Kerry, where monks, who first arrived in 588, built beehive-shaped huts of stone and survived on fish, sea fowl, the produce of small gardens fertilized with seaweed, and rainwater collected in cisterns.

These monastic houses were not the splendid institutions found later during the Middle Ages in continental Europe. Rather, they consisted of an assemblage of rude little dwellings set in the wilderness. Celibate monks lived in individual huts made of wood, of clay and wattle, or of stone. Settlements included a church, an adjoining cemetery, a kitchen, a refectory, and a library. A workshop and forge would have completed

The ruins of Muckross Abbey, County Kerry. Abbeys dotted the Irish landscape and served as the repositories of learning in western Europe in the seventh and eighth centuries. (Library of Congress, LC-DIG-ppmsc-09907)

the cluster of buildings, all of them surrounded by a ring of palisades. The enclosure may have harbored an orchard within while outside would have been found the pasturage and cultivated plots belonging to the monastery, the fields here dotted with farm buildings, a mill, and a limekiln.

Dressed simply in a cape and hood of coarse undyed wool with a white tunic underneath, the monks would have been readily identifiable by their tonsure, which was unique to Ireland—the hair shaved to the front of the head, leaving the hair at the back to grow long. Monks followed a daily routine framed by the schedule of prayer. The canonical hours were kept every day by all save those called to manual labor, and the latter would disperse after morning services—some to the fields to plough, sow, harvest, and thresh or to tend the livestock; some to the workshop to fashion tools and sacred vessels; some, in areas near or on the sea, to boats to catch fish. These tasks were required to sustain life, but no occupation was more central to a monastery's mission than the copying of manuscripts, and some among the scribes of Ireland became artists of exceptional talent. Writing rooms were outfitted both with a plentiful supply of materials—parchment, waxed tablets, inkhorns, quills, and stylos—and with manuscripts—suspended from the walls in satchels—on which to copy texts spiritual and secular.

Monasteries grew to become quite large, some with hundreds of monks, and those that were established by the same founder tended to maintain close contacts with each other. Each community was led by an abbot, whose abode stood slightly apart from the rest, and abbots often nominated their own successors. An abbot was assisted by a vice abbot or prior, in charge of the monastery's material goods, and by *seniores*, a group of older congregants. The *seniores*, unlike the majority of monks who were laymen, were ordained to the priesthood and so were essential for celebration of the Eucharist and administration of the sacraments.

Year after year the liturgical cycle was repeated—Sundays and feast days observed as days of rest, fasting during Lent, and joyous celebrations on Easter and Christmas. The monks subsisted on a simple diet of milk, bread, eggs, and fish, but on Sundays and certain feast days, and on special occasions such as when travelers visited, meat was probably allowed. Discipline was strict and infractions of the rule could be met with severe sanctions. Expulsion and exile were the harshest penalties, the latter imposed for major offenses such as murder. Irish civil law made no provision for corporal punishment, and its use introduced a new measure of chastisement to Ireland. The monks ultimately abandoned it when they met opposition to its extreme nature as well as to harsh fasts and vigils. Resistance to physical violence arose from among recruits on the continent of Europe, where Irish monastics began to move.

Irish Monasticism Abroad

In the same way as monastic founders had traveled across Ireland to found communities in which to practice their piety, so too did Irish sojourners a generation later begin to move beyond the island. Already Irish monasteries had welcomed thousands of foreign students, who returned to their homelands imbued with Irish learning.

The missionary zeal of Irish churchmen brought them first to Scotland. In about 563 Columba (Colm Cille, Columcille, 521–97), from County Donegal, journeyed with a handful of followers first to Iona, a remote island off the west Scottish coast, where he welcomed visitors from across the British Isles. After decreeing a limit of 150 monks, he would send off the surplus in groups of 12 and one—in emulation of Christ and his apostles—to found other congregations. Numbers mounted rapidly, and at his death, communities dotted the mountain heights and rugged coastlines of Scotland, and several dependent communities could be found in Ireland as well, including Durrow, Derry, Drumcliff, Raphoe, and (from 807) Kells.

Columba succeeded in single-handedly establishing a Christian society among the Scots and Picts of Scotland, and his greatest spiritual disciple, Aidan (d. 651), would do the same for all of northern England. The Angles of Northumbria would be brought into the Christian fold, starting from Aidan's base at Lindisfarne.

Taking Columba as their model, monks moved on to the Continent. Columbanus (543–615), born in Leinster and a monk at Bangor for 25 years, departed with the requisite 12 companions in about 590 for Gaul, where he founded three monasteries at Annegray, Fontaines, and Luxeuil. Traveling from Luxeuil to Italy, Columbanus embarked on one of Christianity's great missionary journeys—twice across France, up the Rhine River and across Switzerland to Bregenz in Austria, and thence into northern Italy. By the time he opened his last monastic house at Bobbio in Liguria, where he died, he had been on the Continent a mere 25 years but, in that time, had succeeded in establishing probably at least 60 and perhaps more than 100 monasteries, in the process bringing the faith to the bands of barbarians roving the woods of central Europe.

Adding a third, namely, "white martyrdom"—a missionary path to holiness—to those of red and green martyrdom, Irish monks fanned out across Europe. So-named for their distinctive white woolen robes, they included Cathal (or Cahill), born in Munster, who was elected bishop of Taranto, Italy; Fursa (d. ca. 649–50), the visionary saint who traveled to France; Virgil, archbishop of Salzburg, Austria; and Donetus (ca. 829–76), bishop of Fiesole, Italy. By the end of the eighth century, Irish monks had reached Moravia, and evidence suggests that they journeyed as far as Kiev, Ukraine. Wherever they went, they brought their love of study and their transcription skills.

Learned Irishmen could be found at the court of Charlemagne (742–814), king of the Franks and crowned Emperor of the West in 800, who united much of western Europe and presided over a short-lived cultural flowering. Irish scholars filled posts as masters of the palace schools established at the royal court. Johannes Scotus "Eriugena" (Irish-born) (ca. 815–77) taught philosophy at the Palatine School, a center of learning under the patronage of one of Charlemagne's successors, Charles the Bald (823–77). He earned repute as the earliest philosopher of the Middle Ages, the first truly Christian philosopher since Augustine of Hippo (396–430).

To their native inheritance of Celtic prose and poetry, Irish monks added a mastery of Latin scholarship, honed in the centuries after Patrick introduced systematically, in his own rudimentary words, the language of Rome to the island. They were the first Europeans living beyond the old imperial borders to adopt the Latin script. A heritage both domestic and foreign would be preserved in Ireland—and in Ireland alone—during the centuries when, elsewhere in Europe, learning languished.

Seventh- and Eighth-Century Ireland: Europe's Cultural Repository

At a time when schooling had all but ceased on the European continent, in Ireland education flourished. During the fifth and sixth centuries, instructors in ecclesiastical schools taught Scriptures and Latin grammar to boys, who learned to read the classical authors with ease and to write the language with skill. At the same time, pre-Christian learning in Ireland survived. Secular schools of poets and lawyers kept alive centuries-old systems of education. Stories, histories, laws, family genealogies, and traditions were imparted to new generations, all of it orally transmitted and committed to memory.

The two schooling systems were completely separate, but in the seventh century they began to borrow from each other. Irish-language poets learned to read and write, and the native language was studied in the church schools. Religious authorities drew on secular laws—the lawyers now having been converted—in drafting ecclesiastical legislation. Irish monks, who wrote the lives of the saints in excellent Latin verse, were raised on the old Celtic tales of kings and heroes, and they began to commit them to paper in recognizing that the secular heritage, while not as essential as the spiritual, merited remembering. It is the openness of the early Irish church to secular literature that ensured that the literary heritage passed down orally for generations would be preserved in written form. It is thanks to the scribes that a rich treasury of early literature exists, the earliest vernacular literature in Europe north of the Alps that survives.

Monastic writers composed and maintained works on the lives of the founders of monasteries, including Patrick, Brigid, and Columba, and they penned devotional tracts, homiletic compositions, and much else. Hymns and religious poems appeared in both Latin and Irish, the earliest Irish-language hymn perhaps the seventh-century *Brigit Bé Bithmaith* (Brigid ever excellent woman), also known asUtán's Hymn, in which the poet asks the saint's protection against temptation and evil.

How the classical Old Irish language—the language in use from about 600 to 900—emerged is unknown, perhaps evolving from archaic Old Irish as a single dialect given preferential status or as a standard literary style recognized around the late sixth century. Certainly the monasteries, as the centers of learning, must have served as the sources of its official acceptance. And a considerable degree of interaction must have taken place between Christian clerics and the Celtic poets of Ireland. The poet (*fili,* pl. *filid*) was an important figure among the pre-Christian Irish. Seven grades of *fili* and three subgrades were recognized in law, the highest that of *ollam,* a high poet who was fully versed in the entire body of storytelling, history, and jurisprudence proper to each of the seven grades.

Legal compilation constitutes one of early Christian Ireland's greatest achievements. The Irish church formulated its own law, assembled in the *Collectio canonum Hibernensis* (The collection of Irish canons) by Cú Chuimae of Iona and Rubin MacConnad of Dairinis and dated to the first quarter of the eighth century. Secular legal texts were recorded as well, covering many topics—brehon laws were codified as early as 438. They too were compiled with the assistance of Christian jurists, and so the vernacular laws that were drawn up are not simply ancient customs of a secular legal caste but rather tracts that draw on both foreign and Irish legal materials in devising regulations meant to govern affairs for a Christian society. Both church and secular laws tell us much about ecclesiastical organization and Irish social life in the seventh and eighth centuries.

The earliest evidence of scribal work dates to the end of the sixth century with the Cathach Psalter (ca. 597), a fragmentary copy of the Psalms—reputedly written by Columba—and a copy of the four Gospels of Matthew, Mark, Luke, and John, now in the library of Trinity College Dublin. Historical tales account for a great number of the stories that began to be composed in the eighth century, even in the seventh, and their appearance marks the start of the great tradition of written storytelling in the Irish language. Some tales include stories that the *filid* are said to have known, although we cannot know with certainty the relationship between the written tales and those told and retold by the *filid,* who must have reshaped and redacted the material in the retelling. Stories range from central events in the life of an individual, such as births, wooings, travels, and deaths, to momentous events in social and political history, such as battles, migrations, raids, and natural disasters.

The greatest tales are those of the Ulster Cycle, one among the four great sagas of Irish mythological stories written down in the Middle Ages. They include, besides the *Táin*, the *Compert Conchobuir* (The birth of Conchobar) and the *Compert Con Culainn* (The birth of Cúchulainn). Written in a succinct, realistic style, they vary in quality, but many constitute skillfully crafted compositions. The eighth-century short saga *Echtrae Chonnlai* (The expedition of Chonnlai) uses sophisticated dialogue to relate the story of Connlae, son of Conn, and his love for a woman from the Otherworld, where he ultimately flees to join her. The work is an early example of the *echtrae*—an adventure story describing an Otherworld journey. Mythical Irish Otherworlds include Mag Mell, Ablach, and Tír na nÓg (Land of Eternal Youth), the last the most popular. Considered to lie beyond the edges of the known world on an island far to the west, Tír na nÓg, a place where sickness and death did not exist and youth and beauty reigned forever, could be reached either by an invitation from one of its fairy residents or by undertaking an arduous journey. Voyages by heroes in search of the Otherworld distinguish the *immram* (pl. *immrama*), another class of Old Irish tales. Both *echtrae* and *immram* stories would prove enduringly popular, and it was at this time that patterns in narrative and language were set that would survive for many centuries.

The writings of seventh- and eighth-century Irish authors were preserved not just in Ireland but also on the Continent, and their presence here evinces the pervasiveness of Irish learning in Europe. Many of Europe's earliest libraries were started by Irish monks.

By the seventh and eighth centuries, Irish and Latin culture had entirely fused, the evidence for which is vividly apparent in Irish pictorial art. In earlier centuries, art had existed largely as a by-product of function, but a shift now occurred as craftsmen stressed display as a central element in their productions. The churches, some of which had become wealthy centers of population, were the patrons of, and the showcases for, works of art that grew progressively more splendid. Altars shone with bejeweled book covers, reliquaries, and sacred vessels. Many of these are made of gilt-bronze, decorated with gold filigree in complicated patterns, and inlaid with enamel and precious stones.

Beautifully decorated books and illuminated manuscripts are among the major treasures of the era's cultural flowering. Scribes and painters of miniature scenes drew on varied sources, including, for illustrations,

Byzantine and Mediterranean book paintings brought west in the seventh century, and, for decorations, polychrome enameled and inlaid bronze- and goldwork native to Irish and British society.

Manuscript makers used vellum, and they laid out each page with great care, using rule and compass, and then began the work of copying, the beautiful half-uncial script they devised remaining in use for centuries and forming the basis for many Roman typefaces used today. In their artistry, they joined new depictions of the human face and form—now necessary to represent Christ and the biblical personages—with the interstitial lines and elaborate designs of traditional Celtic display. Text with headings composed of a series of intricately decorated initials appeared in the Book of Durrow, generally dated to the second half of the seventh century and written either in Ireland, in Iona, or in Northumbria. The Lindisfarne Gospels, composed at Lindisfarne in the late seventh century, constitutes the first largely complete luxurious

BOOK OF KELLS

The Book of Kells, less widely known as the Book of Columba, constitutes one of the most splendid examples of illuminated manuscripts housed in Ireland, and the beauty and intricacy of its artwork represents Western calligraphy and illumination at its most magnificent.

The exact date of the manuscript's production is not known. According to tradition, the book was believed to have been created in the time of Columba, perhaps even crafted by him, but because the work encompasses a fully developed style of ornamentation known as Insular style, which is placed in the late eighth or early ninth centuries, it is evidently of a later period.

The place of production is also unknown. The name derives from the Abbey of Kells in County Meath, where the book was kept throughout the Middle Ages. The abbey was founded at the beginning of the ninth century after Viking invasions, and the book may have been composed there or else at Iona or at an unknown monastery in Scotland and then brought to Kells. Regardless, it is undeniably the work of Columban monks closely associated with the foundation at Iona.

In the long and luxuriously decorated book, the four Gospels along with prefatory and explanatory text are copied in Latin on pages elaborately ornamented with colorful flourishes and swirls. The intricately illustrated letters and divine symbols and personages for which Irish

gospel book. Later generations produced progressively more lavish creations. The resplendent script on display would appear again a century later in the Book of Kells, a work that brilliantly exemplifies the merger of Celtic and Christian art.

An equivalent development was achieved about the end of the eighth century by Irish metalworkers. How craftsmen acquired new techniques in making gold filigree is not known, but the mastery of minute detail on display in the Book of Kells is replicated in the glittering gold wire that decorated old pagan motifs of curves and spirals as well as animal ornamentation on goblets, chalices, and brooches. The Ardagh chalice, found at Ardagh, is made of silver and bronze and features gold filigree ornamentation, blue and red glass studs, and rock crystal. It is considered the outstanding example of Irish metalwork of the eighth century.

Elaboration in style is further reflected in the eighth century with the development of stone sculpture. The early Christian Irish customarily set

illuminated manuscripts are renowned are prominently on display, but the book contains some additional features, such as interlinear drawings of common animals and everyday scenes. A relatively small number of motifs and pigments have been combined and recombined repeatedly in webs of ornament and geometry that astound in their degree of minute, complicated detail. The decoration of the opening words of each gospel is so elaborate that the text itself is almost illegible.

The Book of Kells remained in Kells until 1654, when it was sent to Dublin for safekeeping after troops under Oliver Cromwell were quartered in the town. It was presented to Trinity College Dublin in 1661, and it has remained there. It was never finished, and it has been rebound several times.

Portrait of Christ, Book of Kells, ca. 800
(Art Resource, NY)

up a cross, made of wood, in the central enclosure of and at entrances to monasteries and perhaps at graves. Large crosses were also occasionally carried in processions and these, also made of wood, may have been sheeted with metal. From the eighth through the 10th centuries, distinctive crosses of stone appeared, which in time became the characteristic symbol of Celtic Christianity. Great ringed crosses, such as those found at Ossory and Clonmacnoise, are the products of royal patronage, and they constitute the visible expression of the spiritual faith and the physical power of kings. They reproduce, in their elaborate tracings and intricate geometric patterns, the artwork on display in manuscripts and on metal. Craftsmen went on producing a profusion of finely wrought objects, many of which are now lost, in a society ruled by ecclesiastics and kings and where the means of livelihood centered everywhere on the land.

Society in Early Christian Ireland

Monasteries were the institutions that, above all others, distinguished social life in Ireland in the sixth through the eighth centuries. Some of these, such as those at Kildare, Cork, Clonard, Clonmacnoise, and elsewhere, became great ecclesiastical centers. They grew to be ruled by rich and politically powerful clerical aristocrats, and in a society without cities, they became important centers of economic life. Some even became the residence of provincial kings—the king of the northern Uí Néill dynasty maintained a home at Armagh.

Because Armagh claimed Patrick as its founder—the revered saint allegedly received grants of land from the chieftain Daire and built a stone church and monastery—the church here emerged as the greatest of all the ecclesiastical centers in the seventh century when its clergy, in a series of religious tracts, made formal claims to appellate jurisdiction over all Ireland. By this time, Armagh was not a monastic church, the chief cleric no longer an abbot-bishop, but now exclusively a bishop who claimed jurisdiction over many surrounding churches. By the end of the seventh century, its primacy was largely acknowledged everywhere, and the bishop of Armagh took precedence over all the Irish clergy.

Nevertheless, there was no formal structure. In the seventh, eighth, and later centuries, the religious scene was a complex one—great monasteries wielded much influence, but bishops, though often based in a monastery, held considerable power of their own. Church authorities created territorially defined dioceses, their borders often coinciding with those of early Irish kingdoms.

Because the majority of monks were laymen, religious life required not only a stock of priests to conduct services but also churches in which to hold them. Churches varied in the type of status they carried. Some were free, not attached to a monastery or bound by obligations to the original owner or donor of the land on which they stood. Some were unfree, required to pay taxes in being subject to a king or owned by a more powerful church, whereas others were controlled by a wealthy family who founded the church or owned or donated the land. Some churches were large with many dependent churches and abundant revenues. Some were small and these, both free and unfree, were the most numerous. Bishops ruled over all these churches as chief pastors whose duty it was to ordain clergy and oversee their work, consecrate churches, and ensure that religious rites and services were provided to the people.

The people over whom the clergy presided numbered between a half million and a million in the period from the seventh to the ninth centuries. They inhabited an island where large swaths of deciduous forest and great boglands could be found, especially in the midlands and western uplands. Life was everywhere rural—there were no towns or villages—and a mixed farming economy was practiced, concentrated in the lowlands where the great monasteries often supported considerable activity. The poorest lived in isolated huts, while the better-off inhabited farmhouses protected by ring enclosures of dry stone wall or earthen ditches.

Outside the enclosure, tilled fields were fenced off, and the grains cultivated included oats, barley, wheat, and rye, in descending order of importance. Ploughing was done in March, most farmers using a wooden spade with an iron sheath, and they harvested the ripe grain in late summer using a reaping hook. Oats were eaten as gruel and porridge and also as bread, which was the staple of the common people down to the 19th century. Bread made of wheat was a luxury. Barley was malted to make ale. Vegetables were not widely grown, and they consisted chiefly of chives, leeks, parsley, kale, and probably garlic. Likewise, fruits were not in plentiful supply, apart from apples, but wild nuts, especially hazelnuts, were abundant.

Beyond the tilled fields lay the pasturelands. Milk and dairy products were dietary essentials, and cows grazed in summer on upper mountain slopes and in moorland, where they were tended by women. Butter and cheese, heavily salted for preservation, were widely available, and sheep, although raised largely for their wool, supplied much of the milk and butter of the poorer classes. Mutton was eaten by the well-to-do.

Commerce was nonexistent, and survival depended on good harvests and healthy animal herds and flocks. Crop failure could bring hardship that, in its severest form, might mean famine, disease, and social disorder, the last occasioned by internal migration in efforts to survive.

But even good times brought no guarantee that disaster might not strike. Major epidemics swept through the population from the second half of the seventh century to the first quarter of the ninth. Religion brought solace. The poor and the unschooled, however, would turn, on occasion, to the old pagan gods, many beliefs and traditions kept alive in a society in which the oral transmission of Celtic heritage remained important. Religious and secular authorities sought to maintain the social order in enacting laws to ensure respect for the church and its ministers and to keep the civil peace. It was a call for order that was little heeded by secular rulers in relations among themselves.

Royal Dynasties and Early Kingdoms

Kings stood at the top of secular Irish society, and they held considerable power. Irish literature is replete with references to royal rulers. The annals narrate their adventures, the genealogies list their lines of descent, and the sagas tell stories of their heroic deeds and acts of kindness. Pagan traditions imparted much mystical significance to the institution: The installation of a new king was conceived as a sacred marriage with the goddess of the earth, a union that would bring forth life to both the people and the land.

Early Christian Ireland contained many small kingdoms, but their exact number is unknown, perhaps totaling 100. By the seventh century, however, the threefold hierarchy of kingship had evolved such that the petty kings and lesser overkings were disappearing. The annals tell of the conquest of their kingdoms by their superiors in the eighth century. The less powerful kings, each of whom ruled a territory (Irish, *Tír*), were becoming dependent noblemen of the great overkings, whose reach encompassed several kingdoms that gradually evolved over the centuries into Ireland's several provinces.

In the far north in Ulster and in Meath the Uí (pronounced "Ee") Néill emerged in the seventh century from remote origins to dominate the midlands and the northwest. The Uí Néill rulers laid claim to the most prestigious royal title in all Ireland in proclaiming themselves "king of Tara," the sovereign who sat at the seat of supreme power. The Uí Néill split at some unknown date into southern and northern factions. The southern Uí Néill further divided into two major and many minor branches. The Síl nÁeda Sláine and the Clann Cholmáin ruled the fertile lands of Meath, Westmeath, and surrounding areas. The former were powerful in the seventh century, but in the eighth the latter emerged to take the overking of the Uí Néill in 743. By the ninth century, their king claimed the kingship of all Ireland. The northern Uí Néill were also split into two wings—Cenél Conaill in Donegal and Cenél nEógain in Derry—and here too the former dominated from the late sixth to the mid seventh centuries, and then, after a long series of dynastic struggles, the latter emerged the stronger in the late eighth century. They expanded south and east across the mid Ulster plains, subjugating minor kingdoms, until by 800 the Cenél nEógain stood triumphant.

Founded at the beginning of the fourth century by three warlike princes called the Three Collas (Colla Uais [Colla the noble], Colla Meann [Colla the famous], and Colla de Chroich [Colla of the two territories]), Airgialla (Uriel, Oriel, Orialla, among other spellings) emerged in the seventh century as a confederacy of nine kingdoms in present-day counties Louth and Monaghan. The Collas laid waste the kingdom of Ulaid during the fourth century, burning Emain Macha, though the ruling Dál Fiatach dynasty clung to power in County Down and parts of Armagh and Tyrone. Once having reigned over most of Ulster, the Dál Fiatach in the east shared with Cenél Conaill in the west an abiding hatred for the Cenél nEógain, the new strongmen on the scene. The Dál Riata, a kingdom centered equally in County Antrim and on the western seaboard of Scotland, reached its apogee in the late sixth century, but subsequent defeats in Britain led to its gradual decline and eventual disappearance by the 11th century.

In Leinster, the Uí Dúnlainge dynasty held the overlordship of the province, ruling from their powerbase in the Liffey River valley and in the plains of Kildare, from where they had gradually expelled other groups to the province's outer edges, namely, the eastern coastal strip, the Wicklow Mountains, and the northeastern boglands.

From the seventh to the mid 10th centuries the Eóganacht (Eóganachta) ruled Ireland's southern province of Munster. Starting in the fifth century they began to supplant their predecessors the Érainn, and they evolved to become a powerful dynasty, presiding over small kingdoms in the south, east, and west. The Eóganacht were closely connected to the church, and one of their kings, Feidlimid mac Crimthainn (r. 820–46), governed as both bishop and king of Munster. A ruthless ruler who seemed to place material over spiritual matters, he pillaged monasteries and raided Uí Néill territory; but, by the late ninth and early 10th centuries, his dynasty's power crumbled rapidly, replaced by the Dál Cais, who were to dominate in north Munster in the mid 10th century. The kingdom of Osraige existed largely as a buffer state between Leinster and Munster in roughly the area of modern-day County Kilkenny.

In Connacht, the two ruling dynasties were Uí Fiachrach and Uí Briúin (Bréifne), both claiming to be cousins of the Uí Néill. Uí Fiachrach consisted of southern (Uí Fiachrach Aidhe) and northern (Uí Fiachrach Muaidhe) branches. Uí Briúin emerged in the seventh century, ruling in Leitrim and Cavan, and by the first quarter of the eighth, they had become the major dynasty in Connacht.

The law tracts did not recognize a high king of Ireland, although the idea that there existed a king who reigned over the whole island was a pervasive myth assiduously put forth by learned men anxious to promote an awareness of unity. The ancient lawyers spoke of an islandwide custom and law, and clerical supporters of the Uí Néill dynasty pushed the notion of Irish political unity, under the authority, of course, of their patrons. Muirchú, the late seventh-century author of a hagiographical work on Saint Patrick, speaks of Niall, the founder of the Uí Néill, as the ancestral head of the family whose branches came to rule most of the island. Called Niall of the Nine Hostages (Niall Nóigiallach), allegedly for having taken that number of prisoners, Niall (d. ca. 405) was said to have carried out raids on the coasts of Gaul and Britain, and his seven sons all founded dynasties, including the Cenél Conaill, Cenél nEógain, Clann Cholmáin, and Síl nÁeda Sláine. Indisputably the island's most powerful dynasty, the Uí Néill not only laid claim to the overlordship but also were able at various times to make that claim a reality over very wide areas. Their imposing ninth-century king, Maíl Sechnaill mac Maéle Ruanaid (d. 862), made especially strenuous efforts to secure the high kingship. The *Annals of Ulster (Annala Uladh),* a chronicle of Irish history between 431 and 1540, refer to him as such, and he is considered the first definitive high king of historical record. During his reign, however, he was compelled not only to compete with neighboring Irish dynasties but also to treat with a foreign force that had arrived in Ireland from across the sea.

3

FROM VIKING INVASIONS TO ROYAL CONFRONTATIONS (795–1169)

Ireland had known no invaders since prehistoric times. The Vikings, who arrived quite suddenly at the end of the eighth century, sent shock waves through a society in which Christianity had been left to organize itself, exercise its influence, and cultivate its artistic treasures largely undisturbed for more than three centuries.

Marauding seafarers from Norway and Denmark brought ruin and confusion, but they also made a positive contribution to subsequent Irish history in founding the first towns. They tied the island to a continental empire of far-flung places where the Vikings raided and traded, launching both the first large-scale outside contacts and the beginnings of commercial life. In time, like their predecessors before them, they too conformed to Ireland's demographic pattern in assimilating with the natives, becoming Christians, and adopting the Irish language and Irish customs. Initially an independent force sitting behind the defensive walls of their coastal and riverine settlements, they began trading with the interior and soon found themselves drawn into dynastic struggles, which marked the politics of this period just as they had politics for centuries before.

The Vikings brought a nautical technology and superior weaponry, which facilitated the ability to do battle across wider territories with more deadly means. Irish royal dynasties, fewer in number but richer in resources, fought to acquire whole kingdoms, and the first efforts to claim the title of high king by actually possessing the requisite geographical territory were made. Because the stakes were higher, the clashes grew more intense, and the bitterness engendered by those who found themselves on the losing end of the ceaseless dueling

41

stung with more lasting effect. The enmity harbored by the king of Leinster, banished from Ireland in the summer of 1166, would lead to a train of events that carried consequences for the country unlike any other.

The Era of the Viking Wars

In 795 long low-slung ships, fitted with wide, decoratively patterned sails, appeared from off the ocean's horizon and ran their pointed bows onto the rocky beach at Iona. Warriors wearing round or horned helmets, armed with heavy swords and iron spears, rushed into the monastic village and, in a frenzied fury, ransacked the settlement, carrying away slaves and booty, including altar shrines and vessels, their surfaces glittering with the gems with which they had been so painstakingly inlaid. In the same year, seafaring raiders burned the community at Rathlin and attacked those at Inishmurray and Inishbofin.

The Vikings were bands of warriors from Scandinavia who set sail from its shores with but one purpose in mind—to seize whatever plunder they could find. The ships they manned were the most technically advanced of their time, designed by skilled Nordic craftsmen to provide the maximum in mobility. Whatever the reasons that led the Vikings to set out on their quest for riches—and they remain obscure—raiding that had begun in the Baltic Sea spread outwards from there at the end of the eighth century. Over time these men from the far North (Norsemen) ranged as far east as Moscow and Constantinople and as far west as the North American continent. In the 790s fleets attacked Ireland, Britain, and France simultaneously.

Pagan farmers and fishermen and, at home, many of them dexterous craftsmen, the Vikings were the penultimate pirates. Led by their kings and nobles, they are said to have delighted in destruction for destruction's sake. Wielding their terrifying signature weapon, the broad battleaxe, raiders returned to Iona in 802 and again in 806, this time murdering 68 of the monks. The great monasteries, the centers of wealth, were the targets of attacks again and again during the first 40 years of the ninth century. Fear pervaded the atmosphere wherever they roamed, for the Vikings would appear suddenly without warning at any time, ready to wreak havoc without scruple.

By 823 they had completed the circumnavigation of the Irish coast, in 824 even sacking bleak Skellig Michael. Most of the raiders to Ireland came from the fjords of Norway, and during the first decades of the 800s they never tarried long, operating as small, quick-moving forces striking in hit-and-run attacks. The Irish fought back as best they could. Monks moved to inland areas. After the raid of 806 the abbot at Iona, Cellard, carrying with him the revered relics of Columbanus, traveled with his companions 20 miles inland from the Irish coast to Kells, where they founded a new monastery. Kings from Ulster to Munster battled the invaders when they could catch up with them.

Viking ship, bow and port side view, under sail (Library of Congress, LC-USZC4-7646)

In the end, however, the search for security proved elusive. Raids intensified in the 830s, and now roving bands began moving inland. In 836 the first Viking land raids on record occurred on lands of the southern Uí Néill, and much of Connacht was also devastated. The following year the course of invasions began to change character. A mighty fleet of 60 ships appeared on the river Boyne and another 60 on the Liffey. Norsemen pillaged churches, fortresses, and farms in the Liffey valley, and they sailed up the Shannon and the Erne as well, defeating the forces of the Irish kings wherever they went. Viking ships plied the Shannon lakes in the very heart of the country. They appeared to be unbeatable. In 841, at Linn Duachaill (present-day Annagassan, County Lough) and at Dublin they set up defensive bases as footholds from which to mount invasions deep into the interior. At Dublin, the Vikings wintered for the first time in 841–42, building a stockade around their ships and thus laying the foundation of the city.

In the middle of the ninth century, Vikings from Denmark began to arrive, adding another element to the mayhem. The Vikings on the scene resented the interlopers and battled them in a fighting stew that included old and new combatants both native and foreign—Viking against Viking, Viking against Irish, and Irish against Irish.

No one anywhere was safe, but Irish kings kept up running battles against the invaders. They gradually began to achieve greater success, measured both by victories in battle and by a decline in the number of attacks. In 835 the Vikings were defeated at Derry, and in 845 Mael Sechnaill mac Maéle Runaid, king of Meath, captured and drowned the Viking leader, Turgeís. Fleets were still arriving in 849–51, but by a decade later the great raids were over.

That the Irish had found it difficult to resist the invaders stemmed in part from their inability to unite to meet the common threat. The peak of the Viking incursions found the Uí Néill, based at Tara in Ulster, and the Eóganacht, at Cashel in Munster, clashing for the first time on a large scale. And the Scandinavians proved more than willing to join in the local strife. The Vikings very quickly—by the mid ninth century—assumed an active role in the local interdynastic warfare. The first Viking-Irish alliance is recorded in 842, and accounts speak increasingly of these pacts from 850 on.

Battles followed battles both within and between kingdoms, and the power of kings waxed and waned. The Uí Néill kings at Tara built up their power gradually in the second half of the ninth century, and the Vikings in Ulster were largely brought under control. The Vikings remained strongest at Dublin, where they frequently allied with surrounding rulers.

The close of the ninth century saw a slackening in Viking activity; however, the respite proved but a brief interlude. A second period of major incursions began in the second decade of the 10th century and lasted for 25 years. The storm to come gathered force in 914 when a great fleet of ships massed in Waterford harbor. In 915 they set out to attach Munster and, later, Leinster, yet again laying waste monasteries at Cork, Aghaboe, Lismore, and elsewhere. And once again, the Irish counterattacked. Niall Glúndub mac Áedo (d. 919), overking of the Uí Néill, chased the Viking raiders through Munster in 917 but failed to stop them, his allies from Leinster meeting heavy defeat. He himself fell victim two years later when he and many leading aristocrats of the Uí Néill were defeated and killed by the Vikings at the Battle of Dublin. Triumphant yet again, the Norsemen, secure in their base at Dublin, set about consolidating control of outlying settlements in Limerick and Waterford. By about 950 the second great wave of raids was largely over.

What effect did the Viking invasions have on Irish society? Certainly considerable death and destruction occurred. Much cultural heritage disappeared, and the number of treasures that were irretrievably lost cannot be calculated.

Yet, while life was disrupted, it was not extinguished. The Vikings, in fact, also had a very positive impact. In founding settlements, they introduced commercial activity into a society hitherto based entirely on subsistence agriculture. Once settled in Ireland, the Vikings did not become farmers and fishermen; rather, they became merchants and seamen. Unlike in Britain and France where they moved inland, those in Ireland contented themselves in remaining where they had landed. From their bases that hugged the coastline at Dublin, Cork, Waterford, and on the Shannon at Limerick, they built up a system of seaborne commerce that linked Ireland with markets from Scandinavia to Spain.

Dublin retained its status as the most important Viking settlement, and the town grew swiftly in engaging in a far-flung trade that made it one of the richest in Viking Europe.

Dublin, together with York in Britain, became the most important of the westernmost trading posts. Trade became so significant that a cash-based economy was introduced in 953 when the first silver coins were minted. They continued to be issued until the arrival of the Normans. In introducing commercial life to the country, the Vikings set in motion the shift of the island's political and social fulcrum from the central midlands to east coast urban centers, a move that has endured.

THE BEGINNINGS OF DUBLIN

Dublin (in Irish, Baile Átha Cliath) began as a landing stage near the ford that crossed the Liffey River above its mouth. A port was established on high ground at a spot where the smaller Poddle River enters the Liffey, making a "black pool" (in Irish, *dubhlinn*, pronounced "dove-lin"). Records after 843 refer to a settlement at Áth Cliath, an adjacent site, and habitation may also have taken place on Usher's Island, in the river nearby.

The Viking founders constructed around their settlement a defensive embankment of earth, gravel, and mud, topped by a palisade of wooden posts and wattle, later replaced by a stone wall. Population spread in scattered spots along the banks of the Liffey and its tributaries. The establishment of Dublin, together with other towns, marks the start of urban life in Ireland. Because the outpost served as a chief point of embarkation and debarkation for Viking sailing ships, it operated as a commercial entrepôt from the very beginning, and crafts and manufacturing soon joined trading activities. Close contacts with England began in the 10th century.

Kings of Dublin began to appear in the records as early as 850. By the turn of the 10th century, Dublin was called a town, and in 944 the term *dún* (stronghold) is used to refer to the place. By the end of that century, Dublin began to take on the look of a real community. Streets were surfaced with gravel and stone, wattle mats, or split logs. Over 100 houses stood here, with walls of wooden post and wattle and thatch roofs, along with adjacent plots and yards divided by fences.

Dublin was repeatedly attacked and captured by the Irish, no less than 13 times between 936 and 1015. King Amlaibh Cuaran (in Norse, Olafe kuaran) married a member of the Kildare family and may have spoken Irish, and his reign marks the definitive existence of a Hiberno-Norse town. Defeat of the Dublin Vikings by Brian Boru at Clontarf in 1014 spelled the end of the town's rulers as independent players in Irish statecraft.

Dublin grew to become one of Europe's richest ports in the 11th and 12th centuries. Possession of the town became an important goal of Irish kings, and, later, the English in Ireland established their capital at Dublin.

Excavations at sites around the city have uncovered much evidence about the dwellings, adornment, occupations, and culture of the founders and early residents of the Republic of Ireland's capital and the island's largest city.

Expert traders and sailors, the Vikings introduced their advanced shipbuilding skills to Ireland. Busily plying the coastal waters, the warring wayfarers imprinted their presence on the island's fringes. Not only settlements—Waterford, Wicklow, Strangford, and Dalkey—but also islands and bays—Blaskets, Smerwick, Salters, and Selskou—carry their names.

Although settlements might suffer repeated attacks throughout the upheavals of the ninth and 10th centuries, social life, while subject to disruptions, adhered to familiar patterns. Monastic communities rebuilt or moved to other locales. Irish kings were hard pressed by Viking incursions, and several small kingdoms near Norse settlements were overwhelmed, yet the strife that had for so long characterized native society never abated. Kings continued to war with kings.

Tenth-Century Dynastic Dueling

In the second half of the 10th century, battered by battling both Vikings and tribal rivals, the Eóganacht in Munster fell to the forces of the Dál Cais, rulers of a petty kingdom in east Clare who grew to power in part because they occupied the lands that straddled the Shannon, the strategic waterway facilitating control over southwestern and central Ireland. In 964 their leader Mathgamain captured Cashel, the site of the famed rock that served as the seat of the Eóganacht, and soon after they defeated the Vikings, sacking their city of Limerick. By now the ruler of the Dál Cais was styled "king of north Munster." Mathgamain was assassinated in 976, and he was succeeded by his younger brother Brian Bóruma (or Boru).

Brian avenged the killing of his brother. By 980 he controlled Limerick and all of Munster. Ensconced at Cashel, he swiftly set out gathering power.

He was able to do so partly because, from the 940s to the 960s, the major branches of the Uí Néill in the north were engaged in a bitter interdynastic struggle. The overking, Domnall Ua Néill (956–80), put troops on the ground in garrisoning Meath, thus giving substance to his claim to rule the southern Uí Néill. He was succeeded by Máel Sechnaill II (Máel Sechnaill mac Domnaill, Máel Sechnaill Mór, r. 980–1002, 1014–22). Defeating the Vikings of Dublin at the Battle of Dublin in 980, Máel Sechnaill became the preeminent power in the north. He met the rising power of Brian Boru for the first time at Ossory; here, and subsequently elsewhere, his attempts to contain him failed, as Brian effectively coordinated his land and naval forces,

Royal Dynasties and Viking Territories, ca. 950

ATLANTIC
OCEAN

North Channel

Gwecbarra Bay

Cenél
Conaill

Dál
Riata

Cenél
nEógain

Ulaid

Dál
nAraide

northern Uí Néill

Donegal Bay

Ulster

Lough Neagh

Dál
Fiatach

Uí Finchrach
Muaidhe

Uí Briúin
(Bréifne)

Airgíalla
(Oriel)

Blacksod Bay

Lough Conn

Conaille
Muirtemne

Carlingford Lough

Clew Bay

Lough Mask

Connacht

southern Uí Néill

Irish Sea

Lough Corrib

Lough Ree

Tara •

Meath

Dubhlinn
(Dublin) •

Uí Finchrach
Aidhe

Galway Bay

Uí Dúlainge

Leinster

Lough Derg

Dál Cais

• Limerick

Uí Fidgente

Osraige

Déisi

Munster

Vadrefjord •
(Waterford)

• Weisfjord
(Wexford)

Desmumu

St. George's Channel

Eóganacht

Cork •

━━━━━	Maximum area of influence of Dublin Vikings
Dál Riata	Dynasty/kingdom
- - - - -	Province border
Ulster	Province
▨	Viking territory

N

0   50 miles
0   50 km

© Infobase Publishing

BRIAN BORU

Brian Bóruma mac Cennétig (926 or 941–1014), or Brian Boru, high king of Ireland from 1002 to 1014, has entered Irish lore as one of the country's greatest early leaders. Brian was born in the mid 10th century near Killaloe (Kinora) in present-day County Meath to parents of royal stock. His mother was killed by Vikings when he was young.

Brian Boru belonged to the Dál Cais dynasty, rulers of Thomond, a kingdom astride the Shannon River in parts of present-day counties Clare and Limerick. River-borne raids could be

Brian Boru, high king of Ireland (Library of Congress, LC-USZ62-108229)

made with ease from the territory, and Brian accompanied his father and, after the latter's death, his elder brother, Mathgamain, in making forays into Connacht and Meath and in battling and trading with Limerick, then a Viking settlement.

In 964 Mathgamain captured Cashel, seat of the rival Eóganacht dynasty, and he claimed kingship over all Munster. Defeating both the Eóganacht king, Máelmuad mac Brain (d. 978), and his allies the Limerick Vikings at the Battle of Sulchoid (968), Mathgamain, tricked into a meeting of reconciliation in 976, was seized and murdered by his defeated foes.

Brian set out to avenge the deed and quickly won victories over his brother's assassins, killing them. He went on to win control of all of southern Ireland, putting down rebellions and, in the end, winning the title of high king of Ireland.

Seeking to secure control of Ulster, which would give effect to his title, he defeated regional kings there. Facing rebellion in Leinster, a recurrently recalcitrant region, Brian led his forces against the Leinstermen and their Viking allies at the climactic Battle of Clontarf

(continues)

BRIAN BORU (continued)

on April 23, 1014. In an epic clash that the records say lasted all day, Brian's cause proved triumphant. But Brian and many of the leading men of Munster, including his son Murchadh, fell on the field. He lies buried on the grounds of St. Patrick's Cathedral in Armagh in an unknown location.

Brian Boru was the first king to break the traditional identification of the high kingship with the Uí Néill dynasty, and he was the first to give real effect to the title by conquering lands and winning royal submissions across the whole island. He lives on in Irish consciousness as a powerful nationwide leader of a native dynasty. The national symbol of the Republic of Ireland is called the Brian Boru harp.

the latter an innovative element introduced by the Vikings. In 981 Brian besieged and took Dublin, seizing booty and imposing a heavy tribute. He pushed his armies into Connacht and Leinster, setting up a climactic struggle between the rulers of the northern and southern halves of Ireland for control of the whole island. Rather than battling, however, they reached a compromise, agreeing at Clonfert (997) to divide the country between them.

Two years later, Dublin and Leinster revolted against Brian. Marching north, Boru defeated the Leinstermen and then struck at Dublin in the dead of winter, plundering the town, burning its fortress, and forcing its king, Sigtrygg (Sitric) Silkbeard (d. 1036), into submission. Impressed by these feats, Máel Sechnaill recognized Brian as high king of Ireland in 1002.

His base secure behind him, Brian set out to dominate the entire country. First, he won the influential backing of the church, at Armagh in 1005, winning over the religious authorities, who styled him "Emperor of the Irish." Breaking the traditional claim of the Uí Néill to the high kingship based on their control of Armagh, Brian made it a prize to be won by the most powerful of any among Ireland's provincial kings.

Now king of all Ireland in name, Brian Boru had still to secure that title in fact. Forced during the next 12 years to battle various northern kings, he met persistent, stubborn resistance at his back in Leinster. The king of Leinster, Máel mac Mórda Murchada (d. 1014), allied with the Dublin Vikings, rose in opposition. Late in 1013 Brian's son Murchadh ravaged Leinster and laid siege to Dublin, where Brian joined him. On April 23, 1014, the two sides clashed at Clontarf, just north of Dublin. In Ireland's first great battle of historical record, Brian defeated his foes. The king of Leinster was killed, but Brian also died, having won the victory but lost the prize. Poised on the brink of becoming the first true high king of Ireland, he fell on Good Friday, the day that commemorates the death of the founder of Christianity, the faith long firmly in place across Ireland that now stood poised to undergo major institutional changes.

A Revolution in Church Reorganization

The church in Ireland survived the Viking attacks rattled by the killings and looting but substantially intact. Instruction continued in monastic schools, and powerful abbots retained rulership of great monasteries. It was a church that, in the 11th and 12th centuries, stood apart from the one found in other parts of Christian Europe. An outpost branch of Roman Catholicism on the far western fringes of the Continent, it lay out of bounds of the growing power of the papacy. Largely independent, it looked to itself—and not Rome—in governing religion.

The organization into territorial dioceses headed by bishops that had begun in the years immediately after conversion had been supplanted by the monastic foundations, and so there were no parishes. With no strong administrative base over which to hold jurisdiction, bishops were few in numbers and wielded little clout. In contrast, the abbots held power aplenty. The principle of hereditary succession to certain church benefices meant that many abbots were now laymen, and so clerical control of churches declined. Several kings were also bishops or abbots. Abuses ran rife. Laymen subjected churches to taxation. Churches were burned. Moral standards were lax. Clerics committed simony (buying and selling church offices) and lived with concubines. A church organized on a monastic rather than a diocesan basis, staffed largely by lay monks, lacked sufficient numbers of priests to administer the sacraments and instruct the laity.

Reforms were called for, and the movement for organizational change came initially in urban places. Commercial relations put the newly Christianized trading towns in touch with religious authorities and developments overseas, and the inhabitants sought to establish territorial bishoprics on the English and continental, rather than the Irish, model. In England, the archbishops of Canterbury, Lanfranc (r. 1070–89) and Anselm (r. 1093–1109), not only urged provincial kings to support reform but also established dependent episcopal sees in

Ireland, especially at Dublin. At the same time, Irish travelers to Rome learned of the major series of reforms set in motion by Pope Gregory VII (r. 1073–85). Vigorous in promoting the superiority of the church over the state, Gregory instituted measures, including centralization of ecclesiastical government and compulsory clerical celibacy, designed to advance his goal. The appointment of a papal legate to Ireland in 1101 put in place on the scene an official vested with the authority to enact reforms, and a council at Cashel in that year ruled that the church would henceforth be free from secular taxation and that priestly celibacy would be compulsory.

Appointed papal legate after he was made a bishop in 1106, Gilla, or Gilbert, Espaic (d. 1145) advanced a plan for a diocesan and parochial church organization and for a uniform liturgy for Ireland. Irish kings supported the change, chairing church synods and exerting their considerable political influence. A bishop returned to rule at the chief see at Armagh when Cellach Ua Sínaig (St. Celsus), who had inherited the position of abbot in 1105, was consecrated bishop as *comarba Pádraig* (heir of Patrick). In 1106 Bishop Cellach was consecrated archbishop and recognized as primate of all Ireland. In 1111 Cellach and the high king presided over a national synod at Ráth Bresail at which new geographically based jurisdictions were decreed. Ireland was divided into two provinces—one in the south based at Cashel and one in the north based at Armagh. Each province was divided into 12 dioceses, many of which still exist.

The diocesan organization that the country has today was completed 40 years later, the groundwork for which was laid by Máel Maedóc (Maelmhaedhoc Ó Morgair, 1094–1148), Cellach's successor. Consecrated archbishop at Armagh in 1132, he is known to history as Saint Malachy O'More. Traveling to Rome to negotiate the ongoing work of church reform, he stopped at Clairvaux, where he was impressed by the new monastic movement, in essence a more austere adherence to the rule of the founder of Western monasticism, St. Benedict (ca. 480–ca. 547), launched by the Cistercian monks that he saw at work there. Malachy introduced the order to Ireland, the first monastery founded at Mellifont in 1142. Although the Augustinians and the Benedictines had arrived earlier, the Cistercians proved the most influential in introducing a form of monasticism new to Ireland. Cistercian members formed part of a continentwide fraternity that followed a standard rule. These reform movements were welcomed as vehicles by which to restructure the Irish church and revise its intrinsic monastic tradition after the devastation of the Viking era.

Malachy died at Clairvaux, stopping there again on a second journey to Rome, but his work of reform was completed in 1152 when a synod, convened at Kells and concluded at Mellifont, finished the work of reorganizing the religious map. An episcopal system for the whole country was established, and church organization and practices were standardized along western European lines, Malachy himself introducing the Roman liturgy. Dublin and the other towns were incorporated into a system in which Ireland was divided into 36 bishoprics and four archbishoprics, whose ruling seats were set at Armagh, Cashel, Dublin, and Tuam.

The monastic system continued to flourish, but it was now one run by foreign-based orders and rules. The great independent monasteries that had predominated for so long, which had exported members elsewhere, now declined. Bishops took over much monastic land and many once-prominent monasteries, increasingly empty of members, were transformed over time into lowly parish churches. The downfall of the old monasteries put an end to their economic and social systems. Deprived of their resources, the monastic schools with their ranks of scholars gradually disappeared, and they lost their pride of place as the cultural centers of Irish learning.

Early Medieval Irish Art and Literature

The disruptions in Irish society occasioned by the Viking raids had a damaging effect on Irish art. Monastic workshops were plundered, and books—of no interest to the illiterate invaders—were destroyed. The artistic patrimony from the ninth century is sparse, and objects exhibit a crudeness and coarseness that stand in sharp contrast to the impressive productions of the preceding golden age.

But the Vikings, in introducing trade to Ireland, brought Irish artists into contact with current trends in England and continental Europe. High-quality metalwork reappeared, now based on Scandinavian ornamental styles, and trading links led to increased use of silver, imported largely from North Africa, in manufacturing brooches and other objects. Craftsmen in ninth- and 10th-century metal workshops created shrines and reliquaries. Books, bells, and walking sticks—the distinguishing badge of the cleric—were often enclosed in jeweled metal cases.

Little manuscript decoration survives from the Viking period, but sculpture in stone remained active. In the early ninth century, stonecarvers began to replace the hitherto dominant abstract patterns on high crosses with figure sculpture. Biblical scenes on frescoes and ivories were copied on stone. The crosses became larger, the shafts divided into panels on which scenes from the Old Testament and the life of Christ were depicted. The style attained its apogee in the next century with the great sandstone crosses at Kells, Clonmacnoise, Durrow, and Monasterboice. The massive, nearly 18-foot-tall Muiredach's cross at Monasterboice (ca. 922) is the best-preserved example.

Artwork proliferated in the 11th and 12th centuries. Irish craftsmen integrated Scandinavian styles into their work, the evidence for which is most on display in metalwork, the outstanding field of Irish art in this period. Metalworkers lavished their attention on book shrines, bells, and especially croziers that, in their artistry, were unequaled elsewhere in Europe. Reverence for croziers had long been a distinctive characteristic of Irish Christianity. They served both as symbols of religious authority and as reliquaries, the wooden staff forming the core of the object believed to have belonged to one of Ireland's numerous saints. Bronze was the base metal used, and it formed the foundation for decoration. The processional cross of Cong (ca. 1125) is distinguished by its beautiful, subtly curved outline, emphasized by tubular silver edging and glass-filled, bossed rivets. A circular rock crystal at the center was intended to protect a fragment of the true cross.

Celtic crosses at Monasterboice, County Louth (AP Images)

Irish metalwork drew on links with Viking art, but little influence from England and the Continent is evident. Unlike European art of the period, human figures on Irish metalwork are scarce, and elaborate religious iconography is missing.

With the decline of the monasteries, production of painted manuscripts waned, late examples of which feature abundant foliage and smooth, curving interlacings. The richly colored Psalter of Cormac (ca. 1100) is one of the last illuminated manuscripts from Ireland's early Christian tradition.

The written arts, like the visual, survived the Viking invasions. The literature that encompasses the period defined linguistically as classical Old Irish (ca. 600–900) and Middle Irish (ca. 900–1200) is marked by both continuity and change. Writers looked back to the output of the past in rewriting earlier works, but while composing within a highly developed creative tradition, they also reworked material in innovative and imaginative ways. A significant corpus of narrative literature—estimated to total about 150 extant tales—together with a body of lyric poems were produced in the years framed by the arrival of the Vikings and that of the Normans.

At the beginning of the period, monasteries continued as the sole cultural centers, which is readily apparent from the titles of early religious works. *Liber Ardmachanus* (The book of Armagh), a Latin manuscript on Saint Patrick, was commissioned by Torbach, an abbot of Armagh, and written there in 807 by the scribe Ferdomnach. Vernacular manuscripts are linked to religious houses as well. *Leabhar na h-uidhri (The Book of the Dun Cow)* derives its name from a cowhide belonging to the patron saint of the abbey at Clonmacnoise, to which it is linked.

The Book of Leinster, one of whose scribes, Finn, has traditionally been identified as Finn mac Gormáin, bishop of Kildare (d. 1160), is usually cited as the last major work compiled by monastic scholars before the great church reforms. The changes that began in the second half of the 12th century led to the displacement of monks by members of educated secular families, whose origins may have stemmed from hereditary ecclesiastical families in past generations when clerics were married. Henceforth, the repositories of learning would rest with highly educated laymen. Clerical lawyers became secularized, and secular legal families produced what has survived of Irish vernacular law.

Early medieval authors wrote in both Irish and Latin, either one or the other dominating, but bilingualism is also much in evidence. Lives of the saints, homilies, hymns, and apocryphal tales appeared. Irish came to predominate over Latin as the period progressed, written in an ever-changing variety of styles.

The Irish were among the first in Europe to create vernacular versions of the classical texts of Greece and Rome. In the 12th century, Statius's *Thebaid* and Homer's *Odyssey* assumed Irish forms in *Togail na Tebe* (The destruction of Thebes) and *Merugud Uilix meic Leivtis* (The wanderings of Ulysses), respectively. Irish writers utilized a literary style characterized by much ornamental repetition, a diverse lexicon, and rhythmically arranged alliteration.

A new warrior-king to rank with Cúchulainn arose in the character of Finn Mac Cumaill, but the atmosphere evoked in the world of this youthful hero is different from that depicted at the royal court of the hero of the *Táin*. A series of works featuring Finn (*fínaigecht*) appeared in the 10th century in which he is presented as the greatest of all warriors. In the 10th-century tale *Tochmarc Ailbe* (The wooing of Ailbe), Finn and his royal lord, King Cormac mac Airt, do battle against evil. They do so in a setting in which both natural and supernatural worlds prevail, but one in which dynastic ties are looser than in the *Táin* and in which the youthful Finn never attains the full maturity of Cúchulainn.

The appearance of longer, elaborately descriptive passages marks a bold, new prose style, although brisk, succinct prose also continued to be composed. The *Togail Bruidne Da Derga* (The destruction of Da Derga's hostel), from the 11th century, combines fast flowing short sentences with detailed descriptions.

Prose predominated, but an abundance of narrative literature interspersed with poetic language also appeared. In *Buile Shuibne* (Suibne's frenzy), written in the 12th century, verse passages surpass those of prose in telling of Suibne's inner torment on his journey from being a God-cursing king to becoming a God-fearing poet. The weaving together of prose and verse is most influentially on display in *Lebor gabála Érenn* (The Book of the Taking of Ireland), commonly known as the Book of the Invasions, a multiauthored work written toward the end of the 11th century, in which preexisting historical poems are interspersed with passages of prose to tell the story of the world's history and the part played by Ireland. It was copied, revised, and in the 12th century, brought up to date.

The *Lebor gabála* contains many of the themes popular in early medieval Irish literature, including kingship and genealogies. Genealogies of saints were particularly popular. The *Book of Leinster* and later manuscripts preserve information pertaining to some 20,000 individuals.

In this profoundly religious society, spiritual subjects remained of central importance. Much poetic literature written by *céli De* (servants of God) dates to just before the Viking incursions. Hagiographies (*Betha Adamnáin* [The life of Adamnán], *Vita Tripartita* [Tripartite life of St. Patrick]) are prominent. The *Vita* adopts a geographical format, which was first seen in seventh-century tracts on Patrick, in which the foundations attributed to various saints were listed based on their location across the island. This traveling motif also characterizes the continuing popularity of tales that tell of voyages. The 10th-century narrative *Navigatio sancti Brendani abbatis* (*Voyage of St. Brendan*) relates the journey of St. Brendan (Bréanainn) of Clonfert (ca. 484–ca. 577), an abbot from County Kerry and one of Ireland's renowned "twelve apostles," who is remembered less for any historically verifiable facts about his life than for his semi-mythical exploits. Called "the Navigator," "the Voyager," or "the Bold," Brendan and his pilgrim companions sailed to the Isle of the Blessed, which some allege was North America, on a seven-year journey during which they encountered fantastic wonders. The *Navigatio* is considered one among the Irish *immram* stories, which, though essentially Christian in outlook, preserves elements of Irish mythology. The 10th-century *Acallam na Senórach* (The colloquy of the ancients) features an in-depth journey around Ireland by St. Patrick and his warrior-companions. The *Acallam* arguably represents the high point of efforts by scholars to create a written record of stories passed down orally since before anyone could remember. And it is important to remember that at least until the 12th century texts continued to be more commonly heard than read due to the lack of manuscripts and to large-scale illiteracy.

In the 11th and 12th centuries lay learned families—the successors to the monastic scribes—penned prose narratives and poetry that drew on both a native and a foreign literary inheritance. Given the complex dynastic dealings of Ireland's ruling monarchs, much of the literature focuses on kingship. The preoccupation with kingship so evident in so much writing stemmed from the deliberate intent of writers to direct compositions to a specific audience, namely, readers and listeners among the leading players of the royal dynasties then busily engaged in burnishing their claims to, and their hold on, titles and territories.

Power Shuffles and Scuffles in the 11th and 12th Centuries

Brian Boru's death proved tragic, but the victory of his forces highlighted a major fact, namely, that the Vikings no longer existed as a significant, separate force in the island's martial mix. By the 11th century, they had become largely integrated into Irish life. With settlement came close contacts, and within a few generations, Vikings had intermarried and converted to Christianity, often adopting Irish language, dress, and customs. These "Hiberno-Norse," in turn, influenced the native Irish. At Clontarf, Vikings could be found fighting in both camps, and both sides wielded the superior weaponry—heavy swords, iron spears, and chain mail—together with the swift cavalry tactics first introduced by the Norsemen.

Brian's bid for uncontested title to the high kingship of Ireland could not be sustained by his dynastic successors. His two surviving sons—Tadg and Donnchad—lacked sufficient power, and it fell to Brian's old foe, Máel Sechnaill II, to retake the high kingship, which he claimed until his death in 1022.

He did so in a royal world undergoing profound change. Provincial kings in the 11th and 12th centuries warred with the express purpose of seizing large tracts of adjacent lands. Strong kings emerged who ruled over parts of, or even whole, provinces. Minor kingdoms might be partitioned among victors and their ruling dynasties expelled to be replaced by puppet kings in service to powerful overlords. Now able to draw on greater economic and military resources than those available to their predecessors, local monarchs could acquire much greater degrees of control and authority in their territories. Kings of Leinster, Munster, and Connacht all held dominion over Dublin at different times between 1070 and 1130. By the 12th century only a handful of kings remained, the winners of past struggles, and they proceeded to consolidate their powers. Most had by now abandoned traditional royal sites for the towns, and they now sought counsel from an *oireacht* (an assembly of noble retainers). They kept standing armies. After Clontarf, warfare became more bloody and prolonged as society became increasingly militarized. Castles, cavalry units, naval fleets, and permanent contingents of troops appeared.

Early royal succession had been by alternation between collateral branches of the wider dynasty, but new kings now followed old within a small nuclear family marked by an exclusive surname—father to son, brother to brother, uncle to nephew. These compact families intermarried and competed against each other across the entire island.

The kings decreed laws and imposed taxes, and they made their fiat stick. At Athlone in 1166 the king of Connacht, Rory O'Connor (Ruaidhrí Ua Conchobair, ca. 1116–98) convened a great royal council and levied a tax of 4,000 cows on Ireland—all to buy the loyalty of the Vikings at Dublin. Taxes were needed especially to fund the larger

O' THOSE IRISH SURNAMES

Hereditary surnames appeared very early in Ireland, and many came into common use during the reign of Brian Boru. Names starting with "O" and "Mac" originated as patronyms to distinguish a son from his father or a grandson from his grandfather. "O" derives from "Ua" (pronounced hua), placed before clan names, which evolved into Irish Ó and which English-language clerks in the 16th century rendered as O' to mean another word for *of*. The *O* signifies "grandson" or "descendant" attached to the grandfather's name or trade, and it survives as a linguistic link to the extended patrilineal family units *(derbfhine)* of Irish Celtic society. O'Brien, O'Connell, O'Flaherty, O'Flynn denote the descendants of the aforementioned family groups. *Mac*—or *Mc*—is the Gaelic word for *son* and was attached to the father's name or trade. Another common Irish prefix—*Fitz*—dates from the arrival of the Normans, beginning in the 12th century. It derives from the French word *fils*, meaning "son." Over time, prefixes attached to some names were dropped. Irish surnames were often anglicized by Irish immigrants to English-speaking countries overseas and by English settlers in Ireland. For example, Ó Ceallaigh became O'Kelly; Ó Conchúir, O'Connor; Ó Tuathail, O'Toole; Ó Mealaigh, O'Malley; Mac Cárthaigh, MacCarthy; and Mac Dómhnaill, MacDonnell.

armies of the 12th century, armies that were needed to conquer the larger territories that were now contested for. And monies were used to meet administrative expenses incurred in keeping a tighter hold on the royal domains. Frequent wars kept kings in the field for longer periods, and the lands won proved too extensive to be governed solely from the sovereign's base. Royal officials, many of them once minor kings themselves, were now developing into a feudal aristocracy in heading royal households, commanding armies and navies, and holding posts as governors of royal fortresses and of cities. Kings generously granted wide swaths of territory to their supporters, even carving up whole kingdoms and giving them to their allies. They dispensed land in return for homage and military service in a contractual relationship not unlike that emerging under feudalism in continental Europe. The literary text *Acallam na Senórach* sets the idealized image of the 12th-century royal world, one in which brave nobles loyally follow their lord, willingly dying in battle for him, and partake of his grateful beneficence at a court replete with feasting, fine clothes, and fair ladies. The real-world royal realms were, however, far different.

War, deceit, murder, and mayhem are the bywords to describe the political realities of the era. For 50 years (1022–72) the high kingship was held in abeyance, kings busily jockeying for advantage in a shifting swirl of political and military alignments aimed, as always, at territorial aggrandizement. The annals of the period make for bleak reading in recording bloody quarrels, assassinations, mutilation of rivals by blinding or other means, military quartering, and burning of churches and homesteads, which, though unchanged in kind from what had transpired in earlier times, now grew more widespread.

Twelfth-century kings waged long and complicated struggles, each striving to secure control of as much territory as possible, because the key to winning the high kingship lay in gaining a lock on all the land. But none of those who claimed the title did so without the appellation "king in opposition" attached to his name in the records to denote that none won the submission of all the rulers of all the other provinces.

Despite the singular lack of success of Brian Boru's surviving sons, for about a century after 1014 his descendants maintained a fairly successful claim to supremacy. From 1086 to 1166 the most powerful king in Ireland was Muirchertach O'Brien (Muirchertach Ua Briain, r. 1101–18), grandson of Brian. In a succession of victories, O'Brien secured control of Munster and Leinster. He killed the king of Meath (1094) and won, after a series of rebellions, the allegiance of Connacht. He made astute political deals with church authorities, winning their backing in return for his support for the new reforms, and he used marriage as a diplomatic tool in wedding his daughter to leading English nobles, gaining potential foreign political and military support. O'Brien put in place a national network of subordinate authorities in the provinces who were given power to rule in his name. These regional rulers based themselves not in the traditional seats of power such as Kincora or Cashel but in towns such as Limerick and Waterford, sites that had been fortified by the Vikings and thus were better able to withstand attack by the larger armies using the more advanced weaponry of the 12th century. Dublin became an especially important town to control, a status that enhanced its prestige, which, in turn, promoted its further growth.

O'Brien ruled as high king, but he did so without having won the submission of Ulster, where Domnall Mac Lochlain (r. 1084–1121), king of the Uí Néill who claimed the high kingship as well, held him in check. In the end, betrayed by his brother, who seized the throne in 1114, O'Brien rallied to take it back, but he was promptly thrown off it again. By now, no doubt convinced the prize was not worth the effort, he retired to a monastery.

A new king from another province soon rose to the fore. The province proved to be Connacht, and the king from the west was Turlough O'Connor (Toirdelbach Ua Conchobair, 1106–56), the greatest of the 12th-century warrior-kings. Constructing a ring of fortresses around Connacht, he built up a large army and navy that he used to invade his neighbors in his quest to make himself high king. He gained control of Munster between 1115 and 1131, and then he secured Meath.

O'Connor won a shaky allegiance from Dermot MacMurrough (Diarmait Mac Murchadha, r. 1126–71), king of Leinster, but, like O'Brien before him, he failed to defeat Ulster. Suddenly, in 1156, O'Connor died, once again putting the perennial political game of who's on top back into play. Tops on the list of contenders stood Muirchertach Mac Lochlainn (r. 1156–66), king of the Uí Néill. Between 1156 and 1166, Mac Lochlainn and MacMurrough allied and together faced off against their twin opponents, King Rory O'Connor (r. 1156–98), Turlough's son, and his ally Tienán O'Rourke, ruler of Bréifne, a small kingdom in Munster. The struggle, distinguished by seemingly never-ending campaigns and cattle raids, surged back and forth across the whole island.

Eventually, Mac Lochlainn proclaimed himself high king, and the story continues as a replay of past power struggles. While Mac Lochlainn was busily securing his title in squelching local troubles in Ulster, where he subsequently died, O'Connor kept up his attacks, invading Meath and taking Dublin in 1165. Fortifying the already formidable power base left to him by his father, Rory took the high kingship in 1166. Ireland was now ruled by a stable, solid dynasty, and the country seemed poised to establish a feudal-based hereditary kingship on the model of monarchical dynasties then emerging in other western European countries. Then, in a move bemoaned by generations of native Irish to come, the king of Leinster, MacMurrough, intervened to put an end to this prospect of settled, centralized rule.

MacMurrough ruled a province that, since prehistoric times, proved recurrently rebellious, its leaders resenting and resisting central rule. Having defeated MacMurrough, O'Connor was content to take hostages from him and to leave him in possession of a small kingdom centered on Ferns in County Wexford. But O'Connor's ally O'Rourke seethed with a thirst for revenge, determined to avenge his humiliation at the hands of MacMurrough 14 years earlier when, in 1152, he had abducted his wife Dervorgilla. He grasped his chance in 1166 when, deprived of his great ally Mac Lochlainn, MacMurrough stood isolated. O'Rourke, the Norsemen of Wexford, and other allies destroyed his stone castle at Ferns and drove him to Dublin. The Dubliners would have none of him, and they too forced MacMurrough to flee. O'Connor banished MacMurrough from Ireland on August 1, 1166. Leinster's defeated king fled to Bristol, England. Bitterly resentful, he appealed to King Henry II (1133–89) for help. The invitation would lead to an invasion that would change Ireland forever.

4

FROM THE NORMAN INVASION TO THE ANGLO-IRISH ADMINISTRATION (1169–1534)

One of those events that can truly be said to "make" history, although contemporaries would surely not have seen it that way, the Norman invasion profoundly altered the course of Irish affairs. Themselves immigrants to England, the Normans arrived in Ireland in 1169, and they set about, slowly and on a piecemeal basis, to reshape society in Britain's neighboring island as thoroughly as they were doing in England after settling there 100 years earlier. Their castles, churches, and abbeys gradually dotted the landscape as they proceeded westward, by fits and starts, on their campaigns of conquest. They brought a foreign government, with its powerbase outside the country, to rule the island. They introduced a political ideology, law, and culture that tied Ireland to the wider world of western Europe.

They tended to take for themselves the best terrain, but they never succeeded in settling in sufficient numbers to secure all the land. Although it was the Normans who initiated inland town life in Ireland, large swaths of territory remained subject to rule by the native Irish. However, Gaelic rulers no longer presided over whole kingdoms as in pre-Norman times. They formally submitted now to the overlordship of English kings, who occasionally, but very rarely, came to Ireland in the Middle Ages. Irish leaders competed for title to land of varying sizes with Norman aristocrats, who had seized equally varied tracts from them. The Normans, like the Vikings before them, soon settled into the local scene in constituting just another competing player in the perennial scheming for wealth and influence.

In time what the Irish lost in territory they gained back in influence, taking the initiative in building up powerful dynastic realms equal, and in some cases superior, to the great earldoms that, by the 14th century, emerged in parts of eastern, southern, and central Ireland. Many of these earldoms were ruled by families who were by now "Anglo-Irish," having become, through intermarriage and close cultural contacts, almost indistinguishable from the Gaelic Irish in customs and manners. The Irish sought maximum independence from English rule, the Anglo-Irish maximum autonomy under that rule, and the English crown, its retainers clustered in Dublin and its environs, maximum control over both.

A land that proved initially profitable to the Crown, Ireland by the 14th century became a place where the English had a precarious hold. Saddled with wars foreign and civil, the government lacked the manpower and the money to make royal rule a reality. Relying at first on governors weak for want of the resources needed to give them clout and then on powerful Anglo-Irish magnates who sought to control administration more often to advance their own interests, English rulers by the end of the Middle Ages reigned largely in name only. Only when they found the will to give Ireland adequate attention, in the 16th century, would monarchs in London begin to make their writ firmly stick.

Norman Invasion, 1169–1175

The events that surround the coming of the Normans to Ireland constitute neither high drama nor sweeping history. The story begins with a grudge between warrior-kings, and its opening stage culminates not in the arrival of a massive army but rather in the landing of a small armed band. The invasion was provoked by a train of events personal to the instigators, but underlying political and economic considerations would soon draw in the major players in both lands.

In 1166 the defeated king of Leinster, Dermot MacMurrough—"Dermot of the foreigners" as he would subsequently be styled—fled to Bristol, England, then the main port for trade with Ireland. But he soon sailed away again, this time to France, where the king he was seeking could usually be found. Henry II (r. 1154–89) was a Norman Frenchman, born in Normandy and speaking Norman French, who spent most of his time on the Continent striving to keep intact his far-flung Angevin Empire, which stretched from southern France to England. Dermot caught up with Henry in the far south in Aquitaine, and his request for help in recovering his lands did not fall on unreceptive ears. The king harbored an interest in Ireland, an idea that actually predated his reign. An invasion of the island had been discussed at the royal court since the time of the first Norman king, William the Conqueror (r. 1066–87). In 1155 Henry actually secured a papal blessing for an expedition. Though some historians question the idea, it is highly probable that the English pope Adrian IV (r. 1154–59) issued the bull *Laudabiliter* investing Henry with lordship over Ireland. But a decade later Henry's hold on England itself was still too insecure for him to divert forces to the far-off western isle. He stopped short of setting off in 1166, but a shrewd and highly intelligent ruler, he reasoned he had nothing to lose by encouraging the exile. Dermot offered him homage and fealty, which Henry accepted, sending him on his way with gifts and a letter inviting English subjects to lend aid to the Irish supplicant.

Dermot returned to Bristol, where he found no takers, but extending his search across the Severn River, he found the perfect place to sign up volunteers. In the borderlands of Wales, Normans had long been battling the native Welsh. Ever anxious to secure land and the wealth such possession afforded, the Normans were insatiable in their pursuit of property, and Ireland beckoned to them—fertile new turf just a short voyage away. In Wales, Dermot also found the perfect candidate to lead an invasion force. He offered command to one of the great Norman leaders, Richard FitzGilbert de Clare (ca. 1130–76), the second earl of Pembroke, known as "Strongbow." A battle-tested member of a prestigious Norman family, but a restless man with neither a wife nor Henry's royal favor to sustain him, Strongbow relished the prospect of the fortune to be had from Irish adventuring, but he drove a hard bargain. He agreed to lead an army to restore Dermot to power on condition Dermot give him both his eldest daughter, Aoife, in marriage and the right of succession to the kingdom of Leinster.

Dermot consented and, anxious to recover his lands, gathered a motley army of knights and sailed before Strongbow in 1167. But he failed yet again, bested by Rory O'Connor, king of Connacht, and Tienán O'Rourke, ruler of Bréifne, in a short fight that left him sending urgent pleas to Wales for help, offering enticements in land and riches.

In early May 1169 the first wave of invaders arrived, beaching their boats on the sandy shore at Bannow Bay. Numbering about 600, the Norman knights—clad in glittering chain mail, armed with long lances and spears, and bolstered by a squadron of cavalry—routed the Norsemen of Wexford. O'Connor and O'Rourke recognized MacMurrough as king of Leinster south of Dublin, and the restored king acknowledged O'Connor as Ireland's high king. Intent on expanding his power, MacMurrough urged Strongbow not to delay.

Aware by now of the large-scale enterprise afoot, and fearful of the potential threat power-hungry nobles posed to his own rule, Henry II withdrew his consent, placing an embargo on exports to Ireland to cut off supplies. But it was too late. On August 23, 1170, Strongbow landed near Waterford at a place called the Passage, with an army said to have included 200 knights and 1,000 foot soldiers. The Normans took Waterford, Strongbow married MacMurrough's daughter, and together the warriors marched on Dublin, then a semi-independent Hiberno-Norse kingdom. The town fell on September 21, 1170, after a daring surprise raid by a small band of knights broke through the defenses. MacMurrough died in May 1171, leaving Strongbow heir to his kingdom and forcing him to face all by himself a string of challenges—from Leinster tribes in revolt, Norsemen from Norway led by the deposed king of Dublin, and native Irish led by O'Connor, O'Rourke, and others. Bold and daring, Strongbow remained undaunted and succeeded in defeating all his enemies.

But he faced his toughest foe in King Henry. Alarmed by Strongbow's success, his sovereign lord could not abide the threat of an independent Norman kingdom on his western flank. Now backed, chroniclers relate, by calls for help from the Irish themselves, Henry came himself, landing at Crook, near Waterford, on October 17, 1171, bringing with him a fully equipped army of knights, foot soldiers, and archers. In the end, the army proved more useful as a royal honor guard. Marching at a leisurely pace through Munster toward Dublin, Henry won submission from Strongbow, now begging pardon for his disobedience in offering to hold his kingdom of Leinster as a royal fief. Offerings to do homage and pledges of hostages, with the promise of tribute to come, were freely proffered as well by Irish kings from across the country, save from the rulers of the Cenél nEógain and Cenél Conaill dynasties in the distant north, too far away and too preoccupied with their own squabbles to care.

Whatever doubts may have been entertained about the legitimacy of the papal grant of 1155, they were put aside when Pope Alexander III (r. 1159–81) reconfirmed Henry as "lord of Ireland" in 1172 and wrote to Irish kings enjoining fealty to Henry. Echoing the pope's move, the Irish bishops assembled at Cashel made submission to him. The kings duly followed suit, acknowledging the title of "lord" that English monarchs would claim until 1541.

Once in Dublin, Henry granted the city by charter to his backers from Bristol, who had aided him in his own succession to the throne. To one follower alone, Hugh de Lacy (d. 1186), he granted the entire province

SUBMISSIONS BY IRISH KINGS

The Irish kings who made submission to King Henry II during his campaign in Ireland followed a standard set of procedures that would be repeated by Irish chieftains later in the Middle Ages, when subsequent monarchs, John I and Richard II, visited Ireland.

The man making the submission would first remove his cap, belt, and weapons. He would go down on his knees before the king, placing his hands, palms together, between the hands of the king. A prescribed oath would be taken in Irish and then translated by an interpreter into English before being formally recorded in Latin by a public notary. By taking the oath, an Irish leader bound himself to be faithful to the king and his heirs, to obey royal laws and commands, and, in general, to agree to do everything that a good and faithful subject of the king ought to do. In most cases, those making submission pledged themselves to pay large sums of money if they violated the oath.

In the king's opinion, submission turned Irish rebels into faithful subjects. From the Irish rulers' point of view, submissions meant that the king would grant them security in their properties and protection against any rivals in Ireland. Neither expectation proved forthcoming.

of Meath as a counterbalance to Strongbow, subsequently appointing de Lacy both constable of Dublin, with the right to recruit tenants on royal lands there, and justiciar, or representative of royal government in Ireland. Garrisons were set up in all the seaports. And after having done all this, compelled by pressing demands requiring his attention in his other lands, Henry sailed from Wexford on April 17, 1172.

By 1175 Strongbow and de Lacy had quelled Irish resistance in their vast territories, allowing them to parcel out plots among their chief vassals. In 1176 Maurice Fitzgerald, the "Invader" (ca. 1100–76), a Norman baron and key backer of Strongbow, obtained lands in Kildare, laying the basis for the rise of a powerful family dynasty. In an attempt to impose some order onto the political scene, King Henry and Rory O'Connor signed the Treaty of Windsor on October 6, 1175, by which Rory was recognized as high king of Ireland outside Leinster, Meath, and the area around Waterford, a title that gave him the authority to enforce and collect from the other kings the tribute Henry demanded. The treaty, however, remained valid only to the degree to which its signers were able to enforce its terms, and neither party could keep a rein on its respective subjects. Rory's hold on his own title extended no farther than the land he himself controlled in Connacht. South Munster was torn by dynastic strife. Henry's barons itched to take more land, and in the end, even the king himself could not refrain from making grants of sizable tracts, consulting neither O'Connor nor the Irish kings.

Norman Colonization, 1175–ca. 1250

After 1175 the Norman conquest of Ireland proceeded steadily but unsystematically. A newly arrived Norman knight, John de Courcy (ca. 1160–1219), exceeding his instructions, mounted an expedition into the northeastern Ulster kingdom of Ulaid. De Courcy swiftly captured Downpatrick, the capital, and in June 1177 he defeated a large Irish army. Garrisons were founded at Downpatrick, Dundalk, Newry, Carlingford, Carrickfergus, and elsewhere.

Strongbow's death in June 1176 left only a boy who was shortly to die and an infant daughter as heirs, and the entire province of Leinster became a temporary ward of the king. The Crown now moved to play a more direct part in Irish affairs, which were growing increasingly fluid, though Henry himself paid little attention to the island outside of ensuring that his Norman-Welsh vassals there did not grow too powerful and independent. Transferring all his rights as lord of Ireland to his son, John (1167–1216), Henry reserved to the Crown the city-states of Cork and Limerick.

John made his first visit to Ireland as a young prince in 1185. Haughty and rude to the Irish chieftains who came to do him homage, he granted northeastern portions of the kingdom of Limerick (in and around present-day County Tipperary) to Theobald Walter (d. ca. 1206), whom he created the hereditary first baron Butler; to William de Burgh (1157–1206); and to Philip of Worcester (fl. 1185). Both Butler and de Burgh (subsequently anglicized to Burke) would found important Anglo-Irish family dynasties.

Under King John (r. 1199–1216), territorial grants were divided into smaller shares among a large number of tenants-in-chief. Wherever they settled, the Normans built strong fortresses, which proved a highly effective instrument in ensuring that they kept a tight hold on the lands they controlled. These fortresses, whose ruins today visibly recall their presence, were usually sited at some populated place, such as a great abbey, that offered economic contacts. After 1200, when stone replaced wood for construction, the Norman castles emerged as formidable edifices, all but invulnerable to Irish attacks.

Reconstruction of Kilkenny Castle. The Normans built castles wherever they settled in Ireland. (Library of Congress, LC-USZ62-104598)

There was no central direction to the Norman takeover—the English kings were too busy battling elsewhere—but they would intervene in Ireland when greedy lords threatened to become too powerful. When John de Courcy began moving west across the river Bann to meddle in the affairs of the Irish kings in Connacht, King John disinherited him, granting all the lands he held to the ambitious younger brother of the lord of Meath, Hugh de Lacy, whom he created Hugh, palatine earl of Ulster in 1205. In 1209 the absentee landlord in Munster, William de Braose, a favorite at court, quarreled with the king and fled to Ireland, where he was sheltered by de Lacy. Riled by this disloyalty, John returned to Ireland a second time, landing at Waterford on June 20,

1210. The king marched to Ulster, capturing Carrickfergus and forcing de Lacy to flee. The lordship of Meath and the earldom of Ulster were declared forfeit to the Crown.

John laid the foundations of royal government in Ireland. Modern-day Ireland's political and legal systems owe their origins to the settlers from England and Wales. As early as King Henry's reign the justiciar—his chief representative in Ireland—relied on the advice of a council of feudal tenants-in-chief before acting, and under John and succeeding monarchs a King's Council in Ireland gradually evolved, assisted by a growing number of permanent salaried officials. Great Councils, composed of the king's officials and the barons in general, developed in the course of the 13th century into parliamentary sessions on the model of those in England. In 1204, on orders of King John, Dublin Castle was built, which became the seat of English government in Ireland. A coinage system was introduced, and royal revenues were collected by exchequer clerks working under the justiciar. Over time the liberties held by territorial lords diminished, to be supplanted by establishment of counties (shires) staffed by their legal apparatuses—sheriffs, courts, and itinerant justices. A shire court for Dublin appeared as early as the 1190s. By 1260 there existed, in addition to Dublin, seven counties—Waterford, Cork, Limerick, Louth, Tipperary, Kerry, and Connacht—and they were joined by Kildare in 1297 and by Carlow in 1306.

The increasingly complex system of government required clerks trained to run it. As feudal overlords of ecclesiastical properties, English kings drew on the English church to recruit staff in a society in which education was largely limited to the clergy. The practice of appointing English religious leaders as servants of both the church and the state was established in all colonized parts of Ireland. Saint Laurence O'Toole was the last native archbishop of Dublin, and after his death in 1180 candidates were usually royal appointees, often combining the office of archbishop with that of chancellor, treasurer, or even justiciar. King John worked assiduously to put Anglo-Norman bishops in place in all dioceses under royal control, a move resisted at Armagh, which maintained native Irish prelates for a century. But after the death of Archbishop Nicholas Mac Maoilíosa in 1303, almost always an Anglo-Irish high cleric sat in permanent residence at Ireland's primatial see.

The Normans were generous in donating lands both to endow bishoprics and to found chapters of the new monastic orders just then being introduced to Ireland. At the time of the invasion, parishes in Ireland were being territorially defined to fill out the diocesan organization introduced a century earlier. In the east, boundaries often coincided with those of the Norman lord's manor—the fundamental unit of colonization—while in the west they varied greatly in size, often following ancient tribal bounds or encompassing the area around a particular shrine. In those parts of Ireland remaining under native Irish control, large tracts of church-owned land existed apart from territory owned by the diocesan clergy and the monasteries, and tenants here paid rents to the local bishops. Where the Normans did not settle, the native Irish clergy predominated, and they kept alive many features characteristic of the pre-reformed church, including clerical marriage and concubinage, hereditary office-holding by clerics, and patronage by clerics of the bardic classes of poets. Religious contrasts between the territories colonized by Normans and those that were not make manifest that the native Irish, where they could, tried to survive the Norman onslaught. The ruthless greed of the barons was bound to engender opposition, but it was slow in forming because provincial Irish kings enjoyed long reigns in the mid 13th century. Cathal Craibhdhearg O'Connor (ca. 1195–1224) of Connacht, Donough Cairbreach O'Brien (Donnchadh Cairbreach Ó Briain, r. 1210–42) of Thomond in north Munster, and Dermot MacCarthy (Diarmait Mac Carthaigh, r. 1209–29) and his brother Cormac Fionn (r. 1230–47) of Desmond in south Munster kept title to their lands by paying rent or tribute and obeying the strictures of the English king and his justiciar.

They resorted to arms only to maintain the status quo, but when they did they faced a formidable foe. From the arrival of the Normans, the native Irish are usually referred to as the Gaelic Irish, the name the Irish called themselves (*Goídil*, or modern Irish *Gaoidhil*). Though they far outnumbered the Normans, the newcomers made use of superior fighting tactics. When drawn up to do battle, the Gaelic Irish could initially expect to meet a shower of deadly arrows loosed from the longbows of Welsh archers, followed by a charge of mounted knights carrying long lances, and then by a wave of foot soldiers, marching steadily forward in ranks and wielding long, heavy swords. The Irish, clad in their light tunics with their short swords and axes and accustomed to charging in no particular order, stood decidedly at a disadvantage, although by the end of the 13th century, Anglo-Norman barons began to wear lighter armor in fighting on Ireland's rough terrain while, at the same time, some Irish chieftains took to donning chain mail.

No episode displays the effectiveness of Norman arms and methods more vividly than the conquest of Connacht. During the minority of King Henry III (r. 1216–72), government was run by Hubert de Burgh

(d. 1243), brother of the late William de Burgh. All of Connacht was declared forfeit in 1226 and granted to William's son Richard de Burgh. The proud O'Connor kings, leaders of the dynasty whose forbear Rory had only recently been high king, had clung to their title as faithful English allies, but now they struck back. They resisted fiercely the young English barons who crossed the river Shannon in force, but in the end they proved no match for the invaders. By 1235 only the present-day counties of Leitrim and Roscommon were left to the Gaelic Irish.

By 1250 the Normans held three-fourths of Ireland. In general, they secured the best lands, including the plains, coasts, and riverine regions, leaving the hills, boglands, and woods to the natives. Great swaths of territory were held as feudal grants. When leading lords achieved a secure hold on their land, they subdivided it, bringing in vassals who, in turn, became lesser lords over tenants. Many lords set aside portions of their property adjacent to their castles as sites on which to found a town. Frequently a church and often a monastery or friary would be founded by the new settlers. A lasting achievement of the Normans, inland towns found in Ireland today largely date from this time, and their names reflect their Norman, English, and Welsh origins—Longford, Hollywood, Newcastle, Newton.

Towns both new and old grew on the strength of trade, both domestic and foreign. A money economy was introduced, and coins came into general circulation. Customs duties on wool and hides brought great sums into the royal treasury.

Gaelic Revival and Anglo-Irish Survival, ca. 1250–ca. 1350

For all their earnestness in seizing lands, the Normans settled themselves in piecemeal fashion. Outside of Leinster and parts of Munster, they occupied only bits of territory, often the choicest ones indeed but scattered here and there, and nowhere were they thickly planted. Few in number, great families might be further reduced both by the lack of male heirs and by the loss occasioned by the steady slipping away of men to fight wars in Scotland, Wales, and on the Continent. By the mid 13th century, in the absence of an organized plan of control for the country as a whole, the Normans began to slacken their drive. They did so also because they met growing, more effective opposition from the Irish, who, by this time, had stiffened their will to resist.

Penned into the extreme southwest corner of Ireland, the MacCarthys struck out against the holders of north Kerry, the FitzThomas branch of the Fitzgerald (or Geraldine) family. A force under Finghim

MacCarthy defeated the latter's troops at the Battle of Callann, near Kenmare in County Kerry, in 1261. A great Gaelic victory, it secured the MacCarthys' claim as virtual independent rulers of their lands for several centuries. The O'Donnells of Donegal stood their ground in halting Geraldine expansion in the northwest at the ford of Áth in Chip on the Shannon in 1270. The Irish were now fighting with highly effective military forces equal to those of their Norman foes. Most innovatively, they began to employ "gallowglasses," Norse-Scottish mercenaries who first arrived to fight on behalf of the O'Connors.

In the second half of the 13th century, the Irish made their final attempts to impart some degree of political unity among themselves by reviving the old high kingship. The claim of Brian O'Neill (d. 1260) of Cenél nEógain, named high king in 1258, was, however, disputed by his closest neighbor, O'Donnell of Donegal, and with diminished native support Brian was defeated by local Norman colonists near Downpatrick in 1260. In 1262–63, an innovative step was taken. In attempting to find help wherever they could, the Irish for the first time proffered the high kingship to an outsider, offering the crown to King Haakon IV of Norway (1204–63). Haakon died before he could land, but the offer was repeated in 1315, this time to Edward Bruce (ca. 1275–1318), brother of King Richard Bruce of Scotland (1274–1329). Edward landed with an army of Scots in May 1315 as an ally of Donal O'Neill (Domhnall Ó Néill, d. 1325), son of Brian. For three years Edward's forces ravaged the Anglo-Norman colony, weakening the grip of the great lords, until he was defeated and killed at the Battle of Faughart (County Louth) in 1318. With his death ended the last attempt to create a united kingdom of Ireland by which to collectively expel the invaders. The effort in search of a national leader would not be revived, and endeavors by the Irish to survive throughout the rest of the Middle Ages would be waged by and on behalf of local chieftains or local confederations of chieftains.

By 1270 much territory had been recovered by the Irish, but the Normans' colonizing drive went on. In the second half of the 13th century, the by now well-established lordships (Irish, *oireacht* or *pobal*) in eastern Ireland moved to settle the west. Castles were built, and the land divided into baronies among a military aristocracy. Still, with little surplus population in the east from which to draw, the countryside in the west remained overwhelmingly Irish. Irish tenants tilled the land on which Anglo-Norman manors were founded, and despite the best efforts of the colonizers, large tracts here continued to be ruled by native chiefs, subject only to the giving of tribute. But now payment of tribute, namely, rent and hosting services, was given not by agreement with the royal administration but rather with the great lords themselves. Close personal bonds developed between many Irish and Norman families, their members even intermarrying on occasion. Norman landlords consolidated their holdings not only by battling and allying with native leaders but also by feuding among themselves. A quarrel between the de Burghs and the Fitzgeralds from 1264 to 1296 led to an exchange of lands that left Richard de Burgh, the "Red Earl" of Ulster (d. 1326), supreme in both Ulster and Connacht. De Burgh set about colonizing with zest from the peninsula of Inishowen to the tiny port of Derry, which he wrested from control by the church.

During the course of the 14th century, by now many generations into settlement, the Normans were gradually becoming "Anglo-Irish," a population long resident in Ireland with interests distinct from those of England. Within the Anglo-Irish domains, society settled down, modeling its political and judicial systems entirely on the English pattern. The assemblies that began to emerge in the 11th century were attended, at first, exclusively by the great secular and ecclesiastical lords. In time, delegates from the counties and towns as well as representatives from the lower diocesan clergy (proctors) were elected on the basis of an extremely narrow franchise. When members from the counties first sat in 1297, Ireland acquired its first parliament, a title it earned as a body that mirrored the makeup of its English counterpart. Paralleling the one evolving in England, a bicameral legislature emerged, divided between a House of Lords, composed of the bishops and the titled aristocrats, and a House of Commons, consisting of members directly elected from rural and urban constituencies. Members first sat from the towns in 1299.

The parliament of 1297 met during the reign of King Edward I (r. 1272–1307). Endowed with responsibility for Ireland in 1254, when he was still heir apparent to the throne, Edward showed little interest in the country throughout his long reign. He viewed the island largely as a source of men, money, and victuals to provision his armies on campaigns he waged in Scotland, Wales, and France. The English in Ireland were largely left to their own devices, and the parliamentarians in 1297 assumed responsibility for maintaining order and applying English common law. The members enacted the first measures legislating against adoption by English residents of Irish habits and customs, the use of which was increasingly seen as undermining efforts to establish English hegemony. Based on kinship relations, Irish society was exclusively agricultural, featuring a highly mobile tenancy, the prevalence of

Norman Territories in Ireland, ca. 1300

ATLANTIC
OCEAN

Aran I.

Gwecbarra Bay

Uí Néill

Donegal Bay

Lough Neagh

Innisfree I.

Blacksod Bay

Lough Conn

Carlingford Lough

Achill I.

Clew Bay

Clare I.

Longford

Irish Sea

Lough Mask

Lough Ree

Lough Corrib

Dublin

Galway Bay

Hollywood

Aran Is.

Lough Derg

Newton

Newcastle

Carlow

Limerick

Tipperary

Waterford

Wexford

Blasket Is.

Saltee Is.

St. George's Channel

Valentia I.

Munster

Cork

Bear I.

N

Clear I.

☐ Land held by Normans

▥ Land held by native Irish

Munster Province label

0   50 miles

0   50 km

© Infobase Publishing

pastoral over arable farming, and the use of cattle as the prime unity of exchange and the measure of wealth. English urban life and political and judicial institutions were nonexistent in areas ruled by Gaelic lords. Powerful cultural and ethnic identifiers distinguished Irish from English, and the latter sought to forbid adoption by their countrymen and women of characteristics of Irish daily life ranging from use of the Gaelic language to Irish modes of dress (rough cloth and mantles, often unshod) and moral standards (prenuptial trial marriages, sale and bartering of wives, ease of divorce).

Irish parliaments that sat from 1310 to 1366 granted growing powers to leaders of the great Anglo-Irish families whom they counted among their members, a delegation of authority that met with little counter-reaction from a distant royal government in London.

In the early 14th century these families acquired titles, elevated to the peerage as earls, from which to base their pretensions to power. John Butler (d. 1337) was created first earl of Ormond (or Ormonde) in 1329. The Fitzgeralds (Geraldines) comprised two family branches: In Kildare, John FitzThomas Fitzgerald became first earl of Kildare in 1316; in Munster, Maurice fitzThomas Fitzgerald (d. 1356) was created first earl of Desmond in 1329. Over time the heads of these and other major aristocracies were granted wide-ranging powers in their territories.

English-settled areas acquired codes of law and municipal government, the latter replete with town councils, mayors, and clerks. The first municipal charter in Ireland was granted to Dublin by Henry II in 1171–72, and it served as the model for subsequent writs of urban governance. Manors and villages appeared. Fields were cleared and the broad farm-lands tilled in strips. Castles and small cottages dotted the landscape, and parish churches, abbeys, and friaries were numerous. Towns were ringed by defensive walls, a necessity in this age of nonstop wars and raids. Commercial life expanded in old ports, notably in Dublin and Waterford, and in new ones, such as Galway and Drogheda.

The delegation of powers to local authorities so characteristic of the reign of Edward I continued under his son Edward II (r. 1307–27) and grandson Edward III (r. 1327–77). Irish resources were drained away to finance costly foreign ventures, including the Hundred Years' War (1337–1453), a lengthy conflict with France that left the Irish exchequer near bankruptcy. The royal administration in Dublin, manned by the very barest staff, was incompetent and corrupt. A government run largely by the great landlords saved the Crown the expense of maintaining a large administration in Ireland, but it did not guarantee effective rule.

The magnates were often driven to place their own interests above those of the colony. Private wars among the leading families were endemic, and they were bitter enough that barons might turn on their own Anglo-Irish kinsmen in inciting Irish vassals to revolt against them. Many of the colony's landholders no longer even lived in Ireland—almost half of the English colony's lands were owned by absentee owners at the end of Edward II's reign—and much of the wealth of their estates would be either undeveloped or drained away. Landlords not in residence left behind run-down castles and unmanned defenses, encouraging the Irish to encroach on their properties.

Resurgent Gaelic leaders were a force to contend with throughout the 14th century. Saddled with insufficient defensive forces, justiciars in office at Dublin were unable even to guarantee the security of areas nearby. The O'Bryne (Ó Broun) and O'Toole chiefs waged constant guerrilla war on Dublin's very doorstep in the Wicklow Mountains.

By the 14th century three groups of actors jostled for position in laying claim to power in Ireland. The first were the Gaelic Irish, who sought maximum independence to run their own affairs. Irish leaders would acknowledge the king of England as lord of Ireland as long as he remained largely an absentee lord, leaving them alone and free to maintain their old traditions, follow the ancient Irish system of laws, and settle scores the old way, namely, by doing battle. Because of their recalcitrance in refusing to recognize English law, in challenging the authority of the royal administration and in declining to participate in parliamentary affairs, in time they lost their eligibility to vote and stand for office, and they were viewed by the English as aliens and, often, as outlaws. The second group comprised the representatives of the English crown, who, from their base in Dublin, sought to impose royal authority. Though always on the defensive, the government never wavered in its resolve to occupy the country on behalf of, and for the benefit of, the monarchy. In between these two extremes stood the third group, the Anglo-Irish, the descendants of the early Norman settlers. English by blood, they remained loyal to England, but as English subjects in residence, they also understood the complex character of society here. Many had assimilated to a considerable degree, intermarrying and working within Irish legal and dynastic traditions. Some families, such as the de Burghs, who by the 14th century had become the Burkes, became almost indistinguishable from their Gaelic neighbors. Subjects of the king with a centuries-old stake in the country but ever fearful of attack from their Gaelic neighbors, the Anglo-Irish counted on powerful bands of armed retainers, which they diligently maintained, to protect them, and they built strong castles to defend themselves against the rising Gaelic tide that threatened to swamp them. Many saw themselves as upholders of European civilization in its remote westernmost outpost of Ireland. Their presence did, indeed, impact the world of arts and letters.

Culture in the High and Late Middle Ages

The coming of the Normans introduced an intellectual and artistic variety to add to the economic and political diversity of Ireland. However, amid a welter of new influences, Gaelic Irish literature also survived; indeed, it thrived in the 14th and 15th centuries, always remaining distinct from, though by no means unaffected by, aspects of English and French culture brought by the newcomers.

Poetry proved preeminent in the four centuries following the Norman conquest, and the formal and highly stylized verse known as bardic, or praise, poetry came to dominate. Bardic poetry was composed by a professional learned class whose ranks were filled by the merger of the *filid*, the pre-Norman poets rooted in ancient Gaelic life who were linked closely with the monasteries, and the secular, nonliterate poets known as the *baird* (bards). During the 12th century, educated families of bards emerged, learned in poetry, history, and law. They arose from among the minor nobility, church tenants, and pre-Norman professionals during a time of political, religious, and cultural flux occasioned both by the reorganization of the Irish church and the accompanying rise of lay scholarship and by the Norman invasion. After the invasion, the bards became the main purveyors of poetic tradition in Gaelic areas of Ireland.

In an act of remarkable cultural inventiveness, a standard poetic language appeared in the second half of the 12th century based on the spoken Irish of the period that featured standardized linguistic characteristics, including strict versification in syllabic meters, using assonance, alliteration, and half rhymes, that would remain in use until the first half of the 17th century. The bards became a hereditary caste of learned poets, schooled in the traditions and histories of Gaelic dynasties and in the technical demands of the verse technique.

Bardic poetry was composed for the social elite of Gaelic Ireland. The poets were supported at the courts of the great Irish chiefs, and the products of their labors were conceived as commodities that could be bought or sold. Because the poet served as a client of a lord, he labored to create works that endorsed the social and political legitimacy of his patrons and his patron's kinsmen. The *Metrical Dindshenchas* (also spelled *dindsenchas* or *dinnsheanchas*, from Old/Middle Irish for "tradition or lore of places"), an anthology of significant legends in Irish poetic history, consists of about 176 poems, the earliest of which date from the 11th century. These poems served probably as important sources of both fictional and nonfictional information about local places in Ireland and, as such, are major surviving examples of Irish bardic verse. Gaelic literary production flourished from the 13th through the 15th centuries. Genres such as eulogy and elegy were employed by poets, who created for themselves an exclusive, formal role as political counselors in upholding the dynastic rationale of Gaelic leadership. Poets served thus as central agents in the revival of Gaelic fortunes. In so doing, they earned for themselves the enmity of the English administration in Dublin, intent as always on imposing royal authority. Through their compositions, they contributed to the development of an ethnic Irish consciousness, which culminated in a nascent sense of Irish nationality that English rulers would be forced to confront by the 16th century.

The Normans introduced an entirely separate literary presence brought from their homelands in England and France, whose first expressions appeared in Norman French, the dialect spoken by Strongbow and Henry II. Surviving samples of works written are few, the earliest that of a verse chronicle titled "The Song of Dermot and the Earl," composed possibly between 1200 and 1235, which entails an account of Dermot MacMurrough's abduction of Derbforgaill, wife of Tigernán Ua Ruaire, king of Bréifne.

Norman literature in Ireland appeared most noticeably in the early 1300s, most impressively in the British Library Manuscript Harley 913, compiled about 1390, that comprises a compendium of religious and satirical writings in English, French, and Latin. Much poetry consisted of moralizing maxims, reflecting the popularity of proverbs in an age marked by the pervasive presence of religion. In addition to religious poetry, devotional prose works were also written. Of the limited number of compositions that have survived, few contain the author's name, but much material was undoubtedly written by members of the new religious orders, among them the Dominicans and, most notably, the Franciscans, who arrived in Ireland in the 13th century.

The Franciscans spread rapidly throughout Ireland in two distinct waves—in the Anglo-Irish colony soon after the order's founding by Saint Francis of Assisi (ca. 1180–1226) in the 13th century and across the island to Gaelic areas in the 14th and 15th centuries. They served as local agents of a European-wide religious and cultural network in transmitting continental devotional texts and beliefs to Ireland, and Franciscan preachers proved to be central vehicles of cultural interchange. Traversing the country, mendicant friars, such as the mid 13th-century Franciscan Tomás Ó Cuinn, transcended ethnic, political, and dynastic boundaries in preaching the gospel. Some friars were bilingual, and they contributed further to cultural intermixing in Ireland. Polib Bocht Ó hUgin (d. 1487) was a poet whose works exhibit a synthesis of both bardic and Christian traditions. Described in the *Annals of Ulster* as the best and most productive religious poet of the period, he reveals a mastery in the use of syllabic meters in his works while he draws on Scriptures and references to Saint Francis and Saint Michael for themes. Polib Bocht also treats of quintessential Irish subjects such as the mission of Saint Patrick, and his writings and those of others, while exemplifying the vitality of the bardic craft, demonstrate the link between Gaelic culture and the church.

By the 14th century it was the culture of the Gaelic Irish that had assumed a position of unchallenged supremacy in most of Ireland. By now English had displaced Norman French as the idiom to be upheld in prohibiting the use of Irish by English and Anglo-Irish residents. However, such prescriptions continued to be largely ignored, and members of the great Anglo-Irish families became as good consumers and patrons of Gaelic literature as were their Irish counterparts. In the late 1300s, the degree to which some among the Anglo-Irish elite had been thoroughly enmeshed within a Gaelic cultural milieu is evidenced in the work of Anglo-Irish landowner Gerald Fitzgerald (1357–98), third earl of Desmond, whose poetry reveals a familiarity with the heroic saga lore of Cúchulainn.

While Gaelic Irish literature survived the Norman invasion and evolved in subsequent centuries, native styles and techniques in architectural and jewelry design, metalworking, and manuscript illumination did not. The arrival of the Normans did not lead to the sudden extinction of these traditional native artistic skills because the colonization of Ireland was a slow process—the elaborate ornamentation distinctive of Irish Romanesque style continued to be produced in carving and painting at least until the first quarter of the 13th century—but the ultimate effect was the extinction of Gaelic craftsmanship. Certainly some of the invaders must have valued Irish work, but records show no Norman patrons employing Irish artists in the decades after the invasion. In areas where Normans settled, cathedrals and abbeys were built in the early English Gothic style—Dublin's cathedrals, Christ Church (ca. 1186–ca. 1235) and St. Patrick (1220–ca. 1260) were designed by English masons. They featured pointed arches, flying buttresses, and simple decoration. Romanesque arches and doorways and Gothic windows distinguish St. Mary's Cathedral in Limerick, built between 1172 and 1194. Irish metalworkers in towns such as Dublin met intensive competition from Norman immigrant craftsmen.

The Gaelic revival that took place in the 15th century did produce a renewed interest in preserving ancient manuscripts, which were transmitted in large compendia such as the *Leabhar Breac* and the *Leabhar Mór Leacáin*. The *Book of Ballymote*, compiled about 1390 at the manor of a Gaelic lord, includes early texts—genealogies, histories, clerical tales, poems, and legal treatises—although, after 200 years of Anglo-Norman influence, the skills on display in the intricate interlacings so characteristic of manuscript illumination of the golden age were forgotten, now replaced by simple designs. During this period, ancient relics and shrines were also restored, although the work was often crudely and clumsily done.

The Norman variant of Romanesque architectural style, distinguished by rounded arches and massive dimensions, is featured in the design of castles, abbeys, and churches in areas where Normans settled, primarily in the east, where notable examples include Dublin Castle and Trim Castle. Much ecclesiastical building took place in the 15th century, especially in Gaelic areas in the west, although the finest church architecture is found in the territories of the earl of Ormond, centered at Kilkenny. The reconstruction of the Cistercian abbey of Holycross at Thurles in County Tipperary, founded in the late 12th century, carried out by James Butler, fourth earl of Ormond (ca. 1392–1452), in about 1450, includes exquisite carved stonework, featuring many foliage patterns cut in dark limestone in crisp and bold relief.

Of all Irish art forms, music alone continued in an unbroken tradition unaffected by the Anglo-Norman intervention. The quick and lively techniques of the Irish harpist regaled listeners throughout the Middle Ages just as they had audiences of many centuries past. Irish society conceded high status to musicians, and harps were very valuable, constructed by expert woodworkers and often elaborately decorated. Musicians, too, along with the bards, were viewed with suspicion by the English authorities. An ordinance of 1435 excluded both groups from Anglo-Irish areas, these artists considered to be seditious individuals who sought to advance Irish cultural ways and so to aid in aborting English pretensions to rule. By the middle of the 14th century those pretensions stood at their lowest ebb.

Irish Resurgence and the Emergence of the Geraldines, ca. 1350–1534

Lands devastated by the Scots in 1315–18, when Edward Bruce's forces, allied with Donal O'Neill (d. 1325), lord of the O'Neills, invaded the English colony, lay derelict for decades, and the effects, in combination with distress engendered by the north European famine that struck

Ireland at the same time in 1315–17, lingered for many years after. The outstanding demographic tragedy of the 14th century, the Black Death, which struck in 1348–49, stung as swiftly and sharply in Ireland as elsewhere—Dublin and Drogheda were reportedly depopulated within weeks—and panic swept the Anglo-Irish colony, where villages and towns were more numerous, the crowded conditions there proving more propitious in spreading bubonic plague than in rural Gaelic areas. Residents fled, some even returning to England. And plague would return at recurring intervals, notably in 1384. Rory O'Connor (1368–84), king of Connacht, became one among the most distinguished victims, his death initiating a debilitating feud between O'Connor factions. Plague and pestilence brought misery, and constant warfare added to the hardship, which could come at any time. Conflict never ceased, the Irish battling not only each other but also the Anglo-Irish, leaving borderlands everywhere always insecure. The resurgence of Gaelic power and culture steadily proceeded, placing the English increasingly on the defensive.

By the mid 14th century conditions among the English in Ireland had reached crisis levels, and many in the colony feared their eventual extinction. They appealed to the Crown for help, and the government responded in two very different ways—through the dispatch of expeditions and the promulgation of laws. The Treaty of Brétigny (1360) brought a lull in the fighting in the Hundred Years' War, allowing greater resources to be devoted to Ireland. King Edward III dispatched his son, Lionel, prince and later duke of Clarence (1338–68), at the head of an expedition 1,500 strong, which arrived in September 1361. The prince spent five years in Ireland, and he joined his military endeavors with legislative efforts. In his capacity as governor of Ireland, he summoned a parliament in 1366. The Statutes of Kilkenny, promulgated by the legislators on February 19, 1366, represented, at long last, the government's recognition of the plight of the Anglo-Irish. The ordinances codified colonial legislation in forbidding the English in Ireland to intermarry, wear Irish costume, speak the Irish language, use Irish brehon law in place of English common law, wage private wars or make private peace with Irish rebels, or sell weapons to the Irish in wartime or food and horses to them in peacetime. The statutes also recognized a formal division between Gaelic and Anglo-Irish church sectors in disallowing the appointment of Gaelic ecclesiastics to positions in English areas. While they give evidence of the government's intent to impose order, the statutes, over time, proved largely unenforceable.

In the end, Lionel's military campaigns failed to achieve royal control even over his own lands, much less those of any others across the island. Within a few years of his departure, complaints were again heard that English rule lay in ruins. An expedition led by William of Windsor, an experienced veteran in service to the Crown, arrived in 1369. Windsor remained until 1372 and returned from 1373 to 1376, his tenure dependent upon heavy taxes levied against the Anglo-Irish to finance his forces, sums that the Anglo-Irish in time proved unwilling to pay. Any grand design to reconquer the island gave way to a much less ambitious agenda, namely, waging small, defensive wars together with creating and maintaining local garrisons in key areas. Military actions amounted to the equivalent of putting out brush fires—when one was extinguished another would spring up. In the summer of 1370, Windsor's forces had to break off engaging those of the O'Tooles of Leinster because of threats from the earls of O'Brien and McNamara in Munster, and Windsor failed to prevent the burning of Limerick, a key royal stronghold.

According a higher priority to the wars in France, the English government clung to the hope that the Anglo-Irish lords would contribute substantially to their own defense. Thus, the large sums that had gone to the Crown in the 12th century were no longer available in the 15th because monies were withheld by local lords intent on building up their own private forces. To recoup losses, the Crown sought to compel absentee lords to return, a statute of 1368 requiring that they do so on pain of forfeiture of their lands to the Crown. It failed. Most absentees preferred to sell their properties rather than return or pay for forces to defend them. Lands so surrendered were often quickly occupied by the Irish, taking advantage of the vacuum of control the absentees left behind.

The Irish soon waxed strong across the country. By 1375 the MacMurroughs, under the leader who ruled the family for 40 years and styled himself king, Art MacMurrough Kavanagh (1357–1417), reigned supreme in Leinster, and the O'Briens styled themselves kings of Munster. Among the great Anglo-Irish lords, the Burkes provided only the very thinnest veneer of an English presence in Connacht, and only a few isolated Anglo-Irish settlements remained in the once-thriving colony in eastern Ulster. Radical measures were needed to restore Ireland to English control, but they had to await the coming of age of Richard II (r. 1377–99), the grandson of Edward III, who succeeded to the kingship as a 10-year-old boy in June 1377.

When Richard in due course turned his attention to Ireland, he did so in a spectacular way. The first monarch to come to Ireland since 1210,

Richard II sets out for Ireland. (HIP/Art Resource, NY)

the king arrived in summer 1394. He commanded a force of 8,000 to 10,000 men, the most substantial Ireland had yet seen. A truce with France in the Hundred Years' War and another with Scotland gave the king an opportunity to apply some muscle in efforts to impose royal authority. He waged war successfully, forcing MacMurrough to treat for terms, and the great leader formally submitted on January 5, 1395, agreeing to leave Leinster. From January to April 1395, all of the great Gaelic lords—O'Bryne, O'Toole, O'Nolan, and O'Neill—made submissions to Richard in ceremonies whose pomp and splendor recalled those held in the days of Henry II. The king sailed back to England on May 15, 1395, confident that he had left a land at peace and in good order.

But war soon broke out again. The king's own heir-presumptive Roger Mortimer (1374–98) was killed in battle, and Richard sailed back in June 1399, anxious to renew the fight. The Irish proved a frustratingly elusive foe. A chronicler observed: "It is often impossible to come to grips with the people, for they are quite ready to desert their towns and take refuge in the woods, and live in huts made of branches, or even among the bushes and hedges, like wild beasts. And when they hear of the approach of an invader, they retire into such remote and impenetrable fortresses that it is impossible to come up with them" (Froissart 1967, 363).

Leading a much smaller expedition this time, Richard, busy battling in Leinster, was forced to return home hastily in July to meet the threat posed by Henry Bolingbroke (1367–1413) of Lancaster, who, as Henry IV (r. 1399–1413), had seized the throne. For the remainder of the Middle Ages, no English ruler would ever again come to the island in an effort to make meaningful his title of "lord of Ireland." Richard subsequently lost his throne, and his successors would sit insecurely on theirs, English kings finding themselves embroiled in dynastic wars both foreign (Hundred Years' War) and domestic (Wars of the Roses) that left the monarchy greatly weakened, with little time, men, or money to devote to Irish concerns.

Left largely to its own devices, the English colony stood entirely on the defensive throughout the 15th century. Kavanagh renounced his fealty to Richard on the latter's departure. Gaelic armies easily matched English and Anglo-Irish forces, and both Anglo-Irish assimilation and loss of lands proceeded apace. By the mid 1400s, Gaelic lords had taken back all but 35 percent of the island. Anglo-Irish landlords adopted any means they could to survive, resorting to so-called black rents, bribes paid to Gaelic chieftains to refrain from launching attacks, and, shorn of any outside aid, forcing local populations to provide both provisions and quarters for the troops in their private armies, a practice defined as "coign and livery." Gaelic leaders adopted coign and livery as well, the losers everywhere the peasants and craftsmen forced to endure the burdensome exactions. Landowners grew increasingly dependent on Irish tenants as English residents moved out of border areas.

Rule by the government in London became largely confined to the Pale—Dublin and lands within approximately 20 miles (32 km)— so-called in connoting a stake or fence and, by extension, a terri-

Irish and Anglo-Irish Territories, ca. 1450

ATLANTIC OCEAN

North Channel

MacDonnell

Earldom of Ulster

O'Donnell

O'Neill

Donegal Bay

Magennis

Mayo

O'Rourke

Burke

O'Reilly

O'Connor

Irish Sea

O'Farrell

O'Flaherty

The Pale

Burke

Dempsey

Galway Bay

Earldom of Kildare

Aran Is.

O'Brien

Earldom of Ormond

MacMurrough

Blasket Is.

Wexford Lordship

Earldom of Desmond

Saltee Is.

MacCarthy

St. George's Channel

Land held by Anglo-Irish lords	- - - -	Borders
Land held by English king	*O'Brien*	Clan name
Land held by native Irish		

N

0   50 miles
0   50 km

© Infobase Publishing

tory closed off and subject to a particular jurisdiction. The term first appeared in 1446–47, when Gaelic leader Hugh Roe McMahon agreed that he would "carry nothing out of the English Pale" (Cosgrove 1981, 72). Despite his promise, Gaelic raiders would occasionally penetrate even here.

Elsewhere, Ireland was divided into a patchwork quilt of territories of varying sizes ruled by local lords. The three great earldoms—Ormond, Desmond, and Kildare—became the power brokers of note. In north Munster, the earls of Desmond, who had intermarried with the families of the MacCarthy chiefs, had amassed power such that even the towns became subject to their authority, royal writs here having been largely extinguished. Elsewhere, from his base in Tipperary, James Butler (1392–1452), the fourth (or "White") earl of Ormond, effectively annexed the royal city of Kilkenny, including lands of the church, and he even convened local assemblies that exercised powers of legislation and taxation equivalent to those of parliaments. In Meath the earls of Kildare wielded a considerable degree of lordship over Irish chiefs, and they began to extend their influence in the mid 15th century northward over the O'Neill chiefs of Tyrone in return for lending military aid to the latter. In the absence of a strong royal authority, each of these families harbored an ambition to become the sole protector of English interests in Ireland, and rivalries among them could become so intense that they eclipsed efforts to repel and contain their Gaelic neighbors.

The Anglo-Irish made, broke, and remade alliances with their Gaelic neighbors, who, flexing their renewed strength, in turn employed both diplomatic and military means of their own, including waging savage battles among themselves. Gaelic dynasties still claimed title to provincial kingships, but feuding within families, squabbling between rival branches of families, and limited military forces ensured that each family's control extended no farther than its ability to enforce it. The O'Neills of Tyrone (Tír Eóghain) sought recognition as kings of Ulster, but they were challenged by the O'Donnells of Tyrconnell (Tír Conaill). The O'Connors claimed the kingship of Connacht, but internal bickering left them largely powerless to back up their assertion. Pretensions to the kingship of Munster all but ceased, not only the old royal families of O'Brien and MacCarthy at odds with each other but also the Anglo-Irish earldoms of Desmond and Ormond too powerful here for any viable revival of native royal rule. No Irish lord anywhere in Ireland possessed sufficient power to challenge the great Anglo-Irish landlords, and they became, in effect, landholders like the latter.

Since none succeeded on his own in resurrecting the kingships of old, confederations among various Irish chiefs were about the best that could be expected in efforts to combat the Anglo-Irish challenge. Attempts at confederation were made in the 15th century, but they ultimately failed, due partly to the inability to achieve alliances that lasted long enough to have any effect and partly to the power of the resident Anglo-Irish landowners who, though they occupied scattered territories, held the more agriculturally profitable and most populous parts of the country.

Agriculture remained the mainstay of Ireland's economy throughout the period from 1200 to 1500, although significant changes took place. The concentration on tillage during the height of the Norman settlement produced a surplus of grain crops for exports, which earned revenues for the royal treasury, but a trend toward pastoral farming in the later medieval period led to an emphasis on cattle and sheep products. Exports of cattle hides were especially important, while wool exports declined due in part to development of a domestic cloth industry, notably the Irish mantle, which now became a distinguishing article of wear. Animal skins—squirrel, fox, otter, and hare—were also exported, along with timber from the still plentiful forests.

Toward the end of the 15th century an expanding linen industry produced much product sold abroad. Fish, always a staple export, brought prosperity to the western and southern seaboards toward the end of the 15th century when English and Spanish fishing fleets paid money sums to coastal communities for fishing rights in exploiting the great shoals of herring that would travel from the Baltic Sea to the coastal waters off Ireland. Salt to preserve meat and fish and iron with which to fashion tools were major imports, together with wine. Wine became increasingly important, and coastal ports played a key role in trade with Spain, Portugal, and southern France. Most trade was carried on by English and Anglo-Irish merchant families in seaside towns, although native Irish consumers and a few producers, who managed to acquire licenses, became essential participants in many urban markets.

The Anglo-Irish never contemplated a complete break with the English crown, but they always sought maximum autonomy. To that end, they made sure to put in place their own partisans among government officials, in effect privatizing and monopolizing the royal administration in Dublin on their behalf. By the 15th century the post of justiciar was referred to as the lord lieutenant—the chief governor of the colony. The holder of that office from the 1420s to the 1440s, the White earl of Ormond, stacked the House of Commons with his own retainers, even with Irish backers, and even inciting English and Irish allies to take up arms in his support whenever a political opponent held the governor's post.

That opponent, at intervals between 1419 and 1449, was the lord lieutenant, Sir John Talbot (ca. 1384–1453), first earl of Shrewsbury, in alliance with his formidable brother, Richard Talbot (d. 1449), archbishop of Dublin. The rivalry between the Butlers and the Talbots split the English colony for a generation, a split that mirrored and became mired in the English Wars of the Roses (1455–85), the civil war pitting rival aristocratic houses—the "red" rose of Lancaster versus the "white" rose of York—for title to the throne. Ormond's sons sided with the losing Lancastrian faction, whose standard-bearer King Henry VI (r. 1422–61

LORD LIEUTENANT OF IRELAND

The lord lieutenant of Ireland was the representative of the English monarchy and head of the Irish executive during the period from the Norman conquest (1171) to the creation of the Irish Free State (1922). During the early Middle Ages he was referred to as the justiciar, and until the 17th century he was also known as the lord deputy. His various names also included that of viceroy (French *vice roi*, deputy king).

The lord lieutenant represented the English crown, and he answered only to it. Lords lieutenant were appointed for no set term but served at the sovereign's pleasure. He was advised by the King's Council and later the Privy Council, a body of appointed officials and hereditary titleholders headed by the chief secretary for Ireland. Lords lieutenant wielded considerable control over the Irish parliament through exercise of the power of patronage, appointing loyal retainers in early centuries, and later awarding peerages, baronetcies, and state honors to members of parliament in return for their support of government policies.

Until the 1500s Anglo-Irish noblemen held the post. After the Protestant plantations in the 1600s, English noblemen filled the office. Following the Glorious Revolution of 1689, Roman Catholics were excluded from holding the title, the position restricted to members of the Anglican faith alone. The office rose and fell in importance, serving on occasion as a form of exile for prominent politicians who had fallen afoul of the Crown and at times as a stepping-stone to a higher career.

and 1470–71) had been deposed and his armies defeated in 1461. In 1462 Ormond forces under Sir John Butler suffered the same fate as their English allies in meeting defeat in Ireland at the Battle of Pilltown in County Tipperary. The victor, Thomas Fitzgerald (d. 1468), now became the most powerful lord in Ireland. He followed up his triumph here by succeeding his father as the eighth earl of Desmond and winning appointment in April 1463 as lord lieutenant of Ireland by the newly installed Yorkist king Edward IV (r. 1461–70 and 1471–83).

Aligned with the victorious Yorkists, Desmond proved very popular, and using the tried-and-true method of allying with the Gaelic Irish, he amassed great power. But he did so against the express command of the king. In time, his actions incurred the hostility of the English residents of the Pale, who accused Desmond of extorting coign and livery to support his forces. In a move to reassert royal control, Edward IV actively intervened, appointing Sir John Tiptoft (or Tibetot) (ca. 1427–70), earl of Worcester, as chief governor. Cold, calculating, and a ruthless executioner of the king's enemies, who was known as the "butcher," Worcester lived up to his reputation as head of administration in Ireland. He accused the earl of Desmond and his brother-in-law the seventh earl of Kildare of treason for consorting with the native Irish. Summoning both men to Drogheda to answer the charge, he had them summarily beheaded on February 14, 1468.

Appalled, both Anglo-Irish and Irish Gaelic lords rose in rebellion, forcing the king to recall Worcester and, in 1478, to put the eighth earl of Kildare in the governor's seat. Alone among the triumvirate of preeminent Anglo-Irish aristocratic houses to remain in favor, Kildare now took center stage. From his castle stronghold at Maynooth, Gerald, "Garret Mor" (Gearóid Mór = Big Garret) Fitzgerald, famous as Garret the Great or the "great earl," set out to secure absolute control. Hitherto not the most powerful among the Anglo-Irish lordships, the earldom of Kildare enjoyed one great advantage: its geographical proximity to Dublin. Fitzgerald used that strategic position to quickly and firmly clasp power. He all but annexed the Pale. As lord lieutenant, he controlled the parliament and membership of the King's Council, an advisory body, and he used his almost unshakeable hold on the instruments of power not so much to set himself up as an independent ruler as to advance the Yorkist cause, to which he remained loyally attached.

The earl of Kildare played kingmaker in 1487. Following the victory at Bosworth Field in England (1483) of the Lancastrian claimant of the House of Tudor, who was crowned King Henry VII (r. 1485–1509), Kildare acknowledged neither the outcome of the battle nor the act of coronation. He welcomed to Ireland the purported nephew of Edward IV, Lambert Simnel (1475–1535), who, on May 24, 1487, was crowned king of England in Dublin. Returning to England, Simnel failed to secure title, but, undaunted, in 1491 Fizgerald welcomed another Yorkist claimant, Perkin Warbeck (ca. 1474–99), and both the earl of Desmond and the earl of Kildare conspired to place him on the English throne before Warbeck departed in the spring of 1492 to meet eventual defeat.

Alarmed by the plotting on his western flank and sitting as yet insecurely on his throne, Henry VII dispatched Sir Edward Poynings (1459–1521), who arrived in September 1494. An excellent soldier and a capable administrator, Poynings summoned a parliament that sat at Drogheda in December. Proceeding to enact Ireland's most famous legislation of the medieval period, the legislators reaffirmed the Statutes of Kilkenny in proscribing the use of Irish laws and customs by the Anglo-Irish, though not the Irish language. By now, Irish was widely spoken, English largely restricted to the Pale and the larger towns. The law accentuated the difference between the Pale and the rest of Ireland in mandating that inhabitants in the border counties of Louth, Meath, Dublin, and Kildare build a six-foot-high double ditch as a defensive barrier against Irish attacks. The most celebrated provision and one that would last until its virtual repeal in 1782, Poynings's Law forbade the holding of any future Irish parliament without the king's consent and required that royal approval be given to all legislation before its passage by the parliament in Dublin.

In securing adoption of this last provision, the Crown sought to strike at the heart of Kildare's—and Desmond's before him—method of control, namely, to take away the lord lieutenant's ability to control parliament and to use it as a possible tool against the king's interest, as Kildare had done in the Lambert Simnel episode. Suspecting the great earl of allying himself with the Gaelic lords in northern Ireland, Poynings proceeded to secure his dismissal, arrest, and imprisonment for treason. Once again, in a replay of the past, the seizure of the earl sparked large-scale border raids by the Irish, and once again the Crown, unable to commit significant financial and military resources to Ireland, was forced to back down. Henry VII restored the earl to power in 1499, and he served as lord lieutenant until his death in 1513, when he was succeeded by his son, Gerald, "Garret Og" (Gairóid Óg = Young Garret) Fitzgerald (1487–1534).

The power of local lords in both Anglo-Irish and Gaelic areas of Ireland remained the central fact of political life at the turn of the 16th century. Still feeling a need to consolidate his family's hold on the royal throne and inclined, in the early years of his reign, to favor continental ventures, King Henry VIII (r. 1509–47) at first continued the policy of nonintervention in Ireland followed by so many of his forebears. Young, intelligent, brimming with confidence, and eager to govern, the new king would soon begin, however, to reverse past policies in setting in motion a train of events that would culminate in a determined effort to put in place in Ireland a lasting English presence.

5

THE PLANTING OF
PROTESTANT POWER
(1534–1691)

The arrival of the House of Tudor brought a new breed of monarch to the throne of England. Calculating, intelligent, and ruthless, King Henry VIII (r. 1509–47) and his daughter Elizabeth I (r. 1558–1603)—the two rulers who reigned the longest—sought to make firm their dynasty's hold on sovereignty, and they began the conquest of Ireland in earnest, conscious of the need, following Henry's break in 1534 with the Roman Catholic Church, to make a Protestant England safe in a Europe divided by religion.

The quelling of insurrections in Munster and elsewhere in the mid 16th century spelled an end to the power of the great Anglo-Irish earls, who, as loyal partisans of Rome, now assumed, in the English view, a status equally disloyal as that of the Gaelic Irish, whom the English had long regarded as willfully rebellious and culturally inferior. A deliberate drive to settle Protestant English colonists on confiscated lands inaugurated a new kind of policy, one of plantation, with the aim to remove the native stock and replace the population with loyal English subjects, to be rooted firmly on the spot.

But the subjugation of the country envisioned by the plantation plan remained a work in progress, the goal of replacing the natives never completely achieved. Even the defeat of the great earl of Ulster, Hugh O'Neill, in 1598, which marked the zenith of Irish resistance, and the Protestant settlement of Ulster that ensued, failed to break the Catholic will to resist. Bitterly resentful at their displacement, Catholics in Ulster rebelled in 1641 in a furious backlash against the "New English" arrivals. Soon they were joined by Anglo-Irish Catholic landowners and Gaelic Irish allies all across Ireland. Overshadowed by, and subsumed within, the civil war between King Charles I and the English parliament, the Irish struggles ended in defeat for the Catholic insurgents, their power broken by loss of most of their lands and their religion ruthlessly repressed after brutal conquest by the fanatically fervent Protestant Puritans of Oliver Cromwell's armies.

Charles II's restoration to the throne in 1660 brought a respite long enough for Catholicism to regain its dominant hold as the majority religion and for Catholic landowners to recover a portion of their inheritance, but the threat to Protestants in both Ireland and Britain posed by the Catholic king James II proved too dangerous to countenance. The dynastic overthrow engineered by the English parliament, in sanctioning the transfer of the Crown to the Protestant William III, gave both Catholics and Protestants in Ireland a clear-cut cause for which to fight.

The defeat of James and his Catholic armies at the Battle of the Boyne—the third great loss for Catholics in the 17th century—led to the elimination once and for all of the Catholic landed class, both Anglo-Irish and Gaelic, that had sustained the challenge to Protestant power during most of the century now ending.

The upheavals of the preceding 150 years left Irish society as divided as it had always been, but now religion would be added to distinctions defining the divisions between English and Irish. The settlement of 1691 gave political and economic control of Ireland to the Protestants, shutting out the dispossessed Catholics from playing all but a sullenly resentful role.

Irish Society in the Early Sixteenth Century

Ireland in the early 16th century consisted of segmented, separate societies living side by side. The Gaelic Irish comprised 60 or more lords, of greater or lesser status, some the descendants of provincial kings and all exercising authority completely independent of England. They were especially powerful in Ulster, where the English presence had been reduced to a few scattered outposts. The O'Neill, O'Donnell, MacMahon, and other Ulster lords maintained unfettered control in their lands. Their compatriots could be found also all across Ireland— O'Brien and MacCarthy in Munster, O'Connor and O'Kelly in Connacht, and Kavanagh and O'Bryne in Leinster. The Irish who resided on these lands knew of no lord over them but their immediate ruler. They were viewed by the English as virtual enemies, alien in language and lifestyle and inveterately hostile in attitude.

Gaelic Irish lords shared rule over most of the island with the great Anglo-Irish lords, whom contemporary Englishmen took to calling

"English rebels" because they had become largely Gaelicized. Led by the powerful Fitzgeralds of Kildare, whose eighth and ninth earls served as lords lieutenant early in Henry VIII's reign, they included the Butlers, Dillons, and Tyrrells in Leinster; the Burkes in Connacht; the Barrys, Powers, and Desmond Fitzgeralds in Munster; and a few isolated families in eastern Ulster. Although loyal to the Crown, they, too, operated independently.

Royal rule embraced, in effect, only the English Pale together with river valleys in the east and southeast of Ireland. In this area merchants, lower gentry, professionals, and government administrators—descendants of Anglo-Normans—made up the "Old English" residents. Their economic and civil positions made them relatively cosmopolitan, and eager to expand their jurisdictional and trading activities, they opposed both the native Irish and the Gaelicized Anglo-Irish lords. They welcomed efforts to impose royal control, which they hoped would put an end to the incessant warfare and so reverse Gaelic encroachments and promote commercial growth.

Stark economic divisions characterized Irish and English regions. Although rural life prevailed everywhere, semi-nomadic pastoral farming of the most rudimentary sort predominated in Gaelic Ireland just as it had for more than a millennia. Enormous herds of sheep and cattle roamed the countryside. The animals were valued primarily for their skins and for their wool rather than for their meat, and also as sources of milk—an essential nutrient—that was often converted into butter.

Scattered isolated farm dwellings existed, but the most common type of rural settlement remained a disorderly arranged cluster of from half a dozen to several hundred farmhouses (clachans) inhabited by families, usually related, that leased and farmed the surrounding land in common. In this communal system, called rundale, every household secured a small scattered unfenced share of tillage and nearby pastureland that would be redistributed on the death of the head of a household or on a permanent, annual basis, ensuring that all members of the clachan possessed sufficient land for subsistence.

Semi-nomadic herding on unenclosed countryside proved eminently practicable under conditions of constant warfare in allowing for quick movement of animals out of harm's way, but it was also wasteful of resources, limiting population growth in Gaelic areas.

Trade was exclusively by barter. The Irish masses were clearly distinguishable by their dress—poorly shod or often barefoot, they wore heavy woolen mantles and linen shirts that became their trademark.

An Irish banquet in the 1500s. Irish modes of dress and manners differed markedly from those of the English. (North Wind Picture Archives)

Life remained as insecure as it had always been in Ireland, partly because the age-old internecine warfare had never abated.

In contrast, more advanced agricultural practices prevailed on the lands of Anglo-Irish lords. Tenants here occupied the island's most fertile ground, and a familiarity with the agricultural economy of southern England allowed for cultivation of the full range of cereal crops. Unlike in Gaelic areas where the spade remained the primary farming tool, the plough was in widespread use for tilling the soil. The population lived in permanent village communities, replete with shops, markets, and churches that were located near the large manor houses.

Commercial life was restricted to the towns, which were largely English in population. The heavy exactions demanded for trading transactions by Gaelic chieftains in their territories made it impossible for towns to survive there. English merchants in the port towns handled overseas trade, which was largely limited to an exchange of domestic hides, tallow, and linen yarn for salt, wine, and manufactured goods.

Greedy earls and chieftains restricted the rights of town residents as well as the liberties of the church; in fact, the religious hierarchy had been almost completely usurped by secular powers. In Gaelic areas, which were largely isolated from contact with Rome, the priesthood had become widely hereditary and Irish leaders made provision to support clerics just as they did the families of lawyers and bardic poets, all of whom they considered to be their clients. They strove to secure appointments to episcopal vacancies from among their close kinsmen. Lay control of ecclesiastical affairs was not as brazen in English areas, but here, too, lords sought to fill bishoprics with members of their noble houses.

Religious reforms began to be demanded in the closing decades of the 15th century. The Observant Friars, Franciscan monks who called for spiritual renewal and who concentrated their efforts in the Gaelic territories, were the first to agitate for an end to church control by grasping lords. Because they demanded greater clerical independence from lay authorities, once King Henry began to institute radical institutional changes to impose royal rule over the church, they would be the first in Ireland to oppose the monarch's moves.

Henry VIII Takes Title as King of Ireland

Henry VIII had as his principal aim, like his father before him, to settle himself securely on the throne. Preoccupied with military and diplomatic ventures in Europe during the early years of his reign, he paid little heed to affairs in Ireland. By the 1530s, however, the fragility of whatever authority the Crown possessed on the island, evident in the monopolization of power by the largely independent earls of Kildare, demanded the attention of a monarch anxious to hold the reins of rule in all of his lands firmly in his own hands. He needed control in Ireland in order to safeguard any threats to the monarchy that might arise from there. Although not averse to waging war to unify the country under his authority, he was conscious of his far-flung commitments elsewhere, and so with royal resources stretched thin, he preferred peaceful persuasion to achieve his goals. In the end, he pursued policies that mixed martial means with artful diplomacy.

Henry resolved to curb independent-acting Anglo-Irish and Irish subjects, chief among them the leading family, the Geraldines of Kildare. Lord Lieutenant Gerald, "Garret Og" Fitzgerald proved as diligent a promoter of his family interests as had been his father and, opposing the pretensions of his rivals the Butlers, he worked to convert the chief governorship into an hereditary office for his own Geraldine kin. When Gerald left for England in 1534, he saw to it that his son, Thomas, Lord Offaly ("Silken" Thomas, 1513–37), was appointed lord lieutenant.

Thomas lost no time in challenging royal authority, launching a rebellion in June 1534. The uprising lasted a year and two months, quelled by forces led by Sir William Skeffington (ca. 1465–1535), the king's representative. In August 1535 Silken Thomas surrendered, and in an action with few precedents up to that time, the king employed bloody means without compunction in administering "the pardon of Maynooth"—he executed Thomas and five of his uncles in London on February 3, 1537.

The rebellion spelled the downfall of the House of Kildare and, with it, the beginning of the end of Anglo-Irish predominance. Lords lieutenant serving in Ireland would henceforth be Englishmen. On June 18, 1541, an enthusiastic Irish parliament, with Anglo-Irish and Gaelic Irish in attendance, passed an oath declaring that Henry VIII and future monarchs would no longer be referred to as "lord of Ireland," the title in place since 1172, but rather "His Majesty, his heirs and successors [would], be from henceforth named, called, accepted, reputed, and taken to be Kings of this land of Ireland" ("An Act That the King of England" 1786, 176).

Henry assumed the Irish crown because it suited his ambition to see the island securely under English rule, and he now set about alternately cajoling and coercing both Anglo-Irish and Irish leaders to accept that fact. Lord lieutenant Anthony St. Leger (ca. 1496–1559) tried to reconcile landowners to the English crown by legitimizing the status quo through a policy of "Surrender and Regrant," namely, by persuading Irish lords to give up their lands to the Crown on the guarantee that Henry would give them back again as feudal fiefs. Those who made the gesture were ennobled for their efforts—O'Brien, for example, was made earl of Thomond. In return the grantees agreed to obey English laws and customs. The policy placed the Irish lords in the same relationship with the English government as the Anglo-Irish lords, with rights of access to royal courts and the full protection afforded by English law. In place of native Irish brehon law, based on family ownership of land, the new arrangement followed that practiced in England, whereby all land was held in theory by the king, which the individual occupied in return for fulfilling certain obligations to him. The Surrender and Regrant policy managed to achieve a degree of success. Even Conal O'Neill (ca. 1484–ca. 1559), Ulster's proudly defiant greatest lord, traveled all the way to London to swear allegiance to the king, who made him earl of Tyrone. By the end of Henry's reign, 40 of the chief Gaelic lords had made their submissions to him.

However, hopes soon faded that persuasion would suffice. Acceptance of Surrender and Regrant was often only nominal and, in any case, had barely begun before more militant royal officials arrived to undermine the approach in favor of new policies of confiscation and reconquest.

Seizure by eager English land seekers of territories in mid Leinster convinced many Irish lords that the Crown's ultimate goal was to secure their properties.

There had been no such thoroughgoing change in the relationship between the English crown and Irish leaders since the days of Richard II. In conjunction with his efforts to make all the Irish—like the English—his good subjects, Henry went further. To match his insistence on their allegiance in matters of state, he introduced a reformation in religion to bring about conformity in matters of faith. But here he would meet much resistance.

The English Reformation and Ireland

Henry VIII's self-willed drive to sustain his family dynasty led him to claim the right to divorce his wife, Queen Catherine of Aragon (1485–1536), who, having failed to bear the male heir Henry believed essential to ensure the Tudor succession, countered his demand by appealing to Rome to uphold the marriage. Pope Clement VII (r. 1523–34) disallowed Henry's request, and the king turned a disputatious personal debate into an outright institutional break in 1534 when he abolished the English jurisdiction of the pope, assuming for himself the title "supreme head on earth of the church of England." In 1536, Roman Catholic connections were severed. The ruler of Ireland as well as England, Henry moved to impose the same changes across the Irish Sea. The Irish parliament dutifully passed an act acknowledging Henry as the sole head of the church of Ireland, and the royal government began efforts to close Irish monasteries, a step that in England had given the Crown, in one fell swoop, undreamed-of wealth and a group of loyal backers, buyers of the real estate with a lucrative stake in the new order.

But in Ireland, outside the more Anglicized parts of the country, conversion and confiscation would stall. Demands for reforms such as those made by the Observant Friars were made on behalf of restoration, not dissolution, of church power. Unlike in England, there were no currents of heretical thought swirling through society nor did church or clerical abuses arouse popular ire. The impulse for religious change in Ireland came entirely from outside the country, and its imposition came from above, by royal will alone.

Observant Friars mobilized support in the Gaelic lordships for the revolt of the Geraldines of Kildare by depicting it as a crusade against religious change. Resistance stiffened in areas ruled by the native Irish, where the church was separately organized. For the ever self-assertive chieftains here, religion now became an additional reason around which to rally support in upholding claims to independence from England.

While opposition to the Reformation might have been anticipated among the Gaelic Irish (long accepted as incorrigibly rebellious) and among the Gaelicized Anglo-Irish (long regarded by the English as willfully obstreperous), acquiescence would have been expected from the Old English, long accustomed to professing their loyalty to the Crown. That it proved otherwise would carry consequences fateful to Irish history. Confronted by the Reformation, many among the Old English balked. Clergymen in English-controlled areas resigned their positions rather than accede to the religious transformation. Officials and lawyers withdrew their sons from English universities, now staffed by Protestant preachers, and sent them to Catholic colleges in continental Europe where they were taught by new teaching orders—most especially the Jesuits, founded in 1540—imbued with the zeal of Counter-Reformation Catholicism.

With the exception of Mary I (r. 1553–58), a devout Catholic who officially restored the old faith, doctrinal changes were carried forward during the reigns of Henry's successors Edward VI (r. 1547–53) and Elizabeth I. The new state-sanctioned Church of Ireland would be headed by an exact copy of the Roman Catholic prelate, namely, the archbishop of Armagh, who as primate of all Ireland would lead the church islandwide as well as serve the diocese of Armagh as resident bishop. He would enjoy the privileges accorded the established church that were once held by Catholic high clergymen, who now, during the succeeding two centuries, would endure degrees of persecution.

The precise religious convictions of Queen Elizabeth were unknown—they still are—but it was politics and not religion on which her attention centered. For her, as for her father, maintaining the royal supremacy was the central concern. An inexperienced young woman, the daughter of Anne Boleyn (ca. 1507–36), Henry VIII's second wife, she started her reign seated insecurely on her throne. Although she had no burning zeal for Protestant principles and could tolerate Catholics among her subjects, she could not abide disloyal ones. Because many Catholics believed her to be illegitimate, the queen had everything to gain in upholding religious change. Under what came to be known as the Elizabethan settlement, the English monarch was declared to be the only supreme "governor" in ecclesiastical as well as temporal matters. Central precepts of worship were laid down in the Second Book of Common Prayer (1552) and the Thirty-nine Articles (1563).

Religious divisions now hardened. The Act of Supremacy passed by the Irish parliament summoned in 1560 declared the queen the head on earth of the Church of Ireland. All officeholders, both civil and religious; all mayors of towns; matriculants at university; and all tenants-in-chief of the Crown, including those who had newly gained their title through "Surrender and Regrant" were compelled to swear an oath acknowledging her status. The parliament passed an Act of Uniformity, which required the clergy to use only the Book of Common Prayer, decreed English the language of the prayer book, and made attendance at the state Church of Ireland mandatory on pain of a fine. Because these changes in religious beliefs and practices were much more thorough than those instigated by Henry VIII, who, save for papal supremacy, had remained an orthodox Catholic in most doctrinal matters, the resistance the queen encountered was much greater than that which her father had met. In 1570 Elizabeth was excommunicated by Pope Pius V (r. 1566–72), a ruling that absolved Catholics of obedience to her. Gaelic Irish opponents of what had long been considered an alien government now added to their grievances the reformed religion. Anglo-Irish and Old English joined them in their refusal to accept the reforms. By remaining faithful to Catholicism, the Old English deprived the government of the one element of the Irish population hitherto loyal to the Crown. Their refusal to participate in the state religion made them ineligible for appointment to state offices, compelling the government to fill positions that became vacant in the Dublin administration with English-born Protestants. With Anglo-Irish lords now displaced from office, the government in London could take a more direct and forceful role in Irish affairs.

Elizabethan Strategies of Control

In an age of intensive state-building by monarchies in western Europe, religious uniformity became a central prop of government. Under Queen Elizabeth, an emergent English nationalism, made up of economic expansionism, militant Protestantism, and cultural arrogance, lent an aggressiveness to English policy in Ireland that grew increasingly intense. Calls mounted in England that recalcitrant Catholic landowners, their loyalty suspect, should be dispossessed. Elizabeth, however, moved at first with restraint, motivated, like monarchs before her, in part by a desire to advance English interests in Ireland at minimal cost to her government.

Thomas Radclyffe (or Ratclyffe, ca. 1575–83), the third earl of Sussex, lord lieutenant from 1560 to 1564, called for military settlement of

BLARNEY

In conjunction with her efforts to consolidate the monarchy's rule in Ireland, Queen Elizabeth demanded that Irish chieftains agree to hold title to their lands under her royal consent. Cormac Teige McCarthy, the lord of Blarney Castle in County Cork, met every royal remonstrance with effusive promises of loyal support, but by skillful use of words both subtle and sly, he managed to avoid giving a definitive reply. His evasiveness raised the royal ire, and a frustrated Elizabeth declared that McCarthy was giving her "a lot of Blarney." The story of the loquacious lord entered popular lore, and "blarney" passed into popular parlance as a synonym for "smoothly flattering talk" and for "the gift of the gab."

Blarney Castle became a symbol of Irish pride. It began to attract pilgrims. The Blarney stone, the reputed source of the lord's verbal abilities, has a host of legendary origins, including the pillow of either the Old Testament prophet Jacob or that of Saint Columba. The stone is set in the ruined wall on a parapet open to the sky, and visitors who hope to grow eloquent perform the required ritual of kissing it.

Blarney Castle, County Cork (Library of Congress, LC-DIG-ppmsc-009986)

midland areas and the restoration of English legal practices in Anglo-Irish lordships. He launched an unprecedented buildup of armed forces, but English residents of the Pale, fearful that the taxes they were forced to pay for the military machine—wrung from them without parliamentary approval—would prove permanent, succeeded in securing his recall in 1564.

Sussex was succeeded by Sir Henry Sidney (1529–86), who served as lord lieutenant from 1565 to 1571. Sidney set about quashing a stubbornly vexatious chieftain in Ulster. Shane O'Neill (Seán Ó Néill, ca. 1530–67) refused to hold title as vassal to the English crown, preferring to remain an Irish chieftain. Sidney failed to capture him, but O'Neill was defeated by the O'Donnells of Tyrconnell and subsequently murdered. With his death, his second cousin Turlough Luineach O'Neill (ca. 1530–95), the Tanist, succeeded as Irish chieftain of Tyrone.

In 1573 a five-year revolt by James Fitzmaurice Fitzgerald (d. 1579) in Munster was suppressed—Fitzgerald was banished to the Continent—and, in the same year, an expedition to subdue Ulster was launched by one of the queen's favorites, Walter Devereux, the first earl of Essex (1541–76). But Essex's campaign against the great Gaelic lords of Ulster soon bogged down, harassed by guerrilla-style skirmishers, and he switched tactics to include large-scale raids and brutal massacres. In July 1575 he ordered amphibious forces under the command of Sir Francis Drake (ca. 1540–96) and John Norreys (ca. 1547–97) to land on Rathlin Island. Hundreds of women and children of the MacDonnell clan, who had taken refuge in caves, were slain. In the end, the English expedition ended in failure.

Sidney, who had left Ireland in 1571, was recalled to serve a second term as lord lieutenant from 1575 to 1578. An old nemesis returned in July 1579 when Fitzmaurice Fitzgerald landed on the Dingle Peninsula with a small military force, intent on launching a second rebellion. The revolt drew considerable support, both in Munster among Gaelic and Anglo-Irish lords who had supported the earlier action—including a reluctant earl of Desmond—and in the Pale among Gaelic residents there. This time the government acted with dispatch. By 1583 royal forces had captured and executed the ringleaders. The earl of Desmond died in November 1583, and his lands were declared forfeit to the Crown. The once mighty earldom had been destroyed, and intent on forestalling any future attempts at unrest, the government put in place a scheme of deliberate settlement of the territory by loyal English subjects. A series of Acts of Attainment made millions of acres in Munster

Sir Henry Sidney's return to Dublin after a victory over Irish rebels (North Wind Picture Archives)

available for settlement, and by the 1590s, 4,000 English residents had been installed on Desmond lands. The acts inaugurated a new policy, one called "plantation," by which property confiscated from Catholic landowners was transferred to English settlers, a process in which no longer just English but now specifically Protestant English interests acquired a stake in Ireland.

English control gained ground throughout the 1580s and 1590s. Officials carried out a series of freebooting schemes to found English settlements in Connacht and in the southern borderlands of Ulster. However, engaged in war with Spain, the Crown, in general, favored temporizing measures, anxious not to provoke further armed resistance in Ireland. Only when a large-scale challenge to her rule arose in Ulster would Elizabeth countenance intervention in a major way.

The Rebellion of Hugh O'Neill, 1594–1603

By the 1590s Queen Elizabeth had clearly gained ground in successfully subduing Ireland, with one outstanding exception. The heartland of the province of Ulster remained unaffected, entirely Gaelic in government and culture. English authorities had looked for some time to opening at least part of the province to settlement. The two strongest Ulster families ruled virtually independent states: the O'Neills over Tyrone (Tír Eóghain) in central Ulster and the O'Donnells over Tyrconnell (Tír Conaill) in Donegal and adjacent areas. They were allies and, at times, rivals of each other, but in the eyes of the English they were both chieftains in a stubbornly recalcitrant region that posed a threat to English security, both as an outpost that potential rebels elsewhere in Ireland could look to for support and as a back door through which continental enemies could breach England's security. For their part, Ulster lords looked with unease on encroaching English land seekers, who would introduce English laws and customs and thereby supplant Gaelic power.

Hugh O'Neill (Aodh Mór Ó Neill, 1540–1616), the second among the powerful earls of Tyrone, set about busily consolidating control over his patrimony, which had been established when his grandfather Conn surrendered to the Crown in 1542. Hugh's father, Matthew (d. 1558), had lost title by failing to best a challenge from his brother, Shane O'Neill, and the young Hugh, who had been protected by the queen and spent much of his youth in England, honed his skills to avenge his father by learning modern methods of warfare. A client of English adventurers, he secured, with their help, southeast portions of the Tyrone lordship under his control. The English had supported O'Neill's elevation as second earl of Tyrone, and it had been hoped he might prove a pliant partner in Ulster, but shrewd and calculating, he judged the English a greater potential threat to his ambitions than were any of the O'Neills. In 1593 Hugh took over leadership on the abdication of his cousin Turlough Luineach O'Neill, who had succeeded Shane (d. 1567) but had never been recognized as earl of Tyrone by the English. In 1595 he assumed the title "The O'Neill," or the chieftain, in a deliberate challenge to English rule.

O'Neill's push for power drew mounting opposition, first from minor English officials and then from the lord lieutenant. A brilliant organizer, the "great earl" as he became known raised an army of defense and equipped it with English weapons. In 1595 he openly joined forces with his rebellious neighbors, notably "Red" Hugh O'Donnell (Aodh Rua Ó Domhnaill, 1541–1602), prince of Tyrconnell, and he sought support from throughout Ireland, realizing that, in the end, only by expelling the English from the entire island could he make his title secure.

At the outset of the rebellion, the Ulstermen remained on the offensive. Employing musketmen, cavalrymen, and pikemen in imitation of the English, together with Bonnaghts (Bonaghts)—native Irish mercenary soldiers—and gallowglasses from Scotland, O'Neill fought in the traditional Irish way, harassing and ambushing English columns. Until 1597 the English, under inept commanders, marched cautiously into Irish areas, leaving behind garrisons in castles and in hastily built forts.

105

O'Neill's great victory at Yellow Ford, north of Armagh, on August 14, 1598, awakened the English to the formidable opponent they faced. An alarmed Queen Elizabeth dispatched Sir Robert Devereux (1566–1601), the second earl of Essex and a court favorite like his father before him, as lord lieutenant. Arriving in April 1599 with an army of 17,000, he met defeat on every occasion. Furious at his fumblings, in September the queen ordered his return to England. Charles Blount (ca. 1562–1606), Baron Mountjoy, appointed lord lieutenant in 1600, next arrived to personally lead a campaign that saw multiple garrisons established and the adoption of ruthless, scorched-earth tactics—burning crops and houses—and use of seapower to land behind O'Neill's back at Derry.

For his part, O'Neill sought to broaden his appeal across Ireland by making a claim as champion of the Counter-Reformation, a call that, while it failed to impress the Anglo-Irish, did succeed in drawing the attention of Philip IV of Spain (r. 1598–1616), England's 16th-century national enemy. The king dispatched a well-armed troop of about 4,400 men, which landed at Kinsale on September 21, 1601. The injection of foreign forces added a new urgency to English efforts to dampen the insurrection—the old fear of England's foes using Ireland as a back door to the home shore now a reality in the union of Irish rebels and fighters from Spain.

When the Spanish arrived, O'Neill's ally Hugh O'Donnell marched south to Kinsale. Mountjoy also moved south, detaching forces from the Ulster campaign to besiege the Spanish there. On Christmas Eve 1601, O'Neill and O'Donnell's forces of 6,500 laid siege to a comparable number of men under Mountjoy, who were themselves besieging the Spanish. The Irish proved clumsy and slow in moving into position, and their cavalry deserted. Mountjoy's forces were able to overrun the Irish divisions, picking them off one by one, completely defeating both Irish and Spanish. The latter were allowed to sail home. O'Donnell panicked at the defeat and left for Spain as well, hoping to secure further assistance, but he died in Spain the following year.

O'Neill led a forced retreat back to Ulster. Joined by Hugh O'Donnell's younger brother, Rory (Rudhraighe Ó Domhnaill, 1575–1608), they suffered many defeats, unable to live off the countryside because Mountjoy's ruthless campaigns of destruction had left only starving populations in their wake. O'Neill opened negotiations in March 1603. The Nine Years' War that had been waged by O'Neill and his allies constituted the fiercest armed opposition to English rule yet raised in 16th-century Ireland, and fittingly, its failure would mean adoption of the most comprehensive program to secure control ever enacted by the government in London.

Protestant Plantation, 1603–1641

The war transformed the Irish scene. For the first time since the early Normans had arrived, English authority was now everywhere on the offensive. No part of Ireland was beyond English control, and the landscape of Ulster, the province that had previously proved a solid bastion of Gaelic separatism, now sported English forts and garrisons. But O'Neill and his ally O'Donnell retained their prestige among the province's Irish populace, and the government preferred not to stoke a renewal of unrest by imposing a harsh peace. By terms of the treaty signed at Mellifont on March 30, 1603, O'Neill and his allies were allowed to retain their titles and lands, and O'Donnell was elevated to the peerage as the first earl of Tyrconnell.

Fiercely proud and independent, O'Neill and O'Donnell spent the next four years sulking in submission, resentful at having surrendered their former power as ruling princes for the status of simple, if substantial, landlords. O'Neill was summoned to London in July 1607 over a land dispute. Aware that he was under suspicion because his son served as a colonel of a Spanish regiment and knowing that others who had been called to the capital never returned, he joined O'Donnell in boarding a ship at Rathmullen in Lough Swilly and departed on September 14, 1607, to go into voluntary exile on the Continent. Ninety of Ulster's leading nobility went with them.

Evidence suggests that the northern earls had every intention of returning with assistance to resume the effort to drive out the English. But exile proved permanent. O'Donnell died several months after arrival, and O'Neill traveled to Rome, dying there in 1616. Their departure proved to be a watershed event, opening the way for the definitive end of the Gaelic order in Ireland.

The "flight of the earls" left Ulster leaderless and its people defenseless. The vacuum of power they left behind gave the English a gift beyond their wildest dreams—the opportunity to refashion society to eliminate once and for all the thorn in their side that Ulster had for so long proved to be. Plantation, a policy that had been tried in a small and unsystematic way in Munster and parts of Connacht in the previous century, would now be implemented in earnest.

Dispossession of the Irish Catholics in depriving them of their land, the one source of wealth and power in Ireland since before historical times, would weaken their resistance to English rule while the presence of a large population of Protestants would put loyal subjects on the ground in numbers sufficient to guarantee the state's security.

During the reign of the first of the Stuart kings, James I (r. 1603–25), plans were drafted to confiscate a half million acres of the best land in the six Ulster counties of Armagh, Cavan, Coleraine, Donegal, Fermanagh, and Tyrone. The land would be granted on easy purchase terms to either "Undertakers"—English or lowland Scots—or "Servitors"— usually Scots—who would hold their land from the king for a specified rent and who were expected to bring in Protestant tenant farmers and build defenses (usually a castle and a fort) for the residents' safety.

Plans were drawn up to found towns as well. The city of London was recruited as a collective "Undertaker" for the area between the rivers Foyle and Bann, with special obligations and privileges that included extending help in rebuilding the ruined city of Derry. Hence, Derry was renamed Londonderry, and the surrounding region—the county of Coleraine together with bits of territory from Tyrone— became the county of Londonderry. The city of Belfast (from Gaelic *Beal Feirste,* "mouth of the Feirste River") was founded by charter on April 27, 1613.

The early 16th century saw thousands arrive. Some came from England and many more from the Scottish lowlands, including Anglicans from the former and Presbyterians from the latter, but all of them Protestants who brought with them their own institutions and traditions. So many arrived in so systematic a manner that a whole new way of life was created in Ulster, one that was distinctive from that in every other part of Ireland.

Not enough, however, came to displace entirely the Irish Catholic natives. Many Undertakers and Servitors found it easier to recruit natives to work as agricultural laborers, leaving a religiously mixed population in many places. Those among the Catholics who remained as tenants were forced onto the least productive lands, leaving Ulster riddled with resentful Catholics waiting for an opportunity for revenge.

The Ulster Protestants constituted the largest of the cohorts who made up the so-called New English, namely, those who arrived in Ireland from Britain in the 16th and 17th centuries, adding another element to the complex population mix. The Old English were distinguished from the New English by their religion. Having remained Catholic, the former no longer controlled government in Ireland, but they still owned one-third of the island's land. Although they continued to express their centuries-old pledge of loyalty to the Crown, their

status as Catholics made them suspect as subjects who harbored trea-
sonous sentiments.

Ill-disposed as it might be to trust them, authorities were well aware
of the wealth they controlled, and the government drew on the material means they could provide when conditions warranted. In the 17th
century, Ireland was repeatedly drawn into the struggle in England
between the king, who needed Parliament's consent for revenues, and
the parliamentarians, who were anxious to check royal claims to abso-
lutist rule. The Irish sought concessions from the king, which made
English parliamentarians suspect collusion between the two aimed at
undermining both their ruling powers and the Protestant religion.

Desperate to secure financial aid denied him by the English parliament, James found himself forced to alternately resist and grant concessions to the Catholics in Ireland. Likewise his son and successor
Charles I (r. 1625–49), having entered into war with Spain and France,
found himself as badly in need of money as his father had been, and
he too turned to the Old English. In 1627 he met a delegation of eight
Catholics and three Protestants, who agreed to grant him a subsidy of
40,000 pounds annually in return for concessions called *Graces*, which
included a suspension of fines and the abolition of religious tests for
inheritance. But his prompt repudiation of these Graces when the wars
ended made all too plain the precarious position of the Old English
as being entirely at the mercy of the royal whim. Catholic landlords
could look to the Irish parliament as the sole institution in which they
retained sufficient control to frustrate any attempt by the government
to introduce anti-Catholic legislation. But even here Protestants constituted an increasingly powerful political elite, their numbers augmented
after the Ulster plantations. Adding to their woes, the Catholics faced a
formidable challenge in the new lord lieutenant appointed in 1633.

Thomas Wentworth (1593–1641), later earl of Strafford, has earned
a reputation as one of England's foremost administrators in Ireland.
Cunning, ruthless, and ambitious, he built up an efficient and independent administration whose sole aim was to advance the Crown's
interest while at the same time amassing an immense fortune for
himself through land investments. Securing the election of a group of
pliant government officials to the Irish parliament, he succeeded in
playing off Catholics versus Protestants, earning the distrust of both.
Disregarding local interests, the government confiscated one-quarter of
Catholic lands in Connacht. In an ominous move for English Catholics,
no distinction was made between the Old English and the Irish, both
suffering equally from the land grab. Protestants, too, felt Wentworth's

sting: Ulster planters were penalized for failing to meet conditions set down in land grants, and Ulster Scots were subjected to restrictions in the practice of their Presbyterianism. Unwilling to join in opposition to him while he remained in Ireland, Old English Catholics and Protestant planters readily came together to destroy his system of government after Wentworth was recalled in 1639 by Charles, one among a series of demands made by the English parliament as a condition for extending financial sums needed for the king's war against the Presbyterian Scots next door. Parliaments—both English and Irish—secured a charge of treason against Wentworth, and he was executed in 1641.

Faced with open war in Scotland and a parliament in London growing increasingly impatient at royal claims to the monarch's right to rule unrestrained, Charles could not afford to antagonize his Irish subjects. Once again, he granted the Graces. By 1641 confusion reigned in Ireland among the various factions. Old English Catholics were fearful of militant Protestantism gathering strength in the Irish parliament. New English settlers sat insecurely on their recently acquired properties, unsure of where their loyalties between king and Parliament should lie. The native Irish gentry and peasantry stirred with rebellious sentiments. In the end, it would be the native Irish, in flouting the ruling authorities, who would force the parties to sort themselves out.

The Great Rebellion, 1641–1660

The Old English now went further, seeking to win from the king wider independent powers for the Irish parliament, believing that only by securing greater self-government could they be assured of their rights to property and freedom of worship. The king balked at agreeing to any further diminution of his authority, unwilling to give to the Irish rights he had refused to relinquish to English parliamentarians, whose demands also grew more pressing. By the early 1640s, the parliament in London, in alliance with the Presbyterian Scots, emerged as an increasingly militant body, impatient at the king's intransigence. Growing numbers of Old English Catholics in Ireland began to focus their fears on the English parliament, whose members, reflecting their move to make common cause with the rabidly anti-Catholic Scottish Protestants, appeared increasingly disposed to taking measures injurious to them. They now viewed it, and not the Crown, as the greater danger. In fact, many saw the Crown as a bulwark against, rather than an instigator of, anti-Catholic actions, and they had grounds for thinking so. James I and Charles I had permitted Catholic worship. Anxious to maintain cordial diplomatic relations with Catholic foreign powers, the early Stuart monarchs restrained governments in Dublin from fully enforcing strictures against Catholics.

Throughout the early 17th century, the Catholic Church in Ireland thrived. A church that heretofore had been dominated by secular chieftains, in which the public's participation was extremely lax—the sacraments of Holy Communion and confession and the study of the catechism were not widely practiced—became a well-ordered, doctrinaire, papal-directed institution following a vigorous missionary offensive launched by reforming Jesuits and others on fire with the fervor of the Counter-Reformation. An unofficial parish and diocesan structure was set up, and Rome made sure the church was well taken care of. The faithful were serviced by a steady supply of priests, trained at some 20 colleges staffed by Irish prelates in exile located across Catholic Europe.

Fear of persecution for their faith led Old English to find common cause with the Gaelic Irish of Ulster, simmering with bitterness at the New English who had stripped them of their property and position. In 1641, the Ulster Irish hatched a plot to seize Dublin Castle, capture the government's chief officials, and in a series of local uprisings, occupy central strongholds in Ulster. Launched on October 23, 1641, the insurgents failed in their plans to take Dublin, but they succeeded in gaining control of most of Ulster. Declaring that they were not rebels but rather defenders of the king against the English parliament, the insurrectionists laid waste the Ulster planters' properties; as many as 2,000 Protestant settlers were killed and tens of thousands stripped of their clothing and possessions and driven to the few remaining Protestant-controlled places. Moving south, gathering supporters as they marched, the Ulstermen laid siege to Drogheda, where they were joined by Old English from the area. Adherence of the latter transformed a struggle particular to Ulster into a nationwide insurrection. Calling themselves the "Catholic Army," the insurgents defeated government troops at the Battle of Julianstown (November 29, 1641), and they reached Limerick by January 1642.

Incensed by what they believed to have been a general massacre of Protestants, the English and Scottish populace called for strong government action. However, King Charles and the English parliament were now preoccupied by quarrels that led, in 1642, to open civil war. Parliament had suspected the king of conspiring with the Irish rebels and so had withheld the monies needed to raise an army to go to Ireland. Not until April 1642 did Parliament approve the dispatch to

Ulster of a Scottish expeditionary force under General Robert Munro (or Monro, d. ca. 1680).

Old English and Gaelic Irish met in a formal body in October 1642. Called the Kilkenny Assembly, it mirrored the existing parliaments in comprising an upper house, composed of bishops, abbots, and Catholic gentry, and a lower house, whose members represented counties and towns. This alliance of Old English Catholics and native Irish Catholics marked the first appearance of Irish nationalism in its sectarian form. They agreed to side with the rebels, but only after hesitating for six weeks. The Catholics still held two-thirds of the cultivable land in the country, and the Old English were fearful of losing their property and, with it, their remaining political influence. Joined in principle in a Catholic Confederacy (also known as the Confederation of Kilkenny) under the motto "Ireland united to God, King, and Country," they cautiously but, in the end, decisively made common cause with the royalists in Britain against the English parliament and its soldiers and servants in Ireland in seeking not an independent nation but rather a Catholic Ireland loyal to the Stuart crown.

Experienced professional soldiers—Colonel Owen Roe O'Neill (1590–1649), the nephew of Hugh O'Neill, prominent among them— arrived from the Continent. O'Neill knew from a career spent in the Spanish army that no compromise was possible in fighting religiously inspired conflicts and that Irish Catholics had no choice but to drive the English—both royalists and parliamentarians—out of Ireland. But Old Catholics wavered, reluctant to part company from a sovereign who was also battling the Protestant parliamentarians and who had shown them a degree of tolerance. Seven years of confusion ensued. O'Neill won a major victory against Munro's Scottish army at Benburb in 1646, but failure by the Old English to provide sufficient, consistent support forestalled his efforts to score a decisive blow. Lords in Leinster, unwilling to call on O'Neill's aid, were unable to dislodge government forces from Dublin. Having wasted years in wrangling and bargaining with King Charles, Irish Catholics faced their ultimate nightmare when in 1649 the parliamentary armies emerged victorious in the English civil war.

After the parliament in London had deposed and executed the king (January 1649) and abolished the monarchy, the newly installed republican Commonwealth turned its attention to Ireland. Oliver Cromwell (1599–1658), the leader of the parliamentary forces, now headed a government rabidly anti-Catholic, its ire inflamed by exaggerated reports of the brutality meted out to Ulster settlers in 1641.

Arriving as commander in chief and lord lieutenant of Ireland in August 1649, Cromwell launched a three-part program to eliminate all military resistance to government authority, to extirpate all landowners and priests implicated in the insurrection, and to convert the entire population to the Protestant faith. Under a doctrine commonly called "frightfulness," Protestant forces carried out military reprisals and attacks on civilians, which they justified as vengeance against the actions of the Catholic Confederacy. Commanding

Oliver Cromwell (Library of Congress, LC-USZ62-38482)

20,000 men, wielding fighting skills honed to perfection during the English civil war, and proclaiming the religious righteousness of his cause, Cromwell proceeded to summarily crush all opposition. His battle-hardened troops stormed the walls of Drogheda on September 11, 1649, and they proceeded to slaughter more than 2,000 of the 3,000 defenders, an action meant to instill terror in the remaining rebel garrisons in Ireland in setting an example that would shorten the campaign. Another massacre took place at Wexford on October 11.

The events at Drogheda and Wexford would remain bitterly imprinted in the folk memory of Irish Catholics. Remembrance of Cromwell's campaign lingered so long—even today—not so much because of his army's cruelty—cruelty was standard during that time—but because of the no-holds-barred efficiency with which his cohorts carried out their actions and, above all, because of the implacable anti-Catholicism that drove them. A zealous Puritan, brought up to hate and fear Roman Catholicism, Cromwell led his troops, dubbed the "Ironsides," on a mission of retribution for the atrocities committed against Protestants, deeply persuaded "that this is a righteous judgment of God upon these barbarous wretches, who have imbrued their hands in so much innocent blood" (Hastings 1985, 137).

The army of the Catholic Confederacy was defeated at Scarrifhollis, near Letterkenny, County Donegal, on June 21, 1650. On the conclusion of hostilities, men at arms were treated relatively leniently; they were permitted to emigrate, and 30,000 left for the Continent. A general pardon was issued to those who had served in the rebel armies. After nine months in Ireland, Cromwell returned to England, trusting that the island had been subdued. The Cromwellian settlement subsequently imposed on Ireland focused its fury on two central elements of opposition—faith and wealth. The entire organizational structure of the church, so carefully crafted over the years, was now dismantled. An act of May 6, 1653, compelled all priests and other religious leaders to leave Ireland on pain of imprisonment and death. Priests who stayed were ruthlessly tracked down.

Forfeited and seized lands were redistributed by terms of the Act for the Settling of Ireland (1652) and the Act of Satisfaction (1653). In a policy succinctly called "To Hell or Connacht," Catholic landowners were divided into two groups. Those who were guilty of involvement in the rebellion lost their estates and their property rights; those who had not participated were hustled across the Shannon and left to scramble for whatever parcels of property they could occupy. The lands vacated were assigned to Cromwell's soldiers and to English financial backers, called the Adventurers, of the Irish campaign. A colony of soldier settlers, occupying a four-mile-wide line along the western coast and the Shannon, were to serve as a barrier, cutting off Catholic proprietors of small estates west of the river from outside contacts. In an act unprecedented in its sweep, the Catholic landowning aristocracy ceased to exist, the wealth and power they had held for so long transferred to a Protestant upper class, who now formed the major landowning aristocracy of Ireland. Brehon law, officially proscribed in 1607, would be largely eradicated by the end of the century, replaced everywhere by English customary law and the English court system.

For all the zeal employed in implementing the Cromwellian scheme, however, it did not succeed entirely. Promotion of Protestantism duly went forward—schools were founded and clergymen brought from Britain—but problems arose both because preachers could not speak Irish and because many Anglican clergy resident in Ireland could not abide working with a Cromwellian-run church that favored Puritan and Presbyterian sects. The Roman Catholic faith remained firmly in place. Officers and Adventurers awarded large tracts of land took up residence, but many ordinary soldiers never settled on the small plots allotted them, selling out their interests and returning to England. And, overall, Cromwellians enjoyed less than a decade to put their programs in place. Following Cromwell's death on September 3, 1658, his son

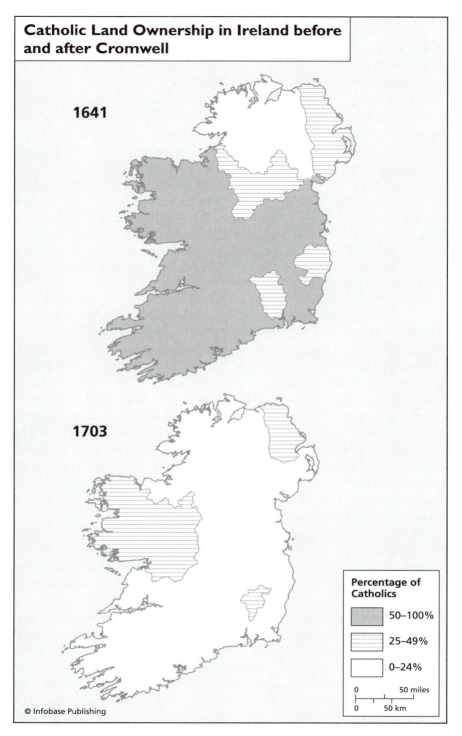

Catholic Land Ownership in Ireland before and after Cromwell

1641

1703

Percentage of Catholics

50–100%

25–49%

0–24%

0   50 miles

0   50 km

© Infobase Publishing

Richard (1626–1712), a far less commanding figure, assumed power as lord protector, and Cromwell's passionate partisans gave way to more accommodating men.

The politically prominent having abandoned their support for the regime, the Cromwellian government collapsed in England, and with the return from exile and restoration to the throne of Charles Stuart (r. 1660–85), all Protestant elements in Ireland welcomed the reimposition of royal rule. Charles II was proclaimed king in Dublin on May 14, 1660, and expectations ran high that the military and political tumult of the previous 20 years had finally been ended. But just as in Ulster at the beginning of the century, so now all across Ireland, those who had been displaced remained unreconciled. Resentment simmered among them, and many waited for another chance to exact revenge. Within a few short years, they would once again back a king fighting to retain the throne of England.

Royal Restoration and Replacement, 1660–1691

While Protestant proprietors supported Stuart restoration, they never fully earned the trust of a monarch forced into exile by the government to whom the Protestants owed their good fortune. In 1662 Charles II appointed James Butler, the earl of Ormond (1610-88), to the lord lieutenancy, a post to which he returned, having occupied it under Charles I in the 1640s. A Protestant from an impeccable Old English family, who had tried in vain to reach agreement with rebels of the Catholic Confederacy, Ormond had gone into exile with Charles and was highly amenable to reversing the Cromwellian land settlements. Claims courts were set up, and about 500 Catholics who could prove themselves innocent of insurrection secured title to portions of their former lands, made available by compelling Protestants to surrender about a third of their holdings.

Recovery proved slow and troubling, however, and in the end no one felt satisfied. Angry Cromwellians took offense at having to give up any part of their newly acquired lands. Ormond would have welcomed a drastic reversal of the settlement, but on reflection he balked at imposing a radical redistribution scheme, convincing Charles that it would provoke a Protestant backlash. The king's acceptance of his advice left dispossessed Catholic landowners sorely distressed. Some took to the hills and woods and raided the new settlements. They became an important lawless element in rural areas throughout the rest of the 17th century, and a few became Irish folk heroes.

By the late 1660s Catholic landowners, who had owned about three-fifths of the land in 1641, were left holding a little over one-fifth. Many felt that a king to whom they had remained loyal had repaid them by ratifying the results of a rebellion against his own royal house.

But they had less cause for complaint in matters of religion. Ormond was willing to grant toleration to Catholics if they would sign a declaration recognizing the state's authority and disallowing the right of the pope to depose a king. Though these terms proved unacceptable to the church, Catholics were left nevertheless largely undisturbed to worship. The extreme religious persecution of the Cromwellian regime ended. A Royal Declaration of Indulgence in 1672 suspended laws that imposed penalties against Catholics and Protestants (mostly Presbyterians) for nonconformity to the established Church of Ireland. Catholic exiles on the Continent returned to resume their missionary work, restoring the church's infrastructure to a considerable degree everywhere except where Protestants had settled most intensively.

Outraged members of the House of Commons in London struck back. In 1673 they declared the Declaration of Indulgence invalid and imposed a Test Act, requiring all officeholders to take communion in the established church. In October all Catholic bishops and clergy who were members of religious orders were commanded to leave Ireland. The measure was not strictly enforced, but fear of Catholicism persisted. In the late 1670s hysteria spread from England to Ireland, sparked by the Popish Plot, an alleged Catholic conspiracy to kill King Charles and subvert Protestantism concocted by Titus Oates (1649–1705), who was later exposed as a liar. In Ireland scores of Catholics were arrested and imprisoned.

An uneasy peace prevailed across Ireland during Charles II's reign. Catholics remained anxious and frustrated, and Protestants held a precarious dominance, their prominence still too shaky for them to feel secure. Owning most of the land, they controlled the country's civil administration and also its commerce. In the 1660s English trading policy imposed restrictions on Irish commercial activities, banning export of Irish cattle, limiting trade with the colonies, and allowing export of wool exclusively to England. Still, trade in meat and butter flourished, and prosperity prevailed in the seaports, notably Dublin, where the population, which swelled to 60,000 by the end of the century, made it the second-largest city in the British Isles.

By 1685 Ireland counted nearly 2 million inhabitants. Three-fourths of them were Roman Catholics, most of them native Irish, eking out a meager existence as agricultural laborers; they included the evicted landlords who now held small plots in Connacht. There remained a small core of Catholic landed gentry, lawyers, and merchants who could form the vanguard of a Catholic resurgence should a favorable occasion arise.

Such an occasion seemed ready-made in 1685. Whatever the sympathies for Catholics held by Charles II—he may have converted to Catholicism on his deathbed—they were plainly evident in his successor, James II (r. 1685–88), Charles's younger brother and a Catholic by conviction. James was inclined to lean for advice on one of his longtime favorites, Richard Talbot (1630–91) whom, in 1685, he made first earl of Tyrconnell and commander in chief in Ireland and, in 1687, lord lieutenant.

The first Catholic lord lieutenant in more than 100 years, Tyrconnell lost no time in restoring Catholics to public office in Ireland, appointing Catholic judges, privy councillors, and key administrators. He began to raise a Catholic army to put at the disposal of the king, and he made plans to call a parliament packed with Catholic enthusiasts eager to overturn the Cromwellian confiscation. Protestants grew alarmed.

Tyrconnell's actions constituted one more cause for concern to add to the growing unease among Protestants in both England and Ireland. The blatant preference shown to Catholics helped to encourage those in Britain who favored offering the throne to the Dutch ruler, Prince William of Orange (1650–1702) and his wife, Mary (1662–94), the daughter of James, who, as a Stuart, would guarantee the stability of the succession and, as a Protestant, would keep the throne safely in the hands of the established religion. The birth of a son to the king and, with it, the prospect of a Catholic dynasty galvanized opponents into shaking off whatever lingering hesitancy they harbored. Seven English notables invited William to England to drive his father-in-law from power. On November 5, 1688, William obliged, landing at Torbay, in Devonshire, with a Dutch army and marching from there to take London in a Glorious Revolution that proved a victory both for a new ruling couple and for principles of expanded rights of parliamentary self-government. James departed for France, leaving his Catholic subjects in Ireland frustrated in their failed hopes.

But Tyrconnell remained in Ireland, holding the country for him and doing so on behalf of Catholics who counted on the exiled king to uphold their rights to land and religion. Protestants in Ireland, now thoroughly panicked, prepared for armed resistance.

James landed at Kinsale on March 12, 1689, bringing with him French money and troops. The deposed king traveled to Dublin, where he summoned a parliament whose attendees were overwhelmingly Catholic. Rectifying old grievances constituted their main agenda; thus, the land settlement was reversed and liberty of conscience decreed with tithes paid to the church of one's choice. The assembly was viewed by Catholics as a triumph for freedom of religion. Protestants saw it rather as a body driven solely to deprive them of their land. For his part, James refused to officially disestablish the Church of Ireland, and he upheld Poynings's Law—which required royal approval for legislation before its passage by the Irish parliament—thus, in the eyes of many of his coreligionists, failing to support fully their legitimate interests. In any case, no legislative writ could be signed and sealed until the issue of the disputed throne had been decisively settled on the battlefield.

The parliament met in session while Catholic compatriots besieged Londonderry, where thousands of Protestants had taken refuge. A boom erected by the besiegers on the river Foyle made it impossible for relief troops and supplies to enter the city, and disease and starvation threatened. After 105 days, on July 28, 1689, the siege was lifted, the defense of the town subsequently assuming legendary status for Ulster Protestants, the commemoration of which continues today. It is estimated that about 4,000 residents—roughly half of those within the town—perished.

In holding out against the authority of King James, Londonderry, together with Enniskillen, provided a bridgehead for the army that William brought to Ireland. Landing at Carrickfergus on June 14, 1690, William III assembled his cohorts (Williamites) and set off south toward Dublin to meet the opposing army of James (Jacobites) drawn up in a defensive line on the river Boyne. Here the forces of the two rival kings made initial contact.

At the Battle of the Boyne, James's armies failed to stop William's southward march. Dublin fell to William, and James, losing heart, fled back to France.

Jacobite forces retreated to the line of the Shannon, determined to defend the Catholic estates that lay to the west. They put up a stern resistance. William went back to England, and Tyrconnell departed for France, taking French troops with him. In 1691 the latter returned, bringing with him a French commander but no French troops. Williamite forces crossed the Shannon after a desperate struggle on the bridge at Athlone, and the decisive showdown took place on the field at Aughrim in County Galway on July 12, 1691, when William's troops, poised for defeat, rallied and inflicted heavy losses on confused Irish forces. Limerick, under siege for a second time, held out to the last.

THE BATTLE OF THE BOYNE

On July 1, 1690 (Old Style), at Oldbridge, just outside Drogheda, at a ford on opposite banks of the river Boyne, the deposed Catholic king of England, Scotland, and Ireland, James II, commanding approximately 25,000 Irish and French troops, faced newly installed Protestant king William III, who led about 36,000 soldiers, including contingents from England, Ulster, Scotland, the Netherlands, Denmark, and France. Both armies were, in fact, religiously mixed. Both commanders were seasoned generals, but the armies were not evenly matched. William could count on experienced professional troops armed with the latest flintlock muskets, whereas James, although possessed of a high-caliber cavalry, relied on poorly trained infantry, largely Irish peasants equipped with inferior weapons ranging from outdated matchlock muskets to pitchforks and scythes.

At Oldbridge William's elite Blue Guard forced its way across the river, driving back James's foot soldiers, but, pinned down by Jacobite cavalry, they could not resume the advance until William's cavalry had crossed the river. James's forces retreated in good order, and casualties were low on both sides—about 1,500 for James versus half that number for William—but the Jacobites were badly demoralized by their defeat, and many Irish deserted. The defeat put an end to James's hopes of regaining his throne by military force, and William's victory launched the drive that would lead to complete defeat of Catholic armies in Ireland within a year.

The Battle of the Boyne marked a turning point in the struggle for supremacy in Ireland, and it remains the battle most freighted with meaning for Protestants in Northern Ireland. The first ritualized observance of the battle was held on July 12, 1796. Every year

Desperate to tie down William's army in Ireland to prevent it from joining the Anglo-Dutch coalition fighting France on the Continent, French officers promised aid. But it never came, and with Tyrconnell gone—he died of apoplexy on August 14 just before the fall of Limerick—the Catholic Irish felt it pointless to continue.

The Treaty of Limerick, signed on October 3, 1691, granted liberty to Irish soldiers to be transported to France to carry on the fight there, and about 14,000 did so. They formed the vanguard of many Irish soldiers who, as the "Wild Geese," would distinguish themselves on Europe's battlefields throughout the 18th century. For those remaining behind,

The Battle of the Boyne (Library of Congress, LL-DIG-pga-02074)

on July 12—the corrected date after adoption of the Gregorian calendar in 1752—Orange Order marchers, replete with banners and bands, pass along traditional routes in Ulster in prideful remembrance of the triumph of "King Billy," the victory that solidified their claim to legitimacy of place on the island. Conversely, Catholics in Northern Ireland view Battle of the Boyne commemorative parades as provocative, staged acts meant to impress on them their minority status.

the terms of the treaty allowed them the privilege to retain their property, the freedom to practice their professions, and the liberty of such rights to worship as they had enjoyed under Charles II. Some individuals did keep their property, but the lands of those who had gone to France or who had perished were confiscated. The Catholic share of land ownership would drop to about one-seventh of Irish territory. The outcome of the struggle confirmed the stark division of Ireland as a country English and Protestant in government, and now in landed wealth, but still largely Irish and Catholic in population. It was a division also reflected in Irish culture.

The Emergence of a Two-Language Literature

The political control so assiduously begun by Tudor monarchs was accompanied by active policies of cultural anglicization, leading to the emergence of the first indigenous Anglophone Irish culture. The arrival of the printing press about 1550 opened up wider reading opportunities in making available greater volumes of works. Polemicists on both sides of the religious divide eagerly adopted print technology to produce religious material in the vernacular language; indeed, printing in Irish owes its origins to the Reformation.

By 1690 a distinctive and diverse body of works existed, written by Old English residents and New English colonists, by English travelers and soldiers who spent time in the country, and by Irish authors. The wars, rebellions, and political upheavals of the era, and the clashing cultural and ideological currents engendered by English Protestant arrivals and displaced native Catholics, shaped much of the literature of the period; but while polemics abounded, some early modern writings tended also to straddle boundaries, both geographic and cultural.

The poet and printer William Baldwin (ca. 1518–ca. 1563) is credited with writing the first English prose fiction in Ireland, *A Marvelous Hystory Intitulede, Beware the Cat*, completed by 1553. A Protestant apologist, Baldwin portrayed the violent unruliness of the feline world as exemplifying the potential danger that Roman Catholicism posed to the emerging English independent church. Negative stereotypes about the Irish that had evolved over the previous centuries were given powerful reinforcement by the Reformation, and they became increasingly evident in mid-16th-century writings.

In line with the vogue in the Renaissance for producing descriptive narratives, Raphael Holinshed (ca. 1529–ca. 1580) produced *Chronicles of England, Scotlande and Irelande* (1577). English travelers, soldiers, and administrators produced an abundance of texts debating how best to subdue Ireland. Edmund Spenser (1552–99), in *A View of the Present State of Ireland* (1598), argued that only "by the sword" could reform come about, although he veered from portraying the Irish as irremediably barbarous to acknowledge that they were amenable to becoming law-abiding subjects. Spenser presents a debate on the era's moral and theological questions in *The Fairie Queene* (1590–96), an allegorical epic poem written against the backdrop of the Munster rebellion and plantations of the 1570s.

Partisanship peaked during the years of warfare in the 1640s and 1650s. Sir John Temple (1600–77) wrote *The Irish Rebellion* (1646) as a polemic to be used in rousing English animosity toward Catholic insurgents, and his graphic portrayal of the atrocities perpetrated against Protestants in Ulster in 1641 served as a contemporary authoritative account. Leading theologian and scholar James Ussher (1581–1650), an Old English Protestant who lost his lands to Catholic depredations, proclaimed anti-Catholicism as a central tenet of his viewpoints (*An Answer to a Challenge Made by a Jesuite in Ireland* [1624]).

The tumult of midcentury haunted the writings of Restoration authors. Roger Boyle (1621–79), first earl of Derry and a member of one of the most powerful New English families, compiled a prolific literary output, including poetry, drama, romances, and political tracts. His six-volume fictional work, *Parthenissa, A Romance in Four Parts* (1651–69), recounts the complex romantic and military adventures of four platonic heroes, and the political exchanges of the protagonists repeat the key issues that dominated Irish and English affairs, with Derry's overriding theme that of order and union within a monarchical state. The political messages interjected into so much writing of the period blurs the borderlines of literature and polemic throughout the period.

At the same time, these years saw the introduction of theater into Ireland. Although plays on religious themes were probably performed as early as the 14th century, the first documented performance is that of *Gorboduc*, a play written by Thomas Sackville and Thomas Norton in 1561 and staged in the Great Hall of Dublin Castle in 1601. Here also the story draws reference to politics in telling of a divided kingdom descending into anarchy. Playwrights, too, depicted Ireland in a bad light as a place of vice. London-born David Barry (1580–1629), or Lord Barry, reputedly of Irish descent, set his comedy *Ram-Alley, or Merrie Tricks* (1611), in an amoral underworld of scheming tricksters and prostitutes. Performed by the boys' theater company, the Children of the King's Revels, it is traditionally viewed as the first Irish-themed play on the London stage.

The first public theater was constructed about 1635 in Werburgh Street in Dublin. It lasted only until about 1640, but indicative of a culture of theatergoing in vogue at the Stuart court, a new theater—Smock Alley—was built as part of an effort to establish a viceregal court of cultural substance in Dublin. Plays dealing with themes of insurrection and upheaval mark the Restoration theater.

Irish-language literature of the period consisted of two quite distinctive strands, both of which had religion as their underlying motivation. The first comprised religious works in Irish produced as part of the state's efforts to spread Protestantism, which it believed essential to its civilizing role, a role that included the founding of Trinity College Dublin in 1592 to serve as an island-based Protestant university; and the second included Catholic tracts produced by an exile community, which were directed at countering that religious propaganda.

The first book printed in Irish is a Protestant tract, though produced not in Ireland but in Scotland. *Foirm ná n=Urrnuidheadh*, printed in Edinburgh in 1567, is a translation of the Book of Common Order, in turn a revision of the Geneva Book, a Presbyterian primer. In 1571, the first Irish-language book to be printed in Ireland, *Aibidil Gaoidheilge & Caiticiosma* (Irish primer of religion), was published by Seán Ó Cearnaigh, treasurer of St. Patrick's Cathedral in Dublin. Ó Cearnaigh was also involved in the translation of the New Testament into Irish, a project that he began in the 1560s and which was completed in 1602.

Initial Catholic reaction to Protestant proselytizing was slow and spotty. Not until the second decade of the 17th century did systematic Catholic efforts to counteract Protestant preaching begin. The Observant Franciscans spearheaded the literary drive. Based at the Irish Franciscan College in the university town of Leuven in the Spanish Netherlands (present-day Belgium), then the leading intellectual center of the Catholic Counter-Reformation in northern Europe, the order counted several talented Gaelic writers, including Eoghan Ó Dubhthaigh (d. 1590), a famous preacher who wrote poems in praise of Catholicism and against the Reformation as alien to Gaelic Ireland, and the former professional poet Giolla Brighde Ó hEodhasa (d. 1614), who wrote prolifically, producing a catechism, *An Teagasg Croíosdaidhe,* widely disseminated among the Irish.

The Franciscans secured their own printing press, and it was the printing revolution that led to a change in Irish concepts of learning and literacy. Spurred by the Counter-Reformation's need to reach the common people, writers in Irish opted for the vernacular, no longer employing the artificial language of poets *(beíla na bhfileadh)* that writers had employed in the past, when knowledge had been the preserve of an intellectual elite. The new conditions led to a fusion of bardic strict, rhyming schemes (the *dán díreach*, or strict poem) with informal meters *(amhrán)* characteristic of the popular language to produce, among the best poets, a fine synthesis of rigorous and relaxed traditions.

The invention of printing and the cultivation of the vernacular led to the standardization of the language, introducing the need for grammars and dictionaries. A Franciscan at Leuven, Micheál Ó Cléirigh (ca. 1592–1643), produced the first Irish dictionary (*Foclóir nó Sanasán Nua)* in 1643.

Vernacular writing in promotion of Catholic doctrine constituted only one aspect of the literary output of the Leuven Franciscans. Histories also assumed special importance. Astute observers took the temper of the times, and under the patronage of Irish gentlemen and aristocrats, priests and learned poets compiled the lore of Ireland, launching a vibrant burst of creativity in tribute to Gaelic culture. Ó Cléirigh returned to Ireland to compile civil histories—*Réim Ríoghraidh* (Succession of the kings, 1630) and a revision of the *Lebor gabála Érenn*, *Leabhar gabhála* (*The Book of Conquests of Ireland*, 1631). His major work, *Annála Ríoghachta Éireann* (Annals of the kingdom of Ireland, 1632), also known as the *Annals of the Four Masters*, which he compiled together with three other clerics, includes material relating to early saints as well as genealogies of kings. It serves as a major Irish-language source for history up to 1616.

It was in Leuven also that arguably the first concept of the Irish "nation" appeared in print. Irish chronicler Tadhg Ó Cianain kept a record of the travels of the Ulster earls following their flight in 1607, and in a letter of November 1607 describing Irish refugees, he uses the word *Éireannach* (Irish person) rather than the ethnic signifier *Gael* and the words *Éireannach* and *nasión* (nation) together. The use of *Éireannach* in conjunction with, and as a description of, members of the "nation" appears to have emerged in the early 17th century among Catholic émigrés in the Spanish Netherlands as part of an effort to overcome ethnic tensions between those of native Irish and those of Old English stock in favor of an appeal to unity based on a common religion and homeland.

In Ireland itself, a new group of nonprofessional poets broke with traditional bardic poetic material in taking up the cause of religion, fusing Catholicism with Irish culture, now viewed as the patrimony of both Gaelic and Old English. The flight of the earls and the destruction of the Catholic landlord class curtailed the patronage available to the poets, and by the mid 17th century bardic schools were extinct. New versifiers, both lay and clerical, emerged in the second quarter of the 17th century. Love poems and verses extolling the virtues of friendship, composed by poets such as Piaras Feirltéar (ca. 1600–53) and Pádraigin Haicéad (ca. 1604–54), attest to the rise in popularity of these heretofore nontraditional topics.

The catastrophe that struck Catholic Ireland at century's end had a profound impact on the world of letters. Dáibhí Ó Bruadair (1625–98) stands as the outstanding poet of the second half of the 17th century, both in the quantity and in the quality of his work. Possibly a native of

Cork, he had a lively awareness of current events in experiencing first-hand the upheavals of the period. His writings bear witness to the effect of these events both on the Irish Catholic landed class and on his own life, which left him embittered. His greatest poem, *An Lengbhriseadh* (Shipwreck), probably written after the fall of Limerick, where he had relocated in the 1660s, epitomizes his belief that there was no reason to continue the struggle. The poem expresses the recognition that in 1691 Irish indigenous culture had suffered a defeat as traumatic as the military and political beating.

Despite the national and personal catastrophe to the native Irish occasioned by surrender and conquest, poets did succeed in preserving a tradition that would be revived two centuries later. The literati of the 16th and 17th centuries succeeded in forging an Irish identity that equated Irishness with the Roman Catholic faith, an identity that would prove a lasting legacy. The Irish masses would cling to their Catholicism in the years after 1691, when Protestantism surged triumphant in Ireland.

6

ASCENDANCY IRELAND
(1691–1800)

The defeated Irish Catholic armies sailed away to France in the autumn of 1691, leaving behind triumphant English Protestants eager to secure and consolidate the victory so tenaciously and bloodily won. The "Ascendancy" or the "Protestant Ascendancy" is the term familiarly used to describe the governing system and the social milieu of the long 18th century that ensued. Although coined late in the period—in 1792 by Orangeman John Giffard, editor of *Faulkner's Dublin Journal*—and widely used only in the 1800s, the label serves, nevertheless, to succinctly identify an era in which Protestant communicants of the Church of Ireland exercised total control over Irish affairs, subject only to the Crown and Parliament of England (Great Britain after 1707, when the Act of Union joined England and Scotland). The Protestant elite created an exclusive world whose physical legacy remains on splendid display in Dublin—a capital city they quite literally rebuilt—and in stately town and country houses across the landscape.

Two distinct societies emerged: a minority Protestant class enjoying varying degrees of privilege and a majority Catholic community enduring wholesale oppression. Its defining rationale based on belief in the inherent threat of Roman Catholicism to the public order, the Ascendancy depended for its survival both on enactment and enforcement of Penal Laws, legislation that effectively shut Catholics out of all avenues to influence and power, and on continuing close links with the English crown.

In the 1700s, in one of the longest periods of peace in the country's modern history, Ireland achieved a degree of prosperity through its participation, albeit limited, in transatlantic trade, but the political links to Britain began to weaken late in the century. Watching closely the democratic stirrings in North America, some among the ruling elite began to agitate for a change in political relationships. Resentful of economic constraints imposed on Ireland and mindful of the country's proud, independent history, members of the Irish parliament—the political nerve center of the Ascendancy—affirmed that Irish interests were separate from those of Great Britain. Moderate reforming Whigs—all loyal Protestants but of a tolerant temperament—joined cautious members of a Catholic Committee in agitating for reform. Bands of armed citizens—Protestant Volunteers and Catholic Defenders—appeared. Catholics won relaxation of many strictures, and Parliament secured its virtual independence.

The changes emboldened calls for more radical action. Societies of United Irishmen, launched by Presbyterian malcontents in Ulster, emerged. Joined by Catholics anxious to break the grip of Protestant predominance, they rose in rebellion in 1798 in an insurgency nonsectarian in its character, republican in its purpose, and separatist in its intent. The rebels meant to create an independent Irish republic in carrying out a revolution on the model of those waged successfully in America and France.

They failed, and defeat led to the loss of the institutional embodiment of Irish separatism. The Irish parliament was dissolved, and union with Britain decreed in 1800. Irish national hopes would survive, memorialized in recollections of the rising of "Ninety-Eight," but the affairs of Ireland would henceforth compete for attention in a legislature occupied with imperial concerns of worldwide dimensions.

Irish Society at the Turn of the Eighteenth Century

The surrender of the Catholic landed interests in 1691 left the majority of Ireland's approximately 2 million people—the Catholic rural dwellers—devoid of leadership. Most of the prominent families who had not conformed to English ways had either been killed in battle or had fled the country following one or another of the defeats of the preceding years. The bulk of the people of Ireland still lived much as their ancestors had done. Apart from the commercial classes in the towns and those inhabitants of eastern areas in Leinster, where English feudal practices had long held sway, most native rural residents held all or part of their lands in common, carried on primarily subsistence farming, paid rents in kind rather than cash, and engaged only tangentially in market activities beyond their immediate localities.

In common with European peasants in general, the poorer Irish tenants and subtenants lived precariously, and poor harvests, famines, and epidemics would not infrequently produce dire adversity. But distinguishing Ireland from all other western European societies, here landowners and senior ruling officials were of a different ethnic background and practiced a different religion from the majority population.

In 1700 Ireland's social superiors consisted largely of first-generation English settlers together with the descendants of English colonists who had prospered in Ireland during the reigns of Elizabeth I and James I, including, among the latter, landowners and tenants of Scottish descent who were concentrated overwhelmingly in Ulster. They also included a scattering of landlords of Anglo-Irish and even Gaelic origin who had adopted English ways, converted, and began marrying into settler families. All were Protestants, all members of the established Anglican Church of Ireland, save for the Presbyterian Ulster Scots and a sprinkling of other Protestant nonconforming sects, and, as such, all staunchly upheld the English commercial, legal, and political systems.

In 1695 the Irish parliament abolished customary Irish tenure, mandating that tenants enter into formal lease agreements with landlords. A process that had begun earlier after the Cromwellian conquest now speedily went forward, resulting in abolition of *clachan* settlements and enclosure of the land within walls and fences. The bulk of the country's wealth, which was generated by the rural population, went toward payment of rent to the landowners, very few of whom diversified their incomes by investing in commercial enterprises.

Some rural residents held titles as subtenants to tenants higher up the social scale, these last receiving rent from them and paying rent, in turn, to head landlords. In the 18th century the landlord class comprised less than 10,000 families, and even fewer, only several hundred of the wealthiest magnates, monopolized most of the land, save for parcels reserved for the established church. The great landlords owned vast estates encompassing thousands of acres on which they built elaborate country mansions. They alone ran the political system. Those who participated in affairs of state needed city residences, which spurred the development of Dublin. The city would expand throughout the century, counting about 180,000 inhabitants by 1800, and the presence of an affluent leisure class promoted commercial growth in turn.

The polarization between the Protestant ruling elite and the tenants, who were predominantly Catholic in religion and Irish in origin, language, and culture, was everywhere apparent, and the stereotypes engendered became deeply embedded on both sides of the religious and cultural divide. To the English the Irish were lazy, ignorant, superstitious, and duplicitous. The Irish saw the English as arrogant, greedy, intolerant, and cunning.

Ethnic divisions varied in their degrees of visibility. They were less in evidence in areas where plentiful supplies of fertile land allowed proprietors to bring in English Protestant tenants and in places, most especially in Ulster, where formal schemes to settle Protestants had been in place for a century. They were most glaringly on display in the province of Connacht, where land was of poor quality and few Protestants could be found.

But even where Protestants lived in relatively greater numbers, a substantial proportion of native Irish remained, many of whom, while they learned English and accommodated to the ruling regime, retained their knowledge of the Irish language and cultural ways.

They provided patronage to Irish poets and priests, previously privileged members of the old Irish order who had lost their status but who, unlike the landlords, remained in place. Bitter over the loss of their world and holding the Shoneen (*Séoinín*, literally "little Johnny"), that is, the British administration and their supporters in the Protestant Ascendancy, in utter contempt, they fostered a myth of a former golden age, constantly reminding Irish Catholics that they were the descendants of glorious ancestors. Although the myth was a fiction because the land the English now owned had been held previously not by Irish peasants but by ruling Gaelic kinship groups, the notion that they had been unjustly dispossessed of their property became firmly fixed in the minds of the common folk along with the determination to recover what had been lost. No matter their resolve, however, in 1700 Catholics could only dream, having in hand not the slightest means by which to overturn the reality that Protestant power reigned supreme.

The Era of the Penal Laws, 1691–1778

The complete defeat of the Irish Jacobites in 1690–91 left Catholics with little cause for hope. Although the Treaty of Limerick promised some degree of toleration, their fears would be fully justified, exemplified after the surrender by the flight of Dominic Maguire (r. 1683–1707), Catholic primate of all Ireland, who lived in destitution in exile. The see of Armagh remained vacant until 1714, and although a new primate, Hugh MacMahon (r. 1714–37), was appointed, he was forced to serve literally on the run, saying Mass and administering the sacraments in the open air.

The sense of relief felt by Protestants after King William III's victory was linked equally to a profound feeling of insecurity. The speed with which Catholics had regained power between 1685 and 1689 and, indeed, the memories of Catholic betrayals and assaults going all the way back to 1641 were too recent for Protestants to assume that the potential threat to their position had been entirely suppressed. In addition, the international situation remained unsettled. The Nine Years' War (1689–97) between England and France still raged. The defeated king James resided at the court of Louis XIV, king of France (r. 1638–1715), and Protestants believed the possibility very real that Irish soldiers, now serving in great numbers in French armies, might return as part of an invasion force on behalf of the Stuarts, to which the Catholic population would certainly rally.

To maintain Protestant supremacy, Catholics needed to be contained, and to that end, the Irish parliament, now composed entirely of Protestant members, set about legislating a complex series of Penal Laws that formally excluded Catholics from participation in most public affairs. In 1695 "Papist gentlemen" were denied the right to carry arms for self-defense or for hunting. Oaths denying the doctrine of transubstantiation (the bread and wine of the Eucharist become the body and blood of Christ) and of papal supremacy were imposed on members of parliament in the 1690s and, subsequently, on anyone seeking to hold any government office, practice law, or hold commissions in the army or navy. Because no Catholic would take them, the oaths successfully closed these careers to them. In 1729 the right to vote was denied to Catholic freeholders. To cut off their access to landed property, popery bills in 1703–04 and 1709 forbade Catholics from buying land or taking leases for longer then 31 years.

By the late 1770s Catholics, though they constituted about 75 percent of the population, owned about 5 percent of the land. Denied ownership to land—the major means of acquiring wealth—Catholics then suffered indignities that struck at the heart of their religious identity. They were compelled to pay tithes to the established church, and laws were passed that proscribed Catholic worship, teaching, religious organizations, and popular practices ranging from pilgrimages to processions. Protestant missionaries endeavored to promote conversion through education with establishment of charter schools, first founded in October 1733 and given government grants in 1746.

But they achieved minimal effect, Catholics remaining wary and distrustful. In any case, efforts at conversion of the masses to Protestantism were half-hearted at best, the propertied and professional classes aware that to do so would mean loss of their privileged status as a small, separate ruling elite. Their aim to maintain their exclusivity also shaped their policy toward nonconforming Protestants, most especially Presbyterians (Dissenters). While non-Anglican Protestants enjoyed full property rights and were granted legal toleration in 1719, affording them the opportunity to vote and sit in parliament, they, too, were excluded from Crown offices and required to pay tithes to the established church. In the early 18th century some found the pressure to conform too great to resist. A number of Catholic barristers and lawyers converted to the established church, and many among the few remaining Catholic landlords did so as well.

Meant to be harsh so as to keep Catholics in a state of subjection, in practice the Penal Laws produced varying degrees of effectiveness. Support for the legislation was always strongest among members of the Irish parliament (MPs) and less so among English governing officials in Dublin and London.

Landed aristocrats and Church of Ireland communicants held all power in the parliament that sat in Dublin. Parliament was in no way a democratic body. Income and property qualifications limited the electorate to well-off members of the population. Town constituencies were even more undemocratic than those in the counties. Some of the former were "rotten," that is, districts in which elections took place mostly as a formality, where only a handful of voters existed. None of the legislative powers won by the English parliament in the Glorious Revolution applied in Ireland. The requirement that elections to an English parliament be held periodically did not exist in Ireland, where a parliament needed to be elected only when a monarch died. Parliaments met biennially to appropriate additional revenues, since the hereditary revenues received by the government in Ireland did not cover public expenses, part of which were needed to maintain the large army—twice the size of the army in Britain—stationed in the country to quell potential or actual unrest.

All authority ultimately resided with the government in England, and no legislation could be considered by the Irish parliament before first being approved in London. The English government—the British government after 1707—appointed the lord lieutenant, who customarily resided in Dublin Castle only for the biennial parliamentary sessions, as well as his chief secretary. The office of chief secretary assumed increasing importance as the century progressed. In theory subordinate to the lord lieutenant or his deputy, the chief secretary served as the spokesman of the British administration in representing government policy before the Irish House of Commons, and his opinions carried great weight. The lord lieutenant and the chief secretary worked at managing the various private interests of parliamentarians, buying and trading favors and positions with individuals and groups of members, and they acted always in the interest of English, rather than Irish, political considerations. Because lords lieutenant and chief secretaries were so frequently absent, political figures known as Undertakers "undertook" to promote the government's agenda using patronage to guarantee voting in London's interest.

Because the Irish parliament could not act without the approval of the monarch and the parliament in London, the British government could and often did threaten to soften anti-Catholic sanctions, using their power as a bargaining tool in dealing with Irish MPs who resisted supporting London officialdom on issues it deemed important. Penal provisions that proved overly petty—those that forbade Catholics from possessing a gun or owning a horse worth more than five pounds—quickly fell into disuse. Most important, after the first years of strict sanctions, Catholic religious life resumed its course to a remarkable degree. Given that Catholics were in the great majority, it proved impossible to rigidly regulate the private life of so many of the country's inhabitants. About a thousand diocesan priests allowed to remain formed the core leadership of a church that gradually regained strength; masses were being said from early on and by midcentury the hierarchy had been restored to a level not seen since the onset of the Reformation. By the 1750s priests were being trained in seminaries in Ireland.

Catholics worshiped in barns, stables, storehouses, and even in the open fields. Official houses of worship were labeled "chapels" since only the buildings of the established faith could legally be called a "church." By the 1720s Catholic chapels could be found everywhere outside Ulster, clustered in back alleys in the towns and tucked away in quiet corners of the countryside.

Although distrust of Catholics remained intense—the papacy continued to uphold Stuart claims to the throne until 1766, leaving Catholics open to the charge of treason—Catholic prelates were careful to counsel their flocks to respect private property and submit to the rule of the temporal authorities, knowing full well that if they did not, they could be deported. After midcentury a Catholic party began to emerge seeking to disprove the charge that Catholics were inherently disloyal. During the Seven Years' War (1756–63), Catholics in urban centers addressed loyalty petitions to king and Parliament, and the government even considered a scheme to recruit Irish Catholics to form regiments to fight in the army of Portugal, a Catholic power allied to Britain against a coalition of France, Spain, and Austria.

The timing proved unpropitious, however. Both the proposal and an effort to introduce a bill in Parliament allowing Catholics to obtain mortgages on land were dropped after an outburst of agrarian violence in Munster and Ulster. Spurred by grievances against enclosure of common lands, rural unemployment, tithes, and "rack" (i.e., exorbitantly high) rents, against which they had no redress in the courts of law, secret societies launched attacks on the governing class. They included Protestant groups in Ulster such as the Hearts of Oak and Hearts of Steel (Steelboys). Catholic agrarian societies included the Rightboys and, in particular, the Whiteboys or Levellers (Buachaillí Bána), who appeared in Tipperary and Limerick between 1741 and 1762 and then spread to other Munster counties, whose members, identified by their white shirts, were sworn to mutual loyalty by oaths.

The disturbances occurred periodically in the 1760s and 1770s. Militant Protestant opinion insisted that the outbreaks were part of a popish rebellion engineered by the French, but in reality the disturbances were inspired, at least in part, by discontent engendered by economic dislocations produced in conjunction with profound changes taking place in Irish society.

Economy and Society in Georgian Ireland

Although she was a Protestant, Queen Anne (r. 1704–14) was also a Stuart, and on her death British ruling circles, unwilling to countenance the return of her Catholic kinsmen, turned to the House of Hanover, a Protestant branch of the Stuarts who ruled a small territory of that name in central Germany. From 1714 to 1830 four Georges of that family line ruled Britain and Ireland, giving their name to the era. During the reigns of the first three Hanoverian kings, Ireland became linked more closely than ever to Britain. Irish society became increasingly anglicized, and its economy largely commercialized. Integrated into the developing world of English merchant capitalism, the country experienced economic and demographic expansion, which wrought great changes in the physical landscape of both rural and urban Ireland and in the lifestyle of many, but not all, people.

A rapid postwar recovery set in by the late 1690s, though overseas wars caused demand for Irish goods elsewhere to fluctuate considerably, the unpredictability of income thus discouraging investment in Irish land. The growth rate slowed in the early decades of the 18th century when prices for Irish farm products, especially in the important foreign market for butter, stagnated, internal trade languished, and a run of bad harvests in the late 1720s and from 1739 to 1741 produced much rural hardship.

After midcentury, however, the Irish economy expanded rapidly, marked by an inflow of capital, low interest rates, and a rise in agricultural prices. The expansion was driven primarily by Britain's growing need for agricultural produce and textiles to supply its military forces and overseas possessions during the period when, from 1740 to 1815, Britain found itself almost constantly at war, as well as to feed and clothe its urban population, which began to grow rapidly in the mid 18th century. The spate of inventions that followed the harnessing of steam power in the 1760s spawned a revolution that led to the creation of an urban factory environment in Britain, making the country the world's first, and leading, industrial nation. These factors created a growing demand for Irish grain as well as butter, beef, pork, and mutton.

Agricultural outflows accelerated, but Ireland's largest exported items after midcentury were textiles, chiefly linen yarn and cloth. British merchants and officials had encouraged Irish linen production as a complement to English woolens since the early 1600s, but a law of 1696 granting Irish linens duty-free entry to the English market gave the real go-ahead.

By the last quarter of the century, annual linen production reached as much as 40 million yards. The industry was highly regionalized, primarily located in Ulster where life in the many market towns revolved around trade in yarn and cloth and where nearly every rural household was involved in weaving or spinning linen. By the end of the century Belfast had replaced Dublin as the export center for textiles. But also in southeastern Ireland, the state-run Irish Linen Board promoted linen production by conducting training schools and distributing thousands of spinning wheels and hand looms.

Other industries appeared as well. Fishing and distilling supplemented farming activities, especially in Ulster, the country's most densely populated and most prosperous region. The growth in distilleries and breweries promoted local grain production and, at the same time, reflected increased home consumption.

Late in the century cotton mills began to appear, again mostly in Ulster, Ireland's emerging industrial center. In 1783 Waterford entrepreneurs and

GUINNESS GROWS FROM LOCAL TO GLOBAL

Arthur Guinness (1725–1803) arrived in Dublin in December 1759 already experienced in the trade that would earn fame and fortune for himself and his descendants. Born in Leixlip, County Kildare, he learned his brew-making skills from his father. It is said that the archbishop of Cashel was so impressed by the quality of the beer brewed by Arthur that, on Cashel's death in 1752, he left the 27-year-old 100 pounds. Arthur used the legacy to set up his first brewery, leaving it to a younger brother after three years and setting off for Dublin. In the capital, he took over an ailing brewery at St. James's Gate and quickly turned the business into a thriving concern. Arthur grew wealthy, which brought him social standing and political influence. He became a major philanthropist and served on the Dublin City Council.

The use of mostly Irish barley malt gave Guinness brew, a fairly strong black beer with a creamy white head and a smooth, velvety texture, its distinctive quality. It proved popular across the social spectrum, from dockworkers and merchants to soldiers and students to members of Parliament, within whose homes, when the legislature was in session, tables were permanently laid out with food and drink.

By 1865 Guinness Brewery was the fifth largest in the United Kingdom and, by the turn of the 20th century, one of the world's largest. Land was purchased in 1873 extending the properties to the river Liffey so as to facilitate transport downriver to the port, where barrels of brew were loaded onto ships for export to ever-increasing overseas markets. After incorporation in 1876, the company ceased being family-owned. The sale of shares to stockholders left the family with considerable wealth, which they used for charitable and public-interest purposes.

Guinness is brewed today in plants in more than 50 countries. A temperamental brew requiring great care in pouring from the tap into the glass, Guinness stout is still produced on the original site. Even more than Irish whiskey, it is the country's national beverage.

exporters William and George Penrose identified a need for plain and ornamental cut glass. Having no glass manufacturing skills themselves, they engaged John Hill, a fellow Quaker, who arrived from Stourbridge, England, to begin production. Originally known as Penrose Glass,

Waterford would subsequently flourish to become what is today arguably the world's most beautiful lead crystal.

Economic growth produced a marked rise in the amount of money in circulation. The supply of cash increased threefold between 1720 and 1770 and trebled again by 1800. The spread of a cash economy was further encouraged by new and improved transportation links—the most impressive, the Grand Canal and the Royal Canal connecting Dublin to the Shannon—that brought prosperity to inland towns by facilitating the expansion of trade. An elaborate network of markets and fairs spread across the country. Cattle fairs, based on regional specializations in breeding, rearing, and marketing to meet the insatiable English demand, became a rural institution. Growth in foreign trade spurred the prosperity of large ports, such as Dublin, Cork, Limerick, and Waterford.

Throughout the century, the tiny, overwhelmingly Protestant land-owning aristocracy remained at the pinnacle of society. After 1750 increasing numbers of Irish landlords began to invest resources in developing their estates. The enclosure of open fields and medieval common lands continued, leading to the virtual disappearance of *clachan*-style settlements. Enlarged fields closed in by hedgerows or stone walls appeared. Bogs and fens were drained. Where the rural economy expanded, the physical landscape changed dramatically. Roads, bridges, and mills were built. Landlord villages grew up beside the major estates, and on the latter, affluent tenants built two-story farmhouses while the wealthiest landlords constructed spectacular classical-style mansions that showcased the central role of the landed aristocracy in Ascendancy Ireland.

The distinctive Georgian style of architecture was nowhere more magnificently on display than in Dublin, the capital that became, in the 18th century, a structural showpiece, imaginatively laid out with a grandeur befitting its status at this time as the second city of the British Empire. In 1729 the foundation stone for a new parliament building was laid. Designed by architect Edward Lovet Pearce (d. 1733) in College Green, the building opened on October 5, 1731. Trinity College was reconstructed, and the spacious, interconnected patterns of squares, streets, and bridges that would come to characterize late 18th-century Dublin were well under construction even before the Wide Streets Commission was appointed in 1758 to oversee urban development and reconstruction. Creation of these formal spaces marked the continued, steady growth of the city south of the river Liffey, where Merrion Square, probably the best known of all the city's squares, was finished about 1797.

In 1745 Phoenix Park was officially opened to the public on lands that had been leased to an English lord in 1611, who had built a manor house named for the clear spring (*fionn visce*, rendered in English roughly as *phoenix*) on the site. Built between 1785 and 1802, the Four Courts building, designed by architect James Gordon (1743–1823) to house the four central courts of law—Chancery, King's (or Upper) Bench, Common Pleas, and Exchequer—became the architectural embodiment of Ascendancy self-confidence. London-born Gordon had already designed the Custom House (1781–91) and an extension to the parliament building (1782).

Apart from Dublin, there were no other towns of great size. Nearly all large towns were seaports. Urbanization elsewhere proceeded

Custom House, Dublin (Library of Congress, LC-USZ62-112333)

erratically—the commercially expanding economy maintaining its agrarian, export-oriented focus. Most urban dwellers—laborers and artisans—lived barely above subsistence, many of them in filthy, congested slums.

By the late 18th century economic growth and transportation improvements had linked most of the country together into a complex network of trade based on a high degree of regional specialization. The pasture-farming districts that spread through north Munster, Leinster, and eastern Connacht featured intensely commercialized production that sustained a prosperous farming class. Grain cultivation was centered in southeast Leinster with its rich, well-drained soils. Dairy farms proliferated in the Golden Vale of north Munster and in east Connacht, both areas noted for their lush grasses. Sheep-raising predominated on poor, mountainous land in western Ireland. The most widespread poverty could be found along the Atlantic seacoast from west Cork to Donegal and in a corridor featuring poorly drained soils running from Sligo Bay east across north Leinster and southern Ulster to the Mourne Mountains of south Down. Mountains, bogs, and poor agricultural land kept inland southern Ulster, in particular, isolated from major trade routes.

In inland western Ireland the primitive conditions so much remarked upon by visitors were readily apparent. Most dwellings were simple one-room huts or cabins made of mud, turf, or dry stones. Farms here were tiny—most less than 10 acres.

Life proved sustainable, if barely so, through dependence on two elements: the pig and the potato. Both needed only a small plot of land on which to survive and thrive, and the sandy soils and temperate climate suited the potato perfectly. Introduced from South America to Ireland in the 1580s, the tubers took hold slowly, but by the 18th century the "paddies" had proved their worth. By the 1750s it was a staple winter food in Munster and 30 years later an essential food source year-round across the island. The spread of the potato promoted the practice of keeping pigs, which lived off the peelings.

The commercialization of the rural economy brought relative prosperity to some regions and classes, but nowhere uniformly or without substantial dislocations brought about in conjunction with dramatic demographic growth. Already rising at the century's start, the number of inhabitants probably doubled by 10 decades later, approaching nearly 5 million by 1800. Economic expansion and altered farming patterns drove rents upward, which, together with occasional disastrous harvests, forced rural residents in the most densely populated places, such as Ulster, to face a choice of either pauperization or emigration.

AN ENGLISH VISITOR'S IMPRESSION OF EIGHTEENTH-CENTURY IRELAND

Arthur Young (1741–1820) was the leading British agriculturalist of his day. He undertook farming surveys, contributed to and edited the definitive *Annals of Agriculture* (1784–1819), and carried on a correspondence with political leaders, including George Washington and the marquis de Lafayette. Young visited Ireland from 1776 to 1779, and the following is an excerpt from his *A Tour in Ireland* (1780):

> The landlord of an Irish estate, inhabited by Roman Catholics, is a sort of despot who yields obedience, in whatever concerns the poor, to no law but that of his own will. . . . A long series of oppressions, aided by many very ill-judged laws, have brought landlords into the habit of exerting a very lofty superiority and their vassals into that of an almost unlimited submission: speaking a language that is despised, professing a religion that is abhorred, and being disarmed, the poor find themselves in many cases slaves in the bosom of written liberty. . . .
>
> The common Irish are in general clothed so very indifferently that it impresses every stranger with a strong idea of universal poverty. Shoes and stockings are scarcely ever found on the feet of the children of either sex, and great numbers of men and women are without them. . . .

Small numbers, perhaps 50,000 to 100,000, left Ireland in the 1600s as a consequence of the hardships occasioned by wars and rebellions. Many more—some 250,000 to 400,000—left in the 1700s. Three-fourths of all transatlantic emigrants in 1700–75 were Protestants, most conspicuously Presbyterians from Ulster, who departed for the English colonies in North America, places that promised religious freedom and economic opportunity.

Catholics left too, largely because of legal proscriptions, lack of opportunity to acquire capital, and Protestant prejudice. But many fewer did so. Catholics perceived emigration differently from Protestants, a fact that reflected the continuing survival of Gaelic culture throughout the century. In the 18th century the majority of Catholics remained insulated from the impulse to emigrate by the provincialism of Irish culture, which discounted individual effort in favor of communal

The cottages of the Irish, which are called cabins, are the most miserable looking hovels that can well be conceived. They generally consist of only one room. Mud kneaded with straw is the common material of the walls. . . . They are about two feet thick, and have only a door which lets in light instead of a window, and should let the smoke out instead of a chimney but they had rather keep it in. . . .

The furniture of the cabins is as bad as the architecture, in very many consisting only of a pot for boiling their potatoes, a bit of a table, and one or two broken stools. Beds are not found universally, the family lying on straw equally partook of by cows, calves, and pigs, though the luxury of sties is coming in Ireland. . . .

The circumstances which struck me most in the common Irish were vivacity and a great and eloquent volubility of speech. . . . Pleased to enjoyment with a joke, or witty repartee, they will repeat it with such expression that the laugh will be universal. Warm friends and revengeful enemies, they are inviolable in their secrecy and inevitable in their resentment. . . . Hard drinkers and quarrelsome, great liars, but civil, submissive, and obedient. Dancing is so universal among them that there are everywhere itinerant dancing masters. . . . Besides the Irish jig, which they can do with a most luxuriant expression, minuets and country dances are taught. . . .

Source: Arthur Young, *A Tour in Ireland, with General Observations on the Present State of That Kingdom* (London: For T. Cadell and J. Dodsley, 1780), pp. 25–26.

action, honored since Celtic times, and which regarded departure as abandonment of one's family and surrender to greed for material gain. Moreover, Irish Catholics had before them a real-life picture of emigration as compulsory punishment in the picture presented of the banished exiles—the Ulster earls and the Wild Geese.

Gaelic ways remained prevalent throughout most of rural Ireland in the 18th century. Before 1750 the great majority of the rural populace beyond all but a few eastern counties—Dublin, Kildare, Wicklow, and Wexford—spoke little or no English. Irish speakers were intensely devoted to the verbal arts. The Irish love of talk—a fact much commented on by English travelers in the 18th and 19th centuries—helped to keep the language alive even as use of English progressed. The language survived in part because it afforded a means to communicate of which the vast majority of the English were ignorant and in part because of the strong Gaelic literary tradition, both of which made the language one of the few weapons left after the defeats of the 17th century with which to express anti-Englishness.

The archaism of Irish culture, nurtured for centuries in relative isolation in a subsistence economy, gave pride of place to speech and memory. Hereditary storytellers, like their predecessors of old, replicated tales of ancient gods and warriors and memorized family lineages. Deprived of their patrons, they had lost their privileged status, but "courts of poetry" continued to meet, now in farmhouses in Munster and also in Connacht and Ulster, where bards judged the compositions of younger poets.

Music and dancing played a prominent part in rural life, and traditional beliefs still held sway. The world was still one in which modern distinctions between the real and the unreal were blurred, a universe in which all things physical—rocks, trees, crops, houses, and food—had a mystical significance and were believed governed by supernatural forces.

Both Catholics and Protestants believed in the existence of fairies— the "little people" associated with the Tuatha Dé Danaan, the quasi-historical inhabitants of Ireland before the Celts. Fairies could be kind and protective but also malevolent, blighting crops, sickening livestock, or even stealing healthy infants, leaving dead "changelings" in their place. Leprechauns were mischievous, miserly male fairies whose dress varied by region but the color of which was red (it became green in the 20th century). Cobblers or shoemakers by trade, they amassed great riches, which, because they could not escape a viewer's gaze, might be had by those fortunate enough to glimpse one. Some fairies did duty as "banshees," signaling the onset of death by emitting unearthly shrieks, or as "Red Willy," guarding illegal stills from discovery. Distinctive customs revolved around death, and the funeral wakes of rural Catholics, which featured "sitting up" with the corpse until burial, heavy drinking, wailing women, storytelling, and practical jokes, assumed legendary status as a trademark Irish practice.

Though many old beliefs and customs persisted, they began to erode as the century progressed, and by 1800 the communal culture of the Irish was much less in evidence. The links forged by trade and communications and the ideology of rational progress based on advances in science and technology—all emanating from Ireland's ties to Great Britain—broke down not only geographic but cultural barriers as well. Resident landlords, affluent farmers, urban merchants, lawyers and journalists, and clergymen from the middle and upper ranks of

Irish wakes became a well-known cultural marker. (Library of Congress, LC-USZ62-118008)

Protestant and Catholic society served as the agents of change. An increasing conformity to English middle-class standards of speech and manners could be discerned, and, most significantly, by the end of the century the English language was making ever more steady inroads. More and more Irish began to change traditional names to their English equivalents.

A desire to emulate English society spurred change among some, and some were no doubt compelled to do so by the pressure, whether subtle or not, to conform. The end result of the destruction of cultural insularity would be not only to undermine traditional identities but also to impart a growing awareness, among the general populace, of their relative deprivation, an awareness that would stoke discontent. At the same time, the spreading English presence was nowhere more apparent than in a burgeoning literary output, and English-language literature would, paradoxically, help to nurture a rise of pride in Irishness that transcended economic and religious divides.

The World of Eighteenth-Century Arts and Letters

During a century framed at its beginning and end by political and military turmoil, the literary work of English-language writers reflected the temper of the times in Ireland but also in the wider European world, which was then alive with the intellectual energy of Enlightenment thought calling for rational inquiry and stressing human reason as the means to knowledge and morality. Protestant writers produced political, philosophical, theological, and scientific works that found a wide readership beyond Ireland in Britain, continental Europe, and North America.

The legitimization of Protestant power in Ireland began in the very year of final triumph. In 1691, William King (1650–1729), later archbishop of Dublin, condemned Catholic oppression of Protestants in the late 1680s and attributed divine providence to King William's victory in his *State of the Protestants of Ireland under the late King James's Government*.

But while apologists for the new order were prominent among Irish writers, other authors were penning less orthodox views. In the 1690s, the most radical among them was John Toland (1670–1722). Born an Irish-speaking Catholic in Donegal, Toland abandoned the faith of his birth in favor of a wide variety of religious beliefs. In the end, deeply influenced by the work of John Locke (1632–1704), Toland, like his mentor, argued that reason rather than human or divine authority should serve as the guide to true knowledge. Although Toland wrote some 100 published works on subjects ranging from religion to linguistics, *Christianity, not Mysterious* (1696) was his most famous book. Arguing on behalf of a religion entirely reason-based, he provoked immediate controversy, and his work became a central reference source in theological debates across Europe in the 18th century.

Just as controversial but writing on a different topic, lawyer and member of Parliament for Trinity College William Molyneux (1656–98) published his *The Case of Ireland's being bound by Acts of Parliament in England, Stated* in Dublin in April 1698, his last work. Molyneux claimed a direct contract existed between the Irish people, whom he defined as the English who had settled Ireland, and the English crown that bypassed the English parliament in dating back to the reign of King Henry II. In challenging the right of the English parliament to legislate for Ireland, the book was condemned by the House of Commons, but Molyneux's arguments would be referenced not only by Irish reformers but also by North American colonists in the following century. Molyneux founded the Dublin Philosophical Society in 1698, which served as the foundation for the creation of the Dublin Society in June 1731, later the Royal Dublin Society (RDS). A forum for study of the sciences, the RDS continues today as a major center for exhibitions, concerts, lectures, cultural events, and sporting competitions.

Toland was the outstanding figure in Irish Enlightenment thought in the late 17th and early 18th centuries. But the reason-versus-faith divide so characteristic of 18th-century debate fails to neatly accommodate the greatest of all Irish philosophers. George Berkeley (1685–1753), while a political conservative and an opponent, though not a rabidly intolerant one, of Roman Catholicism, was both an anti–free thinker in religion as well as a champion of rational inquiry. Berkeley is remembered for the theory he called "immaterialism." Denying the existence of matter independent of perception, he summed up his philosophy in his dictum "Esse est percipi" ("To be is to be perceived") in affirming that only the sensations and ideas of objects can be known, not any "real" object or matter. In his most widely read books, the *Treatise Concerning the Principle of Human Knowledge* (1713) and *Three Dialogues between Hylas and Philonous* (1713), he raises empiricism—the belief that knowledge is based on observation and experiment—to its most extreme expression. He argued that the existence of the physical world depends entirely on the mind's awareness of it, and that awareness comes to mankind from God, the infinite all-perceiving mind who is the ultimate source of all human perceptions. The novelty of Berkeley's reasoning made a significant, and enduring, impact far beyond Ireland.

Probably no 18th-century Irish writer is more remembered than Jonathan Swift (1667–1745). Even more than Berkeley, he dominated English literature in Ireland in the first half of the 18th century. Arguably the greatest prose satirist in the English language, Swift was a prolific writer who penned satires, essays, political pamphlets, and poems.

Born in Dublin, Swift obtained a degree in divinity at Trinity College before taking priestly orders in the Church of Ireland in 1695, but he preferred a post as secretary to his relative Sir William Temple (1628–99) in Surrey, England. He stayed there, where he published his earliest works, before returning to Ireland after Temple's death to take up the post as dean, in 1713, of St. Patrick's Cathedral, Dublin. His early writings, such as *The Battle of the Books* (1704) and *A Tale of a Tub* (1704), demonstrate a style—funny and teasing while critical and instructive—that he would employ fully in his later works.

Swift acquired a reputation as an Irish patriot in writing several works in support of Irish causes. In 1707 he wrote his first major prose work dealing with Irish affairs, *The Story of the Injured Lady*, in which he depicts Ireland as an unhappy woman jilted by England, her unfaithful lover, with whom she had sought parliamentary union, which Swift supported. *Drapier's Letters* (1724–25), a series of pamphlets in which he decries the monopoly granted by the English government to ironmaster

William Wood to mint coins for Ireland, represents Swift's most outspoken effort to rally Irish resistance to what he came to increasingly see as English political and economic oppression of Ireland. In 1729 he published *A Modest Proposal*, an essay that represents perhaps the most extreme use of irony in the English language. In this biting satire, the narrator, with intentionally grotesque logic, offers a radical solution in confronting the famine years of the 1720s, namely, the raising of Irish children for human consumption.

Swift's memorable masterpiece remains *Travels into Several Remote Nations of the World, in Four Parts, by Lemuel Gulliver, first a surgeon, and then a captain of several ships*, better known as *Gulliver's Travels* (1726). Employing his trademark use of pseudonyms, the author as "Gulliver" narrates for readers his journey into human nature and society. In his culminating tale, Swift's satirical account of the brutish human Yahoos in the land of the rational, horselike Houyhnhnms stands as a monumental argument against moral, religious, and political complacency and in favor of a healthy skepticism toward belief in the human capacity for progress.

A wood engraving from an 1865 edition of Jonathan Swift's Gulliver's Travels *depicts English doctor Lemuel Gulliver in the land of Lilliput. The book has remained enduringly popular.* (Library of Congress, LC-USZ62-71678)

Although less well known for his verse, Swift is considered the most important 18th-century Irish poet, who gathered around him a circle of writers, men such as Thomas Sheridan (1687–1738) and Patrick Delany (c. 1685–1768) and women such as Mary Barber (c. 1685–1755). Poets of the period strove to write stylish, urbane verse linked closely both to classical authors, such as Horace and Martial, and to recent and contemporary English writers, such as John Dryden (1631–1700) and Alexander Pope (1688–1744). Writers of poetry were especially in evidence in the mid and late 18th century. Much poetry composed by Irish middle-class versifiers in mid-century is compiled in *The Shamrock or Hibernian Cresses, a Collection of Poems, Songs, Epigrams, &c. Latin as well as English, the Original Production of Ireland. . .* , a four-volume work edited in 1772 by the famous Dublin schoolmaster and poet Samuel Whyte (1733–1811).

Fiction writing grew in the wake of the rise of the novel, which appeared in the 1740s. Thomas Amory (1690/91–1788) offers a fictional portrayal of western Ireland and the old Gaelic order in his sprawling fantasy *The Life of John Bunde, Esq.* (1756–66), but his anecdotal account is also replete with lively glimpses of contemporary Dublin. *The Fool of Quality; or, the History of Henry, Earl of Moreland* (1765–70) by Henry Brooke presents the first English-language fictional portrayal of childhood. Laurence Sterne (1713–68), though he left Ireland in childhood, profoundly influenced later Irish writers in his *The Life and Opinions of Tristram Shandy, Gentleman* (1759–67) and other works. The English author Jane Austen (1775–1817) acknowledged a debt to Regina Maria Roche (1764–1845), whose *The Children of the Abbey* (1796) was one of more than a dozen historical, sentimental novels she penned between 1789 and 1836.

Visual artists joined English writers in growing numbers. Susanna Drury, later Susanna Warter (ca. 1698–ca. 1770), completed watercolor drawings that did much to influence the development of Irish landscape art, her work earning her an award from the Royal Dublin Society in 1740 for her paintings of the Giant's Causeway. London drew Irish painters of merit throughout the century. Working there, Cork-born painter James Barry (1741–1806) was one of Ireland's preeminent neoclassical artists, whose works drew on the art and culture of ancient Rome and Greece. Landscape painter George Barret (ca. 1730–84) and portrait and miniature painter Nathaniel Hone (1718–84) helped found the Royal Academy of Arts in the British capital in 1768.

In music, no composer proved more enduringly influential than Turlough Carolan (1670–1738). Born in County Meath, Carolan created compositions that drew on both traditional Irish folk influences as well as classical Italian works, many of which are still heard today.

Eighteenth-century theater thrived with plays performed on the stage of Smock Alley Theatre in Dublin and in drawing rooms around the country, where plays were read. Successful Irish dramatists earned their plaudits, however, primarily on the stages of London's theaters. George Farquhar (1678–1707), born in Derry, left Ireland for London in 1697 where he penned plays—his best-known *The Constant Couple*

(1699), *The Recruiting Officer* (1706), and *The Beaux Stratagem* (1707) —in which he pioneered Irish comic characters. His efforts left him penniless yet posthumously perhaps the most successful Irish-born playwright in the first half of the 18th century.

More enduring fame came to Oliver Goldsmith (1728 or 30–74). Born in County Roscommon and a graduate of Trinity College, Goldsmith settled in London in 1756, where he published poetry and prose, including *The Vicar of Wakefield* (1766), often described as a sentimental novel but one that can also be read as a satire on such works and their value. His two well-known plays, *The Good-natur'd Man* (1768) and *She Stoops to Conquer* (1773), are comedies of error, the last of which remains one among few 18th-century plays still popular today. Richard Brinsley Sheridan (1751–1816) came naturally to theater writing. Sheridan was born in Dublin where his father managed the Smock Alley Theatre. Settling in London, he wrote *The Rivals* (1775), his first commercially produced play and now a standard in English literature, and *School for Scandal* (1777), a comedy of manners and his most famous work.

With the progressive spread of English culture, Irish-language writers stressed themes highlighting the decline of their country's, and their own, status. Poet Aogán (Aodhagán) Ó Rathaille (Egan O'Rahilly, 1670–1729) wrote verse reflective of his inability to secure a leasehold in his native County Kerry, obliging him to seek sustenance in traveling constantly through Munster. He is credited with composing the first *aisling* poem in developing the image of Ireland as a woman wronged, waiting for her deliverance, that would prove recurrently popular. A sense of beleaguerment also pervades the poetry of Muircheartach Óg Ó Súilleabháin (ca. 1710–54). Eoghan Ó Suilleabháin (1748–84) learned poetry at a bardic school, but with the destruction of the Gaelic order, he was forced to wander as an occasional teacher and laborer. His poems, especially his *aisling* poems expressing the hope for a restoration of the glory of the old Irish society, earned him fame throughout Munster, and many were written to be set to music.

Prose writings comprise copies of early medieval sagas, including material from all the major mythologies—the Ulster and other cycles— as well as hagiographies and adaptations of foreign classical works.

Dublin stood second to London in the English-speaking world as a center for publishing and printing. The capital boasted an active book-buying public, and journalism began in earnest in catering to the demands of a growing literate population in urban centers. The *Belfast News*, which printed its first number on September 1, 1737, is the oldest English-language newspaper still in existence, followed in 1766 by the *Limerick Chronicle*.

Current events assumed mounting importance in works as the century progressed. The political debates surrounding Irish-British relations and the revolutionary developments in America and France stirred responses in Ireland manifested in a host of pamphlets and rousing songs, each of them partisan but all of them evincing, in expressing pride in Irish roots or connections, a newfound sense of cultural confidence. The period was distinguished by the many figures in the political world who composed verse of literary merit, including such writer-politicians as Henry Grattan (1746–1820), Edmund Burke (1729–97), Henry Flood (1732–91), and Theobald Wolfe Tone (1763–98). However, it would be their roles as players who shaped the course of political events in late 18th-century Ireland that would earn them historic repute.

Years of Discontent, 1778–1789

The economic progress of the mid 18th century led to growing underlying tensions. Income, consumption, and output rose steadily, peaking and then remaining stable in the century's last decades. In an agrarian-based society, stirrings of unrest appeared quite naturally, first and foremost, in landlord-tenant relations. Despite the increase in the number of landlords who invested time and money in improving their estates, one-third or more owners were absentee lords who lived more or less permanently in Britain, where they would expend the bulk of their income. Even among those who remained in Ireland, many diverted their funds into a variety of unproductive purposes, ranging from constructing costly country mansions to purchasing seats in the Irish parliament. In areas dependent on domestic industry, economic ups and downs made life insecure while the population boom put pressure on available resources. The consequences for Irish tenants included higher rents, shorter leases, consolidation of smallholdings, and prohibitions against subletting.

Catholics came to see the Protestant Ascendancy as based on exploitation, but Protestants, too, chafed at restrictions on trade and limitations on their right to govern their affairs. The middle classes—lawyers, merchants, and financiers—held an uneasy position in between wealthy Ascendancy landowners and the Catholic majority. While they aped the manners of their social superiors, they resented the financial levies and trade restrictions imposed on them by the ruling regime.

Resentment of taxation and other exactions that led to outbreaks of violence by the Whiteboys and other groups gave rise to government efforts in the 1760s to outlaw such disturbances, but they failed to quell rural restlessness. The war of words waged by American colonists against perceived injustices found an echo in Ireland, where, in the next decade, political agitation added to the rumblings of discontent. Weapons replaced the words when armed conflict began at Lexington and Concord, Massachusetts, in April 1775, and many Irish malcontents, well aware that the London parliament's claim to legislate for the colonies applied equally to Ireland, sympathized with the rebelling Americans. Antigovernment sentiments surged strongly especially in Ulster where close ties between that province and North America, forged for over a century by emigration, fueled calls for radical action.

Around 1760 an Irish Patriot party of parliamentarians in Dublin began to emerge in opposition to the government. The members formed an unofficial alliance with Whig members of Parliament (MPs) in Britain, opponents of the ruling Tories. The opposition in the British capital was eloquently led by Edmund Burke. Born in Dublin, the son of a Protestant lawyer who had married a Roman Catholic, Burke entered the British House of Commons in 1765, where his career centered on an impassioned assertion of parliamentary rights as well as a defense of the rights of the Americans.

The Patriot group of MPs in Dublin coalesced in the late 1770s in the midst of economic depression, aggravated by high taxes to pay for a war against American colonists with whom many sympathized. While they considered Ireland's well-being to be paramount, they defined that well-being very narrowly, and the word *patriot* as applied to them more aptly implies a devotion to their own, instead of a national, interest.

The Irish parliament's subordination to the government in London had been a legal fact ever since Poynings's Law of 1494. In April 1720 the Declaratory Act reiterated the Irish parliament's unequivocal subordination to the British. The act put to rest a debate that had raged since the 1690s about how much independence the Dublin assembly had in originating legislation. Many Irish MPs remained sullenly resentful, fearing that government changes in London could at any time further erode what liberties remained to them. Patriots called for a Declaration of Rights, a legal guarantee of the Dublin parliament's legislative freedom and of the Irish judiciary's independence. They coalesced around the leadership of Henry Flood, an MP from Kilkenny, and then, after he had accepted a government office in 1775, of Henry Grattan. Grattan employed his superb oratorical skills, manifested immediately in his maiden speech on December 15, 1775, to speedily make himself the Irish House of Commons spokesman. He became parliament's outstanding voice in pressing its claim to an exclusive right to legislate for Ireland.

Passionate in espousing the right of nationhood for Ireland, Grattan never wavered, however, in maintaining the ties to Britain, which he believed to be indissoluble, linked as the country was to Britain's traditions of constitutional liberties. In his most famous speech to the Dublin House of Commons in May 1782, he declared: "This nation is connected with England not only by allegiance to the crown but by liberty—the crown is one great point of unity but Magna Carta is greater—we could get a king anywhere but England is the only country from which we could get a constitution" (McDowell 1979, 284).

Henry Grattan (Library of Congress, LC-USZ62-90198)

The trade dislocations occasioned by the American war added strains to an economy already weakened, and calls for the lifting of commercial restrictions mounted after 1775. In 1778–79 France allied with the Americans, and Spain, too, entered the war against Great Britain, leaving Ireland exposed and, stripped of soldiers off fighting overseas, largely defenseless. Irish Protestants took up arms, and detachments of uniformed, so-called Volunteers were formed that were sponsored by the great magnates or professional associations. The first company was enrolled at Belfast on March 17, 1778.

The public now had control of the only armed forces of any size in the country, a fact that the political opposition soon appreciated, and members of the latter were quick to commandeer the direction of these Volunteers. Meeting on College Green, Dublin, on November 4, 1779, Volunteers demanded the removal of restrictions on Irish trade, and campaigns climaxed in February 1782 when Ulster Volunteers gathered in convention in the parish church of Dungannon to adopt resolutions in favor of legislative and judicial independence and relaxation of the Penal Laws. Noisy outdoor demonstrations, inflammatory rhetoric from politicians such as Grattan, threats of noncooperation in the Irish House of Commons, and declining fortunes in the war in America now combined to put mounting pressure on an increasingly beleaguered British government.

At first unsure about how to respond, officials in London made concessions in a succession of legislative acts following the fall from power in 1782 of the government led by Lord North (1732–92) and the replacement of his Tory ministry by Whigs anxious to mollify Irish opinion. On January 21, 1782, Parliament repealed the Declaratory Act and amended Poynings's Law to allow all bills approved by the Irish parliament to be transmitted unaltered to London. On April 17, 1783, Parliament followed up the measures of the year before in passing the British Renunciation Act, specifically renouncing its claims to legislate for Ireland. Remaining limitations on Irish commerce were removed.

Ireland now became an independent kingdom sharing only a monarch with Great Britain. Self-rule was soon followed by the trappings of sovereignty—the Bank of Ireland was founded in 1783 and a separate post office was set up. In 1786 Dublin acquired its first regular police force. In a spirit of reconciliation, various restrictions on Catholic worship and on Catholic rights to acquire land and practice teaching and other professions were lifted.

But political reality soon intruded. While legally separate and endowed with a parliament that was able to legislate independently, Ireland remained under the control of Britain to the extent that the lord lieutenant, a British government appointee, selected and controlled the Irish executive, which meant power over patronage—appointments to offices and grants of peerages and pensions—that served to powerfully influence MPs in their deliberations. The fragile unity that Grattan was able to maintain among Protestants fractured. Parliament's elevation in status satisfied most of the landed gentry, but the urban middle classes and the religious Dissenters remained estranged. Reformers pressed for deeper changes. Delegates to a national Volunteer convention assembled in Dublin on November 10, 1783, and there they drafted a reform plan to make the House of Commons more representative, but in the face of parliament's refusal to accept their agenda and unwilling to employ violence to advance their objectives, they found no viable way to proceed. Most simply went home. During the mid 1780s politics remained largely quiescent until the example set by a storm that broke over France stirred decidedly more vigorous advances.

Years of Revolutionary Ferment, 1789–1800

The revolution that began in France in May 1789 deepened over time, event building upon event, a precedent-shattering cataclysm breathtaking in its sweep and all-encompassing in its scope. The monarchy of the Bourbons fell, replaced by a republic. The politics of the past were cast aside, and the whole of society was subjected to reconstruction, judged by the criteria of liberty from arbitrary power, equality of rights and opportunity, and efficiency of purpose. Ripples from the great revolution soon reached Ireland, a country linked to France by ties commercial, cultural, religious, and personal.

In Ireland, too, calls to reduce privilege and discrimination and advance democracy made headway, which, albeit gradually, began to break apart the comfortable, confident world of the Ascendancy. Led by Grattan and others, Irish Whigs, paralleling their British counterparts as the party most conducive to clipping monarchical privilege, demanded that parliament be "purified" by shrinking the size of the pension's list and limiting the number of officeholders allowed to sit in the legislative body. Whig Clubs were formed in Dublin in 1789 and in Belfast in 1790 to advocate for limited parliamentary reforms and to organize opposition to any legislative union of Ireland and Britain.

Calls for further radical action were made, emanating from a part of the country and from among a segment of the population that had been astir with democratic sentiments since the American Revolution. Frustrated by the inability, and often the unwillingness, of Patriot MPs in the Irish parliament to advance reform, elements among the Presbyterian bourgeoisie in Ulster, critical of Anglican landlords who ruled supreme, suspicious that their economic interests were being ignored, and predisposed to radical egalitarian ideas on the French model, launched a movement, the spark for which was supplied by a young Protestant barrister from Dublin.

Theobald Wolfe Tone was invited to Belfast, a city alive with political debate, in the autumn of 1791 to address a group of activists. The son of a coach maker, Tone had studied law at Trinity College and was called to the bar in 1789. Attracted early on to the radical republicanism that was proving so successful in France, he published *Hibernicum* in 1790, which called for greater rights to self-government, but the work that caught the attention of the Irish political world was *An Argument on Behalf of the Catholics of Ireland*, published in August 1791. Tone advocated emancipation, although his sentiments were animated less out of respect for Roman Catholicism—a religion he thought destined to fade as a superstitious relic with the advance of Enlightenment thought—than by his

Theobald Wolfe Tone (Library of Congress, LC-USZ62-35816)

belief that only through cooperation of Ireland's two underprivileged groups, Catholics and Protestant radicals, could parliament be truly reformed and the country secure a government completely independent of Great Britain. A fortnight of conversation and debate ended with creation of the Belfast Society of United Irishmen on October 14, 1791. Efforts by Tone's friend James Napper Tandy (1740–1803), a Dublin Protestant ironmonger, land agent, and rent collector, led to establishment of the Dublin Society of United Irishmen in November.

Spawned from sophisticated debating clubs, the United Irishmen represented middle-class, radical Protestantism, most of its members Presbyterians who, though harboring antigovernment sentiments, remained committed to working within Irish constitutional traditions. They sought to utilize the pressure of public opinion to effect change, and they were joined in their campaign by Volunteer corps and political clubs, all of which eagerly passed resolutions of solidarity with the United Irishmen. In mid February 1793 Ulster Volunteers, meeting in convention at Dungannon, called for reform measures that included the abolition of tithes, cuts in` government spending, lower taxes, and trade incentives.

Catholics, too, now began to busily agitate for change, and it would be Catholics, that part of the population most sorely deprived, who would win the greatest gains. A Catholic Committee had been in existence since March 1760. Founded in Dublin, the committee remained largely aristocratic in its membership and conservative in its program, but in the increasingly inflammable atmosphere of the early 1790s, it took on growing radical overtones. In 1791 a petition was presented to King George III (r. 1760–1820) asking for relief for his Irish Catholic subjects. Led now by practical businessmen inclined to get results, the members sought to assuage Protestant fears by engaging Tone as their

THE EMERALD ISLE

Ireland's universal identification as the "Emerald Isle" owes its origin to William Drennan (May 23, 1754–February 5, 1820). Born in Belfast, Drennan studied philosophy and medicine and became a doctor, specializing in obstetrics, who practiced in Belfast, Newry, and then Dublin. A militant radical and an enthusiastic supporter of revolutions in America and France, he drew national attention with publication in 1784–85 of his *Letters of Orellana, an Irish Helot*, which called for constitutional reform and Catholic emancipation. Drennan became one of the leaders of the United Irishmen in Dublin, but he withdrew from association with the society after it turned to more violent tactics, and he played no part in the uprising of 1798. In 1807 he retired from practicing medicine and returned to Belfast, where he became an active supporter of the Belfast Academical Institution, an organization that pioneered the introduction of secondary and higher education in the city.

Although Drennan penned very little verse, his poem "Erin" (1785) is forever remembered for its lines that define Ireland:

> *Nor one feeling of vengeance presume to defile*
> *The cause, or the men, of the Emerald Isle.*

Drennan died in 1820, and he was buried in Clifton Street Cemetery in Belfast, his coffin carried to his tomb by three Catholics and three Protestants in symbolic tribute to the nonsectarian sentiments he had faithfully espoused.

chief secretary, a gesture they hoped would demonstrate their commitment to tolerance.

Catholic delegates from parishes all over Ireland met in convention at Tailor's Hall in Dublin in December 1792, where they agreed to act in concert to secure abolition of the remaining Penal Laws. Bypassing the lord lieutenant, a delegation traveled to London, where it received a sympathetic hearing. Overruling conservative arguments that Catholic emancipation would lead to a reformed parliament, which would proceed to break the connection with Great Britain, the government looked instead to its international position. Facing imminent war with France (war was declared on February 1, 1793), British officialdom feared the threat to Britain's security posed by a hostile Irish public opinion. Consequently, the British parliament put pressure on its Irish counterpart, which had the desired effect.

The Dublin legislature passed the Relief Act of 1793, which removed most of the remaining disabilities against Catholics and gave them the franchise. Catholic disbarment from parliament and from high civil and judicial offices remained in effect, but Catholics could now marry Protestants, buy and sell land, and practice at the bar. The government promoted a native-trained educational class and clergy with the opening in 1793 of St. Patrick's College, Carlow, the first Catholic higher educational institution, and in 1795 of a Catholic seminary, St. Patrick's, at Maynooth. It was hoped that an anglicized Catholic Church would evolve if priests were trained in Ireland and if candidates could be drawn from classes outside the Irish-speaking peasantry.

The fact that Catholics could now buy property led to tensions and sectarian rioting in areas where Catholics and Protestants were equally numerous, such as south Ulster. Both sides became increasingly radicalized.

The Defenders originated in Ulster as a Catholic secret society in opposition to taxation and tithes. Possibly having established links with French revolutionaries, Defenders in 1794 stated their goal to be "[t]o quell all nations, dethrone all kings, and to plant the true religion that was lost at the Reformation" (Newman 1991, 47). By the mid 1790s Defender ideology began to spread among the artisans in the small towns, undoubtedly encouraged by a restructuring and expansion of the taxation system, which spurred resentment.

The Defenders engendered formation of a rival Protestant band called the Peep O'Day Boys, and when Catholics attempted to hold armed demonstrations, the two mutual antagonists clashed at the "Battle of the Diamond" near Loughall in County Armagh on September 21, 1795, an event that led alarmed Protestants to form the Orange Order (also known as the Orange Institution or the Orange Lodge), whose lodges—the members staunch defenders of Protestant prerogatives— soon appeared all over Ulster.

Meanwhile, Irish parliamentarian Whigs, led by Grattan, pushed for new concessions to the Catholics, and they were now actively aided by Lord Lieutenant William Wentworth (1748–1833), the second earl of FitzWilliam, a fellow Whig and friend of Grattan, newly installed in January 1795. FitzWilliam offered complete Catholic emancipation, but that proposal went too far too fast. A fierce political reaction arose against him, and accused of exceeding his instructions, he was dismissed in February. Now keenly aware of the seemingly inexorable trend toward greater Irish independence, the government set about determined to crack down on all radical activity.

But it possessed little means by which to do so. With regular troops out of Ireland fighting in the French wars, the government had set up a militia force in 1793; however, within a few years its political reliability could not be guaranteed, the ranks having been filled by poverty-stricken Catholic peasants and contingents in some areas having been infiltrated and even controlled by active Defenders. To put some dependable military muscle in place, Lord Lieutenant John Jeffreys Pratt (1759–1840), the second earl Camden, set up a new backup force, the Yeomanry Corps ("Yeos") in 1796, composed exclusively of Protestants. Thousands soon joined.

The drift toward crisis moved steadily ahead. Already in May 1794 the Dublin Society of United Irishmen had been suppressed by the authorities. In 1796 the government suspended the Habeas Corpus Act (1679), thereby disallowing the right to petition for relief from unlawful detention, and it passed an insurrection act that gave officials wide powers to search for arms and impose a curfew in areas where troubles threatened. The government's crackdown on all radical activity, prompted in part by the accelerating war with France, led to a speedy evolution in favor of more rebellious ends and means among dissidents. The Dublin United Irishmen went underground, and the members restructured the group into a much tougher, more ruthless organization. Tone now called for a complete break with Great Britain. Catholic Defender and nonsectarian United Irishmen movements drew closer together, even merging in some areas.

Both were aligned in steadfast defense of Catholic emancipation and constitutional reform. By the late 1790s reform meant establishment of a republic, on the model of those in America and France, with a government completely independent of Britain.

Arrayed against these now revolutionary elements stood the government and its supporters in the Orange Order, other Protestant societies, and the Yeomanry militias determined to uphold law and order, to maintain the country's connection with Great Britain, and to resist French aggression. The threat of a French invasion loomed as a distinct possibility, one that the government was well aware of. Wolfe Tone had gone to France, where he actively courted assistance.

Tone used all of his considerable oratorical skills in pressing the French government to take action. He stressed that the French would meet a friendly reception in Ireland, but the government in Paris had its own rationale for intervening, namely, that French control of Irish ports would seriously impede British trade, a lifeline that helped maintain Britain as an active opponent of French ambitions.

At long last, a French fleet set sail from Brest in December 1796 under the command of General Louis-Lazare Hoche (1768–97). Delayed from sailing earlier, the fleet met with winter storms. Heavy seas drove Hoche far out into the Atlantic while another ship, with Tone on board, reached Bantry Bay only to toss about for several days in the swelling surf until, near the end of the month, it and others were forced to turn back.

They left behind a country seething with tension, the fear pervasive that bristling antipathies would break out into open confrontation. Ascendancy politician John Beresford (1738–1805) wrote to William Eden (1744–1814), the first baron Auckland:

> We are in a most desperate situation. The whole north, south, Meath, Westmeath, Longford, Roscommon, Galway, Co. and city Dublin ready to rise in rebellion; an invasion invited by ambassadors; our militia corrupted; the dragoons of Ireland suspected; the united Irishmen all organized; the people armed; while we are without military stores, magazines, etc. and where things will end God only knows. . . . (Beresford 1854, vol. 1: 55)

Predictably enough, things ended in hostilities. In January 1797 a young radical MP, Arthur O'Connor (1763–1852), published his *To the Free Electors of the County of Antrim*, a pamphlet that served as a clarion call inciting United Irishmen to action, and the government moved in military forces to break the back of the movement in Ulster. Militias were purged of United Irishmen and their sympathizers.

Now fearful that the government might regain the initiative, the United Irishmen decided to act. They and their Defender allies apparently planned a rising for the early summer of 1798, but in March government forces arrested leaders of the Leinster provincial branch of the movement in Dublin. On March 30 Lord Camden issued a proclamation declaring the country to be in a state of rebellion, and martial law was effectively imposed. Consequently, when insurrection did break out in May and June 1798, rebel actions were badly coordinated, resulting in localized, isolated skirmishes only.

In Ulster on June 7, United Irishmen—almost entirely Presbyterian in religion and nonsectarian in their sentiment—rose under the leadership of Henry Joy McCracken (1767–98), a Belfast Protestant cotton manufacturer, and Henry Munro (1758–98), a Presbyterian linen draper from Lisburn. They launched an attack on Antrim town, but outnumbered, they were driven off. Armed activities ended in Ulster on June 13 when United Irishmen under Munro met defeat at Ballynahinch. The insurrectionists were slaughtered as they fled or surrendered, and Munro was beheaded two days later.

Rebels achieved their best success in Wexford. On May 31 about 15,000 insurrectionists marched in triumph into the town where a witness described their arrival: "The whole of the rebels wore white bands round their hats. Some of a higher order had the Irish harp drawn in gold leaf on a green ground, encircled with the words 'Erin ga braugh!' signifying 'Ireland for ever!'" (Jackson 1798, 33). Catholic cohorts achieved not only striking victories—at Oulart Hill, Tubberneering, and Enniscorthy—but also defeats, notably at Curragh on May 29, where the defeated rebels were massacred after they had surrendered, and at New Ross, where on June 5 wave after wave of defiant fighters, many armed only with pitchforks and scythes, stormed the defenses, leaving some 2,000 assailants dead. Defeated at Arklow on June 9, the rebels pitched their camp on Vinegar Hill near Enniscorthy, where government columns engaged them in a fiercely fought last stand on June 21, a battle that ended in defeat for the insurgents. The rebellion, which had cost some 30,000 lives, ended by summer's start.

Remaining Irish rebels who looked to France for assistance would be sorely disappointed. Although the French government promised aid, its new military commander, Napoléon Bonaparte (1769–1821), could divert only a few minor squadrons away from his main expeditionary force dispatched to conquer Egypt.

They arrived off Ireland in August, too late to be of any assistance to the insurrectionists. A small French force under General Jean Joseph Amable Humbert (1755–1823) landed at Killala on the coast of Mayo. But French officers serving in the armed forces of a revolutionary French government at odds with the Catholic Church were uncomfortable in being welcomed as religious liberators and surprised at how poorly equipped and disciplined the Irish were. Joined by locals, they managed to defeat a force of Yeomanry and militia on August 27 at Castlebar—a victory derisively termed the Races at Castlebar. They set up a Republic of Connacht, but surrounded by British forces, they were compelled to surrender at Ballinamuck in County Longford on September 8. The French were granted safe passage back to France, but hundreds of the Irish rebels were executed.

On October 12 a British squadron captured the small French vessel *Hoche* at Rathmullan on Lough Swilly in a minor engagement that featured a major player. Serving as a French adjutant-general, Wolfe Tone was found onboard the French flagship. Tried by court-martial, he was sentenced to be hanged. Before sentence was carried out, he suffered a neck wound, believed to be self-inflicted, from which he died on November 19 in Provost Prison, Dublin. Less well known to contemporaries than other rebel leaders, Tone was later lionized after publication of an influential biography and of extracts from his eloquently written journals. Subsequent generations of Irish nationalists considered him to be the father of Irish republicans.

And so the rebellion of 1798 ended. Irish aspirations for self-rule had failed, but the rising in Wexford, in particular, served to stir subsequent nationalist sympathies, despite the doubtful degree to which such sentiments propelled the rebels to act—land hunger, higher taxes, and economic hardships all played a prominent part. Nevertheless, the memory of the "Ninety Eight" burned bright in the minds of later generations of Irish nationalists, giving birth to a mythology surrounding the events of that spring and summer epitomized in the rousing ballad "The Memory of the Dead" with its opening line "Who fears to speak of '98?" and in other songs, notably "The Wearin o' the Green." Those who would lead the next fight for Irish rights would draw on such inspiration to battle with a determination equal to that of their forebears, but they would do so within a completely changed political environment.

The rebellion made manifest that Ireland posed a problem that demanded urgent political action. British prime minister William Pitt the Younger (1759–1806), a Whig who entered office in 1783, offered a solution breathtakingly bold. Brilliant, energetic, and not averse to taking risks, Pitt broached a proposal to create a union of the two parliaments. He argued that joining together the British and Irish legislatures would eliminate Protestant fears of Catholic emancipation because, within a united kingdom, Catholics would be relegated to permanent minority status. Furthermore, a union would promote British investment in Ireland, which would advance Irish economic prosperity, and by eliminating the need to coordinate government efforts between two separate bodies, it would make for greater efficiency.

Pitt's scheme was a purely rational one, a carefully calculated plan to promote more effective government. It was one in which promotion of British imperial interests of good order and national security trumped any consideration of local sentiments, and it was left to the few remaining voices among Irish nationalists to mount a countercharge. Many Irish MPs, although they opposed the recently defeated rebellion, retained a commitment to maintaining Ireland's separate identity. Led by Grattan, they mounted an impassioned defense of Ireland's individuality,

"THE WEARIN' O' THE GREEN"

The "Wearin o' the Green" is an Irish street ballad penned by an unknown author about 1798. Written in the wake of the failure of the rebellion that year, the lyrics identify symbols that would ever after become identified with Irish nationalism, namely, the shamrock, which when worn in the "caubeen" (hat) signified the wearer's anti-British sentiment, and the color green, the color of the Society of United Irishmen. Various versions of the ballad exist, and it remains popular, sung repeatedly on annual St. Patrick's Day celebrations. The first two stanzas follow:

I.

Oh, Paddy dear, and did you hear the news that's going round?
The shamrock is by law forbid to grow on Irish ground;
Saint Patrick's Day no more we'll keep, his colours can't be seen,
For there's a cruel law against the wearin' o' the green.
I met with Napper Tandy, and he took me by the hand,
And he said "How's poor old Ireland, and how does she stand?"
She's the most distressful country that ever yet was seen;
They're hanging men and women there for wearin' o' the green.

II.

Then since the colour we must wear is England's cruel red,
Sure Ireland's sons will ne'er forget the blood that they have shed;
You may take the shamrock from your hand, and cast it in the sod,
But 'twill take root and flourish there, tho' underfoot 'tis trod.
When law can stop the blades of grass from growing as they grow;
And when the leaves in summertime their verdure dare not show,
Then I will change the colour that I wear in my caubeen;
But till that day, please God, I'll stick to wearin' o' the green.

Source: Norman Davies, *The Isles: A History* (Oxford: Oxford University Press, 1999), pp. 1,150–1,151.

which, they affirmed, could be given political expression only in its own parliament. High flown rhetoric rang in debate, which, in 1799 ended in defeat for the government's proposal by a margin of five votes in the Irish House of Commons. Undeterred, the government then set about obtaining a majority, partly by propaganda and persuasion but mostly by employing the tried-and-true tactics of Ascendancy politics—bribery

The last parliament of Ireland, elected in 1790, College Green, Dublin (Library of Congress, LC-USZ62-90206)

and patronage—to secure a majority for its scheme. The Act of Union was passed during the parliamentary session of June 1800, the royal assent was given in August, and Ireland became a part of the United Kingdom officially on January 1, 1801.

The politicians who supported the Act of Union saw it as an eminently practical, logical solution to a pressing political problem. Any sentimental attachment to the fact that Ireland had been served by its own parliament for 600 years was swept aside. But sentiment in favor of Ireland's separateness did not die. The parliament building in Dublin, nostalgically dubbed by some "the old house at College Green," became the symbolic center of an ideal of national independence that, having been aroused at the end of the 1700s, would stir patriotic thoughts and deeds throughout, and beyond, the next century.

7

FROM THE ACT OF UNION
TO THE GREAT FAMINE
(1800–1849)

When the parliament at the Palace of Westminster convened for its 1801 session, it did so with members in the House of Commons and life peers in the House of Lords sitting for Britain's sister island. Ireland's parliament had voted itself out of existence, moving the venue of political debate and decision making to London, thus putting the fate of the country out of the hands of the Irish—a small minority in the combined legislature—while at the same time creating a new cause—repeal of the union—that would constitute one of the central issues of contention in the 19th century.

It would be contested by a resurgent Catholic nationalism that made its appearance early in the century. Disaffected Catholics of all classes coalesced in a unified effort to fight for, and to win, emancipation in 1829, a drive led by a politician of superlative skill. Daniel O'Connell (1775–1847) dominated political life in Ireland in the first 50 years of the 19th century to a degree probably unmatched by any other personality at any other time in modern Irish history. He orchestrated the first mass campaigns to effectively challenge the governing system using nonviolent means. In doing so, he gave an organizational focus to a newfound national pride among Ireland's majority population, one drawing on socioeconomic conditions as well as age-old cultural traditions, that spawned, in turn, a new movement—Young Ireland—whose adherents supplied fresh ideas to advance Ireland's cause.

O'Connell preached and practiced pacific tactics, but his calls appeared as visionary ideals in the wake of the nightmarish realities of mass starvation and disease engendered by the great national calamity that appeared at midcentury. The potato blight that struck with a

163

virulence never before experienced from 1845 to 1849 and the Great Famine that ensued—probably the greatest social calamity of 19th-century western Europe—changed the country profoundly, both physically and psychically. Thousands perished and millions migrated in one of the most tragic, most memorable population declines and shifts in history. The famine turned what had hitherto been a relatively small, if steady, emigration stream into a sudden raging torrent, Irish men and women forced to flee for their very survival.

The famine hardened attitudes and actions. A resort to physical force replaced the persuasive power of moral appeals in 1848 when Young Irelanders switched tactics to strike in a brief, though unsuccessful violent attack on British rule. The widely perceived callousness of the government in failing to combat the famine added one more alleged wrong to the litany of grievances the Irish had been harboring for so long. Many among the defeated rebels fled into exile in the United States. The great republic that had won its independence in a war against Ireland's ruler became the destination place of choice for Irish political refugees. In the New World, they helped inspire impoverished and embittered Irish Americans to seek revenge for the horrific suffering they had endured, thereby giving efforts to secure Irish independence a new, and broader, transatlantic dimension.

Ireland in 1800

Ireland began the 19th century under an entirely new political arrangement, but one in which the levers of power remained unchanged. In effect, the union placed Irish affairs in the hands of the 658 members of the House of Commons, and because only 100 of those members represented Irish constituencies, the country's concerns would have to compete with any number of others, more than five-sixths of the legislators serving localities elsewhere in Great Britain. While the legislative venue was located now in the capital of the British Empire, the Irish lawmakers who sat there and the executors of policy back in Ireland remained the same as the power holders of old. The Ascendancy continued to prevail, and Church of Ireland Protestants ran public administrations from the central executive in Dublin on down to town corporations.

The Irish entered the union greatly divided. The rising of 1798 bitterly split Protestants into rebels and government supporters. Protestant landlords and their supporting social groups—Anglican clergy, judicial officials, and civil officers—generally favored the Act of Union as the best means by which to safeguard their continued dominance. Many rural and urban working-class Protestants, particularly Presbyterians in Ulster—those on whom the United Irishmen had so recently pinned their hopes for support—were, however, deeply opposed, fearing that the British parliament would be more inclined than the old Irish legislature to grant Catholics complete equality.

In 1803 one last echo of the 1798 rebellion reverberated in a brief, localized rising by a small band of United Irishmen. Led by Robert Emmet (1778–1803),

Robert Emmet (Library of Congress, LC-USZ62-123393)

a Dublin-born Protestant, a group of insurgents made plans to seize Dublin Castle. Once again, hopes were placed on French assistance, but this time no help was proffered. On July 23, 1803, after a brief scuffle in the streets of Dublin during which the lord chief justice, Lord Kilwarden (Arthur Wolfe, 1739–1803), and his son-in-law were stabbed to death in their coach, Emmet was captured and executed. Hanged on September 20, he joined the pantheon of Irish martyrs for independence, his parting, stirring words from the dock an eloquent, enduring testimonial cherished by Irish nationalists:

> *I am going to my cold and silent grave; my lamp of life is nearly extinguished. I have parted with everything that was dear to me in this life for my country's cause. . . . I have but one request to ask at my departure from this world—it is the charity of its silence. Let no man write my epitaph; for as no man who knows my motives dares now vindicate them, let not prejudice or ignorance asperse them. Let them rest in obscurity and peace; my memory be left in oblivion, and my tomb remain uninscribed, until other times and other men can do justice to my character. When my country takes her place among the nations of the earth, then, and not till then, let my epitaph be written. I have done. (Emmet, September 19, 1803)*

Protestants in 1800 were divided along class, regional, and denominational lines. But Irish Catholics were possibly even less united politically and socioeconomically than Irish Protestants. On the one hand, lower-class Catholics retained the exclusivist identity that had characterized them for centuries, harboring long-nurtured resentments and looking still for deliverance from oppressive rule. On the other hand, many among the middle classes sought to work within the system as a means to improve their situation. They believed that if they could win political equality within the British constitutional regime, the opportunities afforded by free-market capitalism would offer them the chance to acquire equal economic status. Many prominent lay and clerical Catholic spokesmen had denounced the rebellion of 1798 for the violent track it had taken, and they now supported the Act of Union, an act that, in effect, put an end to Irish claims to nationhood. However, substantial transformations in society in the early 19th century would lead these same conservative Catholic middle classes and their clergymen backers to change their attitudes.

Changing Social Conditions, 1800–1849

During the first 50 years of the 19th century, Catholics and Protestants in Ireland coalesced along distinctly separate sectarian lines. By the mid 19th century, Protestants stood nearly unanimously in support of union with Britain and against Catholic efforts either to weaken Protestant-based rule or to break the link with London altogether. Growing Catholic assertiveness disabused former Patriots and United Irishmen of their tolerant attitudes and drove all Protestants, always acutely aware of their minority status in the country, to depend on British authority for the security of their lives and property.

The economic depression that set in after the close of the Napoleonic wars in 1815 tied Protestant merchants and manufacturers, elements in the population who were inclined to support dissent in the late 18th century, more closely to the British imperial system with its protective tariffs and trade preferences, while growing Catholic competition for wages and leases increased Protestant lower classes' reliance on their employers and landlords for protection. After the Act of Union, the institutional embodiment of loyalty to Great Britain could be found in the Orange Order, a fraternal society patterned after the Masonic Order, uniting upper- and lower-class Protestants in a sectarian alliance that espoused fierce defense of the union as a guarantee of Protestant prerogatives. The Orange Order grew in popularity in the 1820s. By the mid 19th century, under its ruling Grand Lodge, the order emerged stronger than ever, its member lodges reinvigorated by an influx of middle-class Presbyterians, who had hitherto been discouraged from joining.

An injection of ideological fervor supplied by the growth of religious evangelicalism after 1800 gave a further impetus to Protestant solidarity. Evangelical strains in Protestantism, rooted in apocalyptic traditions that stressed the approaching divine destruction of the world and the salvation of the righteous, had occurred periodically since the Reformation; calls to an intense faith with emphasis on personal salvation now found a ready response among Protestants buffeted by the strains of these years, marked by ongoing commercialization and nascent industrialization. In addition, a crusade on behalf of Christian renewal and conversion was deliberately promoted and financed by conservative Anglican, Presbyterian, and Methodist clergy and by Tory landlords and urban businessmen. By the 1820s evangelicalism had touched all classes, sweeping both Anglican and Presbyterian churches in succeeding decades.

Efforts were begun to convert Catholics. The campaign, however, failed utterly, which only served to solidify Protestant prejudices. Secure in their conviction that, by refusing God's grace, Catholics showed their spiritual inferiority, Protestants, having humbly submitted themselves to God's gracious offer of salvation, felt themselves more than ever worthy of divine favor—a worthiness, they believed, made manifest in identifiably Protestant virtues of industry, thrift, and sobriety. French traveler and social theorist Alexis de Tocqueville (1805–59) visited Ireland in 1835 and recorded: "All the rich Protestants whom I saw in Dublin speak of the Catholics with an extraordinary hatred and scorn. The latter, they say, are savages, incapable of recognising a kindness, and fanatics led into all sorts of disorder by their priests" (de Tocqueville 1998, 135). For their part, many Catholics remained deeply embittered at history's verdict. In County Clare, de Tocqueville journeyed with an elderly Catholic traveler who "went on . . . to tell me what had been the fate of a great many families and a great deal of land, passing through the times of Cromwell and of William III, with a terrifying exactitude of local memory. Whatever one does the memory of the great persecutions is not forgotten" (de Tocqueville 1998, 174–175).

Religion colored efforts to create a uniform educational system that first were made during this period. By the 1820s some half million Catholic children were being educated in hedge schools. First emerging in the 17th century, they became widespread in the 18th in willful defiance of legislation that denied Catholics access to education. Held in secret, sometimes literally in hedge bottoms, they were first conducted by instructors, frequently on the run, who were often poorly qualified. When enforcement of the laws lessened, schools were held in cottages and barns. Although textbooks were usually scarce, the classics as well as Irish history and literature were taught, and English replaced Irish as the language of instruction as the schools became less secretive.

A nationwide system of primary schools was set up in 1831, funded by the central government, with salaried teaching staff appointed and supported by local boards of governors. Because control lay at the local level where the clergy usually sat on boards as leading citizens, they proved acceptable to Catholics, and the centuries-old hedge schools subsequently declined. By the turn of the 20th century, Catholic Church–run schools totaled some 9,000, and significant progress had been made in reducing the illiteracy of the population, which by 1900 had dropped to approximately 12 percent (O'Toole 2000, 49).

In the first half of the 19th century, Protestant tenant farmers, laborers, and craftsmen could be found, but Protestantism was usually equated with middle- and upper-class status, and in Ulster and the larger cities, they completely dominated the social scene. Most positions in law, finance, commerce, and industry were held by Protestants. In southern rural areas, Protestants were usually privileged head tenants, and they, together with the landlords, maintained the local administrative machine in ruling over the Catholic majority as magistrates, bailiffs, sheriffs, estate agents, jurors at the local assizes, and Anglican ministers.

Except in northeastern counties, Catholics formed the majority everywhere, accounting for some 80 percent of Ireland's total population of about 6,428,000 in 1834. And they were everywhere rural residents. A small number were "strong farmers," namely, those who held more than 30 acres, and "middling farmers," those who held more than 10 but less than 30 acres. The former enjoyed the security of long leases that often ran for more than 20 years; the latter did not, frequently holding their lands on a year-to-year basis.

By the early 1800s a class called "cottiers" emerged as the largest among Ireland's rural laborers. They were workers who received a cabin and two acres of land or less, enough to graze a cow and grow potatoes, in return for a set number of days' service in the fields or, in Ulster, at the looms of their employers. These bound laborers proliferated especially after enfranchisement in April 1793 of Catholic tenants holding land valued at 40 shillings or more (Hobart's Act), a move that drove landlords eager to increase their political influence to grant thousands of one-acre holdings to these so-called 40-shilling freeholders. Most cottiers had no leases and only rarely handled cash; instead, their employers deducted their wages, usually fairly low, from the amount of rent owed, normally quite high. This system ensured farmers a reliable, controlled labor force, while the cottiers obtained land sufficiently large enough for subsistence—but only just enough. Cottiers' lives teetered on the brink of destitution because their holdings were so small. The 1841 census revealed that 45 percent of holdings in Ireland were less than 5 acres; in Connacht, the figure rose to 64 percent.

Cottiers lived a barely sustainable existence, but below them landless laborers and tiny smallholders constituted the poorest of the poor. They made up about one-half of the rural population, and they lived in dire poverty.

Irish society was everywhere based on strong family and local community ties, reflecting a societal characteristic dating back to before the English conquest. Despite landlords' opposition, middling and small farmers commonly subdivided holdings to provide land for their sons when they married. Trends toward early marriage appeared as land became more easily accessible to the children of farmers and cottiers and as increased cottage manufacturing made it easier for families to subsist on smaller holdings, which also increased the economic importance of women and children.

And Irish society retained the violent character of long-standing notoriety. Fighting in both rural and urban locales was endemic, despite efforts to prevent it that included, from the 1760s through the 1800s, passage of special Coercion Acts and repeated expansion and reorganization of the Irish magistracy and police forces. Some brawling stemmed from individual quarrels, often fueled by whiskey, but much was collective and well-organized. Fights between groups of men numbering from a few hundred to several thousand would break out, held, frequently by prearranged agreement, at fairs, markets, athletic contests, or religious festivals. Many participants employed a shillelagh, a wooden club or cudgel traditionally made from blackthorn wood or oak with a large knob on the end named after the Shillelagh forest in County Wicklow that had evolved over the centuries to become not only an accompaniment to walking but also a weapon of common usage. Fighting followed highly ritualized formulas, and although killings were usually few, on occasion deaths and injuries could be considerable. The causes were usually based on ancient feuds for which the original reasons were long forgotten save for the memory to preserve the family honor; they could stem also from a desire by the defeated to avenge their losing the last encounter or simply from a mere love of fighting. In large towns, mobs of laborers and artisans battled each other or the authorities, and food riots would occur when the poor believed bakers and merchants were overcharging or hoarding.

However, authorities concentrated their attention more directly on the host of secret societies that grew up in rural Ireland in the first half of the 19th century. Often the successor to groups such as the Whiteboys of the late 18th century, associations of farmers and laborers bound together by secret, sworn oaths abounded. The Whiteboys themselves reappeared in Munster, joined there by the Rockites and the Terry Alts, and elsewhere by the Thrashers and Carders in east Connacht and north Leinster, the Whitefeet and the Blackfeet in central and south Leinster, and the Molly Maguires in south Ulster. Defeated in 1798, the Defenders went underground to reemerge as the Ribbonmen. Known alternatively as the Sons of the Shamrock, Society of St. Patrick, and Patriotic Association of the Shamrock, Ribbon lodges could be found across the island in the early 19th century. Grievances over rents, evictions, wages, tithes, and taxes motivated all of these groups. Violence carried out by the secret societies grew in intensity over the period. Open battles with police became common, and by the early 1840s assassins were targeting landlords in certain locations. An added sectarian impulse accompanied the turmoil in Ulster. Intensely anti-Protestant Ribbonmen battled Orangemen in frequent skirmishes at fairs and markets, and their chilling vow "to wade knee-deep in Orange blood" sent a ripple of fear through Protestants everywhere.

That vow indicated how much Protestant-Catholic relations had deteriorated since the nonsectarian sentiments that had found so much favor among some, though never all, in Ireland in the late 18th century. It was not foreordained that the division between Protestants and Catholics in political power, social status, and economic wealth put in place after 1691 would lead inexorably to bitter antagonism between the two. Irish society had been as hierarchical and deferential before the Protestant conquest as after, Catholic tenants and laborers merely acquiring at that time new masters of a different language and religion. That mutual hostility became so engrained is a testament to enduring cultural pride among the native Irish and to changing economic conditions consequent to commercialization, which forced Catholics and Protestants of the same socioeconomic class to compete for land and employment and compelled swelling numbers of poor Catholics to submit to increasingly exploitative conditions in landlord-tenant relations.

The union of interests of Catholics, both well-off and poor, both rural and urban, that formed in the early 19th century engendered powerful sentiments of a shared national pride, sentiments that would fire the course of events from the 1820s to the 1920s. The cultural output that began to appear reflected that emergent pride.

Ireland's Cultural Scene, 1800–1849

The debate surrounding the Act of Union gave rise to a great outpouring of pamphlets, speeches, and poems injecting a lively animus to Irish written arts. Ireland's legislative union with Great Britain created a new context within which to consider the idea of a separate Irish nation, a theme that had exercised writers since at least Swift and Molyneux. Under the influence of new trends in thought—conjoined under the term *romanticism*—in early 19th-century Europe, culture moved to the forefront as the vehicle in which to promote national identity, replacing economics or abstract political concepts that had so dominated patriotic Irish debate in the 18th century. Romanticism, which stressed idealism over realism and trumpeted the primacy of imagination over rationality, spawned in Ireland, as elsewhere in Europe, a nationalism defined by the country's unique cultural heritage. Irish writers of the early 19th century harkened back to the past in being greatly influenced by the cult of the bard, and they made efforts to preserve and revive surviving fragments of native Irish culture in committing oral traditions to print. In addition, the continuing thwarted hopes of Catholics for a greater share in public life imparted a sense of grievance to works produced.

Writers worked in a bilingual culture poised to shift dramatically from the Irish to the English language, a shift occasioned by a number of contributing factors particular to the period. The increasing urbanization and commercialization of the country; the improved infrastructure brought by better roads and new railways; the introduction of a national school system and the consequent increase in literacy in English; the spread of cheap newspapers; the long-established use of English as the language of law, politics, and administration; and, at the end of the period, the sharp drop in population through death or emigration in the wake of the Great Famine, particularly in regions in western Ireland where Irish was widely spoken, all helped promote a dramatic decline in the use of Irish. In the early decades of the 19th century it is estimated that about half the population could speak Irish—in the 1820s, about 3.4 million out of 6.8 million—but by 1900 the figure had dropped to about 14 percent—about 616,000 out of 4.4

million. In the transition, much of the traditional folklore and music transmitted in the Irish language was lost. Irish scholarly activities in Ulster largely ended during the period. The Ulster Gaelic Society ceased to exist in the 1840s.

Writers and other creative craftsmen worked in a society marked as well, in the wake of union, by heightened connections with Britain. Many Irish writers lived and published in Britain, a fact that would carry over to later periods, and the widespread departure of authors helped to spur a major decline in the Irish publishing industry, a decline furthered by the Great Famine, which witnessed the bankruptcies of many printing and publishing firms.

In the early 1800s the novel emerged as the outstanding literary form. At first novels were written exclusively by members of the Ascendancy, since most of the native Irish, as rural residents, lacked a fluent command of English. The century opened with publication of *Castle Rackrent* (1800) by Maria Edgeworth (1767–1842). Innovative in several ways, the book is often viewed as the first truly historical novel written in the English language and the first specifically Irish in subject matter. The story of the Rackrent family is arguably also the first English-language family saga, and the stories of the Anglo-Irish characters—for the first time told by a narrator who stands apart from, rather than acts as a player in, the chronicle—is told using elements of syntax and vocabulary and employing settings that are unmistakably Irish. All of Edgeworth's novels draw on her own life as the daughter of well-known English author and inventor Richard Lovell Edgeworth (1744–1817), who, on his second marriage in 1782, settled with him on his Irish estate, Edgeworthstown in County Longford. The most admired novelist of her day, she acted as manager of the estate, mixing with the Anglo-Irish gentry and writing melodramatic tales that became increasingly realistic, all of which, she affirmed, held a moral lesson behind them. All of Edgeworth's Irish-themed novels (*The Absentee* [1812], *Ormond* [1817]) deal with property transfers, specifically lands that are owned by Protestants that pass to Catholics (or characters strongly associated with Catholics) through marriage, effecting an alliance between English and Irish cultures that portends a happier future for the protagonists and, by inference, for Ireland. Edgeworth also wrote tales for children, thus contributing to the start of literature targeted at very young readers.

Edgeworth's prose laid the groundwork for the Irish national romance, which emerged full-blown in *The Wild Irish Girl: A National Tale* (1806) by Sydney Owenson (later Lady Morgan, ca. 1783–1859).

Owenson combines gothic plots, Irish contested history, and the country's contemporary politics in telling the story of an Englishman banished to his father's Irish estates where he learns of their acquisition during the Cromwellian conquest and where he falls in love with and marries the daughter of the Irish family dispossessed by his ancestors, thus again offering a tale that holds out a promise of a brighter tomorrow in a divided Ireland.

In their writings, Edgeworth and Owenson fully reflect authors' preoccupation with conveying intense feeling and shaping human behavior so characteristic of the romantic period. Novels proliferated, and authors began to turn toward new sources for material. Most especially, writers looked to Irish folklore, collected and published in earnest starting in the 1820s. Cork-born antiquarian Thomas Crofton Croker (1798–1854) is credited with launching publication of folklore studies with his *Researches in the South of Ireland* (1824), *Fairy Legends and Traditions in the Southwest of Ireland* (1825–28), and other works. Others drew on accounts of the recent past. A profusion of novels incorporating the rebellion of 1798 as part of their plots appeared, including *The Insurgent Chief; or, O'Halloran, An Irish Historical Tale of 1798* (1828) by James McHenry and *The Croppy: A Tale of 1798* (1828) by John Banin (1798–1828) and Michael Banin (1796–1824). Middle-class Catholic brothers from Kilkenny, the Banins are acknowledged among the first to write Irish historical fiction. *The Croppy* appeared as part of a series of stories titled *Tales of the O'Hara Family*, collaboratively published throughout the 1820s, encompassing both tales of contemporary life of the Irish peasantry and sweeping fiction set in the past that the brothers published under the name "The O'Hara Family."

The Banin brothers and other writers, such as Gerald Griffin (1803–40), introduced adventure tales to fiction, while stories about society (called "silver-fork" fiction) also marked a new trend. Griffin's *The Collegians* (1829) depicts rural Ireland's complex, interconnected social scene in which landowners, lawyers, strong farmers, and others all appear as characters in a plot whose central theme was murder. Dublin-born Sheridan Le Fanu (1814–73), grandnephew of Richard Brinsley Sheridan, turned from law to journalism to writing novels and short stories, many featuring a ghost character (*The House by the Churchyard* [1863]).

Irish theater thrived in the early 19th century in the major cities, and stages continued to feature plays made famous in the 18th century as well as newly popular Gothic melodramas. Large theaters opened in Dublin with the remodeling of the Theatre Royal (1821) and the new Adelphi (1829). During this period, as in the century before, Irish playwrights achieved their greatest successes on the stages of London. Richard Lalor Sheil (1791–1851) dealt with the subject of religious difference in several dramas, stressing the tragic consequences for both the oppressed and the oppressor in religious persecution.

The major technological innovation of photography arrived in Ireland about September 1839 when Belfast engraver Francis Stewart Beatty took a daguerreotype, that is, an early type of photograph, of the Long Bridge in Belfast. The first commercial portrait studio opened in Dublin's Rotunda building in 1841.

Irish painting is distinguished by both landscape and portrait artists. James Arthur O'Connor (1792–1841) traveled extensively on the Continent and became a prominent landscape painter. Dubliner Sir Martin Archer Shee (1769–1850) turned to painting portraits at a young age to help support his family, impoverished members of the Catholic gentry. He moved to London where he won fame sufficient to win election as president of the Royal Academy in 1830. Working on the Continent also, pianist and composer John Field (1782–1837) wrote 18 nocturnes, beginning in 1812, and he is widely credited with creating the musical composition, which is inspired by, and reminiscent of, the night.

The 1830s saw the launching of a profusion of literary journals, notably the *Dublin University Magazine* (1833), founded by Trinity College students, that survived until 1877, and the London-published *Dublin Review*, begun in 1836 and lasting even longer, until 1969. The same period that witnessed the start of the decline of the Irish language ironically also marked the beginning of scholarly societies devoted to preserving and promoting Irish learning. Members of the Gaelic Society of Dublin (1807) and the Iberno-Celtic Society (1818) dedicated themselves to advancing knowledge of Ireland's ancient traditions through study and publication of old Irish manuscripts. Irish scholars such as poets Peadar Ó Gealacáin (1792–1860) and Aodh Mac Domhnaill (1802–67) aided them in their work.

Native Irish writers expressed themselves best during the 19th century through the medium of poetry and nowhere more than in Munster, where the native tradition of scholarship survived longest. Most of the ancient manuscripts preserved during the period were copied here. *The Poets and Poetry of Munster* (1849), published by John O'Daly (1800–78) and James Clarence Mangan (1803–49), collates a great deal of Irish poetry, translated into English, during the first half of the century. No poet proved more prolific than Micheál Óg Ó Longáin (1766–1837), who penned more than 350 compositions. Máire Bhuí Ní Laoghaire (ca. 1774–ca. 1849) is one of the few female poets who has left a considerable volume of work.

Because its consequences proved so catastrophic, no event of the period was as chronicled and served as source material for so much fiction as the Great Famine. Many eyewitness accounts appeared in Irish and English newspapers, and novelists wove the event into their narratives. *The Black Prophet* (1847) by William Carleton (1794–1869) and *Castle Richmond* (1860) by Anthony Trollope (1812–82) remain the two best-known famine novels. An English novelist from London, Trollope was noted for works set in Irish locales (*The Kellys and the O'Kellys* [1848], *The Landleaguers* [1883]). The most famous poet associated with the famine period was James Clarence Mangan. Mangan lived his entire life in Dublin writing much trite material, often under pseudonyms, to finance a life lived eccentrically, plagued by addictions to alcoholism and opium that contributed to his early death during a cholera epidemic. His poetry is rooted in his translation work from languages as diverse as German and Persian, including Irish, to which he imparts a sense of alienation, of deep personal introspection, and of intense sympathy for his subject. He wrote: ". . . when I translate from the Irish, my heart has no pulses except for the wrongs and sorrows of my own stricken land" (Mangan 2002, 224). His most celebrated poem was "Dark Rosaleen" (1847), which drew admiration from later Irish nationalists.

Fictional works on the famine would appear intermittently through the end of the century, and they would touch on issues surrounding its causes and significance, but no works carried the impact that the nonfictional books by John Mitchel (1815–75) had on Irish public opinion. His accounts of the Great Famine in the autobiographical *Jail Journal* (1854) and in other books such as *The Last Conquest of Ireland (Perhaps)* (1860) were widely read. Born in County Derry the son of a Unitarian minister, Mitchel championed tenant rights, and though his words had no effect on the Protestant community into which he was born, they served to inspire and influence national sentiments now actively at work among Irish Catholics.

The Rise of Catholic Nationalism

In the opening decades of the 19th century, moderate Catholics came to realize that reliance on British benevolence would avail them little in their hopes and efforts to protect and promote their interests. Prime

Minister William Pitt had all but promised, when he carried the union of the two parliaments, that it would be followed by complete Catholic emancipation. But opposition from King George III, from ministers in the government, and from Anglican Tories in the House of Lords proved too strong, and the plans were dropped. Hopes were raised again in August 1821 when King George IV (r. 1820–30) visited Ireland, the first reigning British monarch to do so in four centuries. George suggested that the country's problems be taken seriously, and the new lord lieutenant, Richard Wellesley (1760–1842), the brother of the duke of Wellington, was a known supporter of emancipation. The government showed a greater willingness to stand up to the Protestant establishment—the activities of the Orange Order were curbed—but the politicians in Westminster showed no interest in considering Catholic claims, and expectations of change among Irish Catholics waned.

Consequently, unless they swore an oath denouncing their religion as false and idolatrous, Catholics were still disbarred from holding high offices, from sitting in Parliament or on the judicial bench, from securing posts as sheriff and undersheriff, and from serving in the armed forces above the rank of colonel. In practice, they were unable even to obtain minor positions for which they were legally eligible. Fraud and favoritism against Catholics were pervasive, rankling, in particular, affluent Catholics, who felt that they deserved access to greater career opportunities and who resented the lack of protection for their property in being shut out of legal policy- and decision making.

During the first 50 years of the 19th century, Catholic landlords, merchants, and professional men joined together in agitating for a redress of grievances, but constantly bickering among themselves, they were largely ignored. The drive to win Catholic emancipation could not succeed without creating an effective organization and attracting a wide appeal. Both of these requirements appeared in 1823 when the Catholic Association was founded by Daniel O'Connell.

The association was based on an entirely new organizational premise. O'Connell had learned after a decade of political involvement that cliques of well-to-do Catholics would never carry the impact that a mass movement could. Thus, he set about to create an organization composed of Catholics of all classes, and he did so using two novel tools. First, the priests—the sole authority figures who both knew the people and were trusted by them everywhere in Ireland—were recruited to rally the masses. Both angry at and fearful of Protestant proselytization, the clergy were happy to oblige, openly supporting the campaigns for emancipation. Second, a subscription of a penny a

DANIEL O'CONNELL

Daniel O'Connell (August 6, 1775–May 15, 1847) (in Irish, Dónal Ó Conaill) was born in Carhen, near Cahirciveen in County Kerry into a once wealthy Roman Catholic family. Unable to attend university in Britain because of his religion, he was educated in France and then returned to Ireland, where he studied law and was admitted to the bar in Dublin in 1798, among the first Catholics able to do so after restrictions on entering the legal profession were lifted in 1793. In 1802 he married his cousin Mary O'Connell, and the couple had four sons and three daughters.

Daniel O'Connell (Library of Congress, LC-USZ62-2902)

Sensitized to Irish conditions both as a witness to the rebellions of 1798 and 1803, in which he did not participate, and as a highly successful lawyer who dealt with many cases involving Irish Catholic tenants and their English landlords, O'Connell championed Catholic rights and became active in political circles in the capital in the first two decades of the 19th century. A brilliant organizer, he set up the Catholic Association in 1823.

Elected to the House of Commons for County Clare in 1829, he took his seat a year later after his great success in securing Catholic emancipation. In the 1832 general election he became MP for Dublin. Frequently allied with the Whigs in Parliament, O'Connell turned his attention to winning another great cause—repeal of the Act of Union—but his Repeal Association failed to sway British political opinion. After a mass demonstration at Clontarf in 1843, he was arrested and convicted early in 1844 of seditious conspiracy. The conviction was reversed in September 1844, and O'Connell resumed his legislative career.

The onset of the Great Famine in 1845 split the ranks of his followers, some now advocating violent opposition to British rule, which

(continues)

DANIEL O'CONNELL *(continued)*

dismayed O'Connell, an unwavering proponent of peaceful means to effect change. His term in prison having seriously weakened him, he made a last, sad appearance in Parliament to beg assistance for his famine-stricken people. By now very ill, he set off for Rome in January 1847 but died before arriving in Genoa. According to his dying wish, except for his heart, which was buried in Rome, his mortal remains were interred in Glasnevin Cemetery in Dublin.

By mobilizing the Catholic community of all classes, O'Connell created a mass movement using nonviolent tactics on behalf of Irish nationalism. Immortalized in Irish consciousness for his success in achieving Catholic emancipation, he is known as the "Emancipator" or the "Liberator." Dublin's central thoroughfare, called Sackville Street, was renamed O'Connell Street in his honor in the early 20th century after Irish independence was won.

---

month—the "Catholic rent"—was charged for membership. An amount so low that all but the very poorest could afford to join, the payment brought a pride to the members in knowing that they were participating in a collective effort to effect change, and thousands joined, the sums collected in churches on Sundays. The Catholic Association soon boasted a strength in numbers and wealth unmatched by any previous membership scheme.

O'Connell employed a novel tactic, the "monster meeting," gatherings of great numbers of members in massive shows of solidarity. Drawing on the power of a united drive, Catholics now used the one tool available to them—the franchise—to make their voices heard. In the general election held in the summer of 1826, local clergy rallied the electors and led them to the polls, and the voters, most of them tenant farmers who usually cast compliant ballots for the landlords' nominees, turned out sitting members in four counties—Wexford, Westmeath, Lough, and Monaghan—and replaced them with members of Parliament (MPs) who, though Protestants, supported Catholic emancipation.

Poised to make great gains at the next general election, the association found itself instead battling a by-election. In 1828 William Vesey-Fitzgerald (1783–1843), an MP for Clare, vacated his seat to take a post in the British cabinet, a departure that, by law, necessitated he stand for reelection. Vesey was a 10-year veteran in the House of Commons, a landlord who enjoyed good tenant relations, and a politician not averse to supporting Catholic rights. However, because he accepted a post in the cabinet of Prime Minister Arthur Wellesley (1769–1852), the duke of Wellington, the head of a government opposed to Catholic demands, the Catholic Association could not allow his elections to proceed uncontested. Unable to find a Protestant candidate friendly to Catholic emancipation, the association turned to O'Connell. Although he was unable to sit in Parliament, no law prevented him from running as a candidate. Employing the by now much perfected electioneering machinery, priests shepherded electors in well-ordered bands to the polling places. The organizing skill paid off: O'Connell was elected by 2,057 votes to 982.

The government in London read the results with a mixture of apprehension and resignation. Although disinclined to support Catholic emancipation, Wellington and Home Secretary Robert Peel (1788–1850), whom O'Connell dubbed "Orange" Peel for his staunch Protestantism, recognized that the Clare election marked a watershed in the Catholic electoral campaign. Intensely excited over the victory, Irish Catholics might resort to more forceful efforts. O'Connell disavowed use of violent means, but officials reasoned he might prove unable to restrain the masses, and the loyalty of the forces of order could not be guaranteed in the event of a clash—both the police and the army contained large numbers of Catholics. Because the government could count on support for the status quo only in the House of Lords—a solid majority in the House of Commons favored emancipation—Wellington and Peel bowed to reality and introduced a Catholic emancipation bill in the parliamentary session of 1829, which passed into law on April 13. Catholics were now eligible for all positions in public affairs, save for the government's top executive and judicial posts, namely, the lord lieutenancy and lord chancellorship of Ireland, respectively.

O'Connell, the hero of the hour with the Irish Catholic masses, took his seat in Parliament, where during the next 12 years he used his influence in support of Whig Party initiatives, the party proving more supportive of Irish causes than its major rival, the Tories. Tithe reform stood on a list of reform demands. Catholic clergy and the Catholic public across the socioeconomic spectrum resented compulsory payment of taxes to the established Church of Ireland, which counted only about one-10th of the population among its members. Catholics also rankled at the overabundance of Anglican bishops and churches, many buildings located in heavily Catholic areas and so virtually empty of congregants. O'Connell's followers grew to 39 in the 1832 election, and the Church Temporalities Act brought a modicum of reform. Some surplus bishoprics were eliminated.

The election of 1835 saw O'Connell's parliamentary faction decline to 32, but the election produced the ouster of a brief ministry under Tory Robert Peel and the victory of a Whig ministry under Lord Melbourne (1779–1848), and it brought significant advances for Catholics. The Whigs won the election in part through support from Irish voters, a support promised to them in a preelection pact with O'Connell (Lichfield House compact). A new undersecretary for Ireland was appointed, Thomas Drummond (1797–1840), a Scotsman committed to governing on the basis of absolute impartiality. Blaming landlords in part for the agrarian violence so prevalent in Ireland, he famously remarked that "property has its duties as well as its rights," and he set about in earnest to rectify wrongs. Impartial law enforcement was advanced through establishment of a national police force, the Royal Irish Constabulary, which recruited many Catholics, and through appointment of paid magistrates, which freed them from pressures often exerted by local landlords. Catholics were appointed to senior posts in the public service, and tithes, although not abolished, were much reduced. Local government was reformed with passage of the Irish Municipal Corporations Act of 1840, which, although the electorate remained restricted, widened the numbers of those who could vote for town and city governing boards and mayors. Catholics now came to control many town boards (corporations), a change most prominently in evidence with the election of O'Connell as lord mayor of Dublin in 1841.

Drummond died in 1840, and the Tories (henceforth the Conservatives) under Peel came into office in 1841. Anxious that the momentum for change not slacken in the wake of the achievement of limited reforms and eager to maintain Irish Catholic solidarity in facing the new government's expected obstinacy, O'Connell again raised an issue he had first broached in the early 1830s.

The Act of Union continued to rankle among Irish patriots who longed for the right to deliberate Irish affairs in an Irish parliament. Long ambitious to engineer the repeal of the act, O'Connell started a preliminary organization to advance that goal in 1838. In 1840 he organized the National Repeal Association, which, as a new mass-based movement, aimed to utilize the same tools and tactics that had proved so successful in the emancipation drive. Once again, a token repeal rent was collected from members. Once again, he secured the help of the Catholic clergy.

At the same time, a priest was himself busily mobilizing the masses on behalf of another cause. Father Theobold Mathew (1790–1856), a member of the Capuchin order from County Tipperary, started a temperance crusade in 1838 to combat alcoholism rampant in the Cork area, where he had been administering to the poor and founding schools for 20 years. The effort turned into a nationwide drive, and an estimated 5 million individuals took a pledge to abstain from intoxicating liquor during the next decade. O'Connell regarded the movement as having greatly helped to mobilize the masses in support of his own campaign, whose outstanding tactic was, once again, the monster meeting. He proclaimed 1843 as "the repeal year," and 40 such meetings, attended by enormous crowds, were held at sites all across Ireland, strategically situated so as to draw the maximum number of people. The meeting assembled at Tara on August 15, 1843, to hear O'Connell speak has earned historic repute. An observer recorded: "The whole district was covered with men. The population within a day's march began to arrive on foot shortly after daybreak, and continued to arrive, on all sides, and by every available approach, till noon. . . . It was ordinarily spoken of as a million, and was certainly a muster of men such as had never before assembled on one place in Ireland, in peace or war" (Duffy 1880, 347).

O'Connell hoped that the power of public opinion would sway the government to a decision in support of repeal. But whereas Catholic emancipation found favor among a substantial number of legislators, all members of both parliamentary houses, save for a handful of about 20 O'Connell partisans, stood resolutely against repeal.

The government's determination to go to any lengths to maintain the union, "the dissolution of which would involve not merely the repeal of an act of Parliament but the dismemberment of this great empire," said Peel (Duffy 1880, 217), was made emphatically clear when on October 8, 1843, a monster meeting called to order at Clontarf was summarily banned by the government a few hours before it was set to start. True to his principle of abiding by the law, O'Connell complied and canceled the gathering.

O'Connell's retreat at Clontarf took the wind out of the sails of the movement. The National Repeal Association remained in existence, but torn by growing dissensions and led now by a leader irresolute about what direction to take, it slowly dissipated.

The peaceful power of mass public action had been shown to fail, but the power of an ideal would prove to prevail. The political consciousness of Irish Catholics of all classes had been awakened by O'Connell's campaigns, both successful and unsuccessful, and they spawned a new patriotic association of activists intent on devising means, both pacific and martial, to win Irish rights to self-government. The Young Ireland movement, revolutionary but in a refined way, consisted of a rather amorphous group of young, urban, mostly middle-class intellectuals, many of whom were Protestants, who began to coalesce around readers of and contributors to the journal *Nation*, a weekly newspaper founded in 1842 to assist O'Connell in his repeal campaign. Paralleling the rise of similarly named movements in Italy and central Europe, Young Ireland sought to keep alive a vision of Irish nationalism that encompassed everyone in Ireland regardless of creed or origin, a notion of singular importance to Wolfe Tone and one also stressed by O'Connell, despite the latter's appeal directed largely at Catholics. But Young Irelanders gradually diverged from O'Connell, partly because of suspicion by the latter of more youthful, potential rivals and partly because members of the newer group, although they did not advise use of violence, wanted to keep open the possibility that they might resort to force should it become necessary.

The intellectual leader of Young Ireland was Thomas Osborne Davis (1814–45), whose nationalist writings would continue to inspire succeeding generations. Prominent members associated with the movement included the editor of the *Nation*, Charles Gavan Duffy (1816–1903), a Catholic from County Monaghan; William Smith O'Brien (1803–64), from a County Clare Protestant landowning family and an MP for Limerick; and James Fintan Lalor (1807–49), the son of a strong farmer from Queen's County. Lalor broke with O'Connell's singleminded stress on repeal of the Act of Union in placing land reform on the top of his agenda. Unlike O'Connell, who believed that the issue could be addressed after repeal of the union, Lalor called for an immediate, radical overhaul of ownership, insisting that the land rightly belonged to those who worked it. He called for rent strikes to counter evictions. He was joined in that call by John Mitchel. A particularly zealous member of Young Ireland, Mitchel was a regular contributor to the *Nation* and then started his own paper, the *United Irishman*. An impassioned defender of tenant rights, he moved on to advocate use of sabotage in fighting for the Irish cause. He made the appeal in an article in the *Nation* that appeared in 1846. The call to violence chagrined O'Connell, but by that date, with the country buffeted by economic distress and by a famine of calamitous proportions, Mitchel and others believed conditions warranted far more radical remedies.

Continuity and Contractions in the Irish Economy, 1800–1849

Irish economic conditions changed markedly for the worse in response to a depression that set in when the stimulus provided by wartime demand subsided following the end of the Napoleonic Wars in 1815. Industrial decline and stagnation in southern Ireland led to a call for protective tariffs. Only in eastern Ulster did industries prosper. The markedly different regional conditions contributed, on the one hand, to the firm support for union with Britain among upper- and middle-class Protestants in Ulster and, on the other, to calls by Catholics in southern Ireland for aggressive political activity to redress grievances.

In the early 1800s Irish industry suffered from a decline in prices occasioned by the government's contraction of the money supply, a policy pursued until the two countries' treasuries were merged in 1826. After January of that year British currency replaced the Irish pound that had been in circulation since the 1180s.

By 1800 the Irish economy revolved largely around export of raw materials and highly specialized industrial goods to the British market. British economic considerations took precedence. Without the protection provided by tariffs, Irish industries were open to competition from cheap British imports, which, because of the improved transportation network, could now easily be shipped across the entire island to the detriment of native production.

Charles Bianconi (1786–1875) is widely recognized as the founder of modern transportation means in Ireland. Born Carlo Bianconi in Costa Masnaga, Italy, he arrived in Ireland in 1802 and began the first horsecar service in the country in 1815 from Clonmel to Thurles and Limerick. He ran his "Bianconi coaches" along several routes until the 1850s, by which time railroads had largely displaced his services. A major transportation innovation, the first rail line—the Dublin and Kingston Railway—opened to the public in 1834.

However, the introduction of railroads brought no major economic advancement. On the contrary, by the 1840s, Irish manufacturing activity had plummeted—the woolen industry that once employed thousands ruined. The few major industries to survive—linen production, brewing and distilling, and shipbuilding—did so only because firms consolidated and mechanized and because many concentrated in and near port cities, which provided easy access to external markets.

Urban businesses drew labor away from rural areas, reducing employment in the agricultural sector that, since time immemorial, had constituted Ireland's chief economic activity and which, in 1840, still employed over two-thirds of Irish people. Ireland's population continued to increase, growing from about 5 million in 1800 to 6.8 million in 1821 and jumping to 8.2 million in 1841 (Thomas 1997, 153). It did so in an agrarian-based economy that had not changed to any great degree since the 17th century, leaving more and more of the populace dependent for sustenance and employment on a rural regime controlled by a handful of landlords and long-lease holders motivated to earn profits and so gearing land use largely to production for export markets.

By 1840 most Irish rural laborers were still cottiers, and their numbers still grew due to natural increase, employment by landlords to reclaim mountain and bog terrain, and the economic value of such workers in areas where dairying and textile weaving predominated. But rising land values during the early decades of the century convinced many landlords that granting valuable land to secure workers was no longer efficient. Falling prices forced farmers to increase commercial production at the expense of cottiers' small plots, to reduce labor costs through mechanization, and to reemphasize cattle grazing, which required less labor than field tillage. In addition, Parliament in 1829 abolished the 40-shilling freehold franchise, thus eliminating another incentive to maintaining cottier arrangements. Many were forced out and, together with evicted smallholders, they formed a group of landless, independent laborers who survived solely on the wages they earned when they could find work, which, because of the decline of rural industry, was sparse. They constituted about a quarter of the country's population by 1841. Working sporadically, they could be found traveling from harvest to harvest, squatting on wastelands or beside roads on the edges of estates, some migrating to Britain in search of jobs.

The cottiers and landless workers totaled three-quarters of Ireland's rural population by 1840. The very poorest population, these undernourished masses fell victim in disproportionate numbers to disease, most notably to epidemics of typhus and cholera. They eked out a miserable existence, giving the country the stereotypical image that travelers took away with them. Living in one-room, mud-floored cabins with no chimneys or windows and dressed in rags, few cottiers or laborers by 1845 could keep cows or afford milk. Except in eastern Ulster, where the poor survived largely on oatmeal, their sole food source was the potato. Cheap to grow and amazingly prolific and nutritious, the potato could sustain life on a tiny plot of land, providing food for nine months of the year. By the 1830s the very poor came to rely on potatoes alone for food, supplements of milk and fish becoming by then quite rare. By then, too, the more prolific but less nutritious "cup" and "lumper" were replacing the "apple" and "minion" types as the staple varieties. Even in times of abundant harvests, the rural poor subsisted on one meal every day or every other day, and they often ate potatoes that were half-raw in order to slow their digestions. The potato is perishable and, unlike grain, it cannot be stored for more than a year to be drawn out in periods of scarcity. It is also highly susceptible to bad weather and disease. The month of July 1845 proved wetter than usual, but the potato crop looked promising. Then in August news reports told of a strange disease striking potato plantings in southern England.

The Great Famine

The *Dublin Evening Post* reported in its edition of September 9, 1845, that the disease had spread to Waterford and Wexford. It appeared quite suddenly. The leaves would turn black and crumble into bits at the slightest touch. Ireland had known potato failures before—there had been 14 partial or complete blights from 1816 to 1842 and several in the 18th century, notably the *Bliain an áir* (the year of the slaughter) in 1740–41—but this particular outbreak was unusually virulent. It was caused by a fungus from North America, *Phytophthora infestans*, and because it attacked without warning and very rapidly, it spread terror wherever it struck. The infestation appeared in places across northwestern Europe in 1845, notably in Scotland and Belgium, but nowhere else were so many people so utterly dependent on the potato crop as in Ireland.

Farmers and laborers tried desperately to save their crops by cutting off the blackened leaves and stalks, only to find that the tubers had rotted in the ground. Even potatoes that were harvested and looked to be healthy would later decay into a putrid mass of inedible rot.

In 1845 the blight spread to encompass about half the country, destroying about 30 to 40 percent of the crop. Few starved because rural country folk consumed foodstuffs ordinarily sold at market, sold livestock, and pawned whatever they could to buy food, and because government relief measures were, on the whole, successful. The British authorities under Prime Minister Peel—the Tory politician hated by Irish Catholics for engineering O'Connell's downfall at Clontarf—acted promptly. The system of poor relief introduced under the Poor Relief (Ireland) Act of 1838 set up in Ireland the same administrative machinery put in place in Britain four years earlier. Boards of guardians and Poor Law commissioners oversaw a system that mandated those seeking relief enter workhouses where they toiled in prisonlike conditions for their sustenance. Recognizing that rising numbers of poor would swamp the system and anxious to prevent soaring food prices, the government purchased some £100,000 worth of Indian corn and meal in the United States early in November with which it was hoped it could control the market. A relief commission was set up, local committees to distribute food were created, a bureau to provide employment was put in place, and voluntary contributions were solicited, supplemented by government grants. Mass starvation was averted.

What had been a crisis in 1845 turned into a catastrophe in 1846 when, by early August, it was apparent that the blight had returned, this time destroying almost the entire crop nationwide. An observer traveling from Cork to Dublin in July noted that the potato "bloomed in all the luxuriance of an abundant crop," but that on his return 30 days later, he "beheld with sorrow one wide waste of putrifying vegetation. In many places the wretched people were seated on the fences of their decaying gardens, wringing their hands and wailing bitterly the destruction that had left them foodless" (Harrington 1991, 43).

Government relief efforts were now markedly less in evidence following the fall of Peel's government and its replacement by a Whig ministry in July 1846 under Lord John Russell (1792–1878). Largely ignorant of Irish affairs, and, as a Whig, a staunch proponent of noninterference by the government in economic affairs (laissez-faire), Russell believed that his government should leave relief to the local workhouses and the buying and distributing of food supplies to private merchants and speculators. The administration closed the food warehouses, except on

Failure of the potato crop. From the Pictorial Times *(London), August 1846* (Image courtesy of the National Library of Ireland)

THE IRISH POTATO FAMINE

Many visitors recorded their impressions of the victims of the famine that struck Ireland beginning in 1845. The following is an account dated February 22, 1847, by an observer at Castlehaven, County Cork:

> We entered a stinted den by an aperture about three feet high, and found one or two children lying asleep with their eyes open in the straw. Such, at least, was their appearance, for they scarcely winked while we were before them. The father came in and told his pitiful story of want, saying that not a morsel of food had they tasted for 24 hours. He lighted a wisp of straw and showed us one or two more children lying in another nook of the cave. Their mother had died, and he was obliged to leave them alone during most of the day, in order to glean something for their subsistence. . . . As we proceeded up a rocky hill overlooking the sea, we encountered new sights of wretchedness. Seeing a cabin standing somewhat by itself in a hollow, and surrounded by a moat of green filth, we entered it with some difficulty, and found a single child about three years old lying on a kind of shelf, with its little face resting upon the edge of the board and looking steadfastly out at the door as if for its mother. It never moved its eyes as we entered, but kept them fixed toward the entrance. It is doubtful whether the poor thing had a mother or father left to her; . . . No words can describe this peculiar appearance of the famished children. Never have I seen such bright, blue, clear eyes looking so steadfastly at nothing.

Source: John Carey, ed., *Eyewitness to History* (Cambridge, Mass.: Harvard University Press, 1988), p. 320.

the ravaged western seaboard, suspended public works, and forbade local relief committees from selling food at less than prevailing market prices, which soon soared out of reach of the desperately poor.

Food disappeared entirely in some areas for a time, obliging the government to again launch public works, but because new requirements mandated that each local project receive explicit approval from London, delays caused many thousands to perish. Winter arrived early in 1846 and proved to be one of the harshest in memory. Panic set in. Hungry mobs roamed the countryside, and masses of poor poured into the workhouses. During December 1846 in Skibbereen in County

Cork, nearly 100 bodies were found in lanes and derelict cabins, half-eaten by rats.

So many died that the government was forced to amend the Poor Law and permit public relief outside the workhouses. Some 2,000 relief committees made food available at no charge to more than 3 million people—approximately 40 percent of the population—by mid 1847. And the authorities were compelled to rely on private initiatives as well, including charitable and philanthropic agencies, which provided much assistance. Irish Americans rushed private monies and food aid. The Religious Society of Friends (Quakers) worked tirelessly in running soup kitchens and, through its agents across the island, informing public opinion in Ireland and abroad about the depth of the calamity. Both Catholic and Protestant clergymen ministered to material needs; in an action defined as "Souperism," some Catholics agreed to convert to Protestantism as a condition for receiving food and other aid offered by Protestant groups, although most Protestant agencies did not impose it as a requirement for assistance. A few landlords even went bankrupt in efforts to relieve their starving tenants.

But the blight proved stubbornly recurrent. The new outbreak in 1846 prevented a crop from being sown. The disease declined in 1847 but returned in 1848–49. And so the crisis persisted. For the Great Famine, also known as the Irish Potato Famine or the Great Hunger, no exact mortality figures exist, but at least 775,000 and perhaps as many as 1 million perished. They died from what people called "famine fever," which was actually two separate diseases—typhus and relapsing fever. People ate raw turnips; seaweed; half-cooked Indian meal; nettle tops and wild mustard; the carcasses of dogs, horses, and diseased cattle; and even grass, and so they died of dysentery, the fatal bacillary dysentery called the "bloody flux." Irish men, women, and children succumbed to hunger edema ("famine dropsy") from lack of food, to scurvy from vitamin C deficiency, to exposure to the elements, and to infections caught laboring on public works and in workhouses and soup kitchens.

The Consequences of the Famine

The failure of the crop in July and August 1846 sparked the beginnings of a rush to run away among those sufficiently strong to make departure feasible. Less a movement of emigration than a mass exodus, poor cottiers went in the autumn, followed in the early weeks of 1847 by small farmers. Many walked from western counties to Dublin and crossed to Liverpool, England. By June 1847, approximately 300,000 destitute people had landed, straining the city's poor relief facilities. The very poorest remained in Britain. Those who were a bit better off could afford passage farther afield. Most sailed away to North America, and most sought refuge in the United States. Many among those who were poorer sailed first to Canada, where fares were lowest, and from there made their way south to the American republic. Little knots of emigrants would depart from villages and rural crossroads and, with a parting blessing from their priests, set off with their meager bundles for Dublin or smaller port cities, where they would board coal barges or the infamous "cattle ships," old, often barely seaworthy, converted cargo vessels whose owners engaged in the traffic solely to reap rapid profits. Some cattle ships became coffin ships in 1847 when, of the 100,000 who sailed to Canada, about one-sixth died on the voyage or on arrival. Many fewer died on ships to the United States because of stricter regulations required of vessels sailing to American destinations.

Approximately 2.1 million adults and children fled during the decade from 1845 to 1855, totaling about one-quarter of Ireland's population as recorded in the census of 1841. Catholic, Irish-speaking, and illiterate, they left from everywhere in Ireland, although south Ulster, north Connacht, and midland counties experienced especially high rates of emigration.

The famine transformed Catholic attitudes to emigration. Whereas before, poor Roman Catholics had been reluctant to leave, now not even the prospect of death or disease on the voyage could stem the outflow. They left behind a society that changed dramatically both in its demography and in the character of its agricultural economy. Population declined drastically—down by 30 percent in Connacht. Although decreases would lessen in intensity in succeeding years, they would never abate. A drastic drop in the number of small farm holdings accompanied the loss of population. The cottier class largely disappeared, to be gradually replaced, except in the far west where subsistence levels of poverty persisted, by the modern Irish agricultural pattern, namely, a family farm practicing mixed tillage and livestock production with the latter in the ascendant. Subdivisions of land by tenants—so widespread before the famine—ended, leaving social change in its wake. Late marriage, and with it the prospect of fewer children, became more common, the price paid to be able to keep the family farm intact.

A process that had actually begun before the famine now accelerated with larger farmers growing in number. Large landlords survived, although, with the population declines, rents fell and rates soared, forcing at least 10 percent into bankruptcy in the immediate postfamine

189

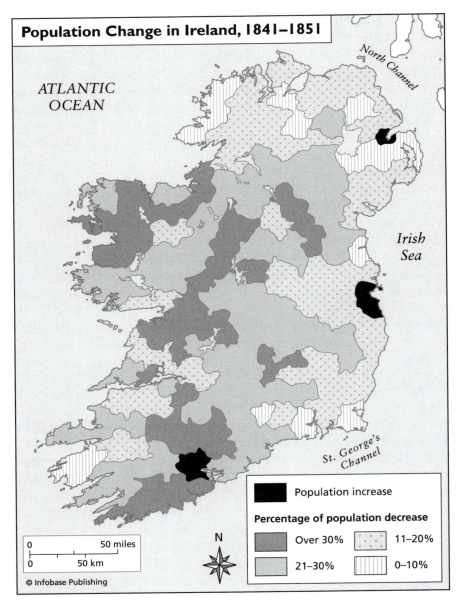

Population Change in Ireland, 1841–1851

ATLANTIC OCEAN

North Channel

Irish Sea

St. George's Channel

N

Population increase

Percentage of population decrease

Over 30% 11–20%

21–30% 0–10%

0   50 miles
0   50 km

© Infobase Publishing

years. The Encumbered Estates Act of 1849 freed landed property from legal obstacles that prevented sales, and many Irish estates were subsequently broken up. But they were not purchased by Irish tenants; rather, local speculators and other well-off landlords picked up the real estate.

Many blamed the landlords and, with them, the British government for the tragedy. Whether justified or not, the criticism bred a bitterness that burned deep. Political reform by constitutional means lost its appeal, replaced by sentiment in favor of drastic action. O'Connell's National Repeal Association broke apart. Driven to radicalism by the appalling condition of the Irish people, William Smith O'Brien and John Mitchel founded the Irish Confederation on January 13, 1847. Made up of a union of clubs across Ireland, the confederation secured the election of two MPs to Parliament in August 1847, and O'Brien publicly advocated the use of force against the British. Traveling to France to congratulate revolutionaries who had succeeded in replacing the monarchy with a republic in February 1848, O'Brien returned home inspired. He and others set up a War Directory, which drafted plans that led to the launching on July 29 of an engagement in County Tipperary called by some the "Battle of Ballingarry" and mockingly by opponents the "Battle of Widow McCormack's Cabbage Patch," because the struggle more nearly resembled a brief scuffle. Although a small skirmish, it ended in disaster for the perpetrators as O'Brien and others were arrested. They joined Mitchel, condemned in May under the Treason-Felony Act (April 1848), in being transported to Tasmania,

Lord Chief Justice John Doherty (d. 1850), standing (left), pronounces sentence of death on Young Ireland members, standing (right), at Clonmel, County Tipperary, on October 22, 1848. Sentences were commuted to transportation to Tasmania. (Library of Congress, LC-USZ62-3096)

a British island colony (now a part of Australia). First introduced in 1791, banishment to the distant Pacific outpost proved to be the fate meted out to thousands of nationalist rebels and land agitators.

The Young Ireland movement collapsed, the one brief action waged by its activists in 1848 serving as yet another link in the by now regularly recurring chain of periodic uprisings. Confederate clubs merged with the Repeal Association and drew back from violent means. Yet the shadow cast by the Great Famine would long linger. The tragedy seared its survivors, both at home and overseas, with unforgettable and, for many, unforgivable memories; and, thus, so too the resort to force would not die. It would only lie dormant, to be revived in 20 years' time.

8

THE DRIVE FOR INDEPENDENCE (1849–1922)

Ireland emerged from the Great Famine diminished demographically but determinedly resolute in spirit. Those segments of the population—and they were in the majority—anxious to secure rights to land and liberty bestirred themselves yet again to win them. Some followed a path of confrontation—the Fenians advocated violent insurrection. Others took a cooperative course—the Home Rulers sought self-government by bringing back Ireland's legislative body, its own parliament. Force failed yet again, redoubling efforts to work within the system. Under the guidance of Charles Stewart Parnell, Ireland found once again a leader of the stature of Daniel O'Connell to shepherd a strategy of fulfilling the dream of independence by constitutional means. Parnell's disgrace and death diminished for a time, but never entirely dimmed, the endeavor, the slack taken up by an Irish cultural revival that sought to instill native pride by promoting and praising Irish linguistic, literary, and leisure activities.

In the early decades of the 20th century, parliamentarians and other activists were joined by a new political party—Sinn Féin—that called for creation of an independent Irish Republic to be won by electoral success. By this time, constitutional efforts had registered some progress. The land issue, which culminated in a virtual war that tore up the countryside in the mid 1800s, was effectively settled with the emergence of a majority of independent small farmers.

By 1910 the many years of political agitation had built to a crescendo, turning Ireland into a tension-filled land. Nationalists and unionists, Catholics and Protestants, republicans and constitutionalists, workers and employers found themselves seething against each other in a country teetering toward disorder. Armed bands stood at the ready on either side of the sectarian divide created by the issue of home rule; but, at the very moment when an Irish parliament was set to win approval, the civil war that was poised to break out between its backers and detractors was deferred by the outbreak of world war.

While unionists across Ireland rushed to the defense of Britain, the violence unleashed on a cataclysmic scale across Europe in 1914 seemingly legitimized the resort to force among some nationalists, who believed the time ripe to strike at a ruling power wholly focused on fighting battles on far-flung fronts elsewhere. The rebellion launched on an Easter Monday morning in 1916 marked a watershed not because of its outcome—like so many before, it was brutally repressed—but because it stirred the public's consciousness in sympathy for the republican brand of nationhood. It was a sentiment remembered when World War I ended, when republican rebels picked up where they had left off, battling British and unionist forces in a war for independence. Hostilities produced a negotiated solution that, though it reflected the realities of Ireland's divided society, left many unsatisfied on either side. The island was partitioned and two constitutional monarchies created, one in the North tied tightly and one in the South linked loosely to the United Kingdom. For the first time in 700 years, the British would quit Irish territory, but the land they left behind remained a deeply unsettled place, its people divided both geographically and among themselves.

Ireland Overseas

Men and women had been leaving Ireland for political and economic reasons ever since the 17th century, but after the Great Famine, emigration acquired an entirely new status. In the wake of the departure of millions of people under the traumatic conditions of the famine, leaving the country became an established, indeed, for young people, an expected route to employment or marriage. Emigration became a great "safety valve," siphoning off surplus population that for the next 80 years saw up to half of each generation depart Ireland, which had the effect of reducing population pressure and giving the country an unusual and highly stable demographic pattern while eliminating potential sources of social unrest.

By 1890 it is estimated that approximately 3 million people born in Ireland were living abroad. After the famine, those who left were compelled to do so not only because of poverty but also because of family considerations—the need to preserve the family farm intact by allowing only one inheritor to take possession necessitated that other

Irish emigrants leaving their home for America (Library of Congress, LC-USZ62-37825)

members depart. Unlike the flight of whole families during the famine, subsequent emigrants were likely to be single and, in contrast to countries in continental Europe, women made up as large a proportion as men. Young, single adults without access to land and untrained in marketable skills left. Irish families produced on average six children, the same as in prefamine Ireland, but now they were reared specifically with the intention that they would emigrate, the remittances they sent home used not only to bring out other family members but also to serve as social insurance for their parents, the monies helping to pay rents, taxes, and debts.

After the famine, too, the conditions of transport improved. Investigations carried out during the famine exposed the nightmarish, overcrowded steerage conditions in transatlantic shipping and led to regulations to mitigate the worst abuses. Brokers, entrepreneurs, and shipping agents entered the trade, which smoothed the traveler's voyage.

Where did the emigrants come from and where did they go? The outflow from Ulster that had characterized Irish emigration since the

18th century gave way to a more widely diffused pattern. In the decades after 1850 nearly every Irish county experienced population losses with poorer and less industrialized areas in Connacht and Munster showing the greatest declines. By the 1890s and the early 20th century, the eastern coastal and northeastern counties, where cities of sufficient size to attract migrants existed, recorded many fewer departures. By tradition, those living in the west of Ireland went to the United States, although small numbers voyaged to New Zealand. Those in Ulster ventured to Canada, though many often moved from there to the United States, whereas others continued the long-established exodus to Scottish mill towns. The southwest and north midlands saw a scattering of emigrants sail for Australia, despite passage fares to so distant a continent that cost four times those charged to cross the Atlantic. The latter's most distinguishing difference lay in its status as a place of destination for Irish convicts. Felons had been sent to Australia ever since the first settlement began there in 1788, and from the late 18th to the mid 19th centuries about 23,000 Irish prisoners were transported.

Beginning in the 1880s, immigrants' place of origin shifted increasingly south and west, and by the turn of the 20th century, heavy emigration was concentrated in Ireland's western counties. Queenstown served as the great port of embarkation to America for those in Munster.

The United States remained the beacon that beckoned the overwhelming majority of Irish men and women. From 1856 to 1921 Ireland lost between 4.1 and 4.5 million inhabitants, and approximately 3.5 million traveled to North America. By 1900 there were more Irish—both first-generation Irish and second-generation Irish Americans—living in the United States than in Ireland itself (Vaughn and Fitzpatrick, pt. 1, 1975: 116–117).

Even a large proportion of Irish emigrants who first settled in Britain eventually moved on to the United States, although many also remained. Britain proved attractive in being close by, and thus cheaper to reach, while also offering the possibility of returning home. And long-established Irish communities existed in Britain that provided a comforting familiarity to newcomers. Most of the Irish were poverty-stricken and working class. Aside from the great metropolis of London, most settled in southwest Scotland and northwest England, where they could be found working in mills and mines, serving in the army and navy, and engaging in trades as tailors and artisans. Small numbers advanced to the ranks of the educated middle class.

Seasonal migration to Britain, which had a long-standing tradition dating back to the 18th century, also remained prominent, and the

AN OBSERVATION OF
IRISH EMIGRANTS

American author Herman Melville (1819–91) is noted for his tales dealing with the sea and seafarers. The following account relates observations of Irish steerage passengers on a voyage from Liverpool to New York made in 1849 and is drawn from his largely autobiographical work, *Redburn: His First Voyage*:

> *They were the most simple people I had ever seen. They seemed to have no adequate idea of distance; and to them, America must have seemed as a place just over a river. Every morning some of them came on deck to see how much nearer we were: and one old man would stand for hours together, looking straight off from the bows, as if he expected to see New York every minute, when, perhaps we were two thousand miles distant, and steering, moreover, against a head wind.*
>
> *The only thing that ever diverted this poor old man from his earnest search for land was the occasional appearance of porpoises under the bows; when he would cry out at the top of his voice—"Look, look, ye divils! Look at the great pigs of the s'a!"*

Source: Herman Melville, *Redburn: His First Voyage* (New York: Harper & Bros., 1850), pp. 324–325.

migrant agricultural laborers (*spailpín*) constituted an essential part of the rural economy in northwest Ireland. Many were owners of tiny farms who were able to retain their holdings through profits earned while working abroad.

Emigrants who settled in Britain and North America met the same set of challenges—a struggle early on to combat prejudice against rural immigrants living in urban environments and against those who professed the Catholic faith. The initial difficulties would later be followed by a slowly improving economic status—which proceeded more quickly in America than in Britain—steady acculturation, and rising political influence, often through leadership in labor organizations. By the end of the 19th century, many Irish immigrants to America had left the factories and mines and could be found in large numbers in the police force, the civil service, and professions such as nursing in major northeastern cities. They purchased property, and they maintained a dense network of Catholic churches and schools.

And they carried on a continuing commitment to politics "at home," because for many the emotional bond with their homeland remained strong even as time lessened personal links with Ireland. Irish immigrants organized pressure groups to influence foreign policy in the United States and government policy in Great Britain toward Ireland, and they established clubs and political associations to advance the cause of Irish liberation. In America especially, the Irish nurtured a brand of nationalism that repudiated the moderate, pragmatic means practiced by O'Connell in favor of radical, revolutionary action based on hatred for Britain, a hatred powerfully motivated by remembrance of oppressive poverty suffered under British rule.

A secret fraternal society—the Fenians (the name alludes to the *fianna* army of ancient Irish mythology)—was founded in Dublin in March 1858 and in New York City in April 1859, although it may have had informal beginnings a decade earlier in Ireland. Later known as the Irish Republican Brotherhood (IRB), the Fenians proposed to establish an independent Ireland with a republican form of government by driving the British forcibly out of the country. In Dublin, it was founded by James Stephens (1825–1901), a Kilkenny-born civil engineer and veteran of the Young Ireland movement, together with Thomas Clarke Luby (1822–1901), a Protestant nationalist. Stephens recruited thousands in a secretive organization that featured a military-style structure with a commander in chief and "circles" of 820 men commanded by sergeants, captains, and colonels. Membership grew, especially among newly arrived town residents and sons of peasant farmers. In New York they were organized under the leadership of John O'Mahony (1816–79), a founder of Young Ireland and an activist in the 1848 rebellion who had escaped to the United States. O'Mahony sought to forge a viable military force in America to serve as a spur in launching a rising in Ireland, but raids into Canada in 1866 and 1870–71 failed. While they showed the strength and determination of the Irish-American Fenian movement, the futile actions led to his discredit.

Another revolutionary organization founded in 1867 in New York as the Napper Tandy Club and later changed to the Clan na Gael ("family of the Gaels") emerged, dedicated, like the Fenians, to undertaking daring exploits on behalf of Irish freedom. In 1876 members employed the ship *Catalpa* to rescue six Fenian prisoners from Australia and take them to America. Both organizations would survive in the United States, where they would recruit men and secure funds for Irish revolutionary activism. Both strands traditional to Irish activism—extralegal, conspiratorial actions waged by groups such as these, and legal, constitutional efforts made by parliamentarians—would vie to win two central goals—rights to land and self-government—that would dominate Irish public affairs from 1849 to 1922.

Demands to Land and for Home Rule Take Shape, 1849–1879

Social, economic, and political power in 19th-century Ireland centered as it always had on access to, and possession of, land. A wide variety of landowning arrangements existed in the second half of the century, although a small number of great landlords—about 800—still owned half the country's acreage. Evictions took place on a large scale in the late 1840s and early 1850s, leaving the image of the heartless landlord firmly fixed in the public's imagination, although the numbers of those thrown off the land dropped steadily as the century progressed. Farms were usually held on yearly leases, which limited landlords' ability to rack-rent, despite popular opinion to the contrary. Rents probably constituted about 25 to 40 percent of tenants' gross income, although in poorer districts in western Ireland amounts at any level were too high. While rich and powerful as a collective class, landlords as individuals varied widely in their economic conditions, some enjoying great wealth but many, in the face of fixed sums in payment of taxation, debt servicing, family encumbrances, and wages for employees, decidedly less well off.

Relations between landlords and tenants grew increasingly embittered as tenants demanded greater security in holding land. On August 9, 1850, the Irish Tenant League was founded. Emerging from localized tenant societies that proliferated in the late 1840s, the league grouped together tenant farmers across Ireland in a united effort to secure realistic rents from landlords. In the general election of 1852, 40 supporters of tenant rights won seats in Parliament. But they failed to effect legislative change, a failure that led to the downfall of the league.

The collapse of constitutional efforts revived interest in both the use of armed might as the preferred means and the pursuit of self-rule as the overriding goal of nationalists. The Fenians believed Britain would never concede Irish rights to self-government, which thus could be won only by resort to force, made possible by secret military preparations and launched at a vulnerable moment when the authorities would find it hardest to respond. Impassioned participants in the 1848 uprising directed the effort. Unlike previous revolutionary leaders, they looked to the working class to fill the ranks, and by 1866

Fenian prisoners being marched through Dublin to Mountjoy Prison by British guards in 1867 (Library of Congress, LC-USZ62-124349)

they had recruited thousands of laborers, artisans, clerks, farmers, and especially schoolteachers in both rural and urban Ireland and in places wherever Irish emigrants had settled, including some 80,000 in Britain who were prepared to start a two-front war. Although nearly all were Catholics, they advocated creating a self-governing country in which a strict separation between church and state would prevail, thus earning the condemnation of the Catholic hierarchy, which also disapproved of the secret nature of the organization not under its own patronage, fearing that its communal, class-based, character might prove a rival to the church. In 1865 plans for a revolt had to be aborted when arms promised by American Fenians failed to arrive. Stephens twice postponed military action in Ireland, leading to his ouster as leader in December 1866. When it finally came, the uprising amounted to a few isolated skirmishes in February 1867, which were easily suppressed.

Another botched attempt at inciting rebellion, the rising of "Sixty-Seven," like that by Young Ireland in 1848, amounted to no more than a token display of action. Undeterred, however, the Fenians soon reorganized. A representative council replaced the supreme authority hitherto exercised by the leader, a position assumed from abroad in 1877 by Jeremiah O'Donovan Rossa (1831–1915), an early Fenian organizer in exile in America. The stress given to use of physical force was downplayed, and the organization, now called the Irish Republican Brotherhood, henceforth sought to inspire, rather than inflame, Irish activism.

But it also produced an immediate, practical effect. The seemingly never-ending efforts by Irish nationalists to trouble British affairs had long touched a chord in British statesman William E. Gladstone (1809–98), but it was the Fenian rising that proved to be the spark that ignited in him a sense of "the vast importance of the Irish question" (Shaw-Lefevre 1912, 18). The leader of the Liberal Party—the successor to the Whigs—and a man who wore his Anglican faith proudly, he never tired of proclaiming that morality must serve to guide policymaking. Gladstone headed his first government as prime minister from 1868 to 1874. His administration brought a new reformist spirit to Anglo-Irish relations, marked by two major legislative changes. The general election of 1868 was fought over the issue of disestablishment of the Church of Ireland, and the Liberals' victory gave Gladstone a mandate to move ahead with legislation. The Disestablishment Act of July 26, 1869, ended the privileges and status of the established Church of Ireland, freeing the church from a connection with the state and placing all

Prime Minister William E. Gladstone (Library of Congress, LC-USZ62-122539)

religious denominations on an equal footing. In removing the favored status of a small minority of communicants who, in 1861, numbered about 500,000 out of a population of about 5.75 million—4.5 million of whom were Roman Catholics—the government dismantled a central prop of the Protestant Ascendancy.

The second major issue—the increasingly contentious quarreling over land—was addressed in the Land Act of August 1, 1870, which provided for compensation to tenants at eviction for improvements made by the tenants. Although largely ineffective, it represented the first recognition by the British parliament of tenants' rights.

Gladstone's backing of constitutional reform for Ireland was paralleled by the revival of moderate nationalist efforts to effect Home Rule for the island. A movement was founded in 1870 by Isaac Butt (1813–79) to advance the cause of giving Ireland back its own parliament. A leading Irish barrister, a Protestant, and, as a former unionist, a supporter of the connection with Britain, Butt had sat as a Conservative MP, but moved by the suffering of the famine and by the resolve of the Young Irelanders and the Fenians, he converted to the cause of Home Rule, which he saw as a necessary solvent to Irish woes. Although far short of the outright independence sought by the Fenians, in the wake of the latter's defeat, a separate parliament seemed a more reachable goal. In the general election of 1874, Butt's new Home Rule League won more than half of the Irish seats to the House of Commons. For the next five years, he and his cohorts would argue the case for Home Rule, trying to convince MPs using the respectful, time-worn means of British parliamentary procedures. Backed in the main by the Catholic middle class, Butt's movement also drew support from a number of influential Fenians. For some, though not all, extreme nationalists the hope of independence seemed a remote possibility in a society that, while unreconciled to existing economic and political conditions, at midcentury remained little disposed to engage in wide-scale, wholesale revolt.

Economic Disparities between North and South

In the mid 1800s society exhibited a level of stability not seen since the century before. The growth in larger tenant farmsteads after the famine years brought a greater prosperity to rural Ireland despite persistent poverty in certain areas, notably in the west. Emigration produced a drop in unemployment by drawing away excess population and helped also to reduce the number of poor. Gladstone's 1870 Land Act inspired hope for a more balanced approach by the state in regulating landlord-tenant relations, while popular repudiation of violence, demonstrated in the indifference to the Fenian rising, offered the prospect of the government's attentiveness to Irish political demands.

Accommodation appeared to be the order of the day. Roman Catholics won a new respectability. A "devotional revolution" was ushered in under Paul Cullen (1803–78), appointed by Pope Pius IX (r. 1846–78), archbishop of Armagh in February 1849, who was transferred to the See of Dublin in 1852 and elevated to the cardinalate in June 1866, Ireland's first prelate to have attained that rank. Cullen convened the Synod of Thurles in 1850, the first national gathering of clerics since the Reformation, at which the attendees oversaw a restoration of vigorous ecclesiastical discipline in the Irish church. Schools were built and Catholic primary education for even the poorest was promoted.

Religious orders proliferated, including, most notably, the Christian Brothers, a lay teaching order founded at Waterford in 1803 by Kilkenny-born merchant Edmund Ignatius Rice (1762–1844). Dublin-born Catherine McAuley (1778–1841) set up a school orphanage in 1827, and her work led to the creation of the Sisters of Mercy, an order of nuns that won Vatican approval in 1835 and which continues its work in nursing and care for the poor worldwide today. The popular faith was enlivened by a spiritual renewal manifested, most startlingly, in the reputed apparitions of the Virgin Mary, St. Joseph, and St. John the Evangelist at a church in the village of Knock in County Mayo in August 1879, which launched a wave of pilgrimages. Knock remains today the center of Irish Marian pilgrimage.

At the same time that the Irish clung to their staunch Catholicism, many became increasingly anglicized, evidenced most significantly in the continued inexorable spread of the English language and the consequent decline of Irish. Estimates suggest that about half of the population could speak Irish during the first half of the 19th century, although in rural communities in the far western peninsulas the proportion attained three-quarters. After the Great Famine, a steady decline took place, driven by population losses due to deaths and emigration and to moves to urban areas where economic and cultural life demanded knowledge of English.

Many in Ireland in the mid 19th century looked forward to the development of a modern industrial society, a dream that appeared to be a real possibility in Ulster. Massive capital investment in manufacturing activity induced an industrial boom in the Belfast area. Already in 1835 Belfast was the premier port in Ireland, handling half of its linen exports.

Power-loom weaving replaced hand looms in the cotton industry in the 1850s with linen surpassing cotton by the 1870s. The city was granted a municipal charter in November 1888. Between 1871 and 1901 the population tripled from 175,000 to 349,000, with sizable increases in the number of Roman Catholics beginning in the late 1850s.

A Harbour Commission was founded in 1847 to facilitate the growing shipbuilding industry, which had begun in the 1790s, and in 1849 the completion of the Victoria Channel gave the shipyards direct access to the deepwater Belfast Lough. In 1858 Edward Harland (1831–95), a native of Yorkshire in England, bought the shipbuilding firm that he managed in partnership with German-born Gustav Wilhelm Wolff (1834–1913). Harland and Wolff grew steadily, earning fame as the company that constructed the White Star line's entire fleet of fabled transatlantic passenger liners, the most renowned of all—RMS *Titanic*—launched on May 31, 1911. Theirs and other firms transformed the economy of northeastern Ireland in making the area the rival of Scotland's Clydeside region as Britain's chief center of engineering and ship construction. Ulster Protestants prospered, but the Catholic middle classes grew as well.

They grew elsewhere in Ireland also but more slowly and despite the failure of industry to expand beyond its northeastern niche. In the greater part of the country, industrial development, urbanization, and agricultural modernization proceeded spottily if at all. Investors remained reluctant to commit their capital in a society still seen as recurrently rebellious. Commercial activity declined in towns such as Galway and Cork, while Dublin continued its development as a mercantile center but without any accompanying major industrial activity.

The island's integration into an international market system as a characteristic colonial economy, which had begun in the 18th century, accelerated in the mid 19th century. Ireland served as a supplier of raw materials, specialized manufactured products such as glassware and linen, and cheap labor to the world's major industrial nations.

The technological innovations that, in the second half of the 19th century, began to so dramatically transform Western society made their appearance in Ireland too. Horse-run trams were introduced in the 1870s, followed by electric streetcars, which first began operating from Portrush to the Giant's Causeway in 1883.

Nevertheless, by the turn of the 20th century, southern Ireland remained essentially what it had always been, a society in which most laborers were engaged in agriculture or casual rural work. Pasturage continued to replace tillage in becoming more commercially attractive

RMS Titanic *under construction at Harland and Wolff shipyards, Belfast, April or May 1911. At Queenstown (Cobh), 123 Irish passengers boarded what was then the world's largest liner on its maiden voyage. Irish survivors totaled 44 of the estimated 712 rescued (about 1,520 perished) after it struck an iceberg on April 14, 1912.* (Library of Congress, LC-USZ62-26743)

at the same time that the elimination of cottiers and the switch to a more diverse diet after the famine made possible use of land for commercial rather than subsistence production. Yet, technological innovation lagged woefully behind developments in Britain.

Agriculture remained mired in backwardness within a structure that offered little opportunity to newcomers. Land rarely changed hands because tenants and holders of expired leases passed farms to their chosen successors by terms of their wills and contracts, in a system that amounted virtually to an established custom, one given some legal standing by Gladstone's Land Act. The prosperity-based, postfamine world of relatively well-ordered, if never entirely tension-free, relations between landlords and tenants began to collapse in the late 1870s in conjunction with a succession of bad harvests and an agricultural depression that ran from 1877 to 1879, accompanied by a temporary slowdown in emigration and a partial drop in food production.

In 1900 rural Ireland looked little different from images prevailing in 1800. The jaunting car or jaunty car was a popular mode of transportation in 19th-century Ireland. County Armagh, ca. 1903 (Library of Congress, LC-USC62-59335)

The Era of Parnell, 1879–1891

In the winter of 1878–79 falling prices, crop failures, and unusually wet weather portended a disaster potentially as devastating as the Great Famine. The hard times forced many landlords into bankruptcy, while others sought to evict tenants who had defaulted on their rent payments. Small farmers faced bankruptcy, eviction, and starvation. To meet the crisis, a meeting of local Fenians held at Irishtown in County Mayo on April 20, 1879, launched a campaign of unrest in the west. Prominent among the leaders at the meeting was Michael Davitt (1846–1906). Proud and passionate, Davitt had been an early member of the Fenians, which earned him in 1870 a term of imprisonment. Released in 1877, he traveled to the United States, where, together with John Devoy (1842–1928), the most prominent among American Fenians, he formulated yet another new policy for Irish nationalists. Labeled the New Departure, it called for an alliance between revolutionary and constitutional partisans to win land reform and self-government.

Davitt looked for support to a rising young Irish politician from County Wicklow. Elected to Parliament in 1875, Charles Stewart Parnell (1846–91) set about to energize the advocates of Home Rule by perfecting obstructionist tactics in refusing to cooperate in the work of the House of Commons, an approach that was vehemently opposed by Isaac Butt, the Home Rule leader who counseled patient, respectful persuasion in keeping with time-honored parliamentary procedures.

Butt died in 1879, and Parnell moved quickly to assume the chairmanship of the Home Rule League. Parnell and Davitt joined forces with formation of the Irish National Land League, founded at Dublin

Charles Stewart Parnell addressing a meeting as president of the Land League (Library of Congress, LC-USZ61-1406)

CHARLES STEWART PARNELL

Charles Stewart Parnell (June 27, 1846–October 6, 1891) was born in Avondale, County Wicklow. His parents separated when he was six, and he spent an unhappy youth at boarding school in England. He attended Cambridge University and visited the United States before becoming high sheriff of County Wicklow in 1874. Drawn to national politics, he was elected to the House of Commons on April 21, 1875, as a Home Rule League member for County Meath, and to the seat for Cork beginning in 1880.

Conservative in social outlook and aloof and aristocratic by nature, Parnell brought an intense passion, clarity of purpose, and pragmatic approach to his goals. In aligning with the radical wing of the Home Rule League, he rose to prominence by adopting militant, obstructionist practices, including use of technical procedures to disrupt the House of Commons's order of business. A brilliant organizer and tactician, though not a great speaker, he was elected chairman of the league in May 1880, after which he transformed it, giving it a grassroots base and a formal structure. In 1882 he changed its name to the Irish Parliamentary Party, and in 1884 he imposed a strict party oath by which all MPs swore to vote as a bloc, thus establishing an effective bargaining machine, which came to dominate British politics in the mid 1880s in extending or withholding support to Liberal and Conservative governments on behalf of Irish Home Rule.

Charles Stewart Parnell (Library of Congress, LC-DIG-cwpbh-03649)

Paralleling his pursuit of Home Rule, Parnell worked

on October 21, 1879. With Parnell as president and Davitt the driving spirit and chief organizer, the league united, in a single great agrarian movement, nationalists of all stripes from moderates to radicals. The

actively for land reform. He was elected president of the Irish National Land League in 1879, and he played a prominent role in the subsequent land war. Winning widespread sympathy after his imprisonment in 1881 for sedition, he continued agitating for both land reform and Home Rule after his release in forming a new constituency organization, the Irish National League.

Parnell's political career was ruined when he was cited as a co-respondent, that is, the legal cause, in a divorce case brought in November 1890 by Captain Willie O'Shea, a Galway MP, against his wife, Katherine ("Kitty," née Wood, 1845–1921), the longtime partner of Parnell and the mother of three of his children. Though their partnership had been widely known privately in political circles, the divorce suit, because it made their relationship public, brought outrage and censure. Prime Minister Gladstone refused to work with Parnell. Devout Roman Catholics, for whom divorce was forbidden, broke with him after he refused to resign as Irish Parliamentary Party chairman, and the majority of members bolted the party.

Parnell fought a bitter battle to secure a political comeback. He issued a Manifesto to the Irish People (November 29, 1890) denouncing English political parties. He married Katherine on June 25, 1891, in the face of near unanimous condemnation by the Catholic hierarchy. He faced hostile crowds on a political tour of Ireland to regain popular support. The struggle broke his health. Contracting pneumonia after addressing a gathering in the pouring rain at Cleggs, County Roscommon, on September 30, he left Dublin for his home in Brighton, England, where he died a week later in his wife's arms. He is buried in Dublin's Glasnevin Cemetery.

Parnell's sudden, tragic death eclipsed the scandal that had destroyed his political and public reputation. Considered the second of Ireland's two outstanding 19th-century nationalists, like his forebear Daniel O'Connell, Parnell was dubbed the "uncrowned king of Ireland." A consummate politician like O'Connell, he, too, created a nationwide organization to effect change by working within the British parliamentary system on behalf of Irish nationalism. That he was willing to accept something less than complete independence is remembered less than his defiant, forthright leadership in the cause of Irish freedom.

Catholic parish clergy backed the organization as did many bishops. A Ladies' Irish National Land League was founded, and branch leagues were established in the United States and Britain. For their part, tenants articulated their demands in a succinct formula when 20,000 Ulster farmers signed a memorial on January 21, 1881, seeking legislation to fulfill the "three Fs," namely, a fair rent, a fair sale, and fixity of tenure.

The league set about to organize resistance to the landlords with the goal, in the short term, to prevent evictions and compel a reduction in rents and, in the long term, to transform tenant holders into property owners. The so-called land war, from 1879 to 1882, pitted tenants against landlords in the greatest mass movement yet seen in Ireland. The "war" featured a variety of actions all backed up by the power of moral force—great demonstrations were staged whenever process-serving and evictions occurred; evicted tenants were sheltered and cared for; an embargo was placed on farms where evictions took place. Tenants made use of an innovative tactic—the boycott—to cut off all economic and social contact of offending landlords, so-named from the action taken in September 1880 against land agent Captain Charles Boycott (d. 1897) in County Mayo, which added a new word to the English language.

Aroused passions erupted inevitably into incidents of violence, against which the government sought to act; however, the Irish National Land League, an organization recognized as a legal body, could not be summarily suppressed. And it was backed by strong parliamentary support, after general elections in April 1880, fought in Ireland on the land issue, were won by Parnell. A degree of sympathy was shown by the new Liberal government, led a second time by Gladstone. But continuing rural agitation, abetted by a league that by now had assumed growing powers in operating local courts that in places took on the functions of a rival government, compelled London to take forceful action at the same time that it sought to resolve the crisis.

Parliament voted exceptional powers of coercion, and arrests of leading members of the league began, starting with Davitt in February 1881. In August Gladstone secured passage of a new land act that legalized the "three F's." Courts were set up to which tenants could apply to obtain a fair rent ruling for their holdings, and a system of shared ownership was introduced. However, the Irish National Land League remained unsatisfied. The government responded by arresting all the principal members, including Parnell in October. Parnell fired back. From his prison cell in Dublin's Kilmainham jail, he issued a No Rent Manifesto, which resurrected earlier calls for a national rent strike. But rank-and-file supporters failed to respond, the majority of them, particularly the large farmers, being satisfied with the act.

With the leaders in prison, the league's auxiliary organization, the Ladies' Land League, assumed control of the campaign, but the women

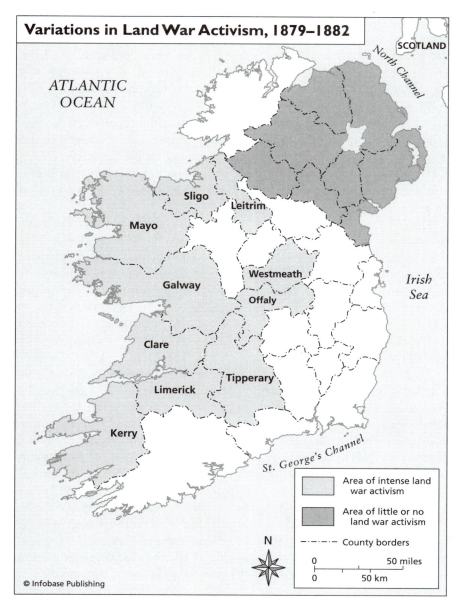

Variations in Land War Activism, 1879–1882

failed to maintain a firm grip, and fearing takeover of the movement by uncontrollable rowdies, Parnell engineered an agreement—the so-called Kilmainham Treaty—in March 1882, by which he agreed to call off disturbances in return for concessions to tenants. The government ceased its arrests, and the prisoners were released. Gladstone remained convinced that the landlord system was no longer defensible, even in the face of the murder on May 6, 1882, of the new chief secretary, Lord Frederick Cavendish (1836–82), and his permanent undersecretary, Thomas Henry Burke (1829–82), in Phoenix Park, Dublin.

The government passed an Arrears of Rent Act in August 1883 that, together with 1881 legislation, progressively reduced owners' interest in holding on to their estates. Growing numbers of landlords found it to their advantage to sell out to their tenants on favorable terms, and under the Asbourne Act (1885) a state-aided land purchase system was put in place under which more and more tenants acquired ownership.

The settlement acts knocked the ground out from under the Irish National Land League, despite continuing calls by Davitt and others for tenant expropriation. Tenants were satisfied in achieving their primary aim, namely, ownership of their holdings. The league was replaced by a new organization, the Irish National League, founded in Dublin on October 17, 1882, an agency that aimed to campaign on broader issues and one dominated thoroughly by the Home Rule League—renamed the Irish Parliamentary Party by Parnell—poised to assume leadership over Irish demands for rights.

By the mid 1880s resort to violent means to secure Irish demands had been relegated largely to the sidelines, although interspersed by occasional flashes of boldly incendiary actions carried on by Fenian revolutionaries. Launched in Britain from 1880 to 1887, the Dynamite War saw several acts made spectacular by use of the newly invented destructive device, including a bombing at the Houses of Parliament in 1885. Financed with monies collected in the United States, the campaign won little support from the Irish Republican Brotherhood.

Sentiments were stirred more by the agrarian movement. The National League's actions demonstrated that Irish national assertiveness was strongly alive, and rights to self-government remained a central focus of the league's leaders. Davitt and Parnell believed that elimination of the landlord class would pave the way for removal of British rule.

Irish activists focused now on obtaining redress of Ireland's other great grievance—reestablishment of a parliament to rule at home. Parnell suppressed factionalism, mobilized public opinion, and, most essentially, secured support from the Catholic hierarchy, which had largely remained aloof from overt commitments to political movements since the days of O'Connell. The general election of November–December 1885—the first in British history in which a substantial portion of adult males could vote—brought Parnell's partisans to a sweeping victory in Ireland. Members pledged to uphold Home Rule were elected to all 85 Irish seats outside eastern Ulster, forming a solid bloc sufficient to hold the balance of power between the Liberals and Conservatives, the two dominant British parties.

Gladstone formed his third government determined to put the issue of Ireland at the top of his agenda. Impressed by the solidarity displayed by Home Rulers, their forces marshaled so effectively by Parnell in the Irish Parliamentary Party, and convinced of the justness of their cause, the prime minister put before the House of Commons a Home Rule bill on April 8, 1886. The bill envisaged devolution of powers over domestic affairs to an Irish parliament.

It won the backing of Parnell and his party and of nationalist opinion overseas, but it drew outraged opposition as well. Conservative Party members saw it as a step toward destruction of the unity of the empire, as a betrayal of the loyalist, Protestant element, and as a sellout to those whose sentiments and actions had for so long sought the ruin of British interests in the country. The Conservatives together with a scattering of disaffected Liberals combined to defeat the bill in voting on June 8, 1886.

Although the measure failed, the attempt marked a milestone in Anglo-Irish relations. A large majority of the Liberal Party was now committed to Home Rule, and nationalist Ireland could count on a loyal ally, no longer necessitating the role of a third party balancing between the two political extremes. The Liberal-Nationalist alliance survived even after Irish nationalists split apart in 1891 when Parnell became involved in a divorce suit that led Gladstone to announce that he would resign as Liberal Party leader unless the Irish party found a new chairman. Parnell refused to quit, and the party broke into Parnellite and anti-Parnellite factions.

Though many former colleagues parted company with him, Parnell retained considerable popular support, and after his death in 1891, he remained very much alive in spirit. Under the leadership of John Redmond (1856–1918), Parnellite constitutional nationalists numbered few in Parliament—only nine in 1892 and 12 in 1895—but a cult of the dead leader developed, in part promoted by Parnell himself who, shortly before his death, had appealed to a much broader segment of nationalist opinion than he had earlier in his constitutional campaign. He supported creation of Fenian associations committed to establishment of an independent republic. That call was taken up as well by Irish intellectuals, who sought to create a nationalism far more sweeping than one limited solely to a campaign for Home Rule. In the 1890s they would launch a cultural revival that would help to inspire a powerful national drive.

Gaelic Literary Revival, 1891–1914

Parnell's death in 1891 splintered the united world of Irish nationalists. Political action appeared to be paralyzed, the charismatic heroism so powerfully personified by Parnell replaced by vicious squabbling among political elites, which, for a decade, produced division and ineffectiveness. Renewed inspiration to take up the Irish cause came, at the turn of the 20th century, not from the practical arena of politics but rather from the world of arts and letters. In a remarkable flowering of artistic creativity, poets, dramatists, and prose writers provided an intellectual underpinning to express and rally pride in Irishness.

The outstanding talent who led what would be called the Gaelic, Celtic, or Anglo-Irish Literary Revival or Renaissance was William Butler Yeats (1865–1939). After Parnell's death, Yeats wrote that "Ireland was to be like soft wax for years to come" (Yeats 1955, 159), and he strove to help shape what he saw as the still evolving consciousness of the country by giving it a cultural legacy of excellence. Ireland's first unquestionably great English-language poet, Yeats was the product of both English and Irish artistic influences, but it was his love for the lore of the Irish countryside that drove his dream to cultivate a national literature that would serve as the cultural cornerstone of an Irish nationality. The poet fashioned a patriotic national picture in deliberate contradistinction to English prejudices of the Irish as a backward, superstitious race. Yeats saw the country's mystical, spiritual traditions and its timeless rural character as qualities not to be disparaged but rather to be glorified, which he undertook to do in writing poetry, the technical quality of which grew with time. In praising the rural peasant life of Ireland, Yeats sought to repudiate the industrial world of modern capitalism, the image of which could be encapsulated for him in a single word: "England."

But other Irish-born writers embraced fully the modern, mercantile world that beckoned in Britain. Oscar Wilde (1854–1900) sought in every respect to cast himself in the exact opposite image of his Irish lineage. Born in Dublin, Wilde fled his home to escape two eccentric parents. In London he became the picture of the urbane, fastidious Englishman who disguised his gigantic, ungainly frame, which, to some observers might have recalled the apelike caricatures of the Irish

WILLIAM BUTLER YEATS

William Butler Yeats (June 13, 1865–January 28, 1939) was born in Sandymount, County Dublin, into a landed, artistically minded Protestant family. Yeats was erratically schooled in England, and his unhappy experience there whetted his Irish loyalties. He acquired a particular love of Sligo, where he had spent two idyllic years as a boy. Yeats studied ancient Irish myths and legends and became thoroughly versed in the lore of the Irish countryside. His anthologies of Irish folklore would include *Fairy and Folk Tales of the Irish Peasantry* (1888) and *Irish Fairy Tales* (1892).

William Butler Yeats (Library of Congress, LC-USZ62-87604)

Yeats's first significant poem was "The Isle of Statues," a fantasy piece modeled on the work of Elizabethan poet Edmund Spenser. His first major volume (1889) with its title poem "The Wanderings of Oisin" manifests a philosophical seriousness and employs a profusion of Gaelic names and ornamental descriptions that mask a hard-nosed realism under the highly imaginative verse. Love themes and mystical subjects predominate in early collections of poems (*Poems*, 1895).

In 1889 Yeats met Maud Gonne (1866–1953), an English-born Anglo-Irish heiress and a feminist and nationalist with whom he fell passionately in love. However, she thrice rejected his marriage proposals, both because she believed him to be insufficiently ardent in his nationalism and because, unlike herself, he would not convert to Catholicism. He consummated an affair with the now-married Gonne in Paris in 1908. Introduced to Lady Augusta Gregory in 1896, he cofounded the Irish Literary Theatre and later the Irish National Theatre Society with her. Both institutions served to support the work of emerging Irish authors.

(continues)

WILLIAM BUTLER YEATS (continued)

The stress in his early works on idealization of rural peasant life and use of conventional poetic diction gave way in the early 20th century to a greater realism and a starker, less ornamental use of rhythm and idiom (*In the Seven Woods*, 1904; *The Green Helmet and Other Poems*, 1910) as well as a more direct engagement with politics, which he had hitherto avoided. In "Easter 1916," with its famous opening lines "All changed, changed utterly / A terrible beauty is born," Yeats, although he detested the hatred and bigotry displayed by some nationalists, admitted his own failure to recognize the worthiness of the cause.

A lifelong devotee of mysticism, spiritualism, and astrology, Yeats wrote many plays that deal with Irish legends (*Deirdre* [1907]). Awarded the Nobel Prize in literature in 1923 chiefly for his dramatic works, he was acutely aware of the symbolic importance of the honor, given in tribute to the literature of a newly independent land. He moved to Galway in 1922, and his later poetry and plays exhibit a return to imaginative mysticism. He died in Menton, on the French Riviera, and was buried nearby. In 1948 his remains were transferred to Drumcliffe, County Sligo.

Yeats achieved great success as a poet and dramatist, but his career encompassed a range of activities, including criticism, autobiography, fiction, fund-raising, politics, and theater management and direction. A master of both free and traditional verse forms, he is considered one of the most versatile, prolific, modern English-language poets. By promoting the writing of plays by and for Irish people, he also helped to earn for Ireland worldwide fame for great drama.

peasant popularized by English cartoonists, through elegant clothes and refined deportment. Just as he had in his personal life, Wilde labored in his writing to reverse the popular images of the national character by inverting the typical stereotypes that held that just because the English were supposed to be industrious and rational, the Irish must, perforce, be indolent and irrational. A brilliant craftsman of poems, plays, novels, and short stories, Wilde earned fame for his ingenious epigrams, barbed wit, and sparkling conversational style in comedic plays such as *Lady Windermere's Fan* (1892) and *The Importance of Being Earnest* (1895). He became one of the most successful celebrities of late Victorian London in presenting in his plays amusing and disillusioning viewpoints on all aspects of English society. An Irishman who became the very image of

English cartoon, ca. 1899. A working-class Irishman admires an upper-class Irishman's stickpin. The Irish were characteristically portrayed in print in demeaning caricatures that featured simianlike features. (Library of Congress, POS-TH-STO, no. 12)

the proper Englishman, Wilde was able to defy and, in the end, reverse the age-old clichés of Ireland.

George Bernard Shaw (1856–1950) also sought to define Irishness from London's central stage. Born and poorly educated in Dublin, Shaw rebelled at his family's snobbery and his landlord father's drunken idleness. In 1876 he moved to London and rarely returned to Ireland, although near the end of a long life spent penning some 50-odd plays, he was to write: "Eternal is the fact that the human creature born in

217

Ireland and brought up in its air is Irish" (Shaw 1962, 248). The greatest English-language modern realist playwright, Shaw wrote only one play directly about Ireland. In *John Bull's Other Island* (1904), it is the Englishman John Broadbent who is the dreaming incompetent whereas Irishman Larry Doyle is the hard-nosed cynic. The play satirized two peoples who persist in maintaining images imposed on each by the other side rather than seeking self-expression.

Whereas Wilde and Shaw built essentially English careers in writing for London audiences, Yeats and others aimed instead to create not only an Irish national literature but also an authentic Irish venue. In the summer of 1897, Yeats spoke to a recent acquaintance—Lady Augusta Gregory (1852–1932)—about his long-held dream of an Irish theater in which plays composed by and for Irish men and women could be performed. Born Isabella Augusta Persse, Lady Augusta, the daughter of an Anglo-Irish landlord, was the widow of a wealthy aristocrat. A trip to Inisheer in the Aran Islands in 1893 reawakened her interest in Irish language and folklore, and she became a dramatist and folklorist herself. In 1899 she funded the money for what came to be called the Irish Literary Theatre.

Lady Isabella Augusta Gregory (Library of Congress, LC-USZ62-104093)

Although regular productions of plays by Irish authors on Irish subjects had been performed in Dublin theaters for 20 years, the Irish Literary Theatre marked the start of a deliberate creative effort to promote native talent. The Irish identity that Yeats and Gregory sought to glorify was one rooted in a highly idealized image of western Ireland—the most Irish of Irish places, they believed, peopled by humble peasants who told stories of fairies in their native tongue. "When we thought of these plays, we thought of everything that was romantic and poetical for the naturalism we had called up, like that generations had called up in moments of discouragement, was romantic and poetical," Yeats later said (Yeats 1923). Plays such as his *Countess Cathleen ni Houlihan* (1899), coauthored by Lady Gregory, and *The Heathen Field* (1899) by Lady Augusta's neighbor Edward Martyns (1859–1923) invoked themes and characters—tenants and landlord strife, kings and glorious battles—of both recent and ancient memory. *Casardh an tSúgáin* (The twisting of the rope, 1901), written by Yeats and Douglas Hyde (1860–1949), was the first play to feature ordinary cottiers speaking in Irish.

Lack of funding led to the collapse of the Irish Literary Theatre project in 1901 and its rebirth in 1903 as the Irish National Theatre Society. Productions staged in a building called the Molesworth Hall were moved to new premises on Lower Abbey Street in 1904, and the first plays to be performed in what became Ireland's premier theater of renown, the Abbey Theatre (Amharclann na Mainistreach), also known as the National Theatre of Ireland (Amharclann Náisiúnta na hÉireann), were performed on December 27. The curtain went up on three one-act plays, including *Countess Cathleen ni Houlihan*. In the play, Ireland is incarnated in the figure of an old woman who mourns for four green fields (provinces) lost to English colonizers and who would regain her queenly splendor only when men in the mold of legendary heroes such as Cúchulainn would risk their lives on her behalf.

The most acclaimed, authoritative plays depicting Irish rural life performed at the Abbey were those written by the revival's greatest playwright, John Millington Synge (1871–1909). Born in Rathfarmham, County Dublin, into an Anglo-Irish Protestant family, and a playwright, poet, prose writer, and collector of folklore, Synge would draw on his recollections of peasant life in the Aran Islands in creating the world of Catholic fishing communities that distinguish his major dramatic works. He injected a realism to rural life that stood in contrast to the idealized peasant folk of Ireland's west so much promoted by Yeats and others. *The Playboy of the Western World* is widely regarded as his masterpiece. A comedy centered on the apparent killing of a kinsman in the west of Ireland, the protagonist refuses to leave off his pursuit of the barmaid heroine, and at its debut on January 26, 1907, members of the audience, incensed at the play's portrayal of harsh, violent pastoral life and of loose womanhood, leapt out of their seats in anger, drowning out the remaining dialogue. Riots ensued for a week. But Synge's style of realistic writing would go on to serve as the basis of much of the training given at the Abbey Theatre's school of acting, and plays dealing with themes of peasant life, both comforting and troubling, would form a staple at the theater until the end of the 1950s. While the Abbey remained the focal stage of Irish dramas, competing societies, such as the Theatre of Ireland (1906), were founded in Dublin and other cities (Cork Dramatic Society).

Poets and prose writers penned a profusion of works. Poets Padraic Colum and Joseph Campbell (1879–1944) both drew on detailed knowledge of folklore in writing verse that highlighted the harsh conditions of rural living. Women poets Ethna Carberry (1872–1902) and Alice Milligan (1866–1953), Ulsterwomen of Catholic and Methodist faiths, respectively, wrote patriotic verse, while Eva Gore-Booth (1870–1926), a lesbian political activist and social worker who lived most of her life in Manchester, England, combined two popular elements of revival verse—nationalistically tinged piety and a mystical sense of the natural world—and, later, musings on public events in her works.

Poet and playwright AE (George William Russell, 1867–1935) rivaled only Yeats as a leading poetic light of the revival. His collections such as *Homeward Thoughts by the Way* (1894) feature highly imaginative and ethereal-like lyrics. AE eagerly promoted the careers of other talented writers, including Seamus O'Sullivan (James Sullivan Starkey, 1879–1958), whose verse is highly descriptive of urban life and intensely patriotic, and James Joyce (1882–1941). Born in the Dublin suburb of Rathgar, Joyce opposed from the start what he saw as the unrealistic romanticism of the literary revivalists. Although he wrote his masterpieces after World War I, already in *Dubliners* (1914) he treated the raw side of life among the Dublin middle class that would become his signature topic.

Writers of novels at the turn of the 20th century were typically preoccupied with stories set in country houses and in telling tales about the Irish gentry. Many popular novelists were women. Many lived in Britain, thereby violating Yeats's assertion made most famously to Synge, whom he chided for residing in Paris and London, that Irish authors should remain home.

Science fiction found a wide audience. Bram Stoker's *Dracula* (1897) perverts, to a monstrous degree, the environment and heredity, themes characteristic of many mainstream Irish novels of the time, a theme also pursued by Oscar Wilde in his specimen of blemished humanity *The Picture of Dorian Gray* (1890), which reads much like science fiction. Stoker (1847–1912), born in the Dublin seaside suburb of Fairview, worked as a civil servant before moving to London, where he became a theater business manager, supplementing his income by writing. The story of the vampire Dracula's dark, medieval threat to the modern world and the triumph of chivalry and love remains the most identified Irish novel of the period. *Dracula* is an invasion story, as is Irish militant nationalist Robert Erskine Childers's (1870–1922) *The Riddle of the Sands* (1903), a fiction thriller in which two young Englishmen play detective in uncovering a German plot to invade Britain, and both novels have never gone out of fashion.

While cultural nationalists writing in English strove to become ever more aware of Ireland's rich literary heritage, Irish-language writers struggled for an audience in the face of the precipitous decline of the idiom. A Society for the Preservation of the Irish Language was set up in 1879, and the Gaelic Union, an offshoot of the society, founded a bilingual periodical *Irisleabhar na Gaedhilge (Gaelic Journal)* in 1882, which appeared after 1893 under the management of the Gaelic League (Conradh na Gaeilge). The league, founded that year by Douglas Hyde and Celtic scholar and revolutionary Eoin Mac Néill (1867–1945) proved the most ambitious vehicle to restore Irish as the language of the country. Hyde strove to re-create an Irish cultural nation by removing all traces of anglicization. From 1899 the league published books, both literary works and language textbooks, conducted language and history classes, and sponsored an annual national festival (An tOireachtas) with cash prizes awarded in competitions for original verse. Translation work was diligently promoted.

Hyde himself produced the first book of original modern poetry in Irish in *Ulla de'n Chraobh* (1901), his only published work. Other scholarly poets included Tadhg (Torna) O'Donnchadha (1874–1949), Piaras Béaslaí (1883–1965), and Peadar O'hAnnrachain (1873–1965), all of whom penned patriotic verse, as did Patrick Henry Pearse (Pádraig Mac Piarais, 1879–1916), a young committed republican scholar. Modern Irish-language poetry begins with Pearse and his contemporaries. Pearse's hope that poetry in Irish would be grounded not only in an in-depth knowledge of Irish traditions but also in contemporary European trends would become fully evident by the mid 20th century.

Author and journalist Pádraic Ó Conaire (1882–1928) achieved his greatest success in writing short stories, the best of which were his tales of life in his native Gaeltacht region. He pioneered modern Irish-language prose with his novel *Deoraiocht* (1910).

Traditional music, customarily passed aurally/orally and only rarely written down, scored a major success for its preservation with publication in the United States of *The Music of Ireland* (1903) by Francis O'Neill, which contained over 1,800 tunes, many contributed by Irish emigrants, and many of which were no longer performed in Ireland. Antiquarian, musician, and painter George Petrie (1790–1866) published *The Ancient Music of Ireland* (1855), and *The Complete Collection of Irish Music by George Petrie*, which included more than 1,600 melodies, was published posthumously in 1902–05. William Perry French (1854–1920) was one of the most prominent songwriters and entertainers of the era, who is recognized today equally for his watercolor paintings. The cultural renaissance helped to revive stepdancing in the Munster or southern style, in which the performers dance in one long line. Invented by the Gaelic League in the 19th century, the *céli* ("kay li") dance is a social dance, often fast-paced with complicated steps, performed by as few as four or as many as 16 dancers, or by an unlimited number of couples.

For all Yeats's and Lady Gregory's musings about a romantically glorified Ireland, the literary revival was, however, limited in its popular appeal. In contrast, sports began to draw both spectators and participants in earnest by the end of the 19th century. In 1874 the Irish Football Union was established. To attract the attention of the masses, the Gaelic League actively promoted Irish music, games, dress, and sports. It did so in conjunction with the Gaelic Athletic Association (GAA), which had been founded at Thurles, County Tipperary, in November 1884. Activities were promoted in deliberate reaction to English sports. Instead of soccer, the Irish were urged to play Gaelic football, which first became popular in the 16th century and remains the most played Gaelic game today. The rules of the modern game were promulgated by the GAA, which continues to regulate the sport. In place of hockey, Irish activists promoted hurling, a stick-and-ball game, said to be the world's fastest, that dates to ancient times, also administered by the GAA. The Irish League urged the Irish to practice their jig assiduously, and it even advised Irishmen to doff trousers and don kilts. By 1903 the league counted some 600 branches.

The literary revival's myth of a timeless praiseworthy Irish peasantry was just that, a myth. It was the creation of urbanized, highly sophisticated aesthetes who ignored the reality of Ireland's complex rural society with its varied interest groups and shadings of classes. Still, the revival managed to both inject and keep alive a renewed sense of pride among nationalists during a period when the political scene was mired in bitterness, confusion, and disillusion. All the revivalist playwrights were advocates of Home Rule, and the Irish literary world served to powerfully promote the struggle for independence that would come to define the first two decades of the 20th century.

Nationalist and Unionist Sentiments Solidify, 1891–1914

The Gaelic League, despite its avowedly nonpolitical aims, did not escape vicious factional fighting among rival claimants to leadership, all of whom had determinedly political motives, during a period at the turn of the 20th century when a politically driven hardening of sectarian sides took place. Protestant leaders in the league were forced out of office in the decade after 1900.

Politics pervaded Irish affairs by 1900. Nationalists remained split between constitutionalists and advocates for the use of physical force, between parliamentarians and republicans, between those who counseled continued patience and those who cried no more waiting for independence. Protestant unionists stood for undiminished ties to Great Britain.

By touting Ireland's cultural uniqueness, the Gaelic League, like the Young Ireland movement before it, provided the best argument for nationalists who, in line with reasoning then in vogue in Europe, affirmed that nations that already existed culturally should be given their political independence. The league's philosophy helped further motivate older established groups, such as the Irish Republican Brotherhood (IRB) and new ones as well. One of the latter appeared in September 1900 in the Cumann na nGaedheal, founded by Arthur Griffith (1871–1922), an ex-Fenian journalist active in the Gaelic League. Griffith shared with Home Rule parliamentarians the belief that the Act of Union of 1800 was illegal, but unlike them, he advocated that its repeal should be accomplished not by waiting for the British parliament to act but simply by Irish members refusing to attend and, instead, reassembling along with elected representatives of the county councils and other local authorities to set up a Council of Three Hundred, an all-Ireland legislative body to legislate domestic policy.

Griffith's assertion that Ireland should become a separate kingdom alongside Great Britain, sharing a monarch but with separate governments, became the cornerstone of his so-called Sinn Féin policy, first proclaimed by him on November 28, 1905. Translated into English usually as "We Ourselves" or "Ourselves Alone," Sinn Féin was launched as a newspaper in May 1906, edited by Griffith, and on April 21, 1907, as an organization called the Sinn Féin League (in 1908 the word *League* was dropped). By then, growing numbers of IRB members were joining, radicalizing the group's objective in moving from advocacy of constitutional monarchy to outright independence as a republic but dropping the IRB's resort to force in favor of support for the use of Parnellite methods to effect change through nonviolent, electoral means. Emerging as a political party, even if at the beginning a relatively amorphous one, Sinn Féin tested the political waters, running a candidate for Parliament in a by-election in 1908. Loss by a vote of two to one demonstrated that the party's call for an independent Irish republic had yet to win wide popular appeal.

Sinn Féin achieved some early success at local elections while gaining additional support from other groups and individuals, notably Constance, Countess Markievicz (or Markiewicz, 1868–1927), born in London and married to a count of Polish descent. In 1909, she launched Fianna Éireann, a movement advocating establishment of an Irish republic, and then joined the feminist Inghinidhe na hÉireann (Daughters of Ireland), founded in 1900 by actress and activist Maud Gonne, which attracted women who believed themselves shut out of male republican groups.

Undeterred by ongoing efforts at the ballot box, others remained committed to the use of violence, the ultimate means to effect change employed at regular intervals in the past. The Irish Republican Brotherhood continued to advocate creation of a republic by force. After the Parnellite split, the IRB suffered internal divisions, but gradually built, from a very small base, a determined, revitalized core of militants. The IRB's activist agenda drew many new recruits. They included Patrick Pearse, the scholar and poet; Thomas MacDonagh (1878–1910), an early associate of Pearse and a lecturer at University College Dublin; Joseph Mary Plunkett (1887–1916), the son of a hereditary papal count; and Seán MacBride (1865–1916), the ex-husband of Maud Gonne.

While Sinn Féin and the IRB both opposed what they believed to be the limited goal of the Irish Parliamentary Party, with its focus solely on winning a separate parliament under British rule, a new force on the scene at the turn of the 20th century professed no interest at all in the political struggle. The emergence of a working class in Ireland reflected the growth in preceding decades of industrial activity, leading, for the first time in Irish history, to a shift in the center of social action away from the countryside to the cities. Hitherto the source of so much agitation for change, in the early 20th century Ireland's rural population withdrew into relative complacency, satisfied that, by means of a series of land laws, culminating in Wyndham's Act of 1903, an estimated three-quarters of farmers owned their own land by 1914. The great landlords largely disappeared as their estates were sold off, and the relations with their tenants, which had comprised so central a theme in Irish affairs since first emerging in the 17th century, no longer aroused Irish passions. The locus of social tensions now shifted to urban places. In the larger towns, many laborers, badly fed and poorly paid, lived in appalling squalor. In October 1913 Pearse reported in *Irish Freedom,* the monthly newspaper of the IRB, that ". . . one third of the people of Dublin are underfed. . . . I suppose there are 20,000 families in Dublin in whose domestic economy milk and butter are all but unknown; black tea and dry bread are their staple diet" (Pearse 1922, 177–178).

To advocate for the redress of workers' grievances, the Irish Transport and General Workers' Union (ITGWU) was founded in 1908 by James Larkin (1876–1947). Larkin had mobilized Belfast dockworkers to create a disciplined, nonsectarian force that had waged a strike against the Belfast Steamship Company the year before. Uninterested in nationalist issues, he espoused only the cause of workers' rights to be advanced by whatever means proved necessary, including violence.

Despite Larkin's efforts to unite workers across political and religious divides, the sectarian divisions bedeviling Irish society seeped into labor relations as well, and the Belfast strike collapsed in 1908 because the unity of Protestants and Catholics could not be sustained. Mutual hatreds here had a long lineage. Catholics and Protestants in Ulster had rioted against each other in 1857, 1864, 1872, and 1886. Protestants rallied around a resurgent Orange Order. In the mid-19th century, it evolved into an essentially urban movement, especially strong in Belfast where many Catholics had moved in search of work. Under the flamboyant leadership of William Johnston (1829–1902), an MP for Belfast, it successfully challenged legislative acts that forbade party processions. Home Rule gave the Orangists a readily identifiable issue on which to focus their enmity.

Never reconciled but often quiescent in the face of Protestantism's all-controlling presence in Ulster, Catholics, too, demonstrated a renewed vigor backed by a resurgent church and a host of parliamentary and extraparliamentary nationalist efforts. The Ancient Order of Hibernians emerged in the 1880s and 1890s, probably drawing its inspiration from the sectarian character of the Ribbon movement earlier in the century. Largely a secretive society and, as such, condemned by the Catholic hierarchy, it appeared strongest at first in Ulster but then found a welcoming reception in the United States. The vigor of the U.S. branches animated Hibernians toward a heightened enthusiasm after 1900. Espousing a militant Catholicism, it helped to maintain and strengthen the rising sectarian rift in Ulster.

Protestants met every Catholic move with their own fraternal efforts, thus ironically giving birth to two similar, yet diametrically opposed, political cultures. Between 1870 and 1910 Protestant workers in Ulster maneuvered Catholics out of more skilled, better paid employment, and they did not hesitate in using violence in doing so. Where elsewhere in Europe workers were uniting to confront employers, in the Belfast shipyards workers clashed with workers instead. Protestants drove out Catholic rivals again and again in the late 19th and early 20th centuries.

Just as it had for the preceding 20 years, in the 1890s Irish political action swirled around the same central axis, namely, the issue of Home Rule. The Liberals, under the by now venerable leadership of Gladstone, had remained true to the cause, introducing a second Home Rule bill in February 1893, which was defeated. A period ensued of Conservative Party rule backed by unionist allies, during which the Irish Parliamentary Party remained split, unable to influence policy with numbers sufficiently large to pressure the two main parties in Parliament. Unity finally returned in 1900 under the leadership of John Redmond (1856–1918), who placed more emphasis than perhaps even Parnell had on the need to win independence through the constitutional processes of the British House of Commons.

The prospects for sectarian violence, simmering now for several years, were set to boil after the Liberals under Herbert Asquith (1852–1928) achieved a marginal victory in the elections of January and February 1910. Conservatives and Liberal Unionists—Liberals who had bolted the party and who would merge with the Conservatives fully in 1912—won equal representation, and only support from the Irish Parliamentary Party made possible formation of a Liberal government. Payment for services rendered was expected. Asquith duly followed Gladstone's example. A third Home Rule bill was introduced in 1912. The measure called for a bicameral Irish parliament (House of Commons and Senate) in Dublin with powers to rule over most domestic issues. The British government would maintain control of the police for six years, and responsibility for defense, foreign policy, religious affairs, and excise and customs duties would rest permanently with the imperial Parliament at London, to which 42 Irish MPs would be elected (down from the current 103).

Alarmed that unionists outside Ulster were weakening in their resolve to combat devolution, unionist MPs and others in Ulster organized themselves in the Ulster Unionist Party in 1905, the successor to the islandwide Irish Unionist Party in existence since 1886.

In the search for a way out of the seemingly intractable divide, the possibility gradually emerged to grant Ulster some type of special status or exemption. Publicly, Home Rulers held firm that a parliamentary act apply to all Ireland, with safeguards built in for Protestant interests, and Ulster unionists likewise insisted on islandwide preservation of the union. However, in private, pressured by their parliamentary allies, both sides considered some kind of solution for Ulster's exclusion. "I have never heard that orange bitters will mix with Irish whiskey," declared Liberal MP Thomas C. Agar-Robartes (1880–1915) in June 1912 in introducing an amendment to the Home Rule bill to exclude the provinces of Antrim, Armagh, Londonderry, and Down—Ireland's most heavily Protestant—from the provisions of the proposed act (BBC, "A Short History"). Irish unionists agreed, but Agar-Robartes's amendment failed in the House of Commons.

Negotiations were made more difficult by the incendiary atmosphere in Ulster. At a massive rally on April 9, 1912, Conservative Party leader Andrew Bonar Law (1858–1923) pledged to Belfast unionists unshakable support for their cause, intimating that he would condone extra-parliamentary means to prevent Home Rule. Unionists made their feelings fully known on September 28 when an estimated three-fourths of all Ulster Protestants signed a pledge to oppose Home Rule, the men in their Solemn League and Covenant affirming that they would use all means necessary to defeat the move and, if enacted, to refuse to recognize a Home Rule government. On January 13, 1913, they put muscle behind their words in creating an Ulster Volunteer Force. Orange Order members flocked to join, and soon 10,000 well-trained men stood ready to resist. They were also well-armed, having illegally imported and distributed, with the tacit consent of the police, thousands of service rifles and millions of rounds of ammunition by April 1914. And they were ready to set up a separate regime to be led by Sir Edward Carson (1854–1935), the militant leader of the Ulster Unionist Party since 1912.

The well-organized moves of the unionists set an impressive example, and not to be outmatched, nationalists fired back. Militants established the Irish (National) Volunteers, patterned on the Ulster model, on November 25, 1913, at Dublin. Within a few months they succeeded in enrolling as many as 75,000 members, twice as many recruits as their northern counterpart, although they were much more poorly armed.

At the very same time, an outbreak of labor strife joined the stew of sectarian tensions in adding strains to Irish life. In August 1913 William Martin Murphy (1844–1919), president of the Dublin Chamber of Commerce and, as such, head of the Employers' Federation, dismissed 40 men for their membership in the ITGWU and went on to organize a lockout against workers who refused to pledge not to join the union. Union leader Larkin urged members not to comply. A strike by tram workers was called in August, and by September 24,000 people were barred from factories, storehouses, and dockyards. Eight months of bitter battling ensued. The so-called revolt of the slums included mass rallies, rioting, arrests, imprisonments, and deaths in the largest and most intense industrial dispute in Irish history. A Citizens' Army, created in November 1913 to protect the strikers, added yet another element to the martial mix in Ireland, and the force remained in existence after the turmoil subsided in January 1914.

Women joined in support. The Women Workers Union, a constituent group within the ITGWU, founded by Delia Larkin (1878–1949), James Larkin's sister, and others ran soup kitchens. Women also began to add their voices to their sisters in Britain and the United States in actively campaigning for the right to vote. They began to organize as early as 1871, when Isabella Tod (1836–96), a Scottish-born journalist, formed in Belfast the first society promoting women's suffrage. Delia Larkin represented laboring ladies in the movement, which, as in other English-speaking countries, was largely led by middle- and upper-class women. Hannah Sheehy Skeffington (1877–1946) founded the Irish Women's Suffrage League and was imprisoned in 1912 for destructive activity. Massive rallies, such as that in Dublin on June 1, 1912, characterized the drive in Ireland as elsewhere. Many suffragists added support for Irish independence to their battles for the ballot, and they became active backers of Sinn Féin.

By summer 1914, threading its way through Parliament in the midst of so much turbulent temperament, the third Home Rule bill had been introduced three times—in April 1912 and July 1913, when it was passed by the House of Commons but thrown out by the Lords, and again in 1914 when the Commons passed it a third time on May 25. Wrangling continued about the powers to be granted a parliament in Dublin, while proposals to exclude Ulster counties also remained alive though vaguely defined, talks having become mired over disagreements about which counties to be included. In July 1914 Carson and the Ulster Unionist Party, with the backing of the Lords, sought an amendment to permanently exclude all of Ulster from the Home Rule provisions. Responding to the threat, Prime Minister Asquith, over the vehement objections of Redmond, introduced a compromise to allow for the "temporary" exclusion of six Ulster counties for an indeterminate period. The Ulster Unionist Council, an umbrella executive founded in 1904 to coordinate the work of local unionist clubs in resisting Home Rule, explicitly identified Ulster's nine counties as the territory to be defended, leaving southern unionists uneasy at being left out and nationalists across the island primed to resist. The Home Rule bill was sent on for the royal assent after it was defeated a third time by the House of Lords, the government using provisions of the Parliament Act of 1911, which stipulated that a veto by the Lords would be automatically overridden for any bill passed by the Commons in three sessions over two years.

Ireland in spring and summer 1914 bristled with tension. Fighting forces aligned with each side stood at the ready, and even the regular standing army had been drawn into the ever-widening divide. In March rumors ran rife that troops at the Curragh, a British army barracks in County Kildare, would be used to coerce the populace into accepting Home Rule; 57 out of 70 officers offered to resign their commissions rather than comply. On July 26 the ship *Asgard*, navigated by Erskine Childers, arrived off Howth with 1,500 rifles for the Irish Volunteers furnished by the German government. Army troops tried unsuccessfully to prevent the landing and distribution, and, then, in harassing a column of Volunteers returning to Dublin, they fired on a crowd of uninvolved civilians, killing four. More guns arrived at Kilcoole, County Wicklow, on August 1. By then, competition between nationalists and unionists was most intense in mid Ulster, the recruiting ground where Protestant and Catholic communities were equally matched. By midsummer 1914 Ireland could be likened to a kettle ready to boil, any incident liable to serve as the flashpoint to spark bloody sectarian conflict. Civil war seemed imminent.

World War and Rebellion, 1914–1918

The Government of Ireland Act was signed by King George V (r. 1910–35) on September 18, 1914. Jubilant Irish nationalists lit bonfires on hilltops all across southern Ireland in celebration. But an event had intruded quite unexpectedly that troubled their joy. The House of Commons voted at the same time to suspend the pending act for a period of one year or for the duration of a war, expected to be short, that now demanded everyone's attention. On August 4 Britain declared war on Germany in protest at the German army's invasion of neutral Belgium, the last act in a monthlong drama that had drawn all of Europe's major powers, save Italy, into hostilities. The need to prepare for fighting Britain's enemies—Germany and Austria-Hungary—preoccupied both the government and the general public, dramatically dampening the threat of conflict in Ireland.

Both nationalists and unionists would answer the call to the colors in significant numbers. In August Redmond offered the Irish Volunteers for home defense, followed in September by a call to his forces to enlist for service. Those among the Irish Volunteers who agreed to do so became known as the National Volunteers. In performing their patriotic duty, he hoped to demonstrate the fitness of nationalists for self-government and to earn the trust of unionists. In the end, he secured neither the single Irish division he sought in hopes of keeping the National Volunteers intact—two were created (the 10th and 16th) under officers of the regular army—nor unionist gratitude.

With suspension of Home Rule assured, Ulster unionists joined wholeheartedly in the war effort. A 36th (Ulster) division was set up under officers nominated by the Ulster Volunteer Force, the very arrangement denied to Redmond. From 1914 to 1918 Ireland counted about 200,000 men—Catholics slightly outnumbering Protestants—who joined the British army, in addition to many expatriates in Britain, the empire, and the United States. Their presence evoked in the popular tune "It's a Long Way to Tipperary," Irish men suffered and bled in numbers equivalent to those that ravaged the ranks of all the belligerents. At the Battle of the Somme beginning on July 1, 1916, the Ulster Division was literally torn to pieces in one of the war's outstanding tragic examples of mass murder by machine gun.

Those who remained at home enjoyed considerable prosperity. After initial economic disruptions, urban unemployment fell below prewar levels as men were drawn into the armed forces and into munitions factories, though women did not enter the workforce in numbers anywhere near those in Britain. Farmers fared best, though the stoppage in emigration added population pressure to small-farmer households, especially in western Ireland. The cutoff of foreign competition for the British market spurred production, and the jump in prices, which doubled between 1914 and 1918, padded producers' pockets even as it hurt consumers. Inflation eased access to agricultural credit and, for the first time, farmers began to buy machinery in earnest and to join cooperatives in large numbers.

For a small coterie of dedicated republicans, the European war brought the prospect of renewed armed resistance. The war's distraction afforded them the opportunity to act on their long-standing premise that Britain's distress would mean Ireland's success, and they jumped at the chance to plan an insurrection. A supreme council of the Irish Republican Brotherhood met in September 1914 and convinced the provisional committee of the Irish Volunteers to repudiate Redmond's conciliatory leadership. The American Clan na Gael offered to finance an uprising. Under its auspices, Roger Casement (1864–1916), a British consul before the war and, from his youth, an Irish nationalist who, after the outbreak of hostilities, worked to secure German aid for Irish independence, traveled

A World War I recruitment poster in Ireland. RMS Lusitania was sunk by a German submarine off Queenstown (Cobh) on May 7, 1915, with the loss of 1,198 lives. The incident led to widespread public outrage in Britain, the United States, and elsewhere. (Library of Congress, LC-USZ62-264-10986)

to Germany to raise an Irish brigade from among British prisoners of war, who were to be sent home together with a shipment of arms.

Planners, however, could not count on the one element they would need to ensure success—support for a rebellion was largely nonexistent among a general public for whom prosperity, military recruitment, and expectation of the impending implementation of Home Rule diminished enthusiasm for fomenting mayhem. At war's start, Sinn Féin and the Gaelic League were largely inactive, though an energetic recruitment drive managed to stem the IRB's decline, its ranks totaling about 2,000 in 1916. With public opinion indifferent if not downright hostile and given the massive wartime forces at the disposal of the government, fanaticism and pent-up frustration alone fueled the drive to proceed among a minority of activists within these organizations.

The government was aware of a brewing conspiracy, but aside from shutting down a few opposition journals and stopping several republican organizations from their recruiting efforts, officials at Dublin Castle employed nothing other than ridicule to counter the threat. Because Home Rule was expected, the administration functioned largely as a caretaker operation, holding secret meetings with Redmond and other nationalists during 1915 while ignoring the unionists in Ulster and actively opposing their efforts in London. Intelligence warnings of imminent rebellion were minimized and seemingly disproved when the only shipload of German arms was sunk, and Casement was arrested promptly when he landed from a German submarine on April 21, 1916, on the Banna Strand in County Kerry. Sentenced to death for treason in June, he was hanged in London in August. Government authorities intended to spend the long upcoming Easter holiday weekend relaxing before rounding up any remaining dispirited conspirators.

Dispirited the conspirators indeed were, but it was their very demoralization that drove them to launch a desperate strike before the weekend was over. Plotters had planned too long for action not to go forward. The Military Council of the IRB, which by early 1916 had managed to unite under its umbrella both idealistic visionaries and hard-headed revolutionaries, reasoned that a bloody sacrifice, however futile, would produce martyrs for the cause and so awaken patriotic sentiments in favor of the dream of an Irish Republic. With that aim in mind, strategists chose not to occupy key sites such as Dublin Castle, where they could cripple institutions of the central government, nor even Trinity College, a strategically situated walled campus offering superb defensive advantages, but rather buildings in the city center and

POBLACHT NA H EIREANN.

THE PROVISIONAL GOVERNMENT
OF THE
IRISH REPUBLIC
TO THE PEOPLE OF IRELAND.

IRISHMEN AND IRISHWOMEN : In the name of God and of the dead generations from which she receives her old tradition of nationhood, Ireland, through us, summons her children to her flag and strikes for her freedom.

Having organised and trained her manhood through her secret revolutionary organisation, the Irish Republican Brotherhood, and through her open military organisations, the Irish Volunteers and the Irish Citizen Army, having patiently perfected her discipline, having resolutely waited for the right moment to reveal itself, she now seizes that moment, and, supported by her exiled children in America and by gallant allies in Europe, but relying in the first on her own strength, she strikes in full confidence of victory.

We declare the right of the people of Ireland to the ownership of Ireland, and to the unfettered control of Irish destinies, to be sovereign and indefeasible. The long usurpation of that right by a foreign people and government has not extinguished the right, nor can it ever be extinguished except by the destruction of the Irish people. In every generation the Irish people have asserted their right to national freedom and sovereignty ; six times during the past three hundred years they have asserted it in arms. Standing on that fundamental right and again asserting it in arms in the face of the world, we hereby proclaim the Irish Republic as a Sovereign Independent State, and we pledge our lives and the lives of our comrades-in-arms to the cause of its freedom, of its welfare, and of its exaltation among the nations.

The Irish Republic is entitled to, and hereby claims, the allegiance of every Irishman and Irishwoman. The Republic guarantees religious and civil liberty, equal rights and equal opportunities to all its citizens, and declares its resolve to pursue the happiness and prosperity of the whole nation and of all its parts, cherishing all the children of the nation equally, and oblivious of the differences carefully fostered by an alien government, which have divided a minority from the majority in the past.

Until our arms have brought the opportune moment for the establishment of a permanent National Government, representative of the whole people of Ireland and elected by the suffrages of all her men and women, the Provisional Government, hereby constituted, will administer the civil and military affairs of the Republic in trust for the people.

We place the cause of the Irish Republic under the protection of the Most High God, Whose blessing we invoke upon our arms, and we pray that no one who serves that cause will dishonour it by cowardice, inhumanity, or rapine. In this supreme hour the Irish nation must, by its valour and discipline and by the readiness of its children to sacrifice themselves for the common good, prove itself worthy of the august destiny to which it is called.

Signed on Behalf of the Provisional Government,

THOMAS J. CLARKE,
SEAN Mac DIARMADA. THOMAS MacDONAGH.
P. H. PEARSE. EAMONN CEANNT.
JAMES CONNOLLY. JOSEPH PLUNKETT.

Proclamation of the Republic of Ireland (Image courtesy of the National Library of Ireland)

elsewhere that boded to garner maximum attention by causing substantial human and property losses.

The Easter Rising of historic repute began Easter Monday morning, April 24, when residents of Dublin awoke to the chatter of machine gun fire. At the General Post Office building in the center of the main shopping district, 1,600 men of the Irish Volunteers and the Irish Citizens' army set up their headquarters. From the steps of the Post Office the proclamation of the Irish republic was read by Patrick Pearse. A scattered assortment of parks, factories, bridges, and public buildings were also seized and defended by small forces. Young women, members of the radically republican Cumann na nBan founded in April 1914 by Constance Markievicz to support the Irish Volunteers, acted as couriers for the rebels. Markievicz herself served as second in command at the rebels' garrison at St. Stephen's Green.

Troops began to be shipped from Britain, and martial law was imposed. Six days of death and devastation ensued. Heavy shelling reduced the rebels' strongholds one by one, the last to fall the position at Boland Mill's held by Eamon de Valera (1882–1975), a 1913 recruit to the Irish Volunteers. Pearse, as commander in chief, surrendered on April 29. The rebels counted only 64 killed against 132 British troops. Civilians fared the worst, suffering 318 killed and 2,217 wounded, in addition to enduring widespread looting, disruption of employment, and destruction of property in central Dublin.

The public responded initially with anger and disgust at the carnage caused by their countrymen. Women threw tomatoes at surrendering rebels. For its part, the British government, stirred to action by the unexpected uprising, moved swiftly in carrying out reprisals. Rebels were rounded up, and 15 ringleaders, including Pearse, were executed by firing squad. Because under martial law the British military could act without clearly defined powers or restrictions and because in a time of war the rising was seen as a vicious stab in the back perpetrated by traitors, the armed forces went further. Arrested indiscriminately, several thousand people of all political persuasions were incarcerated, many without any connections to the conspiracy.

The effect on public opinion was electric, the government's actions ironically achieving the effects the insurgents had so eagerly, and vainly, sought. The movement toward Anglo-Irish reconciliation so steadily in evidence by the prewar Home Rule campaign and wartime conditions now evaporated.

Aware that it had gone too far, the government of Prime Minister Asquith pulled back, stopping further executions, releasing those

Damage in Dublin after the Easter Rising. At right is the O'Connell bridge with the O'Connell monument, at left, and the ruined area around the Eden quay. (AP Images)

interned, and relaxing martial law before its scheduled abrogation in November. But it was too late. Segments of the public previously indifferent to appeals by republicans now made common cause with their brand of nationalism—the ideals of the rebels standing in stark contrast to the realities of a government so ready to persecute Irish nationalists no matter their persuasions. Revolution remained a distinct possibility, and the new coalition government with the Conservatives led by Liberal David Lloyd George (1863–1945) launched negotiations to secure an amended Home Rule settlement under which only six Ulster counties would be excluded from rule by Dublin and for only the duration of the war. The agreement collapsed in face of recalcitrance from some, though not all, among the unionist camp. The deal's demise also led to the definitive end of the Irish Parliamentary Party, Redmond and his legislative cohorts vilified for acquiescing in possible partition, however temporary.

Exasperated, the government gave up the search for a solution while the war still raged. For the republican rebels, defeat did not, as it had so often in the past, lead to renewed efforts for a repeat of the armed struggle. Arguing that another rising, however much tradition dictated that one should be attempted, would lead only to another failure, they affirmed that efforts were better directed at waging a vigorous propaganda campaign aimed at building on the favorable public sentiment now aroused, both at home and abroad.

Insurrection and Independence, 1918–1922

Beginning in early 1917, Sinn Féin worked diligently over the next two years to mobilize popular support for the republican cause. By demonstrating Irish national sentiments the party hoped to win American support for Irish representation when the time came to call a peace conference to settle the worldwide conflict. Dubbed by some the "new" Sinn Féin, the party chose not to repeat armed attacks but rather to use electoral contests as the battleground on which to give convincing proof of republicanism's appeal. However, in keeping with the party's policy, candidates for office pledged to refrain from taking up their parliamentary seats. From February 1917 until the end of the war in November 1918, Sinn Féin candidates won six of seven by-elections in contests in southern counties. In July 1917 Eamon de Valera won the seat for East Clare. In October he was elected president, with Griffith vice president, of Sinn Féin at the party's 10th conference, when a unified organization emerged from what hitherto had been a loose coalition of often quarreling dissidents and when the party formally announced its aim to have Ireland recognized as "an independent republic."

While Sinn Féin firmed up its political base, the IRB, despite the execution of every member of its military council, was reconstructed, largely through the efforts of Michael Collins (1890–1922). Collins, a former London clerk from County Cork, fought in the Easter Rising and was briefly interned. Collins also played a crucial role in the new national executive of the Irish Volunteers, set up in October 1917, as well as on its general headquarters staff in March 1918. The Volunteers remained on defensive alert, ready to rise when the call was given, drilling, parading, and challenging military and judicial authorities while taking care always to refrain from attacking soldiers or police.

The prospect of an insurrection seemed likely when Prime Minister Lloyd George, prompted by panic-stricken generals eager to fill depleted ranks with which to face a renewed German offensive on the war's western front in March 1918, rushed through legislation in April to introduce conscription to Ireland. Home Rule MPs withdrew from

Parliament in protest, and Sinn Féin organized mass opposition. With the backing of the Catholic Church, on April 21 thousands signed a "solemn council pledge" outside churches to resist conscription, followed two days later by a one-day work stoppage. In May the lord lieutenant and supreme commander of the British army in Ireland, John French (Lord French, 1852–1925), arrested Sinn Féin leaders on grounds of a spurious German plot, but acknowledging the extent of opposition, he introduced a quota scheme for voluntary recruitment as an alternative to the hated conscription. The armistice signed in France on November 11 made the entire issue moot.

The conscription threat and Sinn Féin's resolute resistance to it sealed its appeal. The party's presence spread to counties where it had hitherto secured no representation. At the general election of December 24–28, 1918, Sinn Féin swept to victory, claiming 73 out of 106 seats (although 25 victories were in uncontested constituencies) and 48 percent of votes cast—65 percent in southern counties—versus only six seats and 23 percent of votes for Redmond's Irish Parliamentary Party, effectively destroying the Home Rule constitutional nationalists. Although Ireland's largest political party for 40 years, it had not fought a general election since 1910, and its organizational structure had become decrepit in many areas of the country. Shorn of the superlative leadership abilities of Parnell, it had never succeeded in winning the support of the Gaelic League, the IRB, or Sinn Féin.

The Sinn Féin winners were largely young, Catholic, and from the lower middle class, and they included several women, among them Constance Markievicz. Extension of the suffrage in 1918 to all males age 21 and over and females age 30 and over, together with party membership that stood at more than a quarter million, meant that Sinn Féin's electoral success was based on massive, widespread support. In local elections in January 1920, it took 172 seats of the 206 county and city council posts.

Because they were pledged not to take their seats at Westminster, Sinn Féin's newly elected parliamentarians met on January 21, 1919, at the Mansion House, Dublin, where they constituted themselves the first Dáil Éireann—the parliament of Ireland—and declared independence from Britain. Cathal Brugha (1874–1922), an activist from Dublin, was appointed the first acting president, succeeded on April 1 by Eamon de Valera, who quickly dominated affairs. Initially used as a propaganda tool in constituting the visible incarnation of the Irish nation, the Dáil sought to mobilize support for Irish independence abroad. To that effect, de Valera toured the United States for 18 months beginning in June 1919 as "president of the Irish Republic." He raised millions of (U.S.) dollars in support of self-determination, the doctrine that free peoples had the right to rule themselves newly popularized by President Woodrow Wilson (1856–1923) as one among his Fourteen Points, which he hoped would serve as a basis for settlement of World War I.

De Valera's status was increasingly matched by Michael Collins's. Collins became minister for finance when the Dáil was established and, from mid 1919, president of the Supreme Council of the IRB, which, in making him a potential rival to de Valera, highlighted the growing division of authority in the country. Sinn Féin's reach spread throughout 1919, and by summer 1920 the civil authority in many rural areas was effectively subservient to it while it also strengthened its presence in urban areas. The Dáil began the task of setting up new governing institutions, and ministries paralleling those of the official government were put in place. A successful candidate in the 1918 elections, Countess Markievicz was appointed minister of labor, the first woman cabinet member in western Europe.

The gains registered by the republicans did not proceed without a prompt counter-response by unionists. The end of the war saw Protestants resume their prewar opposition to Irish nationalists, but sentiment now swung increasingly toward acceptance by northern unionists of a partition of the country. Convinced that "Home Rule is Rome rule," they believed that a totally separate state was preferable to government under a parliament in Dublin in which they would always be in the minority, their religion, economic interests, and cherished heritage as proud defenders of a British connection forever endangered. In contrast, many Protestants in southern Ireland, long accustomed to life as a minority of less than a 10th of the population, worked strenuously to conciliate the Catholic majority in their midst. They preferred living in a united, self-governing Ireland to residing on an island divided, and so Protestants here proffered proposals to obtain dominion status for Ireland on the model of that obtained in Canada, namely, full self-government in domestic affairs while leaving London in control of foreign relations. In the end, their efforts proved unsuccessful.

In Ulster, diehards revived the Ulster Volunteer Force in June 1920 and hunkered down, determined to maintain a compact, Protestant-dominated state in the North, their resolve made even more resolute in the face of growing opposition by the Catholic minority among them.

Adding to sectarian tensions, labor and agrarian conflict appeared as potential threats after 1917 in the wake of increased trade union

membership and rising unemployment. ITGWU affiliation soared to
about 100,000 by 1920. Strike activities spread from cities to smaller
towns and included not only skilled but also unskilled workers, while
unrest in the countryside emerged when agricultural prices began to

fall as postwar markets opened up once more. By late 1920 civilian unemployment exceeded prewar figures and wages fell, sparking the rise of scattered local "soviets," councils of workers who took over management of industries, so-called after the model that had proved so successful in Russia.

Outside of Ulster, however, labor unrest was too localized and too dispersed to generate any significant threat to the authorities, especially after the defeat of the Dublin lockout in January 1914. Republican leaders began building close, though informal, ties with the Irish Labour Party, founded in 1912 in Clonmel, thus linking labor's grievances to the nationalist cause, a link made evident in a general workers' shutdown called in solidarity with republican hunger strikers in mid April 1920.

In the North, where industry constituted a substantial segment of the economy, a postwar recession worsened unemployment. However, as before the war, economic hardships sparked not labor-management strife but rather sectarian conflict. Under the direction of the Ulster Unionist Labour Association, founded in June 1918, Catholic workers were again expelled from factories and shipyards. Catholics retreated but not without a fight, and riots in Belfast from July to September 1920 led to some 30 deaths.

The status of Ulster constituted the central sticking point to securing a settlement in Ireland just as it had in the immediate prewar period. Lloyd George's second coalition ministry resolved to find a solution to head off growing unionist and nationalist military buildups and the mayhem that by now had become widespread. In February 1920 his government introduced a bill calling for creation of two devolved parliaments in Dublin and Belfast. The Ulster Unionist Council accepted this arrangement in March, and the bill passed into law as the Government of Ireland Act on December 23, 1920. Under the act, executive authority would be vested in the Crown, exercised by a lord lieutenant as chief executive of both Home Rule states. A Council of Ireland would coordinate issues of common concern to the two parliaments, both of which could vote powers to the council, which it was hoped would evolve into a single parliament for all Ireland within 50 years. Both the North and the South would continue to send MPs to the Westminster parliament.

While the parliamentarians parlayed, the government continued to send mixed messages, talking with republican leaders in secret and hinting that the plan was negotiable. At the same time, the administration in Dublin Castle continued to consider a Home Rule scheme for all Ireland under a dominion regime.

Throughout these months as possible political solutions were being bandied about, Ireland slid inexorably into chaos. The Dáil carried on its deliberations, conducting business as a fully functioning government and imposing, on August 20, 1919, an oath of allegiance to the Irish Republic on its members and on the Irish Volunteers. The Volunteers emerged at the end of the war as small, parochial military companies, often without weapons, that, until spring 1920, carried out acts limited to arson, arms raiding, intimidation, and ostracization. Imposition of the oath marked an attempt by the central authorities to beef up their control, and the Irish Volunteers became the Irish Republican Army (IRA), the official army of the republic. At its general headquarters, commanders of the IRA strove to implement a nationwide strategy, which included, most essentially, feverish efforts to import arms.

On September 7 Volunteers openly attacked British army soldiers at Fermoy, County Cork, launching, in effect, an all-out war for independence. On September 12, prompted by the oath of allegiance demanded by the Dáil, the British administration declared the legislature to be an illegal assembly. A campaign of increasingly harsh repression was started. Massive internments forced armed republicans to band more closely together and to go on the run to avoid arrest. They commenced to coalesce into "flying columns" that would strike fast, hit hard, and disappear quickly. The British authorities met the challenge by strengthening their armed forces, compelling republican guerrillas to switch to small-scale attacks that amounted essentially to sniping and murdering of informers.

With de Valera abroad for much of the time, Collins assumed de facto leadership of the armed resistance. His position as president of the IRB, which included among its members leading IRA figures and representatives in the Dáil, gave him considerable prestige while his implementation of successful guerrilla and espionage tactics against the British earned for him legendary status, a status enhanced as a man especially wanted by the British.

Driven by sectarian passions, the "Troubles"—the name the people euphemistically called the conflict—proved especially inflamed because much of the savagery enacted against republicans could be traced not to the regular army but rather to local police forces, namely, the Royal Irish Constabulary (RIC) and, most especially, its branch reinforcements. These latter included both ex-British army regular soldiers, whom locals dubbed "Black and Tans" for their uniforms of dark green or black caps and khaki tunics, and ex-British army officers grouped as Auxiliaries (Auxies). Brutalized by the horrific conditions endured in the world war only recently ended, these recruits proved ruthless in waging war against Irish insurrectionists.

Local authorities chose sides in an atmosphere of raids and ambushes that swept the countryside. On November 21, 1920, a war of reprisals climaxed when, following the assassination of 14 suspected spies for British intelligence by the IRA, Black and Tans opened fire indiscriminately during a football match at Croke Park, Dublin, killing 12 spectators—many dying in the ensuing stampede—in an outrage thereafter remembered as "Bloody Sunday." On November 28 an 18-man Auxiliary patrol was slaughtered by an IRA flying column at Kilmichael, County Cork. In reprisal, the parish priest of Dunmanway was murdered. On December 11–12 the central business district of Cork was sacked by Black and Tans. In Ulster Catholics lived in abject fear of part-time Protestant police officers serving in the "B Specials." The Specials formed one division in a tripartite police force—the Ulster Special Constabulary—set up to back the RIC in its fight against the IRA, and they were given free rein to roam the province "enforcing" order as they saw fit.

Martial law was imposed on December 10, 1920, in the most disturbed southern and western counties and later elsewhere, but the police, military, and IRA intruded increasingly into civilian life everywhere. The IRA raided police barracks and staged demonstrations. They destroyed the Custom House, Dublin's peerless showcase of Georgian architecture, on May 25, 1921. Government forces searched and burned homes and businesses. Both sides ambushed and assassinated opponents and their suspected sympathizers.

The tit-for-tat turmoil elicited mounting anger in Ireland as well as in Britain and the United States. Influential protest groups appeared, such as the Peace with Ireland Council, that worked with British politicians to pursue a settlement. A combination of international protests and military stalemate led to a suspension of hostilities on July 9, 1921, when representatives of the British army in Ireland and the IRA signed a truce.

In the midst of the mayhem, the Government of Ireland Act of 1920 had mandated parliamentary elections for separate bicameral legislatures in the North and the South. The act defined Northern Ireland to include "the parliamentary counties of Antrim, Armagh, Down, Fermanagh, Londonderry, and Tyrone, and the parliamentary boroughs of Belfast and Londonderry." Duly held on May 21, 1921, elections in the North returned 40 unionists, 6 nationalists, and 6 Sinn Féin supporters, the results inaugurating, in effect, a one-party unionist state. A

Northern Ireland House of Commons to govern this area met on June 7, 1921, and a cabinet was appointed with James Craig (1871–1940) as prime minister. The parliament was inaugurated with appropriate pageantry in Belfast City Hall by King George V on June 22.

In the 26 counties in the South, Sinn Féin ran unopposed and triumphed in all but 4 of the 124 seats. Only the four non–Sinn Féiners and 15 appointed senators showed up for the state opening of the southern parliament in June, Sinn Féin members boycotting it as an illegal body, all of them supporters of the Dáil already assembled. The parliament was then suspended. The 1920 act stipulated that southern Ireland was to become a crown colony under martial law, should the parliament fail to meet by July 12. The truce in the fighting went into effect on July 11, and in August the Sinn Féin MPs elected to the southern parliament declared themselves to be Dáil deputies (Teachtaí [sing. Teachta] Dála, TDs). They subsequently convened in the Mansion House with the four non–Sinn Féiners as the second Dáil Éireann, and the assembly confirmed de Valera as president. The killing largely ended while the Dáil oversaw the continued rebuilding of the government's administrative infrastructure. Responding to the virtual breakdown of authority during the months of fighting, local republican organizers took the initiative in setting up institutions modeled on those of the official bodies. The Dáil promulgated a uniform system of civil and criminal courts, tax collection, and local government for the country.

Faced with the distasteful alternative of colonial rule by martial law, Prime Minister Lloyd George let it be known that all options were open for a definitive settlement of the country's political arrangement. On July 14, 1921, he met with de Valera, and two months later a bilateral conference convened in London between representatives of Britain and "Ireland," although delegates from Northern Ireland declined to attend. Lloyd George proposed dominion status in place of Home Rule. De Valera offered "external association," whereby an independent republican Ireland would acknowledge the monarch as head of the British Commonwealth with which Dublin would be linked for certain vaguely stated issues of common concern. Irish negotiators led by Arthur Griffith and Michael Collins thrashed out details and succeeded in winning for their government considerable concessions concerning powers over taxation, tariffs, and national and civil defense, though Irish naval bases were to be retained by Britain and harbor and other facilities were made available should London need them for defensive purposes.

Arthur Griffith and Irish republican sympathizers in London for the Irish-British peace confer-ence, October 1921 (Library of Congress, LC-USZ62-134330)

Under the terms of a draft treaty, signed in London on December 6, 1921, an "Irish Free State" (Saorstát Éireann) would be created. It would not be a republic; rather, it would be a constitutional monarchy with a two-house parliament, given independent powers in matters domestic and foreign. In a dominionlike format, executive authority was vested in the British monarch, represented in Dublin by a governor-general. An oath of allegiance both to the Free State and to the monarch was required to be taken of all members of parliament. The second oath amounted to an indirect vow of fidelity in being given to the king *in* Ireland in reference explicitly to his role as the personification of a con-stituent element of the treaty settlement and not to his status as ruler of a united kingdom. The terms of the oath, largely the work of Collins, were vague enough to satisfy the Irish negotiating team, who found it a tolerable basis on which future progress toward full, unfettered inde-pendence could proceed.

Debate on the draft treaty in the Dáil centered on the controversial oath. De Valera and several ministers vehemently objected to any expres-sion, however symbolic, of loyalty to a British monarch. On January 7,

1922, after 10 days of vigorous debate, the Anglo-Irish Treaty narrowly passed by a vote of 64 to 57. To comply with constitutional norms, the treaty required approval by the parliament of Southern Ireland elected the previous June, the British never having recognized the revolutionary assembly, the Dáil Éireann. The parliament of Southern Ireland thus duly met, on January 14, approved the treaty and elected, as required by that document, a Provisional Government of Ireland charged with accepting the transfer of power from the British government and drafting and approving a constitution for the new state. Michael Collins was selected as the chairman of the Provisional Government. On January 16 Collins received the handover of Dublin Castle from Ireland's last lord lieutenant, Edward Fitzalan-Howard (1855–1947), who had been appointed in April 1921, the first Roman Catholic to hold the post since 1685. Although no proof exists that, on being informed by an impatient Fitzalan-Howard that he was seven minutes late for the ceremony, Collins allegedly replied: "We've been waiting 700 years," the riposte seems a fitting one for so historic an occasion. An act of great symbolic and substantive significance, the transfer of power made vividly real to the average man and woman that political change had truly come.

The legislative union that had engendered so much dissension for more than a century had been dissolved, but the ruling arrangement replacing it was one that none of the protagonists of either the recent or the distant past could have envisaged. An independent republic for all Ireland did not emerge, nor an islandwide constitutional monarchy under British rule. Two separate governments would rule—one in the North and one in the South, both based on parliamentary formats. It was a compromise solution that, given the impassioned atmosphere in which it was reached, was about the best that could be expected; but, because it was a compromise, it was one that left many disappointed. No settlement would have satisfied everyone in an Ireland that had been wracked so strongly by unshakable sentiments, which had suffered for so long under remembered injustices. The turmoil that marked the birth of Ireland's modern political map did not dissipate with the creation of two Irish states. In the South, the resort to force would not abate until the outcome of a bitter civil war settled the lingering division over the governing structure of the new state. In the North, the call to arms subsided, although its appeal remained very much alive. It is a call not entirely absent even today.

9

MAKING MODERN IRELAND (1922–1969)

On January 10, 1922, for the first time in two years, the gates at Dublin Castle stood open and soldiers busied themselves removing the barbed wire strung during the insurrection now ended. British authorities prepared to put a final end to 750 years of colonial rule in Ireland. On the following Sunday, a British civil servant recorded in his diary: "History alone will show whether we have done good work for Ireland. . . . It is clearly now up to Ireland to make a success of it or not" (Sturgis 1999, 224).

It was not, however, a single Ireland but, rather, two separate Irelands that now set out to shape their destinies. The Anglo-Irish Treaty was intended as a dexterous compromise designed to give all parties in Ireland something of what they wanted but none of them all that they had fought for. Partition proved to be the practical solution reflecting the reality that existed in the country following the war for independence. The six counties comprising the enclave of Northern Ireland, with a majority of Protestants on an overwhelmingly Catholic island and with an industrial- rather than a rural-based economy, had long stood apart from the rest of Ireland, its minority population militant in defense of its identity.

The 26 counties to the south, in becoming a dominion within the British Empire as the Irish Free State, were granted far more freedom than Home Rule had promised, but not enough for some. Republicans who were unreconciled to keeping any ties to the United Kingdom launched a brief but bloody civil war that left them sullen in defeat.

The Free State, having triumphed, settled down, despite its rhetoric to the contrary, to de facto recognition of a two-state Ireland. Shorn of the implacably hostile North, the new nation was left at liberty to set about securing its still shaky existence. That security was assured when republicans who had lost the civil war, led by Eamon de Valera, relented in their opposition and entered the political fray.

246

His Fianna Fáil political party in power for most of the period from the 1930s through the 1960s, de Valera engineered a new constitution by which, under a new name—Éire—republicans achieved in large measure their goal of a government unfettered by any links to London. Cherishing a backward-looking, conservative image of Ireland rooted in a rural, peasant-based way of life—an image cast to contrast with urban, globally committed Great Britain—de Valera promoted the creation of an insular, self-sufficient society, thoroughly Catholic in culture and conscience.

But contradictions abounded between de Valera's vision and the realities—economic, political, and cultural—that put limits on the ability to fully implement his concepts. Economically stagnant and having continued to steadily lose people to emigration in the 1920s and 1930s, the country remained neutral during the "Emergency," the word used to refer to the period of World War II. The people of Éire watched on the sidelines while Northern Ireland, bombed and battle-tested, joined with all its resolve and resources in the fight that brought victory to the Allied cause.

Northern Ireland prospered in the postwar years, putting in place a comprehensive welfare state. Adopting its long-sought title in 1949, the now officially named Republic of Ireland, in contrast, struggled to grow its economy. Only with the end of de Valera's rule did new administrations, starting in the 1960s, launch more progressive policies that moved the country toward greater riches. By then, a modern consumer society started to take hold, gradually changing conservative cultural and social outlooks and weakening even the Catholic Church's hitherto solid grip on Irish life.

The Irish were everywhere progressing in the mid 1960s except for the Catholic nationalist minority in the North. The big losers at the time of partition, their minority status locked into the system, Catholics chafed under the de facto ghetto to which they had been confined. Protestant Unionists stood as resolved as ever to keep them there. Discord between the two waxed and waned in intensity over the years, but violent confrontation remained an ever-present possibility. By the end of the 1960s, tensions had mounted to a fever pitch.

Partition in Place in the North, 1920–1923

The Anglo-Irish Treaty of 1921 did not enable partition to take place. Partition had, in fact, preceded the pact, the machinery of a separate Northern Ireland state gradually put in place in 1920. It was done with the active connivance of northern unionists, anxious to secure their base, and the passive indifference of southern nationalists, preoccupied with consolidating their supremacy where it existed and confident that a northern state would prove ultimately unsustainable. In practice, partition appealed therefore to every party but one, the beleaguered Catholics in the North, who, condemned to a minority status in the new state, would become known as nationalists or republicans, namely, those who support an independent, republican Ireland of all 32 counties.

To ensure that Catholics remained permanently in the minority, Ulster unionists insisted on, and won agreement to, a territorial unit made up of the six Ulster counties that together contained a heavily weighted Protestant majority in place of a nine-county Ulster sought by the British government, which hoped that a more religiously balanced state would facilitate eventual reunification.

Under the provisions of the Government of Ireland Act of 1920, northern unionists had elected a parliament, and a fully functioning government existed by the time the Anglo-Irish Treaty was adopted. The treaty applied to all Ireland, but Northern Ireland was given the option to opt out, which it promptly did, on December 7, 1922, the day after the act ratifying the Free State constitution entered the British statute book.

A parliament consisting of the sovereign, a House of Commons, and a Senate constituted the institutions of central government of the constituent unit of the now titled United Kingdom of Great Britain and Northern Ireland. The Senate was given modest powers to amend legislation, while the Commons held power to pass laws on major domestic concerns, with no competence in foreign, imperial, or military matters. It could not make laws aimed at religious discrimination nor could it repeal or alter any existing U.K. statute. A governor for Northern Ireland was appointed with powers to summon, prorogue, and dissolve parliament and to give or withhold the royal assent to bills. Northern Ireland electors sent 13 representatives to the Parliament in London.

The new government erected a formidable, and enduring, state apparatus that aimed to entrench Protestant unionist supremacy. The Ulster Unionist Party (UUP) became the political instrument of control. Considering the compromise solution of partition to be a defeat for his cause, party leader Sir Edward Carson refused the new post of prime minister, and leadership of the party, and that of Northern Ireland, passed to Belfast-born industrialist Sir James Craig (1871–1940), created Viscount Craigavon in 1927. Born in an atmosphere of intense sectarian strife, dissension tore through the North during the years 1920–22. Riots in Londonderry and Belfast occurred regularly. In 1922 alone, 232 people, including two unionist MPs, perished. Twice as many Catholics as Protestants were killed, the casualties condoned and often inflicted by the B Specials. By comparison, Catholic organized action was feeble. The IRA, declared an illegal organization on May 23, 1922, remained small and ineffective in the North.

The government strove hard to impose order. Under provisions of the Civil Authorities (Special Powers) Act of April 1922, the state availed itself of powers of internment, banishment, and summary justice. Relying in part on the British army, it also established a regular police force with creation in May 1922 of the Royal Ulster Constabulary (RUC), the successor to the Royal Irish Constabulary. And because sectarian fraternities such as the Orange Order were strongly in place, the government found itself readily relying on the ability of these Protestant loyalists to mobilize their political and physical forces in its support.

Catholics themselves indirectly helped the government's efforts by abstaining from participation in state institutions. Police quotas of one-third of posts reserved for Catholics remained unfilled. The Nationalist Party, the remnant of the old Irish Parliamentary Party in Ulster, had allied with Sinn Féin to fight the May 21, 1921, parliamentary elections, and they protested that balloting had taken place in an atmosphere of intimidation and violence. The pattern of election results that emerged in Northern Ireland generally saw 33 to 39 Unionists returned among the 52-seat House of Commons, with the rest divided among nationalists, northern Irish Labour Party members, and independents. Angry at a system they believed biased against them and fully expecting that islandwide reunion was imminent, nationalists who were elected to parliament boycotted sessions until 1925, and they participated only spottily in local government, which made it easier for unionists to redraw constituencies and annul proportional representation in favor of single-member districts, which facilitated their ability to retain control.

Several county councils and other local bodies of government that were under the control of nationalists and/or Sinn Féin likewise refused to recognize the Northern Ireland government, and in 1922 the latter moved to quash such recalcitrance in suspending their operations. The government went on to employ blatant gerrymandering to facilitate unionist domination of all local governments outside of areas where overwhelming nationalist and Catholic strength—largely in Fermanagh and Tyrone—made it impossible to do so. Such control opened the way to instituting discriminatory treatment in public affairs, from public employment hiring to the awarding of contracts and of various public benefits, most especially the grant of public housing.

Likewise, the franchise remained undemocratic. Long after restrictions had been dropped in Britain and the Republic of Ireland, the right to vote was limited to householders and their spouses. Adult children residing at home, boarders, live-in domestic servants, and others were disallowed; at the same time, business owners were permitted votes in more than one constituency. Though not aimed specifically to discriminate on the basis of religion, the voting laws disenfranchised disproportionately more Catholics than Protestants.

With creation of a Northern Ireland state, a new educational system was put in place consisting of schools financed entirely by the government, administered by local authorities, and in which religion was taught on a voluntary basis. This arrangement satisfied most Protestants. Catholics remained wary, and they continued to operate their own schools, which received state support.

Fearful and alienated, sheltering behind their church, fraternal societies, and socioeconomic groups, Catholics created their own highly defensive, insular world. Many northern Catholics in 1922 sustained the hope that partition would prove only temporary, a hope shared by many of their coreligionists in the South, who believed Northern Ireland could not survive without southern cooperation. Catholics took comfort in knowing the border had yet to be officially defined. Article 12 of the Anglo-Irish Treaty called for creation of a tripartite Boundary Commission, made up of officials from the Irish Free State, Northern Ireland, and the United Kingdom, charged with determining the island's political division "in accordance with the wishes of the inhabitants, so far as may be accomplished under economic and geographic conditions" (Anglo-Irish Treaty).

The provision of the 1921 treaty most deeply resented by Ulster unionists, Article 12 evoked fears of diminution of territory resulting from the Boundary Commission's rulings that could irrevocably weaken northern authority. Irish delegates to the 1921 treaty negotiations and many in the British cabinet expected the future commission would restore at least the counties of Tyrone and Fermanagh, where Catholics were in the majority, to the Free State. Belfast authorities dithered so as to delay creation of the commission, a delay facilitated by a political power vacuum in Britain occasioned by the fall of the government in October 1923. The unionists thus won time to shore up their strength and make minimum concessions to minority wishes. The breathing space afforded the ruling powers in the North was occasioned also, in part, by the outbreak of civil war in the South.

Civil War in the South, 1922–1923

The Anglo-Irish Treaty that created the Irish Free State split Sinn Féin and its leaders between supporters and opponents of the agreement, launching a divide around which Irish politics would pivot for decades with echoes that would reverberate for much of the 20th century. Unity foundered over one central provision—the oath of allegiance to a British monarch. Acceptance of a constitutional monarchy, argued treaty backers, would give Ireland sufficient self-government from which it could then proceed to win, in time, full, unencumbered independence. Only the immediate realization of a republic, the type of government of which so many had dreamed and on behalf of which so many had died, would suffice, said opponents. Anti-treaty advocates were led by de Valera, who resigned as president of the Dáil after the document was ratified. The Dáil proceeded to elect, as its president, the pro-treaty Arthur Griffith. A cabinet was appointed, and Dáil meetings continued, although the Provisional Government under its chairman Michael Collins took on the important work of drafting a constitution. Griffith and Collins, as the treaty's major Irish negotiators, emerged as de Valera's greatest rivals.

The Provisional Government called a general election to ratify the Dáil's 64 to 57 vote in January 1922 to approve the treaty. At a party convention (*Ard-Fheis*) in February, Sinn Féin agreed to postpone a confrontation between pro- and anti-treaty factions pending the outcome of the election campaign. A bitterly fought political battle helped to coalesce sentiments for and against. In support of the treaty, Arthur Griffith affirmed: "It is the first Treaty between the representatives of the Irish government and the representatives of the English Government since 1172 signed on equal footing. We have brought back (from London) the flag; we have brought back the evacuation of Ireland after 700 years by British troops. . . . We have brought back to Ireland her full rights and powers of fiscal control." Eamon de Valera summarized the position of treaty opponents: "[T]he Treaty . . . gives away Irish independence; it brings us into the British Empire; it acknowledges the head of the British Empire, not merely as the head of an association, but as the direct monarch of Ireland, as the source of executive authority in Ireland" (McLoughlin 1996; 90, 95–96).

The IRA showed no dispensation to debate. In an ominous move in March, an IRA military convention was dominated by anti-treaty partisans. Michael Collins, a key treaty negotiator, worked diligently to avert an open breach by crafting wording in the proposed Free State constitution republican enough to mollify the government's opponents,

Michael Collins (Library of Congress, LC-USZ62-104093)

wording to which, however, the British objected. On June 16, in elections for a third Dáil Éireann, voters approved the pro-treaty position.

The election had been fought in a country just taking shape, still in the process of setting up the machinery of state. The Provisional Government controlled no effective army, police force, or court system. It existed largely as a decentralized administration still staffed mostly by civil servants from the former British regime. The elimination of the threat posed by the common British enemy, together with the weakness of state authority, made it easy for election losers to choose violence as the means by which to achieve what they had failed to win at the ballot box.

Factions within the IRA and the Dáil, each uneasy at the power wielded by the other, grew more mutually menacing. Just as Sinn Féin had split over the treaty's terms, so, too, the IRA had divided. The "Old IRA," whose members were soon incorporated into the Free State army, backed the pro-treaty government, whereas uncompromising republicans, the "Irregulars" or the "Executive," denounced the treaty and renounced allegiance to the Dáil on the grounds that, by accepting the document, it had betrayed the republic. The Irish Republican Brotherhood also split. Military and social anarchy appeared to be a distinct possibility.

In April 1922 the Free State army confronted a direct challenge to the Provisional Government's authority when IRA Irregulars occupied Dublin's judicial center, the Four Courts building, and refused to vacate, demanding that rule be transferred to them. For two months, neither side launched an assault but kept to an uneasy face-off while the politicians wrangled over issues surrounding the draft of a new constitution. On June 22 retired field marshal Henry Wilson (1864–1922) was assassinated by IRA Irregulars, which prompted London to put increased pressure on the Provisional Government to take firm action against the treaty opponents. On June 28 the Free State forces stormed the Four Courts building using artillery bought from the British. They recaptured the ground on June 30. For the third time in eight years, Dublin was convulsed in violence.

Activists quickly lined up on either side. A broad, anti-treaty republican front evolved, uniting politicians such as de Valera and independent IRA units. Civil war spread over the country, breaking out even in areas that had remained untouched in the Anglo-Irish war of 1919–20. The fighting proved ruthlessly brutal. The government secured control of Dublin during the first two weeks, capturing major anti-treaty leaders. Cathal Brugha was fatally wounded when he refused to surrender. By midsummer, the government forces held all the major cities, and the Irregulars confined their military operations to Munster, especially the counties of Kerry, Cork, and Tipperary. Defeated there after three months, they switched tactics, reverting to countryside sniping and assassinations. Seeking to destabilize the country, they declared the Free State government, police, and courts illegal, and they began to shoot on sight Dáil TD's, judges, ex-British army soldiers, and even journalists. The government suffered its most prominent loss when Michael Collins was gunned down in an ambush at Béal na Bláth, County Cork, not far from his birthplace, on August 22. The death of Arthur Griffith 10 days earlier led the Dáil to elect, on September 9, William T. Cosgrave (1880–1965) as its president and head of the Provisional Government. Born in Dublin, Cosgrave had been elected to the Dublin City Council as a Sinn Féin member in 1909, had fought in the Easter Rising, and had served as minister of local government in Collins's Provisional Government. In March 1923 he would go on to found his own political vehicle, Cumann na nGaedheal, as a party in support of the treaty.

Stung by the breathtaking boldness of their republican opponents, the Provisional Government struck back. Authorities executed 77 arrested Irregulars, without trial, in November 1922 and imprisoned about 12,000, leaving a legacy of bitterness among many.

Fighting republican rebels, the government at the same time faced threats of unrest from other quarters. Agrarian discontent simmered in the immediate postwar period after the curtailment of land purchase schemes and despite much real estate redistribution after 1919. Farm owners formed the Irish Farmers' Union to oppose rural laborers, angry over threats of wage cuts. Laborers struck in Meath in 1919, their ranks swollen by returning servicemen, and major confrontations between the union and workers broke out in Waterford in 1921–23.

Industrial labor, too, posed a potential menace. Although labor had to a considerable degree been recruited as an ally of Sinn Féin in the nationalist struggle, politicians grew increasingly apprehensive at the degree of militancy demonstrated by urban workers. Membership in the ITGWU mushroomed during the war. Organized labor's strength was reflected in politics. In 1922, 17 of 18 Labour Party candidates were returned, the party winning 21.4 percent of votes cast, more than the anti-treaty forces.

Both sides in the civil war professed an anti-labor, rural-based conservative nationalism. By 1922 IRA cadres were being used in some areas as strikebreakers, protecting nonunion workers and enforcing rent agreements on behalf of farm owners. The long and bitter strike in Waterford ended in late 1923, won by the farmers with support from the Free State army.

By then the pro-treaty side had won the civil war. Military resistance by the Irregulars collapsed after the death of the republican commander Liam Lynch (1893–1923), shot on April 10, 1923, by Provisional Government forces while preparing to reach a settlement. On May 24, de Valera, president of the revolutionary government that was set up to legitimize the republican side, instructed remaining followers to put down their arms. The end of the fighting left the supporters of a constitutional monarchy free to create an Irish state in their image.

Irish Free State to Éire, 1923–1939

While the government waged the military campaign against the IRA Irregulars, a bill approving the constitution of the 26 counties comprising the Irish Free State was passed by the Dáil on October 25, 1922, and by the British parliament in December. A constitutional monarchy was set up with a three-tiered parliament (Oireachtas) composed of the monarch and a two-body legislature—the lower house, the Chamber of Deputies (Dáil Éireann), the chief legislative body, and the upper house, Senate (Seanad Éireann). The Senate was conceived as a body of elders who could advise the popularly elected lower house, but it could only delay passage of legislation. It was elected by the lower house, except for one-quarter of members nominated by the government. The upper house was intended to ensure a voice for the Protestant minority in the Free State, whose participation was deemed essential in giving credence to the state's claim to rule islandwide. Executive authority was vested in the king, represented by a governor-general (Seanascal), who was appointed by the monarch on the advice of the British government, and executive authority was exercised by a cabinet called the Executive Council, presided over by a prime minister called the president of the Executive Council. Organized in 1924, the legal system—district and circuit courts, high court, court of criminal appeal, and supreme court—followed the model long in place under direct British rule. British police and military forces had speedily departed—all but the Dublin garrison were gone by May 1922. On August 8, 1923, a national police force, the Civic Guard (Garda Síochána, "Guardians of the Peace") was founded, to which the Dublin Metropolitan Police were incorporated in 1925. Irish place-names were restored—Queenstown (renamed in 1849) reverted to Cobh (originally the "Cove of Cork")—or were introduced—King's County became County Offaly and Queen's County became County Laois (Laoighis, Leix) with Maryborough renamed Portlaoise (Portlaoighise). A new currency, the Free State pound, pegged to the British pound sterling, was introduced in 1928. The symbols of sovereignty—a national flag and seal—were adopted.

The constitution mandated that an election be held within a year after the approval of the document. Balloting for a fourth Dáil Éireann at the end of August 1923 led to the governing party—Cumann na nGaedhael—winning the largest number of seats, 66, but only a plurality in a Dáil enlarged to 153 members. Sinn Féin won 44, but because the party had not recognized the legitimacy of the third Dáil, it likewise refused to acknowledge that of its successor, and for the rest of the decade Sinn Féin members who won elections abstained from legislative participation, leaving the country to be governed as a one-party state.

The early work of nation-building thus lay entirely with Cumann na nGaedheal, the party founded in support of the Anglo-Irish treaty, under William Cosgrave as president of the Executive Council. Civil war and military issues demanded the immediate attention of the new government. More than 10,000 prisoners interned during the recent fighting were released by summer 1924, and the National Army, swollen to tens of thousands recruited during the civil war, demobilized. Veteran officers of the war of independence, fearful they would be let go in favor of professionals with British army experience and angry at the government for having failed to more vigorously oppose partition, mutinied in early March 1924, which the government vigorously suppressed.

Irish regimes throughout the 1920s and 1930s strove to give the country a defining identity as a uniquely Irish state, which meant,

THE IRISH FLAG AND HARP

The national flag of Ireland (in Irish, *An Bhratach Náisiúnta*) is a vertical tricolor of green (at the hoist), white, and orange stripes of equal size. Green and orange are the colors traditionally associated with the island's Gaelic and English heritages, respectively, while white signifies lasting peace between these two cultures, whose relationships have been marked by so much conflict.

A green flag featuring a harp dates to at least the 16th century. Green was widely adopted as the color of choice by the United Irishmen in the 1798 rising. Orange dates to 1688 and the "Glorious Revolution" that placed William of Orange of the House of Orange-Nassau in the Netherlands together with his English wife, Mary, on the English throne. William's successful campaign to keep Protestants in power in Ireland led coreligionists on the island to adopt the color as their identifying hue, which they have retained ever since.

The oldest known use of green, white, and orange as a national banner dates to September 1830 when tricolor cockades were worn by those celebrating the successful revolution that year in France, where victors reintroduced the tricolor adopted during the French Revolution of 1789.

Young Irelanders favored the banner in 1848, but until independence in 1922 it was not widely used—the green flag with a harp preferred by the rebels at Easter 1916. Although recognized in 1922 and flown in the Irish Free State, it was not until enactment of the 1937 constitution that the flag was made the nation's official banner.

The harp was chosen as the state emblem on establishment of the Irish Free State, and an image of the harp appeared in the new country's Great Seal. A gold harp with silver strings on a blue background serves as the coat of arms of the Republic of Ireland today. The flag of the pres-

above all, distancing the new nation from the United Kingdom. Governments chipped away at links with London. In the 1920s efforts to weaken the tie focused on the imperial connection. The government from the beginning interpreted the Anglo-Irish Treaty as an international agreement between equals. The Free State joined the League of Nations in 1923, registering the treaty with the league as an international document over the objections of the British government, which considered it an internal pact between the dominion and the United

ident of Ireland today features a harp, and the British royal standard sports an Irish harp in its lower left quadrant. The harp has served as a symbol of Ireland since at least the 13th century. A harp appeared on coins issued by King Henry VIII. Euro coins today feature a harp.

Framed harps first appeared in medieval Europe in the eighth to the 10th centuries. Irish harpers were famed throughout Europe as early as the 12th century. The first harp to feature a hollow soundbox, which amplified the instrument's sound, appeared in Ireland in the 14th century. The oldest surviving Irish harp, dating to the late 14th century, is the Brian Boru harp, or the Trinity College harp.

Irish harp (Victoria & Albert Museum, London/Art Resource, NY)

Prior to 1700 harpists held prestige positions at the courts of Irish kings and chieftains, and they were often consulted before battles. After the breakup of Gaelic society, harpists became itinerant minstrels traveling to the homes of the aristocracy. After World War II the harp was used extensively in popular Irish entertainment, and in the late 1960s an Irish folk music revival gave a prominent place to the harp, which was used in a variety of playing styles and repertoires. Its sounds remain a characteristic feature of Irish music.

Kingdom. Unlike any other dominion, the Free State signed treaties and exchanged ambassadors with other nations. The British government lost the ability to influence domestic legislation when an agreement in 1927 gave to the Irish government alone the power to advise the king on whom to appoint to the position of governor-general.

The yearning to be free of Britain proved impossible, however, in the economic sphere, traditional close links to the large British market unbreakable in the absence of alternative trading partners and in the face of its neighbor's powerful currency. In 1924 approximately 98 percent of goods were exported to the United Kingdom.

At the start of independence, the industrial sector was small, made up largely of manufacturers in traditional sectors—textiles, food, and drink—producing almost exclusively for the home market. Partition skewered the agricultural and industrial character of both the North and the South more heavily in favor of the latter in Northern Ireland and the former in the Free State, where, in the mid 1930s, more than half of the employed population worked directly in the farming sector.

In the 1920s and early 1930s the government pursued a low-tax, low-spending economic policy. Trends in the rural economy in progress ever since the Great Famine—land purchase by small farmers, consolidation of medium and larger farms, growth in pasturage—continued in the 1920s. State-aided programs were initiated in livestock breeding and poultry farming, and an Agricultural Credit Corporation (1927) advanced capital to farmers; still, agricultural productivity remained woefully low by European standards. The state pursued a policy of limited intervention, priority given to maximizing farmers' incomes, considered a precondition to national prosperity. Some import tariffs were imposed to encourage home production, but the government feared high barriers would lead to higher wages for agricultural laborers, thus cutting into farmers' earnings. Social welfare measures such as unemployment benefits were spartan, partly because the government had limited financial resources available. Old age pensions constituted a heavy burden, and cuts were instituted in 1924. Only in the area of energy provision did the state intervene energetically. Under the state-run Electricity Supply Board, set up in July 1925, a hydroelectric scheme to harness the river Shannon put in place a state-of-the-art facility, the Ardnacrusha hydroelectric power station.

Under Cosgrave, real per capita income rose despite a cautious economic strategy that avoided heavy borrowing but that succeeded in balancing budgets, thanks in particular to remittances sent home after resumption of large-scale emigration. Radical change was shunned, local governments manned as late as the mid 1930s by a majority of personnel from the preindependent period and the national government run by highly centralized departments staffed by powerful, professional civil servants. The Department of Finance held the preeminent place, its elite status secured by its successful floating of the first national loan in 1923 and as the department to which all others submitted bills for approval before final drafting.

After years of turmoil, maintaining social and political stability became the central aim, a goal furthered by de Valera's decision to make accommodation with the ruling system. Ready to resume political participation, he seceded from Sinn Féin and launched a new party, Fianna Fáil ("Soldiers of Destiny") in Dublin on May 16, 1926. The party's subtitle, the "Republic Party," left no doubt as to the type of government its founder sought, though parliamentary participation would now be the means to its achievement. Breaking with many colleagues, who continued to deny the lawfulness of the constitution, and reinforced by financial assistance from the Irish-American community, he was able to build up a broad mass of support by articulating policies on a series of grievances, including unemployment, high rates of emigration, small farmers' demands, and republican (nationalist) dissatisfaction with the oath of allegiance, dominion status, and partition. In the June 1927 general elections, the party won 44 seats, a number exceeded only by the 47 won by Cumann na nGaedheal. In August he led the newly elected MPs into the Dáil to take the detested oath, although the deputies took care to let it be known that they viewed it as a meaningless gesture. Politics was at once transformed, a genuine opposition party now in parliament, and a two-party system, based on differing interpretations of republicanism, with roots traceable to the civil war, would emerge to henceforth characterize Irish politics.

Rattled by the assassination in July 1927 of Kevin O'Higgins (1892–1927), the powerful minister of justice, Cumann na nGaedheal struck at its increasingly popular political opponent in suggesting that the new party was a front organization for revolutionaries plotting to destroy the state. No evidence for the validity of such a claim proved forthcoming, however. De Valera became, in fact, a practicing democrat, content to use parliament as the avenue by which to win power. He did just that on February 16, 1931, when Fianna Fáil won the elections and formed its first government with support from the Labour Party, in existence since 1912 to advance the political interests of industrial workers. For the first time, former anti-treaty republicans were in control of the government.

The effect on Anglo-Irish relations was immediate. In place of Cosgrave's policy of reconciliation, de Valera, as president of the Executive Council and as minister of foreign affairs (a post he retained until 1948) proceeded not to abolish but rather to transform parliamentary forms by ingeniously manipulating the system, keeping his aim to undermine the Anglo-Irish Treaty always in mind. First the symbols and then the substance of dominion status were dismantled. In 1933 the oath of loyalty was voided. In 1936 he attempted to use the occasion of

EAMON DE VALERA

E amon de Valera (Edward George De Valera, Éamon de Bhailéara, October 14, 1882–August 29, 1975) was born in New York City to an Irish immigrant mother from County Limerick and a Spanish-Cuban settler and sculptor. Because no records have ever been found of their marriage, it is widely believed he was illegitimate.

Taken to Ireland at age two by an uncle, he was raised in his grandmother's home near Bruree in County Limerick. He attended Blackwood College, County Dublin, on a scholarship and taught mathematics first at Rockwell College, County Tipperary, where a colleague gave him the lifelong nickname of "Dev," and later at other schools.

Drawn to public affairs, in 1908 he joined the Gaelic League. In 1913 he enlisted in the Irish Volunteers. Court-martialed, convicted, and sentenced to death as a rebel leader in the Easter Rising, de Valera's life was saved by a combination of location (he was held in a different prison from other leading insurrectionists) and hesitation by the authorities, who were wary of executing a U.S.-born citizen.

Released in 1917, he was elected that year to the British House of Commons as a candidate of Sinn Féin and also as president of the party. On April 1, 1918, he was elected president of the first Dáil.

Opposed to the Anglo-Irish Treaty of 1921, he resigned from the Dáil when the treaty was approved. Interned during the civil

King Edward VIII's (r. 1935–36) abdication to abolish the governor-generalship and sever ties with the Crown, but warned by legal experts that it was impossible to remove these institutions by simple legislative fiat, he was forced to back down; instead, he opted for the External Relations Act, which reduced the role of the British monarch solely to that of accrediting Irish diplomatic representatives to foreign countries.

The Irish Free State now a republic in all but name, de Valera reached the summit of his ambitions when he introduced in 1937 a new Constitution of Ireland to replace that which he saw as imposed by the Anglo-Irish Treaty. Approved by the Dáil on June 14 and by the public in a referendum on July 1, the document declared the country's new name to be "Éire" (Irish for Ireland). The constitution provided for a directly elected ceremonial president, a prime minister (Taoiseach) as head of government, and a national parliament (Oireachtas) com-

war, de Valera returned to politics in May 1926 when he formed Fianna Fáil. Under the constitution of 1937, a work largely of his own creation, he became the country's first prime minister. He remained in office until stepping down to win elections as president in 1959 and 1966. He retired in 1973 and died two years later at age 92. He is buried in Glasnevin Cemetery, Dublin.

In politics for more than 50 years, the tall, thin, bespectacled de Valera emerged as Ireland's dominant political personality of the 20th century, a status attested to in his being known as the "chief" by

Eamon de Valera (Library of Congress, LC-USZ62-67820)

Irish citizens of all political stripes. A deeply pious man, de Valera sought to shape the country in his image as a Catholic, conservative nation rooted in the habits and outlook of its rural past. It was an image that, as he aged into his 80s, grew increasingly at odds with reality.

posed of a dominant, directly elected lower house (Dáil Éireann) and of a partly appointed, partly indirectly elected upper house (Seanad Éireann), with many fewer powers.

To firm up his foundation of support, de Valera built Fianna Fáil into a formidable force. Drawing on IRA units, the party created strong local organizations that, in combination with skillful use of appointments to reflect cross-country interests, gave it a nationwide spread, unlike Cumann na nGaedheal, which became increasingly confined to Dublin. From its original support base of small farmers, shopkeepers, and IRA anti-treaty advocates, it expanded to include urban workers, small businessmen, moneyed elites, and others. By the 1940s the party had succeeded in achieving a seemingly unassailable grip on Irish national politics.

In the 1930s the IRA became increasingly marginalized, despite occasional outbreaks of violence, including several gruesome murders.

Military tribunals imposed harsh sentences on members found guilty of unlawful acts. On June 18, 1936, the government declared the organization illegal.

Threats to parliamentary rule came not from the IRA but rather from a right-wing paramilitary group that emerged in 1933. De Valera's hold on power reflected the appeal of the political strongman evident in Europe during the economically troubled 1930s. Fascism, with its glorification of the nation and ideology of militant action, proved attractive to some among those fiercely proud of their country's newly won independence. One among a number of fascist movements then in vogue across Europe that arose in the wake of the rise to power in Italy of Benito Mussolini (1883–1945) and in Germany of Adolf Hitler (1889–1945), the National Guard was founded on July 20, 1933. Led by Eoin O'Duffy (1891–1944), outfitted in blue shirts and black berets and aping the European dictators in employing a fascist salute, the Blueshirts—the guard's paramilitary wing—paraded in noisy emulation of continental practices. The guard claimed to uphold Christian, anti-communist values and advocated creation of a fascistlike "corporate" state in which joint government-, employee-, and employer-run industrial organizations would prevail, and it was prepared to use physical force to advance its agenda.

The National Guard was declared illegal in August 1933, but the Blueshirts won for O'Duffy sufficient attention that he agreed to serve as president of a new political party, the United Ireland Party, later known as Fine Gael ("Clan of the Irish People"), created on September 2, 1933, in uniting the National Guard with Cumann na nGaedheal. Claiming Michael Collins as its founding father and with its origins based in the pro-treaty faction of Sinn Féin, the party viewed itself as the protector of the state's institutions and the upholder of law and order. After a year of violence spawned by paramilitary activism, Fine Gael repudiated its links with O'Duffy, who resigned. Both Fine Gael and Fianna Fáil remained firmly committed to working within the parliamentary system. They became, and they remain, Ireland's two main political parties.

Redefining Ireland's political relationship with Britain by enactment of a new constitution represented the fulfillment of one of Fianna Fáil's two goals. Economic and cultural separation constituted the second of its aspirations. Respect for the message of Irish history, namely, that Ireland must secure its liberty, meant that Britain had to be kept at bay even if that meant much of the reality of the past—the progress made by prewar parliamentary nationalism, the many Irish soldiers who fought for Britain in World War I, the retention by the new state of most of the governing forms and ethos of British rule—had to be glossed over.

Economic self-sufficiency was stressed. The government encouraged the setup of native industries with creation of financial and credit institutions to provide, in the absence of private venture capital, start-up funds. State-sponsored corporations were begun in the 1920s. Quotas, licenses, and tariffs were adopted. Efforts were intensified to reorient agricultural production away from pasturage and toward tillage in the hope of lessening dependence on grain imports.

In 1933 de Valera began withholding land annuity payments to the British government, as prescribed by the treaty, in the belief that they should have been included in the settlement, just as the treaty had provided for Ireland's release from payment of its share of the United Kingdom's public debt. London retaliated by imposing duties on Irish agricultural imports, in particular, placing an exorbitantly high tariff on cattle per head. An "economic war" began that continued until 1938, featuring additional duties levied by both countries. The tit-for-tat attacks hit hard. Irish agriculture, the backbone of the economy, suffered greatly in relying on exports to British cities for virtually its entire market. The tariffs led to price increases for many essential manufactured goods, and the cost of living rose. In 1938 an agreement ended the economic duel: The annuities were canceled for a lump-sum payment, trade barriers were greatly lowered, and some preferences were given to U.K. goods.

On entering office, Fianna Fáil made a commitment to raise spending on social services, and sums increased from 36 percent of the government's budget in 1929 to 40 percent by 1939. A scheme for building cottages for agricultural laborers was launched, and outlays for pensions and unemployment relief were increased. Financial support for education remained limited in the interwar years, although opportunities for vocational training were extended in the 1930s. In 1940 the Dublin Institute for Advanced Studies was founded under the sponsorship of de Valera. The institute maintains an international reputation in undertaking research at its three schools of theoretical physics, cosmic physics, and Celtic studies.

National Health Insurance Acts in 1933 and 1941 provided state coverage for the working class against the cost of hospital treatment. Established in 1930, the Irish Hospitals' Sweepstake, known as the Irish Sweepstakes, generated significant revenues, especially from the United States and Great Britain, where lotteries were largely illegal, which led to marked improvements in provision of health care.

In the 1920s and 1930s rural Ireland resembled a land that appeared not to have changed in 100 years, providing the picture-perfect back-drop to the self-reliant, frugal, family-run farm that served as the ideal image of the countryside cherished by de Valera. Single-story cottages predominated, and basic living conditions prevailed. Large families were the rule, though late marriages were common. Population num-bers remained the same as they were in 1900 at just under 3 million, steady emigration from rural areas still the reality of life as it had been ever since the Great Famine. Emigration stood as definite proof that the idealization of rural Ireland so much promoted by the government was largely an illusion. Policies to keep people on the land failed.

But there were signs of change appearing here and there. Two-story slate farmhouses could be seen in growing numbers alongside time-honored thatched cottages, and machinery became increasingly common everywhere. Just as the 1938 Anglo-Irish trade agreement reflected the fact that protectionism could be pursued only so far given the small Irish economy's inextricable links with the major economic and financial power next door, so, too, de Valera's nationalism, centered on idealization of peasant rural life, was to a considerable extent more imagined than real.

In de Valera's idyllic image, urban Ireland was largely ignored, but modernism was spreading rapidly in the cities in the 1930s and 1940s. By 1940 most of urban Ireland was electrified. Anglo-American cultural norms and their agents took firm root. The cinema and radio—the Free State's broadcasting station Radio Éireann opened in Dublin on January 1, 1926—reached all of the country's urban dwellers. Automobiles began to fill the streets of the cities. Aer Lingus was set up as a national airline with the government as the sole shareholder in August 1936. Golf clubs and racecourses proliferated.

Religion constituted the one major factor uniting the country across all regional and class lines. The new state was almost entirely Roman Catholic. The 1937 constitution guaranteed the equality of all religions; in carrying on the tradition of separation of church and state inher-ited from the 19th century, it disallowed establishment of an official national church. Nevertheless, the constitution also recognized the "special position" of the Catholic Church. It was an acknowledgment guaranteed to further frighten Protestants in Northern Ireland, but one that met with little opposition from their southern coreligionists.

Religious and educational rights of southern Protestants were care-fully maintained, and Protestants were awarded weighted represen-tation in the Free State Senate. Even if Protestants were inclined to protest, there were fewer and fewer of them to do so: The proportion of Protestants in the 26 counties fell from about 10 percent in 1920 to about 7.4 percent in 1929, many of them having emigrated.

Legal guarantees aside, independent Ireland was to a considerable degree a confessional state. During the civil war, the pro-treaty forces could count on firm support from the church, whose bishops issued a pastoral letter denouncing IRA Irregulars as murderers. From the beginning, the Free State government consulted the Roman Catholic hierarchy on constitutional matters, and ruling officials were careful to solicit the clergy's opinions in formulating positions and making policies, especially on social and cultural issues. Resolutely against state initiatives in education and welfare during the years of direct rule by Britain, the church continued to oppose any measures that might threaten to curtail its control of these activities. Catholic precepts were rigidly adhered to. Catholic children were taught in Catholic schools by Catholic teachers, children of mixed marriages were raised Catholic, and divorce and birth control were outlawed.

The masses of Irish Catholics stood solidly behind their church, never doubting that the guidance provided by religious leaders reflected the wishes of the vast majority of the population. Their attitudes bolstered newly independent Ireland's air of insularity, and the rigid, restricted climate that resulted profoundly affected cultural life.

The Cultural Scene on a Politically Divided Island

The Irish Free State, as part of its efforts to create a new national identity, sought to put into practice the objectives of the Gaelic Literary Revival of the late 19th and early 20th centuries. During the 1920s and 1930s the regime went to great lengths to emphasize the "Gaelic" nature of the new country. A national language was viewed as an essential attribute of a sovereign people, and the use and diffusion of Irish were diligently promoted, without, however, succeeding in reversing to any considerable degree English as the language universally employed. A government ministry of the Irish language was set up in 1921, it was made a compulsory subject in the schools in 1922, and from 1925 it became a qualification for admittance to certain civil service grades. The 1937 constitution declared it to be the official first language of the country. Instruction in, and promotion of, Irish history and folklore were joined to that of language study. The Irish Folklore Commission, founded in 1927, established the Irish Folklore Institute to preserve the country's oral storytelling traditions. The Irish Manuscripts Commission has

265

since 1928 worked to discover and publish Irish historical and literary writings. Publication of Irish-language works was advanced through foundation in 1926 of An Gúm, the new state's Irish-language publishing agency. An Gúm filled a void left after the Gaelic League largely abandoned its role as a publisher in the late 1910s, putting some 500 titles on the market by the late 1930s.

Independence gave Irish writers the country for which so many among the Gaelic Literary Revival had yearned, but the idealistic, pastoral images so diligently promoted by William Butler Yeats and others failed to inspire many among the best artists in midcentury. They turned away from romanticism and toward realism, away from the tranquil countryside and toward the rough-and-tumble world of the cities. Many did not even live in the country.

James Joyce stands as the towering exemplar of the hard-nosed realist. A lapsed Catholic who from 1912 lived in voluntary exile on the Continent, Joyce joined a cosmopolitan flair with a local focus in his fiction to a degree matched by few other English-language writers anywhere. A complex man who was both a proud, polished practitioner of the English language and a scathing critic of Britain, Joyce could

also be unapologetically anti-Irish, though always in a distinctively Irish way, and he strove deliberately to make a contribution to his new country's cultural heritage. In his *Portrait of the Artist as a Young Man* (1916), the hero proclaims his wish "to forge in the smithy of my soul the uncreated conscience of my race" (Joyce 1991, 276).

His landmark work, *Ulysses* (1922)—arguably the most famous 20th-century English-language novel—broke new ground in employing a "stream of consciousness" narrative, that is, the written equivalent of a character's thought processes in which the author records the spontaneous flow

James Joyce at 22, photographed in Dublin
(Snark/Art Resource, NY)

of conscious experience through the mind. Joyce used the device, together with parody, jokes, literary allusions, and a constantly shifting style, to describe the characters and incidents of the *Odyssey* of Homer during a single day's time (June 16, 1904) in Dublin. Leopold Bloom (Odysseus or Ulysses), Molly Bloom (Penelope), and Stephen Dedalus (Telemachus)—whose inner conflict makes him Joyce's alter ego—stand in parodied contrast to their lofty classical models. In presenting his characters' thoughts in all their diversity and in providing brilliant insights into human nature, Joyce made a major contribution to trends in modern literature then emerging. Joyce brought his literary techniques to full fruition in *Finnegans Wake* (1939), a highly controversial work that discarded all conventions of plot and character building, but the novel proved less influential than his earlier masterpiece.

Writer, teacher, and politician Daniel Corkery (1878–1964) is another realist, an author of plays (*The Yellow Bittern*, 1920) and short stories (*A Munster Twilight*, 1926; *The Storm Hills*, 1929) who, like Joyce, knew well the world of the lower middle classes though, in his case, it was that of Cork, and his characters live lives of quiet commonality in no way resembling the romanticized heroes so much in evidence in revival literature. Also a nonfiction writer, in his classic *The Hidden Ireland: A Study of Gaelic Munster in the Eighteenth Century* (1924), Corkery presents a picture of life as seen by Gaelic poets during the era of the oppressive Penal Laws, one that, because it remained outside the purview of the Anglo-Irish world, contributed to the effort to build a distinctive national identity. Corkery taught Cork-born writer Frank O'Connor (1903–66), the pseudonym of Michael O'Donovan. A veteran of the war for independence and an anti-treaty partisan in the civil war, O'Connor is most famous for his short stories based on his experiences in the former conflict (*Guests of the Nation*, 1931).

The quiet countryside was not altogether neglected, and it was here that novelist and short story writer Liam O'Flaherty (Ó Flaithearta, 1896–1984) placed his works. Born in the Aran Islands, O'Flaherty told tales set in the world of nature in western Ireland (*The Black Soul*, 1924; *Skerrett*, 1932). His only Irish-language writing, *Dúil* (1953), arguably his best work, comprises a collection of short stories, including sketches on nature and life in the Aran Islands. Poet and playwright Sigerson Clifford (1913–85) spent many years of his youth in Cahirciveen, County Kerry, and the experience colored much of his work, including his most popular poem "The Boys of Barr na Straide."

Seán O'Casey (John Casey, 1880–1964) was born into a poor Dublin Protestant family. A nationalist, socialist, and largely self-taught, he served briefly as general secretary of the Irish Citizens' Army in 1914. The impact of the civil war on Dublin's working-class poor is vividly portrayed in his tragicomedy *Juno and the Paycock* (1924), which drew critical and popular praise. However, his subsequent play *The Plough and the Stars* (1926), a drama about life in Dublin during the Easter Rising, caused playgoers to riot on its first performance, relatives and comrades of the 1916 rebels angry at the display of a Citizens' Army flag alongside a prostitute in a pub scene and by O'Casey's refusal to glorify the rebel leaders. The play was banned, but its great character portrayals and the message they conveyed led to its revival, and it became a staple in the Abbey Theatre's repertoire.

The Abbey Theatre managed to survive the years of civil strife despite tight financial constraints. The picture brightened when the incoming de Valera administration granted it public monies, making it the first state-subsidized theater in the English-speaking world. Lennox Robinson (1886–1958) managed the theater from 1911, and in more than 25 plays and 40 years of association with the Abbey, he would be one of the few dramatists to successfully portray middle-class life (*The Big House*, 1926; *Church Street*, 1934).

A growing Irish-language literature emerged, benefiting now from active encouragement by a national government. All major novels before 1929 comprise either history stories or tales about the Irish-speaking Gaeltacht region, an area of the country now defined by a special commission and set up as a division of the Department of Lands to be given assistance in language preservation and social and economic development. Séamus Ó Grianna (1889–1969) wrote of the Easter Rising (*Mo Dhá Róisín*, 1920), Nioclás Tóibín (1890–1966) of the 19th-century landlord oppression (*An Rábaire Bán*, 1928), and Niall Ó Domhnaill (ca. 1907–95) of the Invincibles (*Ar Scáth na Croiche*, 1934).

The most prolific writer of Gaeltacht fiction was Connemara-born Pádhraic Ó Conaire (1893–1971), who published six novels between 1921 and 1939. Seán Ó Ciosáin (ca. 1896–1982) set his short fiction stories mostly in Cork city, while Micheál Mac Liammóir (1899–1978) moved beyond localism in a series of tales set in Dublin but also in France and Italy, peopled by cosmopolitan characters at home in sophisticated society (*Lá agus Oíche*, 1929). A poet, painter, dramatist, and impresario, he managed the Abbey Theatre's alter ego, the Gate Theatre, which he cofounded with theatrical director Hilton Edwards (1903–82) in 1928. Born Alfred Willmore in London, Mac Liammóir became captivated by Irish culture while touring in Ireland and moved to Dublin in the late 1920s, changing his name and learning Irish. He made a major contribution to promotion of the native language in establishing the Irish-language theater An Taibhdheare in Galway in 1928.

In the 1940s Irish-language writer Seosamh Mac Grianna (1901–90) reversed the trend in Irish-language autobiography of the 1920s and 1930s in concentrating on the inner personal in place of external reality. His *Mo Bhealach Féin* (My own way, 1940) comprises a psychological study of a Gaeltacht writer's turmoil in what he sees as an alien and fearsome urban environment, where his quest to live an unconventional life is sadly doomed to frustration. Bilingual writer Flann O'Brien (Brian O'Nolan, Myles na gCopaleen [1910–66]) also concentrated on the individual in *An Beál Bocht* (*The Poor Mouth*, 1941), a comedic parody on early 20th-century Irish-language literature in which the author strongly attacks revival writers who idealized the poverty of Irish speakers.

In the visual arts, Jack Butler Yeats (1871–1957), brother of William Butler Yeats, studied art in London and worked as an illustrator for various newspapers. He settled in Ireland after 1905 and completed landscapes in oil that at first drew on the influence of impressionism in their simplicity of line and color and then after 1920 trended toward expressionism in using paint, applied vigorously and thickly. Yeats painted images particular to the west of Ireland, especially associated with his boyhood home in Sligo, but he also drew on themes universal to humankind, such as loneliness and poverty. One of Northern Ireland's best known artists in the 1920s and 1930s was Paul Henry (1876–1958). Born in Belfast, Henry lived on Achill Island from 1910 to 1919, where he learned to capture the interplay of light and landscape in western Ireland that became defining features of his canvases, which he executed in a postimpressionist style. Other successful Belfast-born landscape artists included Frank McKelvey (1895–1974) and James Humbert Craig (1877–1944), a self-taught painter who abandoned a career in business for his artistic pursuits.

In the world of music no Irish talent won wider acclaim in the early 20th century than did John McCormack (1884–1945). Born in Athlone, McCormack studied in Italy and made his operatic debut at Covent Garden in London in 1907. Thereafter, he performed with a number of American opera companies. His concerts featuring both classical and Irish songs won for him international popular fame. He became a U.S. citizen and epitomized the successful Irish emigrant who, in the end, returned home, dying at Booterstown, Dublin. Herbert Hamilton Harty (1879–1941) left his native County Down and moved to London,

John McCormack standing in front of a poster announcing an upcoming performance. McCormack epitomized the Irish emigrant made good. (Library of Congress, LC-USZ62-123857)

where he established his reputation as a composer and accompanist. His own works include *Irish Symphony* (1910) and a tone poem *With the Wild Geese* (1910).

Paralleling the protectionism so evident in economic affairs, the new state, anxious to promote a uniquely Irish vision of a conservative, insular, family-values nation, condemned any and every form of modernism from jazz to current trends in painting and literature. The government passed a Censorship of Publications Act in 1929, and the board set up to enforce the law did so with the support of and assistance from the Catholic Church, its pervasive influence further implanting a confessional stamp on Irish society in the early years of postindependence. Launched in an atmosphere of lingering insecurity about national identity, a historically poor awareness of cultural works among the public, and the concern of the Catholic hierarchy to protect the faithful from artistic currents thought to harm their spiritual well-being, censorship came as a bitter blow to many intellectuals whose dreams of a country released from the fetters of the past were dashed. The Free State proved decidedly less free than they had expected.

Authors of international standing, such as Kate O'Brien (1897–1974), a major writer of country house novels, saw their works outlawed. Her *The Land of Spices* (1941), a novel of two women's flight from love into religious life, was banned based on a single reference to homosexuality. Many major works were proscribed, Joyce's *Ulysses* virtually the only exemplar of modernism exempted. Even Irish-language classics were scrupulously reviewed. Many artists—George Russell, classicist Stephen MacKenna (1872–1934), and poet Thomas MacGreevey (1893–1967)—preferred to leave the country.

Austin Clarke's (1896–1974) first novel *The Bright Temptation* was banned on publication in 1932. Despite a successful career in London, Clarke was one artist who chose to return, producing a wide array of poems, plays, and essays while managing the Lyric Theatre Company. Patrick Kavanagh (1904–67) penned works distinguished by the coinage of new words and that included perhaps his best poem "Great Hunger" (1942) and his classic novel *Tarry Flynn* (1948) which were at first poorly received but are now considered masterpieces. Kavanagh is acknowledged as one of Ireland's greatest modern-day poets.

Other voices spoke out in opposition. Seán O'Faolain (John Whelan, 1900–91), an anti-treaty republican in the civil war, saw his books *Midsummer Night Madness* (1932) and *Bird Alone* (1936) banned as works highly critical of Free State society. In a censored country surrounded by a world waging global war, O'Faolain founded *The Bell* in 1940, a periodical in which he boldly set about attacking government restrictions. No facet of Irish life escaped criticism.

271

In Northern Ireland, writers who had made reputations before partition, such as St. John Ervine (1883–1971), a novelist who expressed
the sometimes torn allegiance of Ulster Protestants in their affection
for both England and Ireland (*Changing Wind*, 1917), and Forrest Reid
(1875–1948), continued to write after 1922 and some remained active
into the 1930s. Belfast-born Reid, a fiction writer, literary critic, and
translator of Greek, is acclaimed by some as Ulster's greatest novelist (*Peter Waring*, 1937). Also born in Belfast, C. S. (Clive Staples)
Lewis (1898–1963) wrote several works in defense of Christianity
(*The Screwtape Letters*, 1940) as well as children's fantasy stories, most
notably the seven-volume *Chronicles of Narnia* (1950–56) that proved
popular among general readers. Many new writers who appeared in the
1930s were women. Derry-born Kathleen Coyle (1886–1952) wrote
novels whose outstanding quality lies in the intense, emotional inner
life of her heroines (*Liv* [1929]; *A Flock of Birds* [1930]). Constance
Malleson (1895–1975), from County Down and famous in Britain as
the actress Colette O'Neil, wrote works characteristic of the country
house genre peopled with characters struggling through emotional
traumas (*The Coming Back*, 1933). Country house life is also featured
in the novels of D. G. Waring (ca. 1891–1977), who wrote 11 books
between 1936 and 1942 (*Fortune Must Follow*, 1937). The romantic
subplots and political backdrops of the country house stories are far
away from the world created by Olga Fielden (ca. 1903– ?) in which
the characters, preoccupied with personal crises, live in remote places.
Island Story (1933) concerns the battles waged to the death among
members of a family on an Ulster island. The story almost serves as a
metaphor for Ulster itself, which, as a tiny, remote outpost of the United
Kingdom, clung to its separate existence during the interwar years,
never totally sure that its status would remain undisturbed.

Northern Ireland: Stability through Immobility, 1923–1939

In the early 1920s the greatest threat to Northern Ireland's separate
existence remained the Boundary Commission, which was created as
stipulated by the Anglo-Irish Treaty consequent to Northern Ireland's
decision to opt out of union with the Free State. Belfast chafed at
cooperation, but the commission held its first meeting in London on
December 6, 1924. Free State officials and nationalists in the North
were confident boundary makers would redraw lines to the benefit of
the new nation. Aware of the danger, Northern leaders declared their
resolve not to surrender one bit of land. The commission duly found in

favor of the Free State, but the adjustments that were suggested were relatively minor. The proposed terms were leaked to the *Morning Post,* a conservative London daily, in an article disclosing only small changes were contemplated and these largely in favor of Northern Ireland. They caused a furor in Dublin. The official report remained unpublished (until 1969), and the Free State government, anxious not to incite a new round of violence while preoccupied with laying the groundwork of the new nation, hastily arranged meetings in London. The Anglo-Irish Treaty was amended, and the existing border confirmed in an agreement signed in December 1925, which, because it accorded with their fondest wishes, representatives of Northern Ireland were happy to ratify.

Partition was now officially confirmed. The Belfast government relaxed its guard—the Special Constabulary was partially disbanded—but only just a bit. Northern Ireland was too small, too dependent on the whims of the parliament in Westminster, whose interests did not always converge with its own, for officials to let their defenses entirely down. Most especially, the danger from Dublin could never be discounted. Articles 2 and 3 of the 1937 Constitution of Ireland specifically stipulated that the whole of Ireland formed a single "national territory," and an advance column of supporters of a united island stubbornly resided in the six counties of Northern Ireland.

Fully one-third of Northern Ireland's population was committed to its demise. They were easily identifiable because the nationalists were, without exception, Roman Catholics, religion the one certain marker by which to distinguish their sentiments. A fully functioning parliamentary democracy never developed in Northern Ireland because the very basis on which such a democracy operates—the legitimacy of the government—was never accepted by the nationalist side. It was inconceivable for nationalists, who aimed not to change the government but to destroy the state, to play the role of loyal opposition. Political parties committed to advancing various causes and issues could not emerge where there existed no floating blocks of voters to whom to appeal. Only two broad coalitions existed—Protestant unionists and Catholic nationalists—that bound together people of all ranks, including both middle and lower classes, where in other places they might have splintered along differing social and economic interests. Elections were determined solely in terms of on which of these two sides of the political line electors found themselves aligned.

The Boundary Commission having failed to effect geographic change, nationalists grudgingly ended their boycott of parliament, and minority political and religious leaders worked for the betterment of their constituents' interests. In May 1924, their parliamentary leader, Joseph Devlin (1871–1934) formed the National League of the North to unite nationalists, but without, he affirmed, the intention to force unionists into the Free State. Political operations were set up at central and local levels to seek justice and equitable treatment, but because rank-and-file nationalists never abandoned their ultimate goal to achieve islandwide unity, unionists never wavered in their wariness. Nationalists had, by word and deed, shown their hostility to the ruling authority and could not be given positions of trust in government, unionists argued, and so Catholics were excluded from positions of power and avenues of advancement, and their political representatives were marginalized.

Sectarian violence, especially in Belfast, swelled and subsided, but it was never altogether absent during the interwar years. Extreme Protestant organizations, such as the Ulster Protestant League, grew in importance in the 1920s and 1930s, helping to keep tensions simmering and occasionally bursting beyond the boiling point. In 1931 an IRA attack on an Orange Order demonstration sparked reprisals. In June 1932 Ulster Catholics traveling to and from Dublin to attend a eucharistic congress were assaulted, the security forces providing little protection. Riots in Belfast in May, June, and July 1935 culminated on July 12 when Orange Order marchers, defying a government ban, were fired on, precipitating 10 days of mayhem. The IRA launched a series of attacks in England itself from January 1939 to March 1940. The continuing violence provided a justification for the government to retain the Special Powers Act, which was made permanent in 1933, to give it the legal basis on which to deal with outbreaks.

The political system remained rigidly inflexible. Housed in new premises completed in November 1932 and known as Stormont because of its location in the Stormont area of Belfast, the Northern Ireland parliament counted usually 40 percent, and often 60 percent, of its members returned unopposed in elections, and personnel who staffed the government changed little. Viscount Craigavon served as prime minister from 1921 until his death in 1940. His successor, John Miller Andrews (1871–1956), appointed octogenarian veterans of Craigavon's administration to his cabinet. Offices were held almost exclusively by wealthy landed gentry and industrial magnates. At the national level, usually all but two of Northern Ireland's 13 seats at Westminster were held by unionists, who voted consistently with Britain's Conservative Party. Over time, the government developed a copycat pattern of adopting laws that aped British legislation.

Never a viable, self-sufficient economic entity, plagued by distance, lack of raw materials, and without an available source of cheap power, Northern Ireland constituted one of the United Kingdom's most depressed regions. The Belfast government faced an intractable problem of securing sufficient funding, its ability to raise revenues limited, while striving to keep social benefits up to U.K. standards. The Great Depression that began in 1929 hit the urbanized, heavy industry–dominated economy hard. The traditional activities of shipbuilding and textiles declined in line with worldwide drops in production. Although agricultural output grew and diversified, encouraged by policies that gave preference to exports to British dominions and imperial domains, and the area profited briefly from the economic war with Éire, the province presented a picture of dire distress in the 1930s. Unemployment rose from 13 percent in 1927 to 28 percent in 1931 and still stood stubbornly high at 20 percent in 1939. Health and sanitary facilities were neglected. Housing remained substandard, the industrial slums of Belfast famed for their squalor. Poor relief schemes and government relief efforts were niggardly. In effect, Northern Ireland existed entirely as a dependency of the United Kingdom, its administration kept afloat by regular injections of funds from London, doled out by an often reluctant British treasury, which viewed partition as a persistent drain on its resources.

In the late 1930s aircraft production began to relocate to the province, the one major industry to do so. In addition, Ulster's role in Britain's marine defenses was boosted when in 1938 facilities were moved north after Dublin secured the return of harbor installations at Cobh, Berehaven, and Lough Swilly that had been retained by Britain under the 1921 treaty. Ironically, these brighter prospects for the local economy emerged at the same time that developments darkened the European scene as the Continent moved steadily toward war.

The North Goes to War, the South Stays Out, 1939–1945

The European war that broke out in September 1939 revealed how far apart north and south Ireland had diverged in 20 years. Northern Ireland gave wholehearted support to waging the conflict that ensued following the U.K.'s declaration of war on Germany on September 3. Anxious to demonstrate his province's loyalty, Prime Minister Craigavon requested that conscription should be implemented. Conscious of the depth of opposition such a step would arouse in the nationalist community and fearing that to apply the policy might require as many troops as it would provide, Winston Churchill (1874–1963), who became prime minister in May 1940, demurred. The concession to nationalist sentiment raised the ire of unionists against their compatriots even further, but enlistments suffered no shortages. They totaled a respectable 23,000 to all the armed forces by late 1941. The Home Guard was manned by the B Specials. Rationing (except for milk), restrictions, and high taxes replicated those endured elsewhere in the United Kingdom. Troops arrived for training, airfields were constructed, and Londonderry became an important naval base. Wartime proved a boon to Northern Ireland's principal industries. Shipbuilding and linen making experienced soaring demand, bringing with it an unaccustomed prosperity.

The Germans drew up plans for an invasion of Northern Ireland, but they were abandoned early on. Northern Ireland was at first assumed to be strategically invulnerable, an assumption rudely overturned on the night of April 14–15, 1941, when 180 German planes dropped more than 100 tons of bombs on Belfast's residential neighborhoods, killing more than 700. In a gesture carrying great symbolic weight, fire brigades from Dublin and other towns rushed across the border to provide assistance. Relief centers for bombed-out refugees were opened across the border. On May 4 German planes returned to drop incendiary bombs that devastated Belfast's harbor facilities, killing 150.

Éire proclaimed its neutrality in September 1939, a policy strongly resented by northern unionists but one rooted in the country's as yet only brief independent history. The war of independence and the long history of oppression still rankled while the continuing British presence in a portion of the island, in violation of Dublin's constitutional claim to the whole of Ireland, mandated that Éire maintain its separation from the former colonial overlord. Vigorous in its efforts to establish its own identity on the world stage, the Irish Free State considered an independent foreign policy an essential attribute of any sovereign state. Ireland sought from the start to emulate Europe's other small countries in following a neutral course. The Irish Free State and Éire played a central role in the League of Nations. De Valera served as president of the League Council in 1932. Seán Lester (1888–1959), the country's chief diplomat at the world organization from 1929, occupied its chief executive post as the league's secretary-general from 1940 to 1945.

Its wartime policies defined by the term "National Emergency," the government pursued a twofold approach in publicly maintaining strict diplomatic nonbelligerent status while privately carrying on secret intelligence and strategic contacts with the United Kingdom and the

United States. In 1940, with British fortunes at their lowest ebb, North-South cooperation in defense matters was discussed, the possibility even raised that Britain would support Irish unity in return for Éire's joining the war. But nothing came of the diplomatic dialogue, and Churchill's demand early in the war for a reoccupation of the treaty ports was rejected.

Dublin became a hotbed of espionage activity, and German spies became a popular preoccupation, everyone on the lookout for them everywhere. Their activities, however, were largely confined to establishing clumsy contacts with the IRA, which was declared a traitor to the Irish state by the Treason Act of 1939 due to its continued advocacy of violent tactics.

Only one incident, aside from a few stray German bombs that fell in eastern counties, brought the war directly to Éire when, on May 30, 1941, German planes, led astray by jammed radio signals, dropped their bombs on Dublin, killing 34. During the Emergency, the country suffered from some food and fuel rationing. Few automobiles ran on the roads. Tillage was expanded and turf production accelerated to meet wartime conditions. The government assumed wide powers to organize the economy, with planning implemented by Seán Lemass (1899–1971), a Dublin-born veteran of the Irish Volunteers, the Easter Rising, and the anti-treaty civil war forces who helped to found Fianna Fáil.

After the United States entered the war in December 1941, Irish neutrality became more blatantly benevolent. Beginning in 1942, Allied—but not German—airmen interned for violating Irish airspace were sent to Northern Ireland, while the government put no obstacles in the way of thousands of its citizens who enlisted in the Allied forces.

Éire spent the war years in self-absorbed, stagnant isolation, closed off from world-shaping events. Formal neutrality was always strictly maintained. The government protested the presence of U.S. troops in Northern Ireland—foreign troops viewed as an affront while Éire's claim of islandwide sovereignty remained in force. De Valera refused to close German and Italian legations. Churchill in his victory speech on May 13, 1945, taunted Éire for its failure to join the great Allied cause, but de Valera's calm, dignified reply later earned him much respect across the entire Irish political spectrum.

The end of the war brought a heightened determination, nurtured by wartime experiences, to leave conditions that prevailed before the war permanently behind. In Northern Ireland, that resolve focused on creating a more prosperous society. A start had already been made during the war both with creation of a Ministry of Health and Local Government,

Eamon de Valera maintained strict neutrality during World War II. In 1944 he refused a U.S. request, personified here by Secretary of State Cordell Hull (1871–1955), to expel German and Japanese diplomats who might have been working as spies. The cartoonist alludes to St. Patrick, who according to legend rid the country of snakes. Drawing by Clifford Berryman (Library of Congress, CD-1, Berryman, no. 248)

established in June 1944 in recognition of the need for better coordination in the provision of health services, and with passage of a spate of housing laws in 1945 to provide government financial assistance to local authorities in building workers' homes. In Éire, the end of the war offered the state the opportunity to take on the definitive form that had been sought for so long.

The Republic Realized, 1945–1966

Discontent pervaded the Irish political and economic scene in 1945. Rationing and shortages continued, inflation loomed, and strikes by farm laborers, industrial workers, and schoolteachers flared despite the creation of a Labour Court in 1946 to adjudicate disputes. Poverty remained endemic in the early postwar years. Housing was largely substandard. Economic protectionism remained largely in place, and the population fell as emigration—the tried-and-true solution for so many who faced distress in the past—resumed. In one bright spot, rural electrification was begun in 1946, to be completed over the next 30 years.

In power now for 16 years, Fianna Fáil saw its claim as the party averse to compromise on behalf of its ideals dimmed by the experience of governing, and a yearning for political change emerged. Small parties proliferated, including, most notably, Clann na Poblachta, founded in July 1946 under the leadership of Seán MacBride (1904–88), a former treaty opponent and IRA chief of staff, as an ultra-republican coalition of anti-partitionists, socialists, and disenchanted ex–Fianna Fáil members with a powerful IRA presence in its inner council.

In the first postwar election in February 1948, Clann na Poblachta won 13 percent of the vote and 10 seats. Though Fianna Fáil remained the largest party, it lost eight seats, and a coalition government—Ireland's first multiparty government—was assembled that included Fine Gael, Clann na Poblachta, smaller parties, and independents under Prime Minister John A. Costello (1891–1976), a Dublin-born barrister who had served as attorney general for the Irish Free State. The new government held together not because of a previously agreed common policy among the partners but solely on grounds of opposition to Fianna Fáil. Ironically, it would be this coalition and not Fianna Fáil that would bring to a conclusion the latter's old obsession with national disassociation from Great Britain that so preoccupied its great leader, de Valera. By the late 1940s the Anglo-Irish Treaty was no longer a divisive issue in Irish politics, the country for all practical purposes having severed all but the most slender links to London. The removal of the statue of Queen Victoria from the courtyard of Leinster House, seat of the Irish parliament, on July 22, 1948, marked a symbolic gesture preceding Costello's sudden announcement, on September 7, during a goodwill tour to Canada, that Éire would leave the Commonwealth and become a republic. On December 21 the Dáil voted to repeal the External Relations Act of 1936, and by the Republic of Ireland Act, Éire was formally declared to be a republic on April 18, 1949. Fine Gael, the party that backed the Anglo-Irish Treaty, succeeded in proving the truth of its civil war assertion that dominion status would in time give the country the freedom to achieve a republic, completely independent of Britain.

The government's action had shown that severing the last link to the Commonwealth took precedence over reunification. Dublin now placed responsibility for ending partition solely with the government of the United Kingdom. For its part, Westminster gave legal recognition to the move in passing the Ireland Act (June 2, 1949), declaring that the Republic of Ireland no longer constituted a dominion but at the same time retaliating in affirming that Northern Ireland would not cease to be a part of the United Kingdom without the consent of its parliament.

Citing London's failure to follow through in ending its rule in the North, the republic declined to join the North Atlantic Treaty Organization, the postwar Western defense alliance set up in April 1949. The country, however, did join with Britain in a number of European regional organizations, including the Council of Europe. Its application for membership in the major new international organization, the United Nations, set up in 1945 as the successor to the League of Nations, was vetoed by the Soviet Union in 1946. Viewed as an avowedly anticommunist power under the pervasive influence of the Catholic Church and as a country politically, economically, and culturally tied to the Western powers, Ireland was denied entry until 1955 when an agreement brokered between the USSR and the United States admitted several protégés on each side of the by then firmly fixed cold war divide.

In the 1950s and 1960s, except for a brief period in 1954–57 under a Fine Gael coalition, Fianna Fáil largely prevailed, succeeding in forming governments under de Valera in 1951 and 1957 and Lemass in 1959, 1961, and 1965 despite holding less than a majority of seats for intermittent periods (1951–54 and 1961–65). Having declined in the 1940s, Fine Gael revived slowly in the 1950s as a party advocating moderate public social and limited economic intervention policies and then recovered fully in the 1960s under the steady direction of its staunchly conservative leader Liam Cosgrave (1920–), the son of William T. Cosgrave. Clann na Poblachta faded, and the Labour Party struggled to win support. Its strength concentrated overwhelmingly in Dublin, the party counted on the nominal backing of the trade unions, but, in fact, it often made deals with Fianna Fáil. The Catholic Church's anticommunist preaching imparted a fear of the Left among the public that kept potential supporters of the party away.

No political party espoused expressly socialist doctrines—Catholic cultural conservatism permeating political life entirely—and ideological differences between the two central parties were negligible. The basis of distinction rested largely on civil war roots—Fianna Fáil trumpeting the fact of its unwavering republicanism and Fine Gael championing a more moderate attitude as the party that, since the inception of the state, had stood for a less ideological, more pragmatic approach to governing. Both parties held solid, core allegiances based on strong family voting traditions, and each wielded powerful local machines to deliver votes. Father to son family dynasties held seats in parliament and posts in cabinets.

Fianna Fáil remained the more dynamic of the two parties, an energy increasingly injected by Seán Lemass on de Valera's decline into semi-blindness and austere old age. As deputy prime minister (Tánaiste) in the 1950s and prime minister (Taoiseach) from 1959—when de Valera was elevated to the presidency—until 1966, Lemass practiced a hands-on, brusque style of government. Fianna Fáil proved adroit at presenting itself as a nationwide party, attracting support from among both trade union leaders and businessmen. It succeeded in securing at least 50 percent of Dáil seats in more than half the elections between 1932 and 1977.

Government administration continued largely unchanged, the civil service retaining its sterling reputation for professional nonpartisanship and incorruptibility. Local government declined in importance with the rise in the number of state-sponsored corporations, the creation of eight regional banks in 1970 for delivery of health services, and the subsequent abolition of local taxes.

The new republic retained commercial preferences with Britain. The Irish pound remained tied to the British, and trade links were dense. With the republic a political fact, the country moved away from economic nationalism. State interventionism assumed a new importance, a move encouraged by Ireland's application for Marshall Plan aid, the U.S. program of financial assistance to Europe's war-battered nations in place from 1947 to 1952 and one the country was made eligible to participate in. Ireland's receipt of approximately $150 million in loans and grants was made contingent on its drawing up a recovery program, involving long-term economic projections. The plan compelled the nation to confront the reality of its low output and productivity rates, to examine more closely its relations with Europe, to begin to turn away from the protectionism and insularity so much cherished before and during the war, and thus to admit that, all wishing aside, the fact of the country's complete economic dependence on British markets could not be denied. The interdependence of the two economies dictated that policies be drafted to mutual advantage.

Observers need only have looked at emigration for evidence that the economy, with its low growth and mounting deficits, was woefully weak. A little less than a half million people left Ireland—chiefly from rural regions and mostly for Britain—in the decade from 1951 to 1961, bringing the population down to a scant 2.8 million. Market patterns and the government's price-support system sustained the stagnant pasturage-based character of the agricultural economy—cattle, beef, and veal accounted for about 70 percent of exports in 1961, up from 51 percent before the war. Economic planning had been demanded by Lemass as early as 1942, but it began in earnest only in the 1950s under the impetus of postwar recovery projections. Called "programming," it often remained, however, haphazard and ineffective because of the absence of close coordination of government objectives and actions.

In the 1950s the Ireland of the 26 counties looked little different from that of the 1920s. In 1960 more than a third of private dwellings lacked a piped water supply and indoor toilets. Central heating and modern appliances were available only to the small numbers of those well-off. Modern roadways were few, and given the absence of a national building program, the growing volume of vehicles strained the limited network in existence. Society remained staid, conventionally conservative, and poor.

Beginning in the early 1950s, the government began moving away from traditional policies promoting economic self-sufficiency in favor of efforts to attract foreign investment, an approach advocated by all political parties by the middle of the decade. Offering tax breaks and subsidies to foreign firms while maintaining a tight, balanced budget, the government induced more than 300 companies—mainly from the United States—to set up operations in the country during the 1960s, with help provided by the Industrial Development Authority, established in 1950. Industrial parks were set up in large towns. Tariff barriers began to be dismantled. Ireland joined the World Bank and the International Monetary Fund. Profitable agricultural sectors were encouraged, and a price-support structure for dairying developed. Farmers educated in scientifically advanced practices produced a dramatic increase in agricultural output in the 1960s. Modern marketing and business management techniques were introduced, spurred by councils for economic and industrial affairs that undertook extensive research.

In consequence, the 1960s to the mid 1970s proved a boom time. Annual growth rates averaged 4 percent, more than double prewar levels. The old pattern of small, often inefficient industrial firms producing largely for a protected home market that had prevailed from the 1920s through the late 1950s began to move, under the impetus of the changing policies, in the direction of larger, capital-intensive, export-oriented industries. Urbanization and public-sector employment expanded. Young people in increasing numbers moved to the cities and towns in search of greater economic and employment opportunities, leading, in places, to the gradual collapse of rural communities. Emigration slowed and the population began to grow. In 1966 the first demographic increase since the Great Famine was registered with a gain of 62,000, and the numbers jumped to 100,000 by 1971. The gap in living standards between the North and the South that had widened in the immediate postwar years began to narrow, an essential step, many affirmed, in any hope for political reunification. Denting the rosy picture, however, unemployment and inflation rates remained stubbornly high, traditional domestic industries expanded little, and the agricultural growth rate lagged far behind—the first sign that the farming sector was losing its predominant status.

Educational opportunities broadened in the 1960s. National spending increased, and free post-primary education was introduced, which led to a jump in attendance rates. Children's allowances were expanded, and occupational benefits and a host of state pensions were introduced. A Social Welfare Act (1952) put in place a national health service, unemployment insurance, and widows' and orphans' schemes.

The pace of life quickened, and Ireland looked increasingly outward. The Irish Tourist Board (Bord Fáilte) was created in 1955. In April 1958 Aer Lingus inaugurated service to North America. The development of Shannon Airport produced a huge influx of American tourists. The first scheduled commercial flight arrived on October 24, 1945. In 1947 the Customs Free Airport Act established Shannon as the world's first duty-free airport, and the modern tourism industry based on mass marketing and coach tours began. In 1961 the country applied for membership in the European Economic Community, the association of western European countries established in 1957 to foster greater unity and prosperity by eliminating barriers to capital, goods, and labor flows. The republic joined the United Nations Educational, Scientific and Cultural Organization (UNESCO) in 1961, and the year before Irish troops served in UN peacekeeping operations in the Congo.

All Ireland seemingly celebrated when U.S. president John F. Kennedy (1917–63) visited the republic in June 1963. Vast crowds turned out to glimpse the first Irish-Catholic president, with forebears from County Wexford, who, as the returning Yank made good, embodied Irish emigrant success, and who, with family in Ireland, personified

Huge crowds greeted U.S. president John F. Kennedy on his visit to Ireland in June 1963. (AP Images)

the possibility that progress could advance in his ancestral homeland as well. Portraits of the president were proudly displayed beside those of the pope in homes everywhere.

On December 31, 1961, Radio Éireann began television service, a communication innovation already launched six years earlier in Northern Ireland, and the authority changed its name to Radio Telefís Éireann in 1966. Television symbolized the arrival of the consumer society, and it helped in a major way to accelerate the breakdown of insular outlooks and unquestioning attitudes.

Church officials found themselves increasingly compelled to confront the social and cultural changes consequent to technological progress. Although the Catholic Church's influence in government and society had remained solidly in place throughout the 1940s and 1950s and conservative values retained their dominant place, fissures in the wall of religious power began to appear. From its inception, the Lemass administration showed a notable disposition to resist the hierarchy's intervention in the legislative process. Licensing laws extending the hours (to 11:30 P.M. on weekdays) that pubs and other establishments selling liquor could stay open were passed over the church's objections.

Though small, such steps exemplified a growing willingness to challenge clerical control, and they reflected the onset of more critical attitudes that would widen as educational and income levels rose. The impact of the Second Vatican Council (1962–65) proved profound in shaking up the structure and operations of the church itself, thus adding a contributing factor to more open attitudes in society at large. The innovations introduced in church practices led to more rapid and extensive changes than at any time since the Reformation. The vernacular replaced Latin as the liturgical language. Lenten and Friday fasts were abandoned. Priests turned to speak directly to their congregations in the celebration of the mass. Religious vocations declined incrementally, and both priests and laypeople began to increasingly criticize social conditions. Church magazines proclaiming a more independent line (*Christus Rex*, *The Furrow*, *Doctrine and Life*) grew more rapidly than did secular, literary ones. Ecumenical services with Protestants were introduced in June 1970. St. Patrick's College, Maynooth, admitted its first lay students in May 1968, and the ban on Catholics attending Trinity College Dublin was removed in June 1970.

At the same time the country remained demographically as solidly Catholic as always. The number of Protestants continued to fall—in 1970, they totaled approximately 196,000 or about 7 percent of the population—the drop due now more to intermarriage and declining birth rates than to emigration.

Whatever the changes under way in Irish Catholic society, Protestants in the North remained unimpressed, firm in their belief that reunion would mean rule by an inflexible, intolerant religion directed by the papacy, a foreign-based entity. Their resolve to vigorously resist any such possibility remained as resolute as ever.

Sectarianism Alive Amid a Prosperity Drive: Northern Ireland, 1945–1969

The war won, Northern Ireland turned with a will to fulfill hopes for a wealthier, more secure society. The conflict highlighted the country's strategic and economic significance to the wartime effort and, together with sympathy for the sufferings endured in the bombings, helped to generate an attentive hearing in London for Ulster's needs. All of the major social welfare schemes, crowned by universal national health insurance (1948), that were launched by Britain's postwar Labour Party government were introduced, with some adaptations for local requirements. Under a financing arrangement that placed most of the cost

285

on the national government, Northern Ireland was spared the heavy expense for social services that had proved so burdensome before the war.

New structures for primary and secondary education in both the state-run and Catholic-run systems were implemented, and by the 1960s both were virtually entirely supported by the state. Numbers enrolled surged. Roadways were built under a central plan, the first expressway on the island opening in 1962 from Belfast to Lisburn. New housing projects appeared together with modern sewage, sanitation, and utility systems.

During the term of Prime Minister Sir Basil Brooke (1888–1974 [later Viscount Brookeborough]) from 1943 to 1963, state intervention and widespread foreign investment brought new industrial ventures. Northern Ireland became Europe's leading producer of man-made fibers, though new endeavors did not entirely make up for a steady decline of old staples—linen, shipbuilding, and agriculture. Living standards, on a par with those in Éire in the 1930s, jumped substantially ahead of the republic by the 1950s. Economic growth rates of 4 percent in the 1960s and early 1970s matched those of the South, though unemployment stayed stubbornly high.

The proclamation of the Republic of Ireland provided an ideal occasion for Belfast to call an election, in January 1949, that led both unionists and nationalists to reaffirm their traditional positions. However, with the former's commitment to British ties undiminished, nationalists in the North for the first time launched a major drive to both defend and advance Catholic interests. The nationalist MPs for Fermanagh and Tyrone took their seats in London for the first time.

Beginning in 1945 Catholics joined in an Anti-Partition League (APL), made up mostly of middle-class professionals, that soon had branches and held rallies across the province. The APL mounted an assault on partition in the 1949 campaign, with financial support extended by southern sympathizers. In reaction, unionists, as always, closed ranks. "Our country is in danger . . . our determination to remain under the Union Jack should be immediately and overwhelmingly reaffirmed" (Brooke 1949), declared Brooke. Unionist (Ulster Unionist Party [UUP]) majorities won by margins of two to one outside of constituencies in Fermanagh and Tyrone where nationalist (Nationalist Party) victories were registered.

Interest in the antipartition campaign subsequently waned, and a spirit of conciliation both within Northern Ireland and in its relations with its southern neighbor appeared in the wind. Public opinion in the

South seemed to have long reconciled with the de facto existence of partition despite the continuing constitutional claim to unification of the island. Most among both the British public and the government in London assumed that partition had definitively solved the Irish problem. Even the IRA failed to rouse much sentiment in support for its continuing campaign to reunite the country by force. A series of border raids mounted between November 1956 and February 1962 netted a few arms hauls but sputtered out, and it was formally called off. Its leaders switched tactics, fashioning a Marxist-style vision to redress socioeconomic issues. They proposed to unite Ireland by ejecting conservative governments in both North and South, with the ballot box rather than the bullet, and establish an ill-defined workers' republic. But they failed to win support from the Irish nationalist community in the North, many of whom had benefited from the economic development in Northern Ireland and from the social welfare and education programs in place, which greatly surpassed those in the republic.

In March 1963 Northern Ireland's new prime minister, Terence O'Neill (1914–90) of the UUP, set two priorities for his administration—to improve community relations both within the province and with the republic. In an effort to build cross-island bridges, Prime Minister Lemass traveled to Stormont in January 1965, and O'Neill reciprocated in coming to Dublin in February in visits that generated much fanfare. In 1965 an Anglo-Irish Free Trade Agreement marked final acceptance of the reality of Irish-British economic interdependence, promoting cooperation as it advanced more open economic borders.

In June 1963 O'Neill broke new ground with a public condolence to Catholic prelates on the death of Pope John XXIII (1881–1963). In April 1964 he visited a Catholic school. The Nationalist Party in parliament accepted the role of official opposition, indicating a willingness to pursue its goals by constitutional means.

But at the same time that the government and the nationalists showed a more accommodating will, voices on the Protestant extreme right grew more shrill. Alarmed by such developments and by the increasing self-confidence of the Catholic community, hard-line unionists roused themselves in opposition. In 1963 O'Neill's right to the premiership began to be questioned, and back benchers in parliament would stage revolts against his leadership throughout his tenure.

Uncompromising diehards rallied around a fundamentalist preacher, the Reverend Ian Paisley (1926–). Born in Armagh and raised in Ballymena, County Antrim, Paisley imbibed the independent Baptist ethos of his preacher father. Ordained an evangelical minister, in 1951 he went on to found his own "Free Presbyterian Church of Ulster." Belligerently anti-Catholic, he would refer to the pope as the "anti-Christ." His stances in defense of ultra-Protestant interests won for him much attention, as did his association with radical fringe political groups. Paisley charged O'Neill with political betrayal, reminding him that Lemass's republic still claimed jurisdiction over the six northern counties. He took chairmanship of the Ulster Constitution Defence Committee, a shadowy body linked with another equally shadowy entity, the Ulster Volunteer Force (UVF), the first of the modern-day Protestant paramilitary organizations, created in the spring of 1966. Militant unionists, members of or allied with groups such as the UVF, many of them from working-class areas, acquired the label of loyalists in denoting their fierce determination to remain apart from the republic to their south.

In the nationalist community, a conservative, disorganized Nationalist Party gave way in 1959 to a reformed, revitalized National Unity movement that in 1965 itself led to a new organization, the National Democratic Party, which would constitute the political vehicle for Catholics throughout the rest of the decade. Increasingly better educated, Catholics grew more aware of and less reconciled to the discriminatory treatment they continued to receive in both the public and the private sectors of the economy and to what they saw as blatant bias against them by law enforcement agencies. At the same time, a pressure group created to highlight the injustices built into the Northern Ireland system, particularly in local government, employment, and housing,

THE RED HAND OF ULSTER

A large red hand is the central symbol on the flag of the province of Ulster and is also featured on the coat of arms of Northern Ireland. Its use as a symbol dates from the coat of arms of the earls of Tyrone. Its origin is reputedly drawn from an ancient legend, according to which, during prehistoric times, rival giants engaged in a swimming race from Scotland to Ulster, the winner of the race to be given a province as a prize. One of the contestants succeeded in winning by cutting off one of his hands and throwing it on the shores of the province. It is used as a rallying symbol most especially by loyalist groups.

emerged in January 1964. The Campaign for Social Justice sought legal redress of grievances. When that process proved too slow, the Northern Ireland Civil Rights Association (NICRA) was born in February 1967. Impressed by the gains scored by blacks in the United States, they borrowed the tactics used so effectively by the civil rights movement there. NICRA activists took to staging marches, protests, and sit-ins in the belief that such actions would evoke a sympathetic response from the more open-minded among the public and within the government throughout the United Kingdom.

Efforts to chip away at the sectarian mold that marked life in Northern Ireland faced a daunting challenge. The division between Protestant and Catholic communities, one that had been hardening for centuries, became thoroughly cemented after partition. By the time the civil rights campaign began in the 1960s, Protestants and Catholics lived in entirely separate worlds. They were divided physically—each side residing in the provinces' towns and cities in strictly segregated districts, whose boundaries, for election purposes, were drawn to ensure permanent minority status for Catholics. They were divided culturally—each side keeping to its own social sphere. Protestant and Catholic children attended separate schools. Catholics learned Irish. Protestants did not. Catholics played Gaelic games, Protestants played cricket. Where lives intersected, at the workplace, Catholics faced discrimination in job placement and promotion. The past was an ever-present reality, both sides seemingly always glancing back at victories and defeats, mythologized by memory, to justify their own attitudes.

On such stony ground, trust and understanding found little opportunity to take root. Tensions steadily mounted. Easter Monday 1966 saw 10,000 nationalists march in Belfast and Armagh to commemorate the 50th anniversary of the Easter Rising. On June 6 Paisley marched with supporters on the General Assembly of the Presbyterian Church, provoking a riot as it passed through a Catholic area.

By 1968 NICRA had grown increasingly less moderate, impatient at the lack of progress in meeting its reform demands, which it had spelled out to include "one man, one vote" in local council elections; an end to gerrymandered electoral boundaries; laws to protect against discrimination by local authorities; more equitable public housing; repeal of the Special Powers Act; and disbandment of the B Specials. When a unionist-controlled council in Caledon, County Tyrone, allocated a house to a single, Protestant woman, Catholics struck back, stung by a decision that took no account of the many Catholic families badly in need of a home. They held a sit-in and march. A series of marches began in August 1968 followed by another planned for October in Londonderry, Ulster's central flashpoint as the place where Catholics were defeated in 1689 and where they remained thereafter defiant in calling the town "Derry."

In an atmosphere marked as well by a lessening of civility between Ulster and the republic—members of the Fianna Fáil ministry were implicated in providing arms to the IRA in 1968–70—O'Neill's government came to see the marches not as civil rights protests but rather as nationalist provocations. The October march was banned, but on October 5, 2,000 demonstrators paraded anyway, meeting with the massed force of the Royal Ulster Constabulary (RUC).

Undeterred, a group calling itself People's Democracy, which had been established in October 1968 by students at Queen's University Belfast in support of civil rights, set off on January 1, 1969, to march from Belfast City Hall to Londonderry. The 60 marchers were joined by others along the way. At Burntollet Bridge in County Londonderry they were ambushed by militant Protestants, who injured many marchers. O'Neill showed no sympathy, condemning not the attackers but the attacked.

A general election in February 1969 confirmed the prime minister in power, but his power base in the Ulster Unionist Party, deeply divided over his conciliatory moves, left him weakened. Angry at his compromising moves, extremists took to bombing electricity and water supply installations in an effort to discredit his policies. O'Neill won for Catholics his cabinet's approval of the one-man, one-vote principle in local elections, and then having done so, he resigned in April, replaced by James Chicester-Clark (1923–), a landowner and MP from South Londonderry.

In the end O'Neill's balancing act between meeting nationalist demands and placating unionist forces had satisfied neither side, but the actions he took in favor of both showed that the pressure supplied by violent street politics had brought some results and might bring more.

The approach of summer 1969 brought with it the traditional marching season. Both sets of extremists remained restless. The police force was small, counting only some 3,000 men in the RUC. The B Specials were untrained for riot control and, with no Catholics in the ranks, would only serve to ignite tensions in Catholic areas. In London a new Northern Ireland Committee of the cabinet had been created, but ignorance of the situation characterized governing officials. In Dublin government fears for the minority in the North mounted.

On July 12 fighting broke out in Londonderry that lasted for three days. On August 2 Protestant militants in Belfast, assembled under the title of the Shankill Defence Association, launched an assault in the Catholic Unity Flats area, which deteriorated into looting and wanton destruction. Catholics were determined to resist another march through one of their districts. Both sides braced, awaiting August 12, the date of the annual Protestant Apprentice Boys' march.

10

TWO IRISH VISIONS IN COLLISION (1969–2000)

As in so many years past, the parade units of the loyalist Apprentice Boys of Derry had assembled near the Catholic residential Bogside area on August 12, 1969, preparing to enact their usual ritual traditional to Northern Ireland's annual marching season. During the yearly taunting time—when Protestants publicly flaunted their sectarian bias before Catholics—tensions were always high, although this year they were ominously so with sporadic outbursts of violence mounting over the preceding months. Both sides were primed—and the security forces were braced—for trouble. But the intensity of the violence that ensued over the next three days and the continuing flare-ups thereafter surprised everyone. A volcano of pent-up frustrations, injustices, and prejudices nursed for generations burst forth in a fury of death and destruction that proved impossible to contain.

Northern Ireland was transformed, its urban places turned into battle zones. With the civil authorities unable to cope and local law and order forces overwhelmed, the British government and the British army stepped in to govern and police the province. Guerrilla war settled in with paramilitaries launching sporadic, horrific attacks in which British troops—and Britain itself—became targets. Moderates on both nationalist and unionist sides strove to find a way out, but those who favored violent solutions found sufficient support to keep their arsenals active for decades. The conflict became embedded in the pattern of life in Ulster, the public going about its business amid roadblocks and checkpoints.

To the world watching outside, the "Troubles" in Northern Ireland appeared a tragic anachronism—a testament to intolerance too long treasured. Such sentiments of dismay were shared by many in the Republic of Ireland, where sympathy for the plight of Northern Ireland's

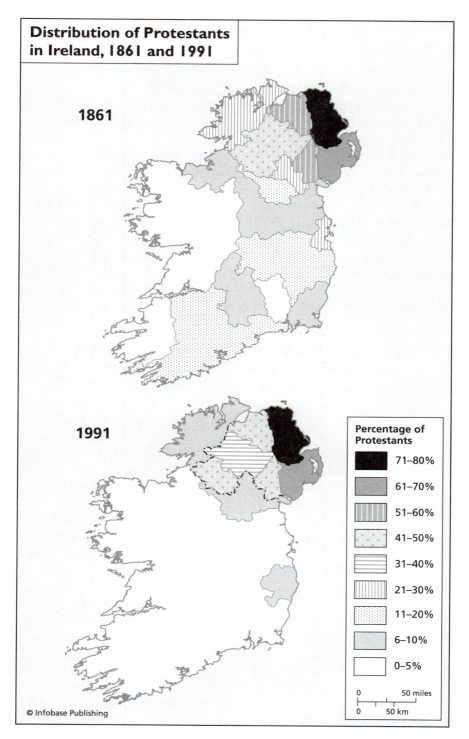

Distribution of Protestants in Ireland, 1861 and 1991

1861

1991

Percentage of Protestants

- 71–80%
- 61–70%
- 51–60%
- 41–50%
- 31–40%
- 21–30%
- 11–20%
- 6–10%
- 0–5%

0   50 miles

0   50 km

© Infobase Publishing

Catholic minority was tempered by utter rejection of the violent tactics of the Provisional IRA. A negotiated settlement satisfactory to both sides replaced reunification as the aim of Irish governments.

Aside from a growing determination to actively assist a resolution of the protracted conflict in the North, the South focused its attention on wealth creation. A succession of ministries in midcentury wrestled with efforts to realize real economic gains. Progress in the 1970s was followed by a downturn in the 1980s and then a turnaround in the 1990s that exceeded all expectations, bringing levels of growth never before achieved. By century's end the Republic of Ireland, too, stood transformed, but unlike in the North, in the South residents were busily engaged in pulling away from the legacy of the past. Utterly different from the staid, stagnant, stereotypical country of old, the South was now a prosperous place alive with social and cultural change. In the North, a settlement brokered with U.S. assistance—the Good Friday Agreement—gave grounds for hope that better times could be had there too.

Northern Ireland: A Vortex of Violence, 1969–1985

Protestant marchers in Londonderry stepped off on August 12, 1969, to parade in proudful commemoration. Tensions had been building for months, which made the atmosphere electric. It is unclear who triggered the violence that day—whether Protestants taunting Catholics with their traditional gesture of throwing pennies at them from the old city walls or Catholics throwing stones at the marchers—but the parade was stopped at the edge of the Catholic Bogside, the residents having erected barricades and stored an arsenal of supplies. Under a hail of stones from Bogside youth, the Protestant Apprentice Boys tried to storm the defenses. Young men hurled gasoline bombs and broken up paving stones against them. Three days of street warfare ensued. Disorders spread to the Catholic Falls Road and the Protestant Shankill Road areas in Belfast. Homes were burned and gunfire exchanged.

A Derry Citizens' Defence Association set up a headquarters, and some Bogside residents expected military aid to arrive from the republic while unionists rallied against what they expected might be an imminent invasion from the South. The Royal Ulster Constabulary (RUC) deployed armored cars with mounted guns to drive back nationalist rioters, and the government mobilized the B Specials, who began burning Catholic homes and businesses, further inflaming the Catholic community.

The RUC, overwhelmed by the mounting mayhem, appealed for further reinforcements, which only the army could provide. On August 15,

British soldiers string barbed-wire fences between Catholic and Protestant neighborhoods in Cupar Street, Belfast, on September 10, 1969. (AP Images)

under an action code-named Operation Banner, British troops moved in to try to separate the two sides. Their presence was at first welcomed by besieged Catholics. To diffuse the situation, the U.K. government issued the Downing Street Declaration on August 19 in which both the British and the Northern Ireland governments reaffirmed that "every citizen of Northern Ireland is entitled to the same equality of treatment and freedom from discrimination as obtains in the rest of the United Kingdom, irrespective of political views or religion" (Harkness 1983, 160). The government moved ahead with plans for reforms that met most of the minority community's demands. Electoral boundaries were to be redrawn, housing to be administered by a nonpartisan authority, and safeguards put in place to end discrimination in public employment. In December the Ulster Defence Regiment (UDR), a part-time security force under British army control, was set up, and in April 1970 the B Specials were disbanded. The hope, however, that Catholics might join the UDR proved stillborn, and it became a de facto Protestant auxiliary military force.

But once unleashed, the pent-up frustrations and resentments that had been building for so long proved impossible to contain. Residents scrawled graffiti on walls in Belfast Catholic neighborhoods interpreting IRA to mean "I Ran Away" in bitterly remarking on the almost total absence of their traditional defenders during the August disturbances. Searching for a response, IRA leaders held a stormy convention in Dublin, and on January 11, 1970, they split into two groups: the Official IRA, which retained its tactics to effect change through conventional politics, and the Provisional IRA (Provos), which committed itself, in returning to the methods practiced by so many of its forebears, to bring about the reunification of Ireland by force. The political party Sinn Féin split also in both the republic and Northern Ireland into Official and Provisional wings.

Recruitment to the Provisional IRA soared when the British army began late-night arms searches in Catholic areas. Anticipating a ban on Orange parades that did not come, disappointed Catholics met the massed presence of the army with nail and gasoline bombs, and residents soon began to view army patrols as part of a deliberate effort to humiliate them and destroy their property. The sympathy first won for the army among many Catholics evaporated, the identification of the army with the Protestant side now complete.

Spring 1970 commemorations of the Easter Rising led to renewed rioting. The Provisional IRA entered the fray for the first time in Belfast in late June. Monies flowed in from the Irish Northern Aid Committee (NORAID) in the United States, an American fund-raising organization founded in 1969 to promote a united 32-county Ireland.

Political forces working for restraint scrambled to avert further deterioration. Unionist Party supporters of Prime Minister Brian Faulkner (1921–77), who succeeded Chicester-Clark in March 1971, held to a moderate line despite growing dissent within the ranks. Compromise-seeking Protestants and Catholics combined in April 1970 to found the Alliance Party, a cooperative effort to effect conciliation. Moderate Catholic MPs, prominent among them Derry-born John Hume (1937–), formed the Social Democratic and Labour Party (SDLP) in August, which, while still seeking a united Ireland by consent, placed stress primarily on reform within the Northern Ireland system and renounced violent tactics.

At the same time that efforts at conciliation were launched, movements in favor of division also appeared, the growing radicalization on the political front reflecting the mounting military buildup. Ian Paisley established the Democratic Unionist Party (DUP) in September 1971, committed to upholding Protestant intransigence. In February 1972 William Craig (1927–), an Ulster Unionist Party MP, formed the Ulster Vanguard Movement in defense of Ulster separatism.

Implementing the government's 1969 reform agenda took time—local government restructuring proving especially complicated—but time was something that, with confrontations mounting month after month, moderate voices and the forces of law and order could little afford. Early in 1971 the IRA took the offensive. The first British soldier was killed in Belfast on February 6, 1971, and bombings multiplied. Other Protestant terrorist and vigilante groups appeared that, in addition to the Ulster Volunteer Force, began to answer attacks with attacks. One of the largest, the Ulster Defense Association, was founded in 1971, and it was later joined by an associated group, the Freedom Fighters.

Protestants put increasing pressure on the government to adopt firmer measures. In August 1971 Faulkner introduced internment, that is, holding without trial suspected IRA members for indefinite periods of imprisonment. A tried-and-true method that had worked successfully in the past, internment had to be applied wholesale given the massive scale of the disorders. More than 300 were arrested. Because only nationalist republicans were held and because some internees were being badly mistreated, Catholic tempers flared. Demonstrations were staged, and even moderates withdrew from their participation in public bodies. Action culminated on January 30, 1972, when 13 people were shot dead by the British army. "Bloody Sunday" caused a wave of revulsion that swept through the nationalist community, spreading across the border where sympathizers burned down the British embassy in Dublin on February 2.

Unable to cope with the crisis, Faulkner's government drew growing criticism from London. In March 1972 London suspended the Northern Ireland government, and Faulkner resigned, refusing to accept the move. Parliament was abolished on July 18, and direct rule from Westminster introduced. A new office in the British cabinet was created, that of secretary of state for Northern Ireland, and William Whitelaw (1918–99), a civil servant noted for his conciliatory abilities, was appointed to the post.

The change to a government run from London failed to change many minds. Encouraged by its successes, the Provisional IRA redoubled its bombing campaign. A brief truce between the IRA and the British army in July collapsed, and on July 21, 1972, a chain of bombs let off by the IRA in Belfast killed nine people and injured 130. "Bloody Friday" marked a high point in the deadly dueling. In the wake of widespread public disgust at the ghastly event, violence slowly subsided, though the year would end with a total of 472 killed

MASSACRE at DERRY

The Dead

Jack Duddy, 17 years.
Kevin McElhinney, 16 years.
Patsy Doherty, 21 years.
Bernard McGuigan, 41 years.
Hugh Gilmore, 17 years.
William Nash, 19 years.
Michael McDaid, 17 years.
John Young, 17 years.
Michael Kelly, 17 years.
Jim Wray, 23 years.
Gerard Donaghy, 17 years.
Gerald McKinney, 35 years.
William McKinney, 27 years.

Poster depicting the victims of the massacre at Derry known as "Bloody Sunday," January 30, 1972 (Library of Congress, POS-6-Ireland, no. 2)

out of a total of 678 since 1969. Though the intensity of the conflict lessened in succeeding years, its range lengthened. Violence spread to London in March 1973 when two car-bomb explosions killed one and injured 180 people.

The army reestablished itself in Catholic districts, and the government set about in earnest to cajole moderates in both camps—the SDLP and Faulkner's Ulster Unionist Party—toward agreement. The SDLP was promised a share in executive power and creation of cross-border cooperative institutions, while Unionist Party members were reassured that Northern Ireland would remain within the United Kingdom as long as the majority of the population so wished. A 78-member Northern Ireland Assembly to be elected by proportional representation was drawn up in May 1973, and in elections in June, both moderate parties won a majority. After lengthy wrangling, they agreed in November to create a joint administration. In December at a conference at Sunningdale in Berkshire, England, members of the executive-designate of the new assembly agreed with representatives of the British and Irish governments to set up a Council of Ireland to oversee matters of common interest. Under the terms of the forthcoming Sunningdale Agreement, on February 1, 1974, the Northern Ireland Executive took office, headed by Faulkner, with Gerard (Gerry) Fitt (1926–), leader of the SDLP, as his deputy.

But the hope that conflict might give way to cooperation proved short-lived. The IRA never relented in launching attacks. Paisley's DUP stood staunchly opposed to any collaborative measures. Faulkner was repudiated by a majority of his own party, including the party's MPs in Westminster, who were overwhelmingly anti-reform. In elections to the British parliament on February 28, 1974, die-hard unionists won in 11 out of 12 constituencies, voters appearing to balk at the prospect of a Council of Ireland, fearing the link might prove a wedge to edge them toward a united Ireland.

On May 14, 1974, the Ulster Workers' Council called a general strike against the Sunningdale Agreement. Walkouts grew slowly, and paramilitaries wholeheartedly backed the strike. On May 28 Faulkner and his Unionist Party colleagues on the Northern Ireland Executive resigned, feeling unable to remain in power in having lost the confidence of their constituents. The executive collapsed. The Northern Ireland Assembly was prorogued, and direct rule from London reimposed. The strike was called off.

Exasperated at having tried and failed to broker a settlement, the British government withdrew, leaving Northern Ireland politicians to work their way out of the by now interminable stew. A 78-member Northern Ireland Constitutional Convention was elected in May 1975, and by the end of August negotiators succeeded in securing a "voluntary coalition" in which the SDLP put their demand for an islandwide Council of Ireland on hold in return for a trial period of power sharing. Again, however, a compromise deal died aborning. Ian Paisley repudiated the proposal, as did the majority of unionists, who drew on fears, embedded after 50 years, that long-time opponents could not be trusted. A broad coalition of unionist groups, including the Ulster Unionist Party, calling itself the United Ulster Unionist Coalition, demanded the return of majority rule as it had existed before suspension of Northern Ireland's government.

From 1975 on a deadlock set in. Stalemate ruled because all sides could not muster sufficient support from beyond their own constituencies to break the impasse. Moderate Catholics in the SDLP and radicals in the IRA were not powerful enough on their own to effect their agenda, and unionists would have no truck with either, distrusting the former and detesting the latter for their violent tactics. The IRA could expect no support from the Dublin government, which abhorred its campaign of killing. Unionists could not restore minority rule on their terms without support from the British government, which would not give it while Protestants sought to regain unchanged their pre-1969 dominance over Catholics. Catholics in turn showed no gratitude to London, believing the government could put more pressure on unionists to make concessions.

The intensity of the violence waxed through the early 1970s with more than 200 killed each year from 1973 through 1975, climbing to 297 in 1976. The savagery diminished thereafter, falling in the early 1980s to an annual count of about 80 deaths. Throughout, horrific incidents shocked the sensibilities of observers in Ireland and worldwide. In response to the killing of six Catholic civilians by loyalists, the Provisional IRA machine-gunned to death 10 Protestant civilians in the so-called Kingsmill massacre of January 1976. The U.K. ambassador to the republic, Christopher Ewart-Biggs (1922–76), and a civil servant were killed by a land mine at Sandyford, County Dublin, on July 21, 1976.

In August 1976 an IRA Provo, shot by a British soldier after having ignored an order to stop the stolen car he was driving, struck and killed three Belfast children. The tragedy led to a campaign called the Peace Movement in Northern Ireland, headed by Mairead Corrigan (1944–), a Roman Catholic and the aunt of the three children, and

Betty Williams (1943–). Later reestablished as the Community of the Peace People, the movement conducted massive cross-border demonstrations, winning for both women the 1976 Nobel Peace Prize, though efforts to build an enduring peace movement failed. In August 1979 the first earl Mountbatten of Burma (1900–79) was assassinated in County Sligo, and IRA Provos ambushed and killed 18 British soldiers at Warrenpoint, County Down.

Terrible scenes played out on television screens across the world while the people of Northern Ireland tried to go on with their lives as best they could. The public carried on in an economy that expanded until 1973 but thereafter declined, caused partly by the violence that discouraged investment but primarily because of drops in economic performance across the United Kingdom with a consequent decline in the ability of London to supply regional aid to Northern Ireland. Throughout the 1970s manufacturing activity plummeted while many recently established industries, such as man-made fiber factories, reduced their workforce or shut down entirely. Unemployment leapt to 20 percent by the end of the 1980s.

What has been called a veritable "deindustrialization" in Northern Ireland hit Protestants hardest, Catholics always having suffered higher rates of joblessness. The growth in white-collar, service jobs meant that educated Catholics could better compete for these positions than could blue-collar Protestants. Growing Catholic mobility took place, while at the same time Catholics were growing in numbers. The Roman Catholic share of the population rose from approximately 35 percent in 1961 to 40 percent in 1981, reflecting a higher birth rate and reduced emigration. These social and economic changes made it that much harder for unionists who sought to return to the pre-1969 status quo to make their case.

In 1979 and 1981 British secretaries of state resumed their peace-making efforts in trying to broker a deal, but they were rebuffed by both the Ulster Unionist Party and the SDLP. In 1980 IRA prisoners began a hunger strike in Maze (Long Kesh) Prison, County Antrim, to protest prison regulations that forbade their being given the special political status allowed to internees before 1976. Treated as common criminals, they refused to wear standard prison garb, covering themselves only in blankets, a gesture copied in marches and demonstrations by sympathizers in the province and worldwide. By October 1980 seven of them moved to begin a hunger strike. Called off in December, it was resumed in March 1981. The first of the strikers was the first to die. In May Robert Gerard "Bobby" Sands (1954–81), who, while in prison, had been elected to the British parliament, succumbed, becoming in death a symbolic martyr to republicans. Altogether 10 prisoners died in 1981.

The early 1980s gave evidence that hard-line attitudes might be gaining ground. The hunger strikers succeeded in securing increasing sympathy from Catholics, growing numbers of whom saw the actions of the British government, in withholding what they viewed as fundamental human rights from republicans, as those of a cruel occupying force. An attempt to relaunch the Northern Ireland Assembly led to elections on October 20, 1982. Provisional Sinn Féin, the Provisional IRA's political vehicle, surprised observers in winning five seats to the Ulster Unionist Party's 26, the Alliance's 10, and the SDLP's 14. The election marked the start of a new campaign by the party, which soon called itself simply Sinn Féin, to combine electoral politics with violent actions by the IRA. Concerns among moderates and their supporters in Dublin and London grew when Sinn Féin's Gerry Adams (1948–) won the June 1983 British general elections as MP for West Belfast. Although he did not take his seat, his party drew 13.4 percent of the vote versus the SDLP's 17.9 percent. Born into a Belfast family whose members had been active in republican politics dating back to the Fenians, Adams joined the NICRA and, subsequently, aligned himself with the Provisional wing of the IRA. Interned for periods in 1971 and 1973, he played an important policy-making role in the 1981 hunger strike campaign and in 1983 was elected president of Sinn Féin.

Anxious to undermine any increased support for the radical IRA among their compatriots, moderate Catholics in the SDLP appealed to the British and Irish governments to relaunch negotiations to achieve a power-sharing arrangement. In consequence, the Irish government established the New Ireland Forum, which brought together representatives of the republic's main political parties with those of the SDLP to fashion a common approach to a political settlement. Meeting in Dublin for the first time on May 30, 1983, the forum produced a report in 1984 that offered a set of options—a unitary 32-county Irish state; a federal islandwide government; or joint Republic of Ireland and U.K. authority over Northern Ireland. Rejected by unionists and the U.K. government, the forum proved influential nevertheless in bringing the republic fully into the search for a solution to the Northern Ireland problem.

The government under Prime Minister Margaret Thatcher (1925–) firmly rejected all of the forum's proposals. Elected in May 1979, Thatcher and her administration were initially inclined to staunchly support the unionists, but realizing that there was no going back to permanent Protestant power holding, Prime Minister Thatcher, too,

A TOUR THROUGH SOUTH ARMAGH IN 1983

Those parts of Northern Ireland where Protestants and Catholics came into the closest contact served as the flashpoints for the most violent attacks during the height of the "Troubles" (Na Trioblóidí), the term resurrected from the Anglo-Irish war of 1919–21 to identify the Northern Ireland conflict. South Armagh is a region where the two communities have lived in proximity for centuries, and it became one of the most battle-tested places in the province. A reporter for *The Times* of London was taken on a tour:

In Northern Ireland I frequently felt that it was impossible for an outsider like myself to understand the hatreds and passions of either side, but Willie took me on a 12-mile dolorosa across South Armagh that went some way towards enlightening me. Every mile we passed the scene of some atrocity. . . .

We passed the Kingsmills Presbyterian Church where in 1980 the "provies" shot Willie's uncle, Clifford Lundy, a former UDR member, as he was returning from his work as a lorry driver.

We drove through the village of Whitecross where Willie was raised until local republicans drove out his family with stones and petrol bombs when he was 12. . . .

Just west is the farm where the IRA ambushed Willie's father one August afternoon in 1975. . . .

A hundred yards beyond . . . was another roadside memorial— this one to a 12-year-old Catholic girl named Majella O'Hare who was caught in the crossfire of a gunfight between soldiers and the IRA as she was on her way to confession.

We had traversed the northern part of South Armagh, where there was still a significant Protestant population, but as we headed south towards the border the towns and villages became almost entirely Catholic and republican. Here the Irish tricolour, not the Union Jack, flies from every flagpole. Here signs are writ- ten in Irish as well as English, and the roadside memorials are to "volunteers" killed by the security forces. . . .

Willie had more or less completed his tour by now. . . . This angry young Protestant dropped me in Crossmaglen with a parting shot. "As far as I'm concerned this is our home," he said. "Ulster belongs to us. No IRA man or anyone else will push me out of it. They may carry me out, but they'll never push me out."

Source: Martin Fletcher, *Silver Linings: Travels around Northern Ireland* (London: Little, Brown, 2000), pp. 115–118.

in time, came to recognize the need for some sort of power-sharing scheme. In seeking to offer the SDLP some show of support so as to thwart the electoral appeal of Sinn Féin, London came to share with Dublin a desire for a solution that acknowledged the rights of both majority and minority communities.

They did so in the face of a continued campaign of violence. The Provisional IRA launched increasingly audacious attacks, exploding bombs in Hyde Park and Regent's Park, London, in July 1982. In a direct threat to the prime minister, a bomb was detonated at the Grand Hotel in Brighton, England, during a Conservative Party conference in October 1984, killing five. Residents in Great Britain grew as accustomed to strict security checks as were Northern Ireland's long-suffering citizens. Ulster's by now intricate network of roadblocks, metal detectors, and army checkpoints stood no more vividly on display than in Belfast, where the "Peace Line"—a 30-foot-high wall topped in places with barbed wire, constantly monitored by British soldiers—cut through and closed off streets to separate the Catholic Falls Road area from the Protestant Shankill neighborhood.

British prime minister Thatcher and Irish prime minister Garret FitzGerald (1926–) held a summit in November 1984 and issued a joint communiqué calling for recognition and respect for both communities. Their meeting produced the Anglo-Irish Hillsborough Agreement, signed on November 15, 1985, which marked a major step forward in bilateral cooperative efforts. No longer would the two governments respond on an occasional basis to specific crises. Now they put in place a mechanism for regular interchanges. London and Dublin affirmed that any change in the status of the province would be made only with the consent of the majority of the people of Northern Ireland and that if, in future, a majority should agree to the establishment of a united Ireland, both governments would introduce and support legislation to that effect in their respective parliaments. The terms of the agreement called for creation of a joint British-Irish Intergovernmental Center to meet regularly as a forum to discuss matters relating to Northern Ireland. For the first time, Dublin had entered the search for a solution to the impasse in Ulster in a major way, its diplomatic drive indicative of a country possessed of a newfound confidence.

The Republic: Social and Economic Progress, 1966–1982

Government and citizens in the republic watched the events unfolding in the North with great concern, but society turned away with dismay at the violence, setting its sights steadfastly on growing the country's wealth. The Second Programme for Economic Expansion, the ambitious plan to move the economy forward launched in 1964, and the third from 1970 to 1972 oversaw an influx of foreign manufacturing investment and vigorous export promotion.

Regional free trade became a major priority. No other milestone marked the way to brighter economic prospects than did the country's entry into the European Community (EC)—the successor organization to the European Economic Community (Common Market)—on January 1, 1973. The Irish people expressed wholehearted support—the venture garnering 83 percent in a popular referendum—for the move, which promised greater prosperity and the possibility of widening the country's economic connections beyond the traditional tight links to Britain.

The surge in foreign investment brought to Ireland firms producing electrical goods, chemicals, and electronics, which helped to diversify the country's export markets. The economy grew at a healthy average annual rate of 4 percent throughout the period, despite slumps, briefly in 1973–74 and a longer recession after 1979, induced in part by rising energy prices that affected Ireland along with the rest of the Western world.

Economic performance was overseen by political regimes that changed more swiftly than at any time since 1922. The ruling parties switched five times from 1966 to 1982. The three traditional parties—Fianna Fáil, Fine Gael, and Labour—still dominated the scene, but the ethos born in the wake of war had long since dissipated. Fianna Fáil had shed its professed radicalism and Fine Gael its conservatism, both parties moving to the center of the political spectrum, their differences on issues now based more on kind than on degree. Labour remained a distant third in popular support, the party unable to induce electors to switch their political habits and vote on the basis of class rather than faction. New leaders replaced old stalwarts, while all the parties became better-funded and well-managed.

Having won an overall majority in the 1965 general election, Fianna Fáil's Seán Lemass retired suddenly in November 1966, opening up a struggle for the party's leadership that led to a deadlock between Charles Haughey (1925–2005) and George Colley (1925–83) and the choice of Jack Lynch (1917–99) as a compromise candidate. Born in Cork, John Mary (Jack) Lynch owed his start in politics to his status as a revered sportsman who earned all-Ireland medals in hurling and Gaelic football. He had served in the Dáil as a member for Cork constituencies since 1948.

In the general election of June 18, 1969, Fianna Fáil secured a gain of two seats. In April 1970 the government was rocked by scandal when customs officials at Dublin airport seized a consignment of arms secretly imported from the Continent to be sent to the Provisional IRA in the North. In May Lynch dismissed two ministers—Minister for Finance Haughey and Minister for Agriculture and Fisheries Neil Blaney (1922–95)—who he believed were implicated in the affair.

By February 1973 the government felt confident enough to call an election, one in which economic issues predominated. Fianna Fáil lost six seats, paving the way for a coalition of Fine Gael and Labour to form a government on the basis of a pact the two parties had made before the election. Liam Cosgrave served as prime minister. The coalition's concerns were dominated by issues of security. In 1974 bombs set off by northern unionists killed 34 people in Dublin and Monaghan, and the government responded with tighter security legislation and the grant of greater powers to the Civic Guard.

Cosgrave's government significantly expanded social welfare benefits, and support for the government held firm in subsequent by-elections. Inflation rose, fueled both by external factors, notably restrictions on oil sales by the Organization of Petroleum-Exporting Countries (OPEC), and by domestic unemployment. Constituency borders, redrawn in the mid 1970s, were expected to accrue to the benefit of the ruling parties, and so the June 1977 election results proved a surprise to election watchers. The economic troubles contributed to a resounding defeat of the Fine Gael–led coalition, and Fianna Fáil returned to power with the largest mandate ever attained in an Irish election—84 seats versus 64 for Fine Gael, Labour, and others.

The government under returning Prime Minister Lynch proceeded to follow through on electioneering promises to abolish certain taxes, but efforts to advance its agenda were stymied by dissension among parliamentary backbenchers over the government's relatively conciliatory policy toward unionists in the North and by mounting economic worries. Having had enough, Lynch resigned in December 1979, opening up a battle for the party's leadership. Old challengers Haughey and Colley renewed their rivalry. Networking assiduously and counting on his considerable charisma to keep the loyalty of party backbenchers, Haughey won a narrow victory. From County Mayo and the son-in-law of Seán Lemass, Haughey had been elected to the Dáil for Dublin East in 1957 and had served as minister of several departments.

Haughey as prime minister carried worrisome implications for efforts to end the Northern Ireland impasse in view of his identification with the wing of Fianna Fáil most strident in its sentiment in favor of islandwide reunification, but once in office he worked for closer coordinated peacemaking efforts with the United Kingdom, and cordial cooperation characterized relations until Haughey's support for imprisoned hunger strikers soured U.K. officials on collaborative ventures. He concentrated diligently on Northern Ireland affairs until sidetracked both by persistent economic problems stemming from the recession that set in after 1980 and by divisions over his leadership among party members, many of whom remained wary of his integrity in remembering his implication in the arms crisis of 1970. In June 1981 he called a general election in an effort to bolster his position. The first election held for a Dáil in which the number of seats had been increased from 148 to 166 to reflect population growth, the results produced no clear victor. Fianna Fáil lost its absolute majority while Fine Gael gained seats. Labour along with three independents held the balance of power, and a coalition composed of Fine Gael, Labour, and the independents formed a government.

The new prime minister, Dr. Garret FitzGerald, had succeeded Cosgrave as leader of Fine Gael in 1977. Born in Dublin, the son of the first foreign minister of the Irish Free State, and a lawyer, businessman, consultant, and journalist, he served in the Dáil from 1969. FitzGerald saw as his first priority redressing the economic distress that had deepened after 1979. From 1973 to the early 1980s Ireland was hit by two oil crises, a series of bank strikes that paralyzed business activity for more than a year, pay raises for public employees, poor industrial relations, and runaway inflation. In hopes that the downturn would prove short-lived, Haughey had borrowed heavily to maintain existing levels of public expenditure, but the economic woes had lingered, leaving FitzGerald to face a massive public sector debt. Severe budget cuts were proposed, but the government's economic package fell one vote short of passage in the Dáil in January 1982.

The country found itself entirely unprepared for the competition from its European partners consequent to membership in the European Community. Heavy industry, located especially in the Cork region, suffered massive shutdowns in the late 1970s and early 1980s. Agriculture, though benefiting from generous European subsidies that saw farmers' incomes grow dramatically, proved unable to take up the economic slack because of production quotas.

The economy would dominate politics throughout the 1980s, and the decade was also one in which, for the first time, issues surrounding fund-raising by political parties emerged. The courting of wealthy corporate donors by Fianna Fáil in particular gave rise to worries about the potential for unhealthy influence on politics by big business contributors given access to the highest levers of power.

The failure of the government's budget proposal preceded by one month the fall from power of the Fine Gael coalition, when several independent supporters balked at voting for a tax increase in February 1982. A general election on February 18 again produced no clear winners. Haughey managed to cobble together a coalition with independents and minor parties, but once again his hold on power proved precarious. Scandals touched some of his closest associates, and divisions riddled Fianna Fáil. TD for Limerick East Desmond O'Malley (1939–) tried but failed to challenge Haughey's leadership of the party in March 1982.

The recession raged on. Government revenues declined further, forcing up the debt to higher than ever levels and necessitating steep tax increases. In November the government lost the support of some independents and that of the Workers' Party, the latter originally Official Sinn Féin and founded in 1982 as a far-left Marxist-inspired republican party in both the republic and Northern Ireland. Haughey, losing a vote of no confidence, was compelled to resign. For the third time in 18 months voters trudged to the polls, but this time a clear result ensued: Fine Gael and Labour won a majority and a coalition government under FitzGerald took office.

They did so in a country in which social change marched relentlessly forward. No other indicator registered the degree to which Ireland was undergoing rapid transformation as dramatically as did demography. From an all-time low of 2.8 million in 1961, the population had jumped to 3.4 million 20 years later. The century of decline had been reversed, and the population now was not only larger but also younger. By 1980 almost half of the republic's people were under the age of 25. They were being educated in a system that had been largely overhauled. Government reports in the 1960s highlighted deficiencies at all schooling levels. New curricula were introduced in the 1970s at primary and secondary levels, and larger and better-equipped schools were built. From 1967 education was provided free for most pupils, and attendance more than doubled between 1960 and 1980. At the university level, a new Higher Education Authority was created in 1968 to advise the minister for education on funds allocation and other issues. Regional technical colleges were established.

Despite the economic woes, modernization brought higher living standards for most, though not all. Poverty persisted among some 20 percent of the population, which helped to spawn a growing crime rate in urban areas, especially Dublin. And the rise in population meant more young people entering the labor force, leading to higher unemployment in the absence of available jobs. Industrial expansion also engendered mounting worries about environmental pollution.

Movement toward more progressive social attitudes proceeded in line with modernization. Traditional Catholic mores that had for so long put a clamp on change continued to loosen. Laws that made the sale and import of contraceptives illegal were changed in 1979 to make them available under certain restrictions. By the early 1980s pressure began to grow for a repeal of the ban on divorce. Abortion remained outlawed, but thousands of women traveled to Britain each year to procure one. These actions reflected a growing activist movement among women during the period, who, despite much lower levels of workforce participation than found elsewhere in western Europe, secured legislation to guarantee equal opportunity and pay and a more gender-equitable tax structure. Marriage levels dropped, and growing numbers of couples were living outside marriage.

The tide of social change fragmented Irish value systems. Devotion to Catholicism remained strong—huge crowds greeted Pope John Paul II (1920–2005) on his three-day visit in September 1979, the first ever by a pontiff to Ireland—but the impact of globalization proved relentless, linking the country ever more closely with trends and perspectives characteristic of the modern Western world. Minds opening to wider outlooks proved equally in evidence in the world of arts.

Ireland's Modern Culture Scene
English-Language Literature

Censorship remained in force in the immediate postwar years, and literary activity suffered correspondingly, but by the 1980s a considerable relaxation set in. Works previously banned were allowed to be republished. Wider freedoms for cultural expression followed inexorably from the steady progress of modern consumerism, from technological advances that shrank barriers to communications, and from growing ties with continental Europe. The second half of the 20th century witnessed a blossoming of creative writing, especially a surge in the appearance of short stories and poetry of international repute, and in an outpouring of superlative dramatic productions.

The claustrophobic culturalism that characterized the early postwar years was succeeded in the late 1950s by the arrival on the scene of a new generation of novelists whose works veered away from preoccupa-tion with national issues and social themes to concentrate on topics in private life. An emphasis on character rather than plot, a more in-depth look at the material realities of daily life, and a self-conscious rejection of inherited moral codes characterized the work of Aidan Higgins (1927–), as in his *Langrishe Go Down* (1966), John McGahern (1934–), and Edna O'Brien (1930–). O'Brien stirred considerable controversy with books such as *The Country Girls* (1960) and *Girl with Green Eyes* (1964) dealing with issues of unhappy marriage and female sexuality far too honest for the censors to allow. Her works were banned, although she was among the most read novelists of the period. McGahern saw his second novel, *The Dark* (1965), banned. He left Ireland but returned in 1974 to write novels and short stories, all dealing with exile, personal relationships, and sexual topics (*The Pornographer* [1979], *Amongst Women* [1990]).

Beginning in the 1980s O'Brien's impact lessened as a new generation of readers hearkened to the irreverent tones of Roddy Doyle (1958–) and Dermot Bolger (1959–). The communities of Bolger's Finglas and Doyle's Barrytown, neither rural nor urban, contain families whose characters undergo crucial experiences of relocation and displacement. In Doyle's Barrytown trilogy—*The Commitments* (1987), *The Snapper* (1990), and *The Van* (1991)—the Rabbitte family departs from the hierarchical, traditional Irish family. Jimmy Rabbitte's title as head of the family is merely titular, the members held together by mutual sup-port and solidarity.

The country house, or the "big house," has proved a popular theme among Irish writers since the 19th century. The site of order and the symbol of power during the Protestant Ascendancy and a place of decay with the decline of the landlord class, the big house has evoked a range of meanings in fiction, poetry, art, and social history, and it has pro-voked some of the most evocative writings in Irish literature as penned by W. B. Yeats and others. Elizabeth Bowen (1899–1973) from Dublin and Mitchelstown, County Cork, gives a picture of the country house and of families and their ancestors in many of her novels (*Bowen's Court* [1942], *A World of Love* [1955]). Another writer from Mitchelstown, William Trevor (1928–) writes novels that include tales based on Irish history and politics as well as black comedies. He treats of the Anglo-Irish big house in works such as *The Silence in the Garden* (1988) and *The Story of Lucy Gault* (2002), a tale that deals with the decay of the country estates.

In Northern Ireland, Brian Moore (1921–99) moved far beyond the well-established lines of the communal divide in his early works

(*The Feast of Lupercal* [1957]) in dealing with issues of family ties and the search for identity set in a variety of international locales and historical periods (*Cold Heaven* [1983], *Black Robe* [1985]). Belfast-born Sam Thompson (1916–65) in his play *Over the Bridge* (1960) vividly depicts the sectarianism rampant in the Belfast shipyards just before the outbreak of violence at decade's end, but the discord in the North has resonated little in the Irish creative mind, whether in prose, poetry, or drama, writers seemingly preferring to avoid concentrating on the unseemly events that so much recall the country's disturbed past. Bernard MacLaverty (1942–) in his short novel *Cal* (1983) tells a tale of a star-crossed love affair across the religious divide, and poet and critic Seamus Deane (1940–) in his semiautobiographical *Readings in the Dark* (1996) treats in a moving way the harrowing ordeals of the narrator's nationalist family and his struggle to put the past to rest.

Deane served as general editor of the *Field Day Anthology of Irish Writing*, the first attempt to create a standard canon of Irish literature from its ancient beginnings. The anthology embodies a cooperative effort by writers in the North and the South, and it was preceded by another cross-border endeavor, the Field Day Theatre Company. The theater was cofounded by playwright Brian Friel (1929–) and actor Stephen Rea (1948–). Staging productions at sights around Ireland, the theater company debuted with Friel's *Translations* (1980). A playwright noted for the quality and range of his works, who explores issues of identity and emigration, Friel closed out a decade of great dramatic achievement with *Dancing at Lughnasa* (1990).

Tom Murphy (1935–) from Tuam, County Galway, who had earlier scored a hit with *A Whistle in the Dark* (1961) with its depictions of violence among the emigrant Irish, wrote his two greatest plays in the 1980s, *The Gigli Concert* (1983), about the sufferings of ordinary men under stress, and *Baile gangaire* (Town without laughter) (1985), dealing with the issue of unwanted pregnancy. The play resonated with audiences in following closely on two key events in 1984—the death in labor of a 15-year-old schoolgirl at the end of a pregnancy concealed from her parents and the discovery of two murdered infants in County Kerry—that spawned constitutional and legal debates in the republic about the issue of control of women's fertility.

The 1980s witnessed the spread of regional playhouses while companies appeared in Dublin that offered alternative theater. By that decade Irish drama posted an abundance of achievements, the production of many quality plays symbolized by a newly redesigned Abbey Theatre (1966) and the appearance of the new Peacock Theatre a year later. The

Peacock became an important venue for Irish-language plays, with its opening production a stage adaptation of Flann O'Brien's satiric novel *An Béal Bocht (The Poor Mouth)*. Appointed artistic director at the Abbey in 1966, Walter Macken (1915–67) wrote prolifically, including a number of plays (*Home Is the Hero* [1953]) and novels, many set in historical venues, such as *The Silent People* (1962), about the Great Famine.

In December 1969 Samuel Beckett's play *Waiting for Godot* was produced on the main stage of the Abbey in acknowledgment of his receipt of the Nobel Prize in literature that year. A novelist, dramatist, and poet, Dublin-born and Trinity College–educated Beckett (1906–89) is one of the outstanding Irish artists of the mid 20th century. His early short-story collection *More Pricks than Kicks* (1934) exhibits the strong influence of James Joyce, whom he knew. Beckett settled in France in 1939, uncomfortable in the stifling creative atmosphere in censored Ireland. His literary career blossomed there in the postwar years. Working in Paris, he wrote in French, which would be the language of most of his works and which he would translate himself into English. His most famous play, *Waiting for Godot* (*En attendant Godot* [1953]), was a critical and popular success, which paved the way to a career in theater (*Endgame* [1957], *Happy Days* [1960]). The plays present characters who despair of their condition but who nevertheless strive to survive in the face of a world that neither understands them nor is understandable to them, and yet who manage oftentimes to retain a wicked sense of humor. Beckett's later plays are written in a sparse syle and feature very few characters (*Catastrophe* [1982]), who often draw on memory in forcing recollections of haunting past events. Beckett died in Paris, an expatriate to the end.

In contrast, another poet, novelist, and playwright lived life in Ireland to the full. Born in Dublin into an educated working-class family, Brendan Behan (Breandán Ó Beacháin, 1923–64) joined the IRA in 1939 and was arrested and imprisoned (1942–46) for the attempted murder of two detectives in Dublin. In prison he learned the Irish language, wrote his first play (*The Landlady*), and began to produce short stories and prose. His breakthrough came with his play *The Quare Fellow* (1954), Irish slang for "condemned man," which chronicles the ups and downs of prison life. His autobiographical novel *Borstal Boy* (1958) is his acclaimed masterpiece. An ardent republican, Behan turned away from violence late in his life, a life that was plagued by the heavy drinking that helped bring him to an early death.

In poetry, Seamus Heaney (1939–) stands preeminent for the range, versatility, and quality of his work, his outstanding skill recognized worldwide on his winning the Nobel Prize in literature in 1995. A Roman Catholic born near Bellaghy, County Derry, Heaney's work, which also includes essays, touches on many aspects of Irish life, always delivered in a congenial, personal voice. In *North* (1975), his most elaborate and controversial volume of verse, he employs myth to give immediacy to the sectarian turmoil, which he conveys in a warm tone based on his independent approach. He includes three moving elegies to friends who died in the violence in a follow-up volume, *Field Work* (1979). A New York–born Irish academic, John Montague (1929–) writes poetry that deals with both personal issues of family and separation as well as public concerns surrounding the turmoil in Northern Ireland (*The Rough Field* [1972], *The Dead Kingdom* [1984]). He held the Ireland Chair of Poetry for many years. Other major poets in the latter part of the century include Thomas Kinsella (1928–), a poet who also published a translation of the *Táin* in 1969; Brendan Kennelly (1936–), who has published more than 20 books of poetry, novels, and translations, including his most popular work *Cromwell* (1983); Derek Mahon (1941–); and Michael Longley (1959–), a Belfast-born poet whose verse centers on life in the conflict-ridden province (*An Exploded View* [1973]).

Revisionism characterized much historical writing from the 1970s through the 1990s, prompted to a degree by the outbreak of so much violence in the North. Some historians sought to downplay the significance of violence in Irish history. Mixed sentiments about the era of rebellion and independence were expressed, some feeling shame at the manner in which the IRA abused the legacy of the past to justify waging a war of terror in the North. Some among historians suggested that glorification of the violent birth of Irish independence had done much to ensure the permanence of partition. Esteemed historian, journalist, and politician Conor Cruise O'Brien (1917–) has made implicit his belief that Ireland would have won its right to self-government without the upheaval of the Easter Rising (*State of Ireland* [1972]).

By the end of the century, many historians broached a more balanced approach to the past. Seeing little need any longer to argue whether past insurrections were necessary or not, they depicted both the noble and the ignoble sides of 20th-century Irish history, freely acknowledging the bloodier, more sinister components of the recent and the more distant past. Social, economic, and cultural history, long neglected as areas of study, grew in importance. University of Dublin historian Margaret MacCurtain helped to launch study of the role of women in Irish history (*Women in Irish Society: The Historical Dimension* [1978]).

The Censorship of Publications Act remains in effect, although amendments in 1946 and 1967 have softened strictures, and today only works that are clearly pornographic tend to be restricted. Public criticisms continue, however, in citing the fact that meetings of the Censorship Board are held in secret and that standards and criteria of judgment are vague and ill-defined.

Irish literature, too, has undergone shifts in focus. The important place rural Ireland traditionally occupied in Irish cultural discourse has been succeeded by a greater concentration on urban Ireland. The clash between tradition and modernity that served as the underlying theme for so many playwrights has been decided in favor of the latter. The Ireland of quaint cottages and hardy peasant folk has been replaced by an Ireland that displays all of the complex realities of advanced societies. Issues of Catholic versus Protestant ideology or moderate versus radical republicanism, which once predominated, are superseded today by topics dealing with women's and gay rights, immigration, and sexual exploitation.

Irish-Language Literature

Modernism emerged full-blown in Irish-language literature when writers joined with those working in other languages in expressing the feelings of loss and alienation in a world in which the old certainties of identities rooted in firm relationships with God, community, and family were vanishing in the midst of rapid change. The poet who first expressed this sentiment is Máirtín Ó Direáin (1910–88) in his precedent-setting *Coinnlea Geala* (1942). His central theme is the spiritual despair accompanying the breakdown of traditional rural communities in the wake of urbanization and modernization. Born in Inishmore, one of the Aran Islands, Ó Direáin wrote poetry that, because it broke with traditional forms and meters, has earned for him the title of the first modern Irish poet. Modernist poets combined a familiarity with the achievements of the Irish literary tradition, an openness to European influences, formal experimentation, and a willingness to employ modern settings, namely, the urban industrial world, as subject matter. Outstanding exemplars include Seán Ó Ríorda (1916–77), a County Cork poet whose deep, afflicted questioning of identity is reflected in his reordering language to suit his own needs, which he called *Riordanu* ("Riordanizing"). He conveys an intensity of feeling through language in his 30-poem collection *Brosna* (1964). Dublin-born Máire Mhac an tSaoi (1922–) displays a tension between personal desire and the wish to adhere to conformist values in drawing on both classical Irish verse and traditional Gaeltacht poetry (*An Cion go dti Seo* [1987]). She is considered by many the most accomplished female Irish poet.

An important spur to production was provided by *Innti*. Founded by Michael Davitt (1950–2000), the literary journal, published from 1970 to 1996, gave Irish poets both an outlet for expression and a means of access to audiences in featuring works of a new generation of poets who included Davitt himself, Nuala Ní Dhomhnaill (1952–), Liam Ó Muirthile (1950–), Gabriel Rosenstock (1949–), and others. Cathal Ó Searcaigh (1950–) has become one of the most popular contemporary poets, the most identifiable feature of his work the celebration of homosexual love (*Suibhne* [Sweeney, 1987]). Ó Searcaigh is unusual in being a native speaker of Irish, most prominent *Innti* poets working from English as their mother tongue.

The impact of the women's movement is confirmed by the presence of talented female voices, including Dhomhnaill, whose works often attest to the continuing psychological validity of traditional folk beliefs (*An Dealg Droighin* [1981]). Biddy Jenkinson (1947–), a poet, novelist, and dramatist, also draws on material from the early Irish literary tradition.

Outstanding dramatists include Ó Tuama, whose controversial plays have been denounced by clerics but applauded by audiences (*Gunna Cam agus Slabhra Óir* [Twisted gun and gold chain, 1950]), and Críostóir Ó Floinn (1927–), who wrote social and political critiques (*Is É a Dúirt Polonius* [1973]).

From 1940 to 1980 two dominant threads emerged in prose writing: a traditional regional stress, linked most often, though not exclusively, with the Gaeltacht region, and a modernist emphasis, characterized by linguistic and stylistic innovation and experimentation. Séamus Ó Grianna, already an established author by 1940, is linked with the former, and his highly sentimentalized short stories of life in Gaeltacht Donegal remained popular through the 1960s. Connemara-born Máirtín Ó Cadhain (1905–70) was a schoolteacher and a member of the IRA who after World War II became a professor of Irish language at Trinity College. He propounded a Marxist approach to cultural relations, affirming that capitalist economic structures must be broken before English cultural dominance could be overcome. His *Cré na Cille* (Church and clay, 1949) gives a detailed insight into class and cultural identification in a poor rural community where relationships with the land and language are the important social factors.

Themes of social change and displacement mark novels of the 1960s and 1970s, reflecting the march of modernity in Ireland. Ó Grianna himself breaks away from romantic depictions in introducing an element of sociocultural criticism to his writing (*Bean Ruadh de Dhálach* [1966]), and critics hailed Pádraig Ua Maoileoin (1913–) for his innovative depiction of Gaeltacht life in *Bríde Bhán* (1968). Diarmid Ó Suilleabháin (1932–85) uses interior monologue to critique contemporary Irish culture and investigate issues of individual identity (*Dianmhuilte Dé* [The sloe thorn, 1964]). In his novels, Eoghan Ó Tuairisc (Eugene Watters, 1919–82), one of the most important writers of the 1960s who was known for both comedies and tragedies, moved beyond descriptions presented solely by Irish speakers. In his first novel, *L'Attaque* (Attack, 1962) he presents a critical, revisionist view of the political, social, and religious causes behind the 1798 rebellion. The autobiography *An Lomnochtán* (1977) presents a view of the world as seen by a young English-speaking boy.

Many new prose writers appeared in the 1980s and 1990s. The trilogy penned by Dublin-born Séamus Mac Annaidh (1961–) involves a multilayered series dealing with themes of teenage culture and identity and intergenerational anxiety set against Northern Ireland's sectarianism. Ciarán Ó Coigligh (1951–) is noted for social realism, which remains a dominant strain in fiction (*Duibhlinn* [1991]), while others, such as Dublin-born Lorcán Ó Treasaigh (1956–) moved on to dispense with conventional narrative structure in using a series of unrelated episodes to create a world of the imagination (*Sracfhéachaint* [1986]).

The 20th century ended with ongoing attempts to promote production of popular fiction beyond the academic community, which has always provided a dependable outlet for Irish-language literature. The annual Oireachtas competition continues, and in addition to literary awards, prizes are given in print and visual media fields.

The Irish language maintains a fragile hold in the country. The language is taught as a compulsory subject in schools, and a major development in education has been the growth of Irish-language immersion schools *(Gael scioleanna)*. Children attend summer immersion courses in Irish language, music, and dancing established in Gaeltacht districts.

In 1956 a new government department, Roinn na Gaeltachta, was created to better promote the culture and economy of the Gaeltacht area. Boundaries were enlarged in 1974 to include areas in counties Kerry and Waterford, but the population of Gaeltacht regions continues to decline as a result of aging and outmigration of younger people. The percentage of those claiming to speak some Irish has grown from a low of 18 percent in 1911 to a current figure of about 30 percent, though levels of fluency vary and nowhere outside of Gaeltacht areas does it constitute the language of daily intercourse. In December 2006 the government launched an ambitious program in education designed to create a bilingual Irish- and English-speaking country over the next 20 years.

The challenge for contemporary Irish-language writers is to find artistic voices and develop creative roles in a new cultural environment, one in which the clear markers of identity that existed in the past have been replaced by a complex, highly fluid, homogenizing modern society, at once both Irish and global. The ability of the language to create its own reading and listening public will mark the measure of its success. In the 21st century the language struggles constantly for cultural survival, but its continuing vitality is essential to the country's national identity. It keeps alive the links to a literary culture that spans more than 14 centuries.

Film

Filmmaking began in Ireland in 1897 when the first known moving picture shots of Sackville (later O'Connell) Street in Dublin were recorded. In 1898 Robert A. Mitchell, a Belfast doctor, became the first Irishman to shoot a film in Ireland, namely, a documentary of a yacht race. Though the first public screening took place in 1896 in the Star of Erin Ballroom on Dublin's Dame Street, films were shown largely as part of music hall variety shows or itinerant showmen tours until 1909 when the first cinema house—the Volta—opened at 45 Mary Street in Dublin, with James Joyce its manager. By 1922 there were 37 cinemas in Dublin.

Hollywood, California–based producer Kalem Company arrived in Killarney, County Kerry, in 1910 and shot approximately 70 films in Ireland, intended mostly for Irish-American audiences, which launched a tradition in which cinematic representations of Ireland were constructed by those coming from outside the country to be directed toward those of Irish heritage elsewhere.

Early film producers were often returning emigrés or children of emigrés. In 1916 Killarney-born James Mark Sullivan (1873–1933), a U.S. lawyer, journalist, and diplomat, came back to set up the Film Company of Ireland, the first professional domestic production company. The company's adaptation of two popular historical novels, *Knocknagow* (1918) and *Willy Reilly and His Colleen Bawn* (1920), remain its greatest cinematic legacy.

The Irish Free State embarked on independence infused with the same spirit of rigid control over films that marked official attitudes

317

toward printed works. A Censorship of Films Act (1923) gave the state the power to determine films appropriate for viewing, and informed by the highly conservative Catholic ethos, many thousands of films were banned or edited in succeeding decades.

The 1920s and 1930s saw only sporadic production. The government information film *Ireland* was released in 1926. Popular representations of Ireland produced in Hollywood or Britain began. John Ford (1894–1973) made the first of his Irish-themed films with *The Informer* (1936), based on Liam O'Flaherty's novel. The British-produced documentary *Man of Aran* (1934) by filmmaker Robert Flaherty (1884–1951), with its depiction of the rustic, self-sufficient life of the islanders, accorded well with de Valera's idealized visions. For his second sound film, Alfred Hitchcock (1899–1980) adapted Sean O'Casey's *Juno and the Paycock* (1930), the first Abbey Theatre play to be filmed.

The image of the country controlled to a large degree by outsiders, a National Film Institute of Ireland (NFI) was established in 1945, funded partially by the state, to produce, distribute, and exhibit educational films in both Irish and English languages to schools and other institutions. Still, until the 1990s, film was seen largely from an economic rather than a cultural perspective. Policy focused on attracting large-scale overseas productions to film in Ireland while development of an indigenous industry was neglected. British and U.S. film companies required that lead roles be played by their own nationals so as to maximize profits through audience recognition of famous stars, even though the ability of these actors to deliver the rhythm and cadence of Irish dramatic speech was not always forthcoming. Though many in Ireland regretted the images in films such as John Ford's *The Quiet Man* (1952), with their depiction of the country as a quaint, timeless place peopled with stereotypically pretty colleens and characters ever ready to brawl and tipple, they were tolerated because they brought employment, and because hugely successful overseas, they engendered revenues from tourists and from sales of Irish exports.

The establishment of Ardmore Studios in 1957 at Bray, County Wicklow, marked the first indigenous production venture. Though it failed to secure a steady supply of clients, it did encourage more overseas filmmakers to shoot films in the country. Film was added to the purview of the Arts Council, established in 1951 to award state grants for cultural projects. Director Bob Quinn (1935–) completed *Poitín* (1977), his first feature with proceeds from the first Arts Council film script award. For three decades he has recorded life in the west of Ireland, especially in the Connemara Gaeltacht.

Maureen O'Hara and John Wayne converse over a rocky wall in a scene from the film The Quiet Man, *which was shot on location in the village of Cong in western Ireland. The film preserves a stereotypical image of Ireland beloved by many who claim Irish heritage in North America and elsewhere.* (AP Images)

The first group of indigenous filmmakers emerged in the 1970s and 1980s, including Kieran Hickey (1936–93) (*Attracta* [1983]), Joe Comerford (1947–) (*Reefer and the Model* [1988]), and Pat Murphy (1947–) (*Anne Devlin* [1984]). State acquisition of Ardmore Studios in 1973 brought an influx of regular clients, and following continuing demands by independent filmmakers, the Irish Film Board was set up in 1981 as an agency expressly enjoined to consider the need to reflect national culture in the allotment of funds. Between 1981 and 1987 the board partially funded 10 feature films, using Irish casts and focusing on local issues. Most were not commercially successful, and the government suspended the board in 1987.

Until the early 1990s virtually no feature films were being produced. A major turnaround came with the film *My Left Foot* (1990), directed by Jim Sheridan (1949–), a film made in the enduringly popular Hollywood populist mode, whose chief performers—Irish citizen Daniel Day-Lewis (1957–) and Dublin-born Brenda Fricker (1945–)—won Best Actor and Best Actress Academy Awards. The film became a tremendous success and gave birth to a formula that other

Irish producers have striven to emulate, namely, the local story with universal appeal.

The Crying Game (1992), directed by Neil Jordan (1950–), was nominated for six Academy Awards, and Jordan won in the Best Screenplay category. The film explores national and gender politics, and as a case study in homosexuality, it helped spawn an international industry in gender and gay studies. Jordan directed other Irish-themed works, including the critically successful *Michael Collins* (1996), arguably the first epic of Irish cinema, and *The Butcher Boy* (1998), from the novel by Pat McCabe (1955–), an author of novels with foreboding, often violence-laden plots set in contemporary small-town Ireland.

Reestablished in 1993, the Film Board funded development of more than 500 films and production of more than 100 by 2003. Tax breaks were made available to any producer using Ireland as a location, which made the country the fastest growing audiovisual producer among European Union members in drawing high-profile, big budget overseas productions (*Braveheart* [1994], *Saving Private Ryan* [1998]). The Irish Film Institute, the successor to the NFI, serves to produce, promote, and distribute film culture backed by Arts Council and lottery funding. The institute operates two art house theaters, which showcase independent and foreign language films not widely available commercially, in Dublin's Temple Bar district, an area redeveloped in the late 1980s and early 1990s as the city's "cultural quarter." A counterpart of the Irish Film Board, the Northern Ireland Film and TV Commission has worked closely with the former, and it has helped fund virtually every feature shot in Northern Ireland since 1997. The documentary *Mise Éire* (I am Ireland [1959]) was the first feature-length Irish-language film made by Gael Linn, an independent but state-aided cultural agency created in 1953 to promote use of the Irish language in media.

Many films have explored conventional themes of Irish identity. Films such as *Eat the Peach* (1986) and *The Field* (1990), which deal with rural Ireland and the struggle to own land, have proved popular with Irish audiences but less so internationally. A film that has won wide acclaim, *Dancing at Lughnasa* (1998), based on the classic play by Brian Friel, features an all-star cast in telling the story of five unmarried sisters and their simple life in County Donegal in the 1930s.

A famous film that focuses on Ireland's war of independence is *Shake Hands with the Devil* (1959), the first U.S. film shot at Ardmore Studios, directed by Michael Anderson (1920–) and starring Irish-American actor James Cagney (1899–1986). Hollywood has exploited the violence in Northern Ireland in fictional narratives that highlight the potential that conflict here holds for global terrorism (*The Patriot Game* [1992]) and which offer little insight into the political and socioeconomic context of the conflict. More sophisticated presentations are provided in *Maeve* (1982), directed by Pat Murphy; *Angel* (1982), Neil Jordan's first feature that began his preoccupation with the theme; and *Some Mother's Son* (1996), directed by Northern Ireland–born Terry George (1952–).

Films such as *Intermission* (2003) by first-time director John Crowley (1969–) appeal to native audiences in treating Irish themes. *The Wind That Shakes the Barley* (2007), a historical drama of two brothers fighting with volunteer guerrillas against brutal squads of Black and Tans in the war for independence, won the 2006 Palme d'Or award at the Cannes Film Festival. Filmed in Ireland, with a script written by Paul Laverty (1957–) and starring Irish actors Cillian Murphy (1976–) and Pádraic Delaney (1977–), the film is the highest grossing Irish-made independent film to date.

Film festivals began at Cork in 1956 and are now held across Ireland. The Irish Film and Television Awards (IFTA)—Ireland's equivalent to the Academy Awards—first began in 1999 to celebrate the country's cinematic talent.

Ireland's presence in film has long been celebrated in the internationally recognized faces of its native-born actors and actresses, who include, among others, Maureen O'Sullivan (1911–98), considered the country's first film star; Barry Fitzgerald (1888–1961); Cyril Cusack (1910–93); Maureen O'Hara (1920–); Siobhán McKenna (1923–86); Richard Harris (1930–2002); Peter O'Toole (1932–); Fionnuala Flanagan (1941–); Liam Neeson (1952–); Pierce Brosnan (1953–); Kenneth Branagh (1960–); and Colin Farrell (1976–).

Despite the success of Irish films, the globalization of film production makes maintenance of a separate national industry increasingly difficult. Because Ireland's majority language is English, Irish cinema is irrevocably drawn to the United States and Britain for sources of finance and target audiences, and since the 1990s a new generation of filmmakers has increasingly explored wider issues, reflecting the country's greater prosperity and growing cosmopolitanism, in efforts to win a more universal appeal. Films such as *Ailsa* (1994), directed by Paddy Breathnach (1964–); *The Snapper* (1993), directed by Stephen Frears (1941–); and *The Commitments* (1990), directed by Alan Parker (1944–) have achieved global box office success. The Irish debate the relative merits of the openness that prosperity has brought. Some criticize the loss of a unique cultural identity. Others welcome a global, in particular American, culture as a positive, liberating force, content to accept even the old stereotypes of romantic Ireland so beloved by Irish descendants abroad as offering a legitimate perspective on the country.

Music, Dance, and Painting

Irish music has maintained its vibrant, native tradition throughout the 20th century. Indeed, Irish sounds have influenced other forms of music, such as country music in the United States. After independence, the teaching of folk music and dancing in schools was stressed, and Radio Éireann devoted considerable airtime to broadcasting cultural programs.

The Irish music scene in midcentury was characterized by a dearth of native composers and little government money made available to promote creative endeavors—until the 1950s the Royal Irish Academy of Music received only paltry grants. Foreign culture was actively embraced. In the early 1960s the touring show band, popular abroad, spread to Ireland, and the first of the big Irish bands, the Clipper Carlton, was followed by others. But already by the mid 1960s they began to decline, overtaken by the rise of discos. And the arrival of the Beatles (1963) and the Rolling Stones (1965) in Dublin, greeted by hordes of screaming fans, attests to Irish youth's close connection to Western popular trends.

Summer music festivals (*Fleadh Cheoil*) helped keep interest in traditional music alive. Folk bands such as the Dubliners and the Clancy Brothers became famous worldwide in the 1960s. Their rebel songs and traditional ballads helped revive interest in these tunes in Ireland itself, where popular music had become preeminent. Beginning in 1962 the Dubliners have endured despite changes in membership, and they have recorded dozens of albums over the years.

Born in Belfast, flutist James Galway (1939–) studied in London and Paris and played with philharmonic orchestras in London and Berlin until 1975, when he launched a solo career. His repertoire ranges from classical works to jazz and modern rock, and his career has been crowned with a knighthood by Queen Elizabeth II (r. 1952–) in 2001.

No one contributed more to developing an awareness of Irish music and its potential than Seán Ó Riada (1931–71). Born in Adare, County Limerick, and educated at University College Cork, he served as assistant music director at Radio Éireann from 1953 to 1955 and then music director of the Abbey Theatre. He launched a traditional Irish group, Ceoltoiri Cualann, many of whose performers later formed the Chieftains. The best known Irish composer in the mid 20th century,

Ó Riada crafted innovative arrangements of the native repertory to be played in the traditional way, and his music scores for films (*The Playboy of the Western World* [1962]) garnered praise. His score for *Mise Éire* is one of the classic pieces of Irish 20th-century music.

During the 1970s and 1980s the distinction between traditional and rock music grew increasingly blurred with performers crossing between the two and mixing elements from each. A creative admixture of folk, blues, country, and rock characterizes Irish traditional and folk music, performed by artists such as County Kildare singer and songwriter Christy Moore (1945–), whose first album, *Prosperous* (1972), led to the formation of a group called Planxty, which combined American folk and traditional Irish sounds. Belfast-born Van Morrison (George Ivan Morrison, 1945–) began performing solo in 1966 and has produced numerous albums (*Astral Weeks* [1968], *Irish Heartbeat* [1988]) to international acclaim. The County Donegal musical group Clannad, who appeared in the 1970s, performed Irish-language songs to traditional tunes, and they spawned artist Eithne Ni Bhraonain, known as Enya, who left the group in 1982 to earn for herself an internationally successful career.

Formed in Dublin in 1976, U2 became Ireland's most successful and one of the world's most popular rock bands in the 1980s and 1990s. The group has consistently performed in support of political and international causes, issuing a song "Sunday Bloody Sunday" in 1972 calling for an end to the violence in Northern Ireland. The band's charity concerts on behalf of peace in Northern Ireland (1998) and aid to Africa (2005) were organized by Dublin-born singer Bob Geldof (1954–), who in 1975 had founded the popular music group the Boomtown Rats. The success of U2 spawned other Irish groups that have won international acclaim, such as the Cranberries from Limerick and the Corrs from Dundalk. County Donegal native Daniel (Danny) O'Donnell (1961–) sings popular religious and traditional music to mainly middle-aged audiences in Ireland and abroad. Dublin-born singer Sinéad O'Connor (1966–) won international success with her album *Nothing Compares 2 U* (1990). Dana Rosemary Scallon, born Rosemary Brown (1951–), earned international fame in 1970 in winning the Eurovision song contest with "All Kinds of Everything." She became a well-known singer of contemporary Catholic music.

Contemporary groups that strive to remain true to traditional sounds include Deántu Danú, the Border Collies, and Dervish Dervish among many others. Traditional music, featuring the sounds of harp, bagpipes (villeann pipe, Irish union pipe), fiddle, flute, concertina, tin whistle,

The dancing and musical spectacular Riverdance *has been performed worldwide before millions.* (AP Images)

guitar, bodhran (a round goatskin tambourine or drum played with a small stick), and Irish banjo (a four-string version of an instrument introduced from the United States in the 19th century) can be heard at venues everywhere in the country, and Dublin, Belfast, and Cork hold major festivals.

Dancing, like music, is actively promoted by public and private initiatives. Set dancing, in which participants dance in "sets" of four couples to a series of figures, each danced to a different type of tune, experienced a revival in counties Kerry and Clare in the 1980s after almost dying out. Stepdancing achieved international fame after the phenomenal success of the Broadway-style musical *Riverdance*, which debuted as an interval act in the 1994 Eurovision Song Contest and has since toured the world with a changing cast of stars, performers launching separate programs of their own.

In painting, Louis Le Brocquy (1916–), Evie Hone (1894–1955), and Mainie Jellett (1897–1944) organized the annual Irish Exhibition of Living Art in 1943 to promote public awareness of contemporary art trends. Hone, a master of cubist principles, turned to production of religious stained glass windows while Jellett, also trained in cubist techniques, completed several outstanding murals. Le Brocquy is a prolific postwar artist producing watercolors, landscapes, tapestries, and book illustrations. Made director of the Irish Museum of Modern Art in 1989, he is considered among Ireland's most accomplished 20th-century painters, acclaimed for his "Tinkers" paintings (1946–48), depictions of these wandering Irish gypsies, and for his evocative portrait heads of famous artists.

Landscape painting continued to dominate in the 20th century as the subject preferred by many Irish painters, as it had in previous eras. Artists include Nora McGuinness (1910–80), a painter of vivid, highly colored landscapes; Daniel (Dan) O'Neill (1920–76), whose canvases are full of romantic imagery evoking images of love, life, and death; and Charles McAuley (1910–99), a largely self-taught painter who is considered one of Northern Ireland's greatest artists.

The Arts Council of Ireland serves to encourage interest in Irish art and to disburse state funding to Irish artists and arts' organizations. An Arts Council of Northern Ireland is charged with the same mandate.

Science

Irish inventive genius built on contributions to technological innovations that characterized the preceding century. The development of the automobile industry was greatly assisted by the work of John Boyd Dunlop (1840–1921), a Belfast veterinarian who in 1887 redeveloped a pneumatic rubber tire. John Robert Gregg (1867–1948) from County Monaghan studied stenography and devised his own system of shorthand, which he promoted in publishing many books after he settled in the United States. His Gregg system of shorthand became the most widely used in North America. Ernest Thomas Sinton Walton (1903–95) was educated in physics at Trinity College and at Cambridge University. At Cambridge, he worked with fellow physicist J. D. Cockcroft to devise an instrument with which they succeeded in splitting the atom and for which they were awarded the 1951 Nobel Prize in physics.

Sports

Sports in Ireland owe their modern-day start to the Gaelic Athletic Association (GAA). Under its aegis, the rules for Gaelic football were rewritten, and it, together with hurling, were transformed into fast team games, which drew large crowds, as did soccer (football), with hundreds of soccer clubs in existence by the mid 20th century. In 1903 the Gordon Bennet motor car race—the first international motor race to be held in the British Isles—launched enthusiasm for automobile racing that would lead to the Irish Grand Prix competitions of the 1920s and 1930s.

While the GAA continued as an important organizing force in Irish sports, after independence it yielded its role in athletics to the National Athletic and Cycling Association of Ireland, which was later amalgamated into the Irish Amateur Athletic Association, the single governing body for Irish athletics. The association included both the North and the South, although Ulster members later left to set up their own Northern Ireland AAA.

Interest in native sports grew with national league games in hurling and Gaelic football held in 1925. Inaugurated in August 1924 and played again in 1928 and 1932, the Tailteann Games featured a 16-day festival of Irish sports and pastimes in marking the culmination of an idea first raised in the 1880s to revive what is claimed as the world's oldest organized sports event, said to have been held from about 1800 B.C.E. to about 1180 C.E. The games continue today as a track-and-field event. Boxing drew fans especially in the 1930s when Jack Doyle (1913–78) became a national champion, defeating a string of heavyweight challengers in 1932–33.

The state supplied only minimal funding support for sport through midcentury, though the public's enthusiasm, then and now, has never dimmed. Gaelic football remains the most popular in terms of fan attendance. Hurling and rugby draw large crowds, and golf and fishing are major recreational sports. Interest in soccer peaked when the Irish team qualified for its first European championships in 1988 and its first World Cup in 1990, when it reached the quarter finals.

Horse racing is as important and popular as ever. The Turf Club oversees licensing and registering of entries at all of the country's current 27 tracks, while the Irish Horse Racing Authority, a semi-state body, was founded in 1994 to supervise the financing of racing. The Curragh, a flat, open plain in County Kildare, remains the center of Irish racing, home to all five classic races, including the Derby, the most lucrative in terms of prize money. Both steeplechases and "on the flat" races are held around the country. They include the Laytown Races north of Dublin, Europe's only official running held on a beach.

The Irish made an early appearance at the Olympic Games. Irishmen living in the United States participated in 1904 and 1908, and in the latter games, native-born Irish contestants won eight gold medals. In recent decades, track and boxing have drawn major Irish talent. Ronnie Delaney (1935–), from Ardmore, County Wicklow, won the gold medal in the 1,500 meter race at the Melbourne Olympics in 1956, a feat credited with reawakening interest in amateur international competitions. Dublin-born middle-distance runner Eamonn Coghlan (1952–) set six world indoor records, and he won the 5,000-meter race at the 1983 World Championship in Helsinki, Finland. John Treacy (1957–) won a silver medal in the marathon at Los Angeles in 1984, and Cobh-born Sonia O'Sullivan (1960–) has surpassed all other Irish athletes in winning world and European gold medal championships as a world-class runner. In 2000 she became the first Irish female athlete to win an Olympic track medal in taking the silver in the 5,000-meter race. Running has become a popular pastime in Ireland with events topped by the Dublin Marathon, held since 1980, and the Belfast Marathon, run since 1982.

Irish men have shined in cycling with Stephen Roche (1959–) garnering the sport's superlative prize in winning the Tour de France on July 26, 1987. Some of the strongest rugby teams of the 20th century were fielded in the 1980s when squads won the Triple Crown in 1982—the first time since 1949—and in 1985.

Most popular sports are operated on an islandwide basis, with the notable exception of soccer, which has separate organizing clubs in the North and the South, although an all-Ireland cup soccer competition—the Setanta Sports Cup—was established in 2005. Athletes from Northern Ireland in Olympic competition can choose to represent teams either from the Republic of Ireland or from Great Britain. The Irish Sports Council oversees the planning, developing, and coordinating of competitive and recreational sports in the republic today, a country in which sports benefits from the growth in both a younger and a wealthier population that has proven to be an outstanding legacy of the past 20 years.

The Republic: Economic Turnaround and Changing Political Ground, 1982–2000

By the early 1980s the social changes sweeping the republic resulted in several referendums that registered public sentiment on newly emergent issues. A campaign in the period 1981–83 to strengthen the constitutional prohibition on abortion in recognizing the right to life of the unborn fetus won a 67 percent vote in favor with 33 percent opposed, though turnout was low (54 percent). Likewise, a bill introduced in the Dáil in May 1986 to remove the constitutional ban on divorce was defeated in a popular referendum. Alarm about the possible harmful effects that divorce might have on property rights together with active opposition by the Catholic Church proved decisive, church pressure proving highly influential in rural areas. But in a sign of changing times, urban constituencies, especially in Dublin, overwhelmingly voted both against tightening abortion restrictions and in favor of allowing divorce.

A general election in February 1987 led to formation of a minority government under Fianna Fáil's Charles Haughey. The opposition included a new party, the Progressive Democrats, which had split from Fianna Fáil in 1985 in response to Fianna Fáil's opposition both to the Anglo-Irish Agreement and to more liberal social policies. Led by ex–Fianna Fáil cabinet minister Desmond O'Malley, who had waged a long-running battle with Haughey, the party secured 14 seats in the Dáil in 1987. The new party championed private enterprise, low taxes, progressive policies on social issues, and government administrative reform. During the same election Sinn Féin ended its more than half-century abstention from participation in politics in the republic in running a vigorous campaign on behalf of 27 candidates, but the party won only a dismal 1.7 percent of votes without gaining a single seat.

The next general election in 1989 saw yet another party enter the political fray. The Green Party (Comhaontas Glas) won its first seat in the Dáil. Supporting socially liberal and ecologically friendly policies, the new grouping, founded in 1981 as the Ecology Party of Ireland by Dublin schoolteacher Christopher Fettes (1937–), paralleled the rise of similar parties then appearing across western Europe. The Workers' Party, a Marxist offshoot of Sinn Féin that had emerged in the 1970s and gathered strength through the economically troubled 1980s, achieved its best showing to date by winning seven seats. The 1989 election marked a watershed in Irish politics as Fianna Fáil, for the first time since taking office in 1932, entered into a coalition. The alliance that it formed with the Progressive Democrats from 1989 to 1992 and with Labour from 1993 to 1995 reflected the new reality that smaller parties were attracting increasing support.

Throughout the mid 1980s Ireland suffered considerably from the effects of worldwide recession. Inflation shot up to 21 percent, and unemployment approached record levels of 20 percent in 1986, just at the time when the country's first large-scale generation of university-educated men and women entered the workforce. Emigration rose steeply, up to 50,000 people a year leaving, which rekindled fears that dreaded old demographic patterns had reappeared. From 1982 to 1986 the national debt doubled, due mostly to outlays for social welfare programs, large subsidies to state and semipublic corporations and public utilities, and measures to reduce inflation and stabilize the currency. The national debt soared, reaching a whopping 94.5 percent of gross domestic production (GDP) by 1993.

Under a cloud of suspicion concerning his knowledge of scandals that plagued the early 1980s, Haughey resigned as prime minister in February 1992, to be succeeded by Albert Reynolds (1932–), a TD for Longford-Westmeath since 1977. In a surprising move between two historically rival parties, after the subsequent election in November, the Labour Party under Dick Spring (1950–) joined in a coalition with Fianna Fáil engineered by Patrick Bartholomew "Bertie" Ahern (1951–), the TD for Dublin Central since 1977. Ahern would succeed Reynolds as head of Fianna Fáil in November 1994. Labour appeared poised to break through to become a major player, winning 33 seats in 1992, garnering major ministerial posts—finance and foreign affairs—and having seen its candidate Mary Robinson (1944–) elected as the first female president of Ireland in 1990. Her election proved dramatic, sparking the liveliest ever campaign for the largely ceremonial office. A scandal engulfed Fianna Fáil candidate Brian Lenihan (1930–95), and weakened by the controversy, the party failed to effectively challenge Robinson, who mounted a bold campaign, calling on voters to turn away from past practices—the presidency was usually seen as a retirement honor for senior Fianna Fáil politicians—and vote for a woman as a sign of support for gender equality. She won the election and proved extraordinarily popular, though her party was less so.

In a continuing sign of the progress made by women, Robinson was succeeded in the presidency in 1997 by Mary McAleese (1951–). An attorney born in Belfast, McAleese was appointed a professor of criminal law at Trinity College Dublin in 1975. She returned to her alma mater as a vice chancellor in 1994 before running as the Fianna Fáil candidate for president, a post to which she was reelected without opposition in 2004. Her approach to the presidency mirrors that taken by Robinson in stressing a role marked by a caring concern for social justice. Both women have transformed the office into one in which the titleholder can make influential gestures in support of a more inclusive, tolerant concept of Irish nationalism.

The Fianna Fáil–Labour government fell following Reynolds's resignation on November 17, 1994, over the planned, though subsequently withdrawn, appointment of a controversial attorney general. For the first time in the history of the republic, the fall of a government was not followed by a general election. Instead, Labour switched sides, Dick Spring leading the party into a "rainbow" coalition government

MARY ROBINSON

Born Mary Therese Winifred Bourke in Bollina, County Mayo, Mary Robinson (Máire Mhic Róibin, May 21, 1944–   ) traces her family roots to an Irish-Norman lineage that dates to the 13th century. She attended Trinity College Dublin and, in her 20s, was appointed a professor of law at the college. In 1970 she married Nicholas Robinson, and together they have three children.

She was elected as an independent to the Senate in 1969, and she used her position to campaign for liberal causes. In the mid 1970s she joined the Labour Party and won election to the Dublin City Council (1979–83). Still a member of the Senate, she decided not to seek reelection in 1989, and she then accepted an offer to run for the Irish presidency as the Labour Party candidate, even though she had resigned from the party earlier in protest at the Anglo-Irish Agreement signed at Hillsborough, which she felt had been reached without the participation of unionists in Northern Ireland. Beating Fianna Fáil candidate Brian Lenihan in a runoff round, she was inaugurated the seventh president of the Republic of Ireland on December 3, 1990, the first woman, the first Labour Party member, and the first non–Fianna Fáil candidate in the country's history.

Robinson proved extremely popular across ideological and political lines. In her duties in the largely ceremonial post, she raised issues and made symbolic gestures that broke new ground. She signed bills to liberalize the availability of contraceptives and decriminalize

with Fine Gael and the Democratic Left, a splinter group of disgruntled former members of the Workers' Party who broke away in 1992 in the wake of media claims that the Official IRA was still operating and after they failed to secure approval of amendments to the party's constitution to dismantle its authoritarian decision-making structure. Fine Gael's John Bruton (1947–   ) became prime minister.

In the general election of June 6, 1997, Fianna Fáil returned to power in a coalition with the Progressive Democrats led by Bertie Ahern as prime minister and Mary Harney (1953–   ) as deputy prime minister. She became the first woman to head a party in Irish history when she replaced Desmond O'Malley as leader of the Progressive Democrats in 1993.

Dick Spring, having presided over the rapid decline of Labour's fortunes, resigned in November 1997, replaced by Ruari Quinn (1946–   ),

homosexuality. The first Irish president to visit Queen Elizabeth II at Buckingham Palace, she also met with political leaders on both sides of Northern Ireland's sectarian divide. She traveled extensively, making regular visits to Irish missionaries overseas as well as to foreign heads of state.

Robinson resigned the presidency a few weeks before the end of her term in 1997 and, on September 12, took up the post of United Nations High Commissioner for Human Rights. Her tenure as high commissioner ended in 2002, and she has since served in academia and on the boards of many chari-

Mary Robinson (AP Images)

table and advocacy groups. Robinson broke new ground in demonstrating the growing presence of women in Irish government affairs.

who served in both the Dáil and the Senate as well as holding the powerful minister of finance portfolio in the rainbow coalition. Quinn engineered a merger of Labour with the Democratic Left to strengthen the party's ability to compete and to bolster the power of the center left.

The Fianna Fáil–Progressive Democrats coalition held firm during the last three years of a decade that saw a series of unfolding scandals. In May 1991 a parliamentary tribunal investigating the beef-processing industry produced revelations of collusion between the Department of Agriculture and the Department of Industry and Commerce with private firms that involved misuse of public taxes. A "passport for sale" scheme in the mid 1990s, though legal, raised eyebrows about the potential for influence peddling and for threats to the nation's security. Judicial tribunals investigated allegations of corporate bribes to politicians. Claims of human rights abuse arose with allegations of police brutality lodged against the Civic Guard, claims first made in the late 1970s that grew with mounting numbers of incarcerations along with several incidents of death.

At the same time the country experienced a remarkable turnaround in economic performance. An about-face began slowly in the late 1980s. The gross national product (GNP) grew 30 percent between 1987 and 1992, the economy expanding in the early 1990s at a rate of about 2 percent a year. Rates then moved ahead at a speed that astonished economy watchers, averaging 9 percent annually between 1995 and 1999. Unemployment dropped to 7.7 percent in 1998 and then to just 3.8 percent in 2000. Inflation fell to 2.4 percent by the end of the century. Living standards measured by GNP per capita were estimated to have caught up with the European average by late 1998.

Many factors, domestic and global, can be credited with creating the upturn. The government maintained tight fiscal controls while pursuing limited intervention policies, at the same time it offered incentives to international businesses, including a low corporate tax of 10 percent and generous grants, to locate in the country. The capital gains tax was cut from 40 to 20 percent. Efforts to attract, in particular, high-tech firms proved successful, and major international computer firms established operations in Ireland. Relatively low wages attracted businesses, hikes in salaries being kept moderate through agreements worked out by the government with businesses and trade unions. The country offered a young, highly educated, English-speaking workforce. Its geographic location made it ideal, especially to U.S. firms, which could conduct business in the morning and then contact head offices in the afternoon thanks to the favorable time zone difference.

Membership in the European Community—the European Union (EU) after adoption of the Maastricht Treaty in 1993—gave the country access to Europe's large and growing market, while cash transfers under the EU's regional development policy, which began in the 1970s, paid off by the 1990s in helping to lay the foundations for substantial growth.

Agricultural production as a percentage of gross domestic product dropped dramatically, falling to about 5 percent at the start of the second millennium. In contrast, industry grew at rates higher than most industrial economies, accounting for about 40 percent of GDP and about 80 percent of exports while employing about a third of the labor force in the late 1990s. The service sector share rose the most, accounting for approximately 50 percent of GDP by 2000.

Public debt was greatly reduced, which enabled public spending to double without the need to raise taxes significantly. The new wealth led to large investments in modernizing the republic's infrastructure. Roads were built and improved. The Dublin area light rail line and the suburban rail line in Cork were constructed, and the national rail network upgraded. Redevelopment in Dublin has transformed the city, although critics have decried the haphazard nature of much of the urban renewal.

Changes in social policies moved more slowly than those that turned Ireland into an economically wealthy country during these years, but legal liberalizations did make headway. The laws relating to homosexuality were harsh in the extreme—dating to 1861 and mandating life imprisonment on conviction. A Supreme Court challenge and a case brought before the European Court of Human Rights led to a law change in 1993, which decriminalized homosexual relations between adults. Divorce was made legal following a referendum on November 24, 1995. Contraceptives, banned in 1935, are now freely available. Abortion remained highly divisive. In 1992 the Supreme Court, confronting the case of a 14-year-old girl who had been raped and was pregnant and suicidal, decided that she had the right to an abortion in Ireland. Referendums to roll back this judgment followed on November 25 with voters approving the right to obtain information and to travel abroad for an abortion, although they continued to disallow the procedure in the republic itself.

In a sign that even the Catholic Church had softened its hitherto definitive opinions, in the abortion referendums bishops advised the faithful to vote their conscience. No longer the authoritative body of old speaking in a monolithic voice on moral issues, the church had been largely marginalized in the debate, indicative of a weakening reflected as well in a continuing decline in church attendance and practice. A booming economy and a more open, secular social outlook presented an image of an Ireland far removed from the poor, backward, cleric-controlled country that had predominated for so long. The reality of that Ireland had long served to justify unionist arguments that the North should remain apart from such a nation. The changes in the republic made such reasoning increasingly difficult to sustain, adding to feelings of unease among Ulster diehards, who, with a growing Catholic population among them and a British government inclined to support greater minority rights, felt their society increasingly under siege. For others in the North, however, developments across the island elicited a growing willingness to participate in finding a solution to the seemingly intractable conundrum that Northern Ireland had become.

Northern Ireland: Gunmen and Statesmen Vie for Center Stage, 1985–2000

The Anglo-Irish Agreement of November 1985 brought the Republic of Ireland fully into the search for an end to the violence in Northern Ireland. To back up the agreement, an International Fund for Ireland was set up in 1986 to provide money for regional development in deprived areas of Ulster and border areas of the republic. Brightening economic prospects for residents, it was hoped, would lessen sectarian tensions.

The 1987 U.K. general election saw the moderate SDLP's share of the vote rise by 3.2 percent and Sinn Féin's fall by 2 percent, but the elections produced no change in the level of violence. Eight IRA men were killed during an attack on a County Armagh police station in May 1987, and 11 killed and 63 injured by a bomb set off by the IRA in November at Enniskillen, County Fermanagh.

The government tried to address the one minority issue that remained, employment discrimination, the other demands of the 1960s civil rights movement having been largely met in the early 1970s. The Northern Ireland Fair Employment Act (1990) created a revised, tougher Fair Employment Commission charged with ensuring equitable employment to guarantee that Catholics receive a fair share of spaces in the workplace.

District council elections in May 1989 continued the trend in slight gains for moderate parties. In 1990 the new secretary of state for Northern Ireland, Peter Brooke (1934–), offered a cautious olive branch to Sinn Féin in suggesting that the British government might talk to its representatives if the IRA abandoned its campaign of violence. In November he reiterated London's efforts to act as honest broker in declaring the government was prepared to accept the decision of a majority of Northern Ireland's residents freely and democratically registered. In what became known as the Brooke initiative, the secretary launched an ambitious effort to build interparty consensus. Three sets of talks were started: among the Northern Ireland constitutional parties (UUP, SDLP, DUP, Alliance); between Dublin and the Northern Ireland parties; and between Dublin and London. The talks proved lengthy, continuing into the administration of Patrick Mayhew (1929–), who became secretary of state in April 1992, and they became more contentious as they progressed to discussion of specifics. While the UUP conceded the principle of power-sharing in the government of Northern Ireland and agreed to some form of vague islandwide cooperation, it balked at the SDLP's proposal that Ulster be governed by a six-person commission, composed of three people elected from Northern Ireland and three nominated by the London government, the Dublin government, and the European Union.

Moderate Catholics continued to gain in strength, the SDLP winning votes at the expense of Sinn Féin, but extremists maintained their determination to pursue their goals using violent means. In 1992 republicans killed 36 people and unionists, 39. Loyalists grew increasingly uneasy with the forces of law and order, hitherto taken for granted as allies. The police strove to curb the violence emanating from every quarter, earning the reputation among some unionists that they were encouraging compromise with nationalists. Friction between loyalists and the RUC mounted, and the government banned the Ulster Defence Association in August 1992.

Both Dublin and London forged ahead in trying to reconcile the competing aspirations of unionists and nationalists by affirming that both communities be afforded equal respect and validity and that the people of Ireland alone had the right and the power to determine their fate. U.K. prime minister John Major (1943–) and Irish prime minister Albert Reynolds issued the joint Downing Street Declaration on December 15, 1993, setting down their governments' position that "it is for the people of Ireland alone, by agreement between the two parts respectively, to exercise their right of self-determination on the basis of consent, freely and concurrently given, North and South, to bring about a united Ireland, if that is their wish" (Downing Street Declaration). For the first time, recognition of the right of all the people of the island to a role in finding a solution, without any outsider interference, was given. Both governments pledged to seek a settlement by peaceful constitutional means, and both promised that parties linked with paramilitaries, such as Sinn Féin, could participate in talks if they would renounce violence.

London's reiteration in the declaration that it had no selfish, strategic, or economic interest in remaining in Northern Ireland, its support of self-determination there, and its acknowledgment of an islandwide Irish dimension to a settlement appeared to knock the wind out of the sails of the IRA's stated reasons put forth to justify its campaign of violence.

The declaration opened the door to moving ahead, a door through which a new player entered to participate in a very direct way in the search for a settlement. Republicans had long been active in securing support, overtly sentimental and covertly financial, from Irish Americans in the United States. The administration of U.S. president William J.

Clinton (1946–), which entered office in January 1993, granted Gerry Adams a 48-hour visa at the end of January 1994, over the objections of the British government. The offer marked a departure from the practice of earlier U.S. administrations, which had shunned Sinn Féin as a supporter of terrorism. Clinton joined with Irish-American interest groups in urging Adams to push republicans to abandon the use of political violence. Continuing U.S. pressure led to an IRA cease-fire on August 31, 1994, matched on October 13 by one announced by the Combined Loyalist Military Command, an umbrella group of the major Protestant paramilitary forces.

The cease-fires gave both the British and the Irish governments the opportunity to enter into direct dialogue with those who were backing a violent solution, namely, Sinn Féin and the two unionist parties with paramilitary links, Paisley's Ulster Democratic Party and the Progressive Unionist Party. In February 1995 Dublin and London published *A New Framework Agreement* ("framework document") that sketched out proposals for a constitutional settlement in laying out plans for new political structures in Northern Ireland, between the North and the South and between Britain and the Republic of Ireland.

In 1995, optimism seemed warranted. In January the U.S. government announced that it would substantially increase its contribution to the International Fund for Ireland, and George Mitchell (1933–), who had retired from the U.S. Senate at the end of 1994, was appointed special ambassador to the president and the secretary of state to deal with the Northern Ireland controversy. Adams was given an unlimited visa to travel in the United States, and he arrived to participate in talks in Washington, D.C. On March 29 the British government announced that while ready to open exploratory talks with Sinn Féin, the IRA would have to decommission its weapons before party representatives would be allowed to participate in all-party discussions. The Forum for Peace and Reconciliation, established by the Dublin government earlier in October 1994, helped to extend dialogue among rival groups in offering a venue for talks, even though unionists failed to attend sessions.

While initiatives at governmental levels moved ahead, expressions and actions in support of sectarian sentiments persisted. Gerry Adams told a republican rally in Belfast in August 1995 that the IRA had not "gone away." Orange Order marches in July and August produced outbreaks of violence in Portadown and Belfast. David Trimble (1944–), the successor to James Molyneaux (1920–) as head of the Ulster Unionist Party, walked with Ian Paisley, hands held aloft in triumph, past sullen Catholic crowds in Portadown.

Protestant Orangemen march through a Catholic area of Portadown on July 11, 1996, after police cleared Catholic demonstrators blocking their path. (AP Images)

An International Body on Decommissioning of Weapons, chaired by Mitchell, published a report on January 26, 1996, urging all parties to commit to six principles to achieve a democratic, nonviolent solution, including the total, verifiable decommissioning of all weapons held by paramilitaries. As if in defiant response, the IRA ended its cease-fire in February and June in detonating massive bombs in London and Manchester, respectively. The work of Mitchell's commission inched forward, slowed by the reluctance of the Conservative Party government in London to irritate unionist MPs, whose support was needed to sustain the government in power. Violence sputtered on into 1997.

Annual Orange Order parades in County Armagh proved a recurrently troublesome flashpoint. Because the parade traversed a Catholic district along the Garvaghy Road north of Portadown, for the third straight year it sparked nationalist riots in July 1997. Turmoil also erupted in Belfast over parade routes through heavily Catholic neighborhoods. The issue of the right to march was, and remains, a contentious one. At times when authorities ban the parades or alter the routes, loyalist retaliatory counter-riots have broken out, Orangemen holding that to march along their traditional route is their civil right. In 1998 a Northern Ireland Parades Commission was set up with the power to ban, restrict, reroute, or otherwise impose conditions on any parade in the province.

The election of a Labour Party government in Britain in May 1997 under Prime Minister Tony Blair (1953–) helped to revive the momentum for progress. The party won a landslide victory, thus completely sidelining unionists, and the new secretary of state for Northern Ireland, Marjorie "Mo" Mowlam (1949–2005), laid less stress on decommissioning as a precondition for talks than did her Conservative predecessor. In June Blair announced his intention to resume all-party talks and gave the IRA a five-week deadline to reinstate a cease-fire. The IRA did so on July 20, and Sinn Féin was admitted to the peace talks on September 9. Intensive negotiations on three levels—between London and Dublin, between Belfast and Dublin, and among the parties in Northern Ireland—proceeded through the fall and winter, guided by Mitchell, who set a deadline of midnight on April 9, 1998, for completion of an agreement. The discussions represented a breakthrough among several, though not all, formally intransigent Northern Ireland politicians. SDLP's John Hume had undertaken a series of private meetings with Gerry Adams beginning in 1992 in an effort to bring Sinn Féin into the political process. His efforts paid off now. Adams proved willing to talk, as did Trimble of the Ulster Unionist Party. A staunch unionist after joining the UUP in 1978, uncompromising in his refusal to talk with Sinn Féin, after his selection as party leader Belfast-born Trimble proved remarkably pragmatic. Final, frenetic discussions among Blair, Ahern, and leaders of the Northern Ireland parties produced an accord unveiled at a plenary session on Good Friday, April 10.

Not a peace settlement but rather the vehicle by which to achieve one, the 65-page Good Friday Agreement (or "Belfast Agreement") restated old principles and put in place new institutional arrangements, providing a framework for a new government, the first since dissolution of the Stormont system in 1972. A declaration reiterated a commitment to nonviolence, partnership, equality, and mutual respect. The governments of Britain and Ireland reemphasized that constitutional changes could come about only on the basis of popular consent, as set down in the Downing Street Declaration. Provisions called for devolution of some central powers to a Northern Ireland Assembly and to the creation of a North-South Ministerial Council and a British-Irish Council, two bodies set up to facilitate consultation on issues of regional importance.

All parties agreed to work to secure decommissioning of weapons by paramilitary groups within two years of approval of the agreement. Northern Ireland police reform, release of prisoners convicted of politically motivated crimes, and a change to the Irish constitution to remove territorial claims to Northern Ireland rounded out the central points.

To gauge popular sentiment for the pact, the people of Ireland, North and South, went to the polls to vote in referenda. On May 22, 1998—for the first time since 1918—an islandwide electorate cast ballots. The results showed a resounding majority in support of the document in the republic and a favorable majority as well, though a less solid one, in the North.

	Northern Ireland	Republic of Ireland
Yes	71.12%	94.39%
No	28.88%	5.61%

Elections for the Northern Ireland Assembly were held on June 25, 1998. The Ulster Unionist Party won the largest share of votes and 28 seats; the DUP, 20; SDLP, 24; Sinn Féin, 18; and others, 18. The DUP participated in the balloting even though its leader, Ian Paisley, refused to countenance the Good Friday Agreement, calling it "treacherous." The assembly convened and on July 1 elected David Trimble as first minister designate and Seámus Mallon (1936–) of the SDLP as deputy first minister designate for the new Northern Ireland Executive, the policy-implementing body created as per the Good Friday Agreement. For their efforts, John Hume and David Trimble were jointly awarded the 1998 Nobel Peace Prize.

Earlier, in his visit to Belfast on November 30, 1995, President Clinton had warned:

> The greatest struggle you face is between those who, deep down inside, are inclined to be peacemakers, and those who, deep down inside, cannot yet embrace the cause of peace. Between those who are in the ship of peace and those who are trying to sink it, old habits die hard. (Clinton 1995)

Events immediately following the Good Friday Agreement would bear out his words, with attempts to form an all-party government counterbalanced by continuing outbursts of violence and by a reluctance among participants to fulfill agreed-on formulas for settlement.

Proof of the difficulty peacemakers faced came within months of the agreement, when terrorist attacks resumed. Three Catholic brothers aged between eight and 10 were killed in July 1998 when union-ists gasoline-bombed their home. In one of the worst outrages of the entire decades-long turmoil, on August 15 a republican splinter group, the "Real IRA," detonated a 500-lb. bomb placed in a parked car in a crowded shopping street in Omagh, killing 29 and injuring 200.

The inability of Sinn Féin to secure IRA decommissioning by the agreed deadline led to a stalled process of government formation, but by November 1999 the Northern Ireland Assembly was in session and the Executive met for the first time on December 2. On that date, the government of the republic voted to amend Articles 2 and 3 of the constitution to remove the controversial claim that the whole island forms a single "national territory" and to affirm that, while the people of Northern Ireland were guaranteed the right to be a "part of the Irish nation," a united Ireland could come about only with the consent of a majority of Ulster's residents. The decade—and the century—ended with cautious optimism that cooperation rather than confrontation would come to characterize public life in Northern Ireland.

11

IRELAND IN THE TWENTY-FIRST CENTURY: THE PAIN-FILLED PAST RECEDES AT LAST?

At the start of the 21st century, optimism and self-confidence characterize the public spirit in Ireland, both North and South. The sectarian divisions still remain an ever-present reality in Northern Ireland, but a seemingly never-ending cycle of dashed hopes and false starts in trying to put a definitive end to the violence has been followed by the resumption of devolved government, this time in a revival that offers a real chance of survival. Leaders in the Northern Ireland government elected in March 2007, for the first time ever, include former diehard unionists and nationalists, avowed enemies who have turned away from confrontation to cooperation in a power-sharing breakthrough.

The new development is welcomed in the Republic of Ireland, whose people have long been reconciled to the reality that any change in the status of the six northern counties will come only by consent of the majority of the inhabitants. The republican rhetoric in praise of national union and the old hatreds kept alive in the memories of so many generations have faded. Yesterday's formative battles—for land and independence—have long been won.

The Ireland of the 21st century little resembles the country of old. The Irish enjoy one of the world's healthiest, wealthiest economies, one that is intricately linked to cutting-edge technologies. In 2008 the country enjoyed Europe's fastest rate of population growth at 1.9 percent (Central Statistics Office), a remarkable turnaround for a nation whose modern history has long been defined by demographic decline. Well-educated young people are no longer forced to leave for other shores, and Ireland draws immigrants for the first time in its modern history. Membership in the European Union links the country to a continent for which, as an island located on its far western fringe, Ireland has historically been a remote outpost. At work in a global economy and attuned to a world of instant communications, the people of Ireland confront the same issues affecting all advanced societies. The country remains socially conservative in many ways—antiabortion and censorship laws still exist, and Catholicism exerts a powerful devotional pull—but today critical attitudes inform public discourse, and no institution is immune from scrutiny. The Irish identity of long repute—one that is rooted in a solid sense of place, that is localized and family-based—is being left behind, regrettable to some but inevitable given the inexorable push of 21st-century social, cultural, and economic forces.

It is to be hoped that the Irish will succeed in maintaining a balance in celebrating their distinctiveness while participating fully in an interdependent world. Certainly an Irish cultural presence remains vividly alive, even if oftentimes a stereotypical and simplistic one, among those of Irish descent worldwide. Recent positive developments in Northern Ireland give promise that the people of this tormented corner of the island will, like their counterparts in the South, demonstrate a willingness to break with the past without forgetting it entirely.

The "Celtic Tiger" Roars

The Republic of Ireland has been called the "Celtic Tiger" (Tíogar Ceilteach), a term reportedly coined in 1994 in a report for the Morgan Stanley investment firm, in reference to the country's rapid growth in the mid and late 1990s. Also called the "Boom" and the "Economic Miracle," the last decade and a half have witnessed a fundamental transformation of the country from one of western Europe's perennially poorest to one of its richest nations. The good economic times were fueled largely by robust exports, powered most especially by high-tech industries, many U.S.-based, and by lower corporate taxation levels and high levels of consumer spending and business investment. A strong construction drive also contributed significantly to the economic advance.

After seven years of consistently steady growth, momentum slowed in mid 2001 and 2002. The country shared in a global downturn in investment in the information technology industry. Traditional activities in textiles registered a slowdown. Tourism revenues dropped in the wake of a drop-off in travel after the terrorist attacks of September 11,

2001, in the United States. Several major companies, faced with rising wages and insurance premiums, moved operations to lower-cost eastern Europe or closed down while the rising value of the euro, which went into general circulation on January 1, 2002, hurt exports to non-euro countries, most especially to the United States, Ireland's second-largest trading partner after EU members.

Nevertheless, the GDP growth rate remained exceptionally high in international terms, moving ahead at a healthy clip of 6 percent in 2001 and 2002. Beginning in 2002 low-interest rates set by the European Central Bank encouraged private-sector consumption. The economy bounced back in late 2003 and 2004 as U.S. investment levels rose again. Referred to by some as "Celtic Tiger 2" or "Celtic Tiger Mach 2," the upturn surged ahead through the middle of the decade. The GDP grew 6.7 percent in the first half of 2007, faster than any other country in the euro zone. Construction remained vigorous through mid decade as the sector strove to catch up with demand for housing and office space. A state policy of low corporate tax rates remains in place, while the public debt continues to decline. Inflation stood at 5.7 percent in 2007, up from recent rates of between 3 and 4 percent, which has raised prices and made Dublin one of Europe's more expensive cities.

The consequences of the economic climb have changed the country more profoundly and more quickly than at any other time in its history. A historically poor country boasts recently an annual per capita gross national income of $45,580 (World Development Indicators Database 2007), the sixth highest in the world, the sixth in Europe, and the third in the EU. Spending has gone up in the wake of rising incomes, and the consumer society so characteristic of advanced economies is equally evident in Ireland. The majority of wealth held by Irish citizens is invested in property, and citizens with the funds to do so have taken to buying choice real estate abroad.

One of the most significant manifestations of the economic upturn has been the changing demographic face of the country. The greatest shortcoming that had long plagued independent Ireland, namely, its inability to provide jobs at home, no longer applies. Unemployment rates are low, at 4.4 percent in 2006, and the country's population stands at a modern-day peak estimated at approximately 4.4 million in 2008.

Reflecting the reversal in the nation's fortunes, for the first time in modern history growing numbers of newcomers have arrived. Immigration in the 20th century had been minimal, but beginning in the 1990s asylum seekers coming from some 100 different nations have sought refuge in the republic. Numbers grew steadily starting from a

The final section of the Spire is raised on Dublin's O'Connell Street on January 21, 2003. Conceived in 2000 as a millennium project, the conical, all-steel Spire is the tallest structure in Ireland, and it is symbolic of the country's soaring economy at the turn of the 21st century. (AP Images)

344

low base in the late 1980s to approximately 52,000 in 2000 and mounting to 109,000 in 2007, with a drop-off to nearly 84,000 for the year ending April 2008. For the same year Ireland saw 45,000 emigrate, an increase over the previous year, with Australia proving especially attractive as a destination place (Central Statistics Office). The immigration figures represented a major turnaround for a traditional outmigration nation. People from places as diverse as Nigeria, Algeria, Moldova, Libya, Romania, and Poland have settled in Ireland. Together with the many thousands of migrant laborers who come to work in the prospering economy, they have transformed the face of Ireland's urban places, especially Dublin, and they pose an entirely new challenge to Irish society in dealing with the reality of multiculturalism.

Though the new wealth is now a fact of life, nevertheless recent developments point to problems that stem from the nature of the Irish economy. The republic's dependence on the United States as an export market and a source of direct capital investment makes the country highly sensitive to American economic trends. Signs of a U.S. recession, such as those that appeared in 2008, can produce a spillover effect in Ireland, with a fall-off in export earnings and investment inflows. The boom in real estate, which saw home prices rise by 12 percent a year in the mid 2000s, cooled precipitately in 2007–08 when prices dropped 7 percent. The downturn in the residential property market led to a slowdown in GDP growth in 2008, and unemployment can be expected to rise given the shrinkage in the construction sector. Wages are rising and are now well above the EU average, especially in the Dublin area, which puts pressure on the ability to maintain corporate competitiveness. Outsourcing of professional jobs has increased since 2004 when the EU opened its membership to many eastern and central European countries with their lower cost economies. The progressive tax system partially redistributes wealth among the poorer segments of society, but there are large disparities between the richest and the poorest citizens, a gap aggravated by increases in property values.

The establishment of high-tech, capital-intensive industries in the republic has had some spillover effect in Northern Ireland, which experienced a sharp rise in manufacturing growth from 1998 to 2001 followed in succeeding years by a leveling off. The signing of the Good Friday Agreement in 1998 and the consequent declining fear of sectarian violence led to an input of foreign investment of the type seen in the republic. Once-dominant industries such as textiles and shipbuilding have continued their long decline. Engineering, especially production in aerospace and heavy machinery, is the largest manufacturing subsector. Just as in the republic, services account for the largest share of employment output, almost 70 percent in the republic and 78 percent in Northern Ireland in 2004. The North's traditional dependence on the public sector remains high—government expenditures contribute to two-thirds of the economy versus one-third in the republic—and subsidy monies from the central government equal about one-fifth of economic output.

Ireland's Ties to Europe Tighten

The Republic of Ireland's membership in the European Union has led to a major shift in its economic and political focus, the connections to an increasingly powerful, continent-wide organization allowing the country to pull away—and stay away—from its historically close links with the United Kingdom. The EU now accounts for two-thirds of Ireland's exports and more than half of its imports. The euro, which replaced the Irish pound (punt) as the country's currency, ties Ireland financially to the huge European market. Agricultural subsidies have boosted farmers' incomes. Accession of new members from eastern and central Europe has brought several thousand workers from Poland and the Baltic states as well as increased competition for business investment in the absence of controls on labor and capital movements. The country has been compelled to adopt EU-wide standards not only in economic matters but also in certain social practices. Thus, the Irish government was forced to give up its policy of dismissing female civil servants on marriage. The exposure to attitudes and practices prevalent elsewhere in Europe has led to growing cosmopolitanism and an increased exposure to wider outlooks in Irish society.

Public enthusiasm for entry into the union was high at the outset, and support has been strong, but with growing prosperity more critical attitudes have recently been registered. In a referendum on June 7, 2001, the electorate voted to reject the proposed Treaty of Nice, which aimed to reform institutional structures in preparation for the admission of new countries in 2004. The voters' decision surprised not only political classes across the EU but also the major Irish political parties. None had mounted a major campaign on the issue, and only smaller parties such as Sinn Féin and the Greens have consistently advanced skeptical European attitudes. Irish voters, having always supported moves toward greater European unity by big majorities, were expected to do so again. But this time the electorate registered a wariness of structural changes that appeared overly complicated, a fear that smaller states would be marginalized, an anxiety about the effects on the economy brought by a potential influx of newcomers, and a worry that Ireland's traditional military neutrality might be compromised.

The government secured, in the Seville Declaration, a reaffirmation of Ireland's policy of neutrality. The terms of a second amendment in October 2002 included explicit exclusion of Ireland from joining a common EU defense policy and a requirement that moves toward "enhanced cooperation" under the treaty would require approval by the Dáil. This time a massive campaign to urge a "yes" vote was mounted. All the major parties backed the referendum, with only the Green Party and Sinn Féin opposed, and a 60 percent vote in favor ensued.

Nevertheless, more critical attitudes can be expected to endure. Opposition to high taxation and heavy regulation, attitudes that find so much favor at EU headquarters in Brussels, remains strong—Charlie McGreevy (1949–), the finance minister at the time of the referendums, earned a rebuke from the European Commission and Council of Ministers for his defiance of EU budgeting policy—and many in Ireland believe such approaches to be not only outmoded but also, in the wake of the pursuit of opposite policies that have proved successful in Ireland, to be wrong for the country. In a sign of continuing skepticism, in June 2008 Irish voters rejected by a margin of 53.4 percent a proposed treaty (Treaty of Lisbon) for modernizing the European Union. Anti-treaty groups marshaled a majority to vote no in claiming the pact would compel Ireland to change core policies, including its low business tax rates, military neutrality, and ban on abortion.

Ireland has long taken an independent stance in international forums, first in the League of Nations and then in the United Nations. No Irish diplomat has won greater acclaim than Seán MacBride, who served as minister for external affairs in the coalition government from 1948 to 1951. A founder and chairman of the human rights organization Amnesty International, in 1973 he was elected by the UN General Assembly to the post of UN Commissioner for Namibia to oversee developments leading to the grant of independence to that southwest African nation, and he was appointed chairman of UNESCO in 1980. He formulated the MacBride Principles, a set of guidelines for foreign investors in Northern Ireland designed to ensure they helped to discourage discriminatory hiring and sectarian tensions in the workplace. His efforts won him the Nobel Peace Prize in 1976.

Membership in European bodies will entail cooperating in securing a regional consensus in policy positions, but Ireland will, like other member countries, continue to pursue freedom of action to varying

THE IRISH DIASPORA

The Irish government defines *diaspora* to mean those of Irish nationality who habitually reside outside the island. The figures include some 3 million persons, including roughly 1.2 million emigrants who were born in Ireland. Though today's prosperity no longer draws thousands away, the prominent place of emigration in Irish social history is starkly apparent in these numbers, which add up to an extraordinarily large ratio for a nation of this size.

The diaspora that readily comes to everyone's mind, however, is not one defined by nationality but rather by ancestry. By the early 21st century, there were estimated to be more than 80 million people worldwide who could claim some degree of Irish lineage, which totals more than 14 times the population of Ireland itself. The government has acknowledged the existence of these many millions in a 1998 amendment to the constitution that states "the Irish nation cherishes its special affinity with people of Irish ancestry living abroad who share its cultural identity and heritage."

The vast majority of Irish descendants live in the United States, Great Britain, Canada, Australia, New Zealand, and South Africa, but they can be found everywhere—from the countries of continental Europe to the islands of the Caribbean and from South America to Asia. The history of many nations is replete with famous Irish names. Ten U.S. presidents starting with Andrew Jackson (1767–1845) and ending with Bill Clinton claim Irish ancestral roots. Patrice MacMahon (1808–93) and Bernardo O'Higgins (1778–1842) served as 19th-century presidents of France and Chile, respectively, and O'Higgins is considered the father of Chilean independence. Eduard Count von Taaffe (1833–95) served twice as prime minister of Austria-Hungary (1868–70, 1879–93).

Long celebrated in Ireland as a religious holiday, St. Patrick's Day became a public holiday in 1903, and today it is celebrated in more countries than any other national holiday, although only in the Caribbean island of Montserrat, founded by Irish refugees from neighboring St. Kitts and Nevis, and the Canadian province of Newfoundland and Labrador is it observed as a public holiday. The first civic celebration in the United States took place in Boston in 1737, and New York City's famous parade started in 1762 when a military procession of Irish troops paraded with fife and drum.

St. Patrick's Day parade, New York City, ca. 1961 (Library of Congress, LC-DIG-ppmsca-61202)

In a bid to draw ever more tourists, in 1996 the Irish government launched a state-sponsored St. Patrick's Festival in Dublin, adding theatrical performances and cultural events to the traditional parade.

Evidence of a global Irish presence is displayed most recently in the explosive growth of Irish "traditional" pubs in places far beyond where the Irish have settled. Beginning in the 1990s, perhaps sparked by Irish fans who gathered in bars everywhere to celebrate the 1994 World Cup, thousands of Irish-themed public houses can now be found in locales from Amsterdam to Abu Dhabi.

Though viewed by some as superficial and tourist-driven, popular culture markers such as leprechauns, shamrocks, shillelaghs, and sentimental songs such as "Danny Boy" and "McNamara's Band" are today immediately identifiable everywhere as being Irish, and as such they attest to the enduring impact made around the world by the people of this small island.

degrees. The republic has tended to abstain rather than vote against resolutions in Brussels with which it disagrees. Ireland's military neutrality—made plain by its nonmembership in NATO—gives cause for national debate given the country's endorsement of the growing foreign policy coordination of EU members and the pressure that might arise for a closer alignment in military matters as well.

Conflicts of interest may arise to the extent that EU foreign policies put pressure on traditionally strong relationships that the republic maintains with countries outside the regional bloc, most especially the United States. Links to the republic across the Atlantic remain close on all levels, governmental and commercial, and they extend to deep bonds, both real and sentimental, maintained by many private citizens in both countries. Irish emigrants have left as their legacy a link between their country of origin and lands across the globe, places that their descendants now call home.

For a small nation, Ireland exerts a considerable presence internationally. Irish soldiers participate in UN peacekeeping missions in trouble spots across the globe. Development aid is distributed to many poor nations, and Irish missionaries and charitable agents are active around the globe.

The Republic: Questioning Traditional Authority

Institutions around which Irish life has long revolved remain preeminent in the 21st century, but prosperity has brought with it a greater public confidence, evident in a willingness to examine and challenge ruling elites.

The political parties dominant since the 1930s remain so. Fianna Fáil (FF), Ireland's largest and most successful party, has tended to advance left-leaning economic policies (spending increases, more government control) and conservative social positions (retention of censorship, opposition to abortion). Coalitions with the free market–advocating Progressive Democrats (PD) have drawn Fianna Fáil toward the center-right in supporting tax cuts favored by the former. The coalition has been in power since 1997.

Under Prime Minister Bertie Ahern, Fianna Fáil came to within a few seats of winning an overall majority in the Dáil elections of June 6, 2002. The return of a FF-PD coalition marks the first time since 1969 that an Irish government has won reelection. Completing its full five-year term, the Dáil was dissolved by President Mary McAleese in April 2007, and elections on May 24 led to a drop of only three seats

Republic of Ireland General Elections 2002 and 2007		
Party	2002 Seats	2007 Seats
Fianna Fáil	81	77
Fine Gael	31	51
Labour Party	20	20
Progressive Democrats	8	2
Green Party	6	6
Sinn Féin	5	4
Socialist Party	1	0
Independent	13	5
Ceann Comhairle (Speaker)	1	1
Total	166	166

for Fianna Fáil, leaving it with sufficient numbers to form the core of a coalition but necessitating a search for an additional partner with which to form a workable alliance, because the PDs suffered a sharp drop in support from eight to two seats. The government formed on June 14, 2007, under Prime Minister Bertie Ahern includes Fianna Fáil, Progressive Democrats, and the Green Party, which, with six seats, held the same number of places as in the 2002 elections. The elections were considered a victory for Fianna Fáil, despite the small drop in seats, the party credited with shepherding the country's vibrant economic performance.

The 2007 elections were fought by Fine Gael on the basis of a proposed "Alliance for Change" coalition with the Labour Party. The two parties have traditionally cooperated, the centrist Fine Gael (spending cuts, less government control) complementing Labour's left-leaning agenda (more social welfare). In the election, Fine Gael rebounded, gaining 20 seats to reverse the 2002 results when it had suffered a loss of a third of its representation. The party has struggled to regain the level of support it enjoyed in the 1980s. Parties such as the Progressive Democrats and the Greens have drawn away middle-class voters, who have formed the core of Fine Gael's support, in offering a wider variety of political choices. The party's 2007 comeback was engineered under the direction of a new leader, Enda Kenny (1951–), who replaced

351

Michael Noonan (1943–) after the latter resigned in the wake of the major losses in 2002. Labour Party support has remained steady, bolstered by backers of the Democratic Left, which merged with the party in 1999, although it, too, experienced a change at the party's helm. Ruari Quinn stepped down to be replaced by Pat Rabbitte (1949–). Smaller parties and candidates running as independents continue to garner a scattering of support. Support for Sinn Féin is meager, and both of the major parties rule out any possibility of forming a government with the party, linked as it has been with the violence in Northern Ireland.

Scandal continued to plague prominent officials in both the public and the private sectors. In 2008 Prime Minister Ahern faced charges that he secretly collected cash from businessmen, and on May 6 he resigned as both head of the government and leader of Fianna Fáil. Brian Cowen (1960–) replaced him as prime minister. Elected as the leader of Fianna Fáil in April, Cowen had served as head of various ministries since 1992 and from 2007–08 as deputy prime minister.

The investigative tribunals that so rocked the country in the 1990s continued into the new century. However troubling, they demonstrate the ability of the country to confront, and rectify, abuses in the system. The public's attention in 2000 focused on money and the misuse of power to obtain it with revelations of corruption by politicians and businessmen that, because many of the incidents occurred in the 1980s when the country found itself in economic recession, proved particularly disturbing. Investigators uncovered that many among the wealthiest were placing their money in offshore accounts to avoid paying taxes, a practice in which banks and accounting firms actively colluded. Fears grew that a culture of tax evasion was brewing as a consequence of Ireland's drive to create more and more wealth.

Efforts at reform went forward. The committee system in the Dáil was altered to make it more open, and calls for reforms in the health service and in education elicited wide public debate. At the same time, abortion remains outlawed. A church-supported amendment to tighten laws further by ruling out the risk of suicide as an acceptable medical reason to allow an abortion was narrowly defeated in a referendum on March 7, 2002, in which a large number of "no" votes were registered in Irish cities, highlighting the continuing urban and rural social divisions in the country.

Religion continues to play a central role for many. Religious rituals and displays, such as processions and venerations of relics, that have always characterized Irish Catholicism remain important. However, the irrepressible advance of consumerism and secularism, in progress in Ireland during the past half-century, has profoundly altered the religious landscape. Church attendance registers steady declines, and vocations to religious life have dropped precipitously. Ordinations to the priesthood fell from a peak of 412 in 1965 to only 44 in 1998, while by 1999 just 21 women entered religious life compared to 227 in 1970 (Donnelly 2000, 12–27).

The institutional church no longer commands unquestioning obedience from the faithful. Better-educated than ever before, Irish Catholics have grown increasingly skeptical of church claims to authority. Beginning in the 1990s the church has been forced to confront a number of scandals that have generated widespread publicity and have led to a collapse of respect for religious institutions and individuals. Paternity suits were lodged, and pedophile cases have appeared in recent years. In the late 1990s television programs began to air allegations of physical, emotional, and sexual abuse at state-funded orphanages and industrial schools run by religious orders that dated back to the 1940s and 1950s. At so-called Magdalene schools, unwed mothers expiated their guilt in working in exploitative conditions. Public revulsion at the revelations was intense, giving rise to a wave of lawsuits and a host of apologies from religious orders and their members.

More critical attitudes reflect the existence of information sources more numerous and diverse than ever before. After 1970 Irish media outlets diversified with domestic private radio and television stations and the British Broadcasting Corporation, giving growing competition to state-run Radio Telefís Éireann (RTÉ), which itself expanded to two channels in 1978. An Irish-language television station, TG4, began operating in 1996, kept on the air by large state subsidies. Use of computers, introduced in the 1990s, has progressed steadily. In print media, the *Irish Times* is the country's preeminent news outlet. Its circulation surpassed 100,000 in the 1990s. Communications links around the world continue to grow. Ryanair, founded in 1985, has grown from a single inaugural flight from Waterford to London into one of the world's major low-cost air carriers. Through all the available means of communication, the people of the Republic of Ireland, just as they had been doing for more than 30 years, kept closely informed of developments across the border in Northern Ireland, where major changes took place in the opening few years of the new century.

Northern Ireland: Devolution Again the Solution?

The ground on which the new governing institutions of Northern Ireland were built proved decidedly shaky from the very beginning. The inability to secure a firm commitment from the IRA to agree to decommission its arms constituted a recurring stumbling block to creating a viable government. In January 2000 Northern Ireland secretary of state Peter Mandelson (1953–), after introducing legislation to create a new police service for the province to replace the Royal Ulster Constabulary, announced that he would suspend the Northern Ireland Assembly in the absence of IRA decommissioning, and, after failing to secure a deal to stave off doing so, he followed through on February 11. Then on May 6 the IRA released a statement expressing a readiness to put its arms completely and verifiably beyond use, a commitment sufficient to put the devolved government back in place on May 29. In June the IRA agreed to open up its arms depots for inspection, and in October inspections were made, although Canadian general John de Chastelain (1937–) of the International Decommissioning Commission, the body charged with overseeing the process, announced that no progress had been made on actual paramilitary disarmament.

The first few years of the new century would prove trying as efforts to get a functioning government going followed a tortuous course. The Northern Ireland Assembly suffered from repeated suspensions—from February 11, 2000, to May 30, 2000, and for two 24-hour periods on August 10, 2001, and September 22, 2001—because of disagreements between the two main unionist parties (Democratic Unionists and Ulster Unionists) and Sinn Féin. The unionist parties refused to participate in the governing institutions set up under the Good Friday Agreement alongside Sinn Féin until they won assurances that the IRA had decommissioned its arms and discontinued its violent activities.

New ugly incidents aroused fears that old, hateful sentiments remained undiminished. Nightly rioting in late September 2001 in north Belfast escalated with gunfire directed at the security forces, and violence spread to east Belfast, which continued into 2002. Unionists made threats against nationalist teachers and postal workers. In August 2002 three IRA men were arrested in Colombia. Linked to radical leftist guerrillas in that country, their presence in South America made manifest that members of the organization who were commited to violent tactics remained active.

In November 2001 a new police force replaced the RUC. The Police Service of Northern Ireland began training recruits, while officers contended with continuing outbreaks of violence in fending off both unionist and nationalist attackers. Sinn Féin refused to endorse the law-and-order reform, and it withheld nominating members to the Policing Board, the new body set up to oversee the reformed force. In October 2002 police raided Sinn Féin offices in Belfast to investigate the possibility that the party was using its position inside government to gather intelligence on opponents. Exasperated at the republican party's seeming reluctance to fully engage in cooperative efforts, the British government suspended the Northern Ireland Assembly on October 14. The Northern Ireland Executive's chief officeholders First Minister David Trimble and Deputy First Minister Mark Durkan (1966–), who, as head of the SDLP had replaced retiring Seamus Mallon in the post in 2001, stepped down. Direct rule from London was resumed until such time as Sinn Féin demonstrated that it had ended its links with the IRA. Symbolic gestures and soothing words were no longer sufficient to build trust, Prime Minister Tony Blair declared, and full implementation of the Good Friday Agreement was needed.

From 2003 to 2006 the work of building confidence among the parties inched forward, coaxed by periodic summits led by Blair and Ahern. In May 2003 the British and Irish governments issued a joint declaration linking the restoration of Northern Ireland's domestic governing institutions to an end to paramilitary activity. A four-person International Monitoring Commission was created in September 2003 charged with scrutinizing paramilitary cease-fires and to report on violations of the Good Friday Agreement.

Prospects at first appeared dim for reviving power-sharing institutions. Extremists on both sides were in the ascendant. The Northern Ireland Assembly remained suspended. Although not in attendance, its members formally disbanded on April 28, 2003, as scheduled, in advance of elections planned for the following month. Those elections were postponed by the British government until November. Held on November 26, they produced triumphs for both the Democratic Unionists and Sinn Féin. The legislative body remained in suspension. Sinn Féin went on to win seats in the June 2004 elections for the European Parliament and again in May 2005 in balloting for the parliament in London when, again, it and the Democratic Unionist Party (DUP) gained at the expense of the moderate parties.

The surge in support for the DUP, which made it now the largest party in Northern Ireland, reflected the belief among Protestants that Sinn Féin offered too little in return for entrusting the party with a place in government. Sinn Féin's rising strength represented sentiments among Roman Catholics that the DUP had to be powerfully challenged in its pretensions. The growing political clout of these two parties meant that only by bringing them into full participation in the peace-making efforts would community reconciliation be secured. The method of verifying decommissioning constituted the central sticking point. The DUP, supported by the British and Irish governments, insisted that documenting the arms' drawdown be done by means of photographs, but Sinn Féin saw this as humiliating to the IRA. Negotiations failed to reach an agreement. Sinn Féin began to give ground only after a bank robbery and a grisly murder outside a bar in January 2005 in Belfast were tied to the Provisional IRA. Tired at the interminable foot dragging and weary at the IRA's stubborn refusal to abandon once and for all the decades-old resort to force, supporters of Sinn Féin across the political spectrum let it be known they expected the party to put pressure on its armed ally. Irish-American political circles, too, condemned Sinn Féin's backing of IRA recalcitrance.

Compelled to act by this concerted drive, Gerry Adams suggested to the Provisional IRA in March that it disband as a paramilitary organization. In July a major breakthrough came when the IRA announced an end to its armed campaign, ordered its units to lay aside their weaponry, and instructed its members henceforth to engage solely in democratic politics. In late September General de Chastelain confirmed that the Provisional IRA had indeed put its arms out of use.

In the early part of 2006 leaders on both sides remained wary of each other. The Northern Ireland Assembly, still suspended, was called together in May to elect a first minister and a deputy first minister and to choose other members of the Northern Ireland Executive, but Ian Paisley refused to serve alongside Sinn Féin's chief negotiator, Martin McGuinness (1950–). Progress continued, however. Violence virtually ceased, and significant reductions in the British military presence were announced.

Northern Ireland watchers both on the island and around the world were stunned when, on March 26, 2007, DUP leader Ian Paisley and Sinn Féin head Gerry Adams appeared together in a televised broadcast—seated side by side for the first time ever—to announce that they had arranged a power-sharing deal. The announcement followed talks held at St. Andrews, Fife, Scotland, on October 11–13, 2006, among the British and Irish governments and all of the major parties in Northern Ireland. Unionist insistence on its aims, backed up by pressure from Dublin, London, and, in the end, Sinn Féin, proved decisive in compelling the IRA to make concessions. In the St. Andrews Agreement, all parties agreed to restoration of the Northern Ireland Assembly, and

Sitting side by side for the first time in history, Democratic Unionist Party leader Ian Paisley *(left)* and Sinn Féin president Gerry Adams (right) give a news conference at the Stormont Assembly building in Belfast on March 26, 2007, to announce a stunning deal to forge a power-sharing administration for Northern Ireland. (AP Images)

Democratic Unionists, as the largest of the loyalist parties, agreed to share power in the Northern Ireland Executive with Sinn Féin, the largest nationalist party. The agreement called for devolution of police and judicial powers to the local instruments of government within two years. Sinn Féin fully accepted the establishment of the Police Service of Northern Ireland.

The third elections to the Northern Ireland Assembly were held on March 7, 2007. Trends of recent years continued with the DUP, Sinn Féin, and the Alliance Party increasing their support while the Ulster Unionists and SDLP registered declines.

Democratic Unionist chief Paisley was elected to head the government as first minister of the Northern Ireland Executive. Sinn Féin deputy leader Martin McGuinness accepted the second post as deputy first minister. McGuinness, a high school dropout from Londonderry, rose to become that city's IRA commander and spent many years on the run from the law as a member of the seven-man IRA ruling "army council." The remaining 12 power-sharing positions in the administration were filled on the basis of the number of seats each party holds in the assembly.

2007 Northern Ireland Election Results	
Party	Assembly Members
Democratic Unionist Party	36
Sinn Féin	28
Ulster Unionist Party	18
Social Democratic and Labour Party	16
Alliance Party	7
Green Party	1
Progressive Unionist Party	1
Kirean Deeny (Independent)	1
Total	108

Paisley pledged to cooperate with nationalists in Northern Ireland and work with the government of the republic, a government he once considered anathema, to promote harmony and healing, and Adams affirmed that the accord marked the beginning of a new era in politics. Paisley resigned as first minister and leader of the DUP in May 2008. He was succeeded in both positions by Peter Robinson (1948–), an MP for East Belfast.

The British army's emergency action in the province—Operation Banner—ended on July 31, 2007. Forces were reduced to a residual level to provide support for public order and specialized ordnance disposal. The longest continuous deployment in the modern history of the army, the operation counted 763 deaths and 6,100 injuries (Evans 2005, 1).

The paraders still assemble for Northern Ireland's traditional demonstrations, but they do so peacefully. The Orange Order still refuses to acknowledge the authority of the Parades Commission, and the marchers in Portadown are blocked from moving through Catholic neighborhoods, but the order's lodges have recently agreed in principle to negotiate, and the July 2007 parade passed without incident. Devolution is once again at work. A government is in place that, for the first time, because it includes those who hitherto steadfastly refused to cooperate with their foes, holds out hope for a lasting end to the decades of political stalemate and bloodshed that has left as many as 3,700 dead. At no time before have all parties proceeded with more confidence that the paramilitaries have put aside their weapons for good and that both majority and minority communities in Northern Ireland will succeed in breaking down once and for all the walls, both physical and mental, that have for so long separated them in learning to live no longer side by side but, indeed, with each other.

In March 2002 David Trimble, former first minister of the Northern Ireland Executive, described the Irish republic as a "pathetic sectarian, mono-ethnic, mono-cultural state" (BBC News, 2002). However, the Republic of Ireland had changed far too much for such sentiments, which reflected long engrained Northern Irish Protestant prejudice, to remain valid. In 1996 Ruari Quinn of the Labour Party, then serving as minister for finance, described Ireland as "a post-Catholic pluralist republic" (Ferriter 2004, 751). That statement, too, missed the mark as a comment that reflected more a future aspiration than it did the current reality. The old negative stereotypes of republican Ireland no longer apply, but the images of a wholly secular, multicultural Ireland are not yet entirely valid. The institutions of state and church that for so long served as powerful inhibitors to social progress remain firmly in place even as they too are affected by the forces of change that are sweeping through the country. Those forces move steadily ahead. Ireland is fast becoming a fully modern nation. Once a backward place on the periphery of Europe, at the beginning of the 21st century the Republic of Ireland is a vibrant, wealthy land totally in touch with and attuned to world affairs. The challenge ahead for the country lies in its ability to preserve its cherished traditions while at the same time remaining fully open to global influences, trends, and technologies.

The Irish have one of Europe's most ancient histories. Mayhem and misfortune make up no small part of their story, and tragedy runs through their narrative, but the often sorrow-filled tale has left in its wake a remarkably resilient race. Endurance and adaptability are the defining traits of the Irish people. They have survived—at home and wherever across the globe they have roamed—to become one of the most readily recognizable of the world's peoples.

The spirits of ancient Celtic warriors might be seen to drift out of the mists that often envelop Ireland's trademark green countryside; given Irish history, their presence down through the centuries has never been far away. But today it is the spirits of Ireland's saints and scholars, its performing artists and wordsmiths, its entrepreneurs and civil servants—both North and South—that hold sway, giving promise of peaceful, prosperous days that, this time, have truly come to stay.

APPENDIX 1

BASIC FACTS ABOUT THE REPUBLIC OF IRELAND

Official Name
Ireland (Irish, Éire)

Government
A republic with a parliamentary system. The national parliament (Oireachtas) consists of the president and two legislative houses: a House of Representatives (Dáil Éireann) and a Senate (Seanad Éireann). The president is largely a ceremonial post elected by popular vote for a term of seven years. The Dáil consists of 166 members returned in 41 constituencies by universal adult suffrage. The Senate has 60 members, nominated by the prime minister and elected by panels of experts. Elections must be held every five years. The prime minister (Taoiseach) is appointed by the president on the nomination of the Dáil, whose confidence he must retain. The Taoiseach appoints members of his cabinet, and members of the government head departments of state. Political parties include the two largest and oldest—Fianna Fáil and Fine Gael—as well as the Labour Party, Democratic Left, Sinn Féin, Progressive Democrats, Green Party, and other small groups. A common law legal system operates.

Political Divisions
Provinces	26 counties; four traditional provinces
Capital	Dublin (1.6 million [metro], 2006 est.)

Geography
Area	26,600 sq. mi. (68,894 sq. km)

Boundaries	Bounded by the Atlantic Ocean on the west and south, the Irish Sea on the east, and by Northern Ireland on the north
Topography	A central plain rimmed by low mountains; small lakes (loughs) in the west and south; short rivers; irregular coastline; numerous small islands
Highest Elevation	Carrantuohill in County Kerry at 3,414 ft. (1,040 m)
Climate	Mild maritime climate tempered by Gulf Stream and prevailing southwesterly winds. Temperatures uniform from 34°F (1°C) to 68°F (20°C). Rain throughout the year, but more frequent in winter and in the western parts of the country.

Demography

Population	4.4 million (2008 est.). Pop. density: 156 persons per sq. mi. (60 per sq. km). Urban: 60%; rural: 40% (2005 est.)
Major Cities	Dublin, Cork, Limerick, Galway, Waterford
Language	English, Irish
Religion	Roman Catholicism (approx. 88%, 2006 est.)

Economy

Currency	euro (€) = 100 cents
GNP per capita	U.S. $45,580 (World Bank, 2006 est.)
Agricultural Products	cattle, beef, dairy products
Industrial Activity	machines, textiles, food processing, chemicals, brewing, computer software, clothing, glass and crystal production, steel, lead, zinc, silver, bauxite and gypsum mining, tourism
Trade	
Main Exports	machinery and equipment, chemicals, foodstuffs, computers and computer parts, pharmaceuticals, animals and animal products
Main Imports	data processing equipment, petroleum and petroleum products, textiles, clothing
Labor Force	services (64%); manufacturing (29%); agriculture (7%) (2005 est.)

Media

Newspapers	*Irish Times* (national daily); *Irish Independent* (national daily); *Irish Examiner* (Cork daily)
Television	RTE, TG4, TV3
Official Web Site	www.irlgov.ie

APPENDIX 2

BASIC FACTS ABOUT NORTHERN IRELAND

Official Name
Northern Ireland

Government
Northern Ireland is an integral part of the United Kingdom. The British monarch is head of state. The British government is represented by the Northern Ireland Office, headed by the secretary of state for Northern Ireland. Northern Ireland sends 18 members to the House of Commons in London. The Northern Ireland Assembly is the legislature of Northern Ireland. The assembly is a unicameral body composed of 108 members elected by universal adult suffrage for 18 six-member constituencies. The executive, the Northern Ireland Executive, is headed by a First Minister and a Deputy First Minister. They are elected by the assembly. A common law legal system operates.

Political Divisions
Provinces	Six provinces. After 1974, divided into 26 districts for administrative purposes.
Capital	Belfast (277,200 [city]; 700,000 [metro], 2005 est.)

Geography
Area	5,452 sq. mi. (14,121 sq. km)
Boundaries	Bounded by the Republic of Ireland on the south and west, the Atlantic Ocean on the

	north, and the North Channel, a strait of the Atlantic Ocean, and the Irish Sea on the east
Topography	A central plain with groups of hills and lakes; small islands off coast
Highest Elevation	Slieve Donard in County Down at 2,782 ft. (848 m)
Climate	Mild maritime climate

Demography

Population	1.7 million (2006 est.)
Major Cities	Belfast, Londonderry
Language	English, Irish, Ulster Scots
Religion	Protestantism (53%, 2006 est.) (Presbyterian, Anglican, Methodist); Roman Catholicism (44%, 2006 est.)

Economy

Currency	pound sterling (£) = 100 pence
Agricultural Products	livestock and dairy products, potatoes, barley, wheat
Industrial Activity	manufacturing: textiles, aircraft, shipbuilding; food processing, machinery

Media

Newspapers	*Belfast Telegraph* (daily) *Irish News* (nationalist daily); *News Letter* (unionist daily)
Television	BBC Northern Ireland, UTV
Official Web Site	www.nio.gov.uk

APPENDIX 3

CHRONOLOGY OF IRELAND

Beginnings to the End of Pagan Ireland

ca. 2,000,000–30,000 B.C.E.	Great ice age of the Pleistocene period; climate warms and temperate topography emerges
ca. 6400 B.C.E.	Rising sea levels separate Ireland from Great Britain
ca. 3800 B.C.E.	Neolithic Ireland; first farmsteads
ca. 2500 B.C.E.	Bronze Age; bronze- and goldwork exported
ca. 700–150 B.C.E.	Celts arrive
100 B.C.E.–500 C.E.	Beginnings of Irish language
77–84 C.E.	Roman governor of Britain considers conquest of Ireland
297–450	Irish raids on settlements in Roman Britain

Christianity Arrives and Thrives

431	Palladius sent as bishop to Christians in Ireland
ca. 432	Patrick begins his mission (traditional date)
ca. 550–650	Monasticism flourishes.
ca. 550–600	Earliest Irish text in writing
ca. 563	Columbanus founds monastery at Iona, Scotland
ca. 590	Columbanus begins mission on the European continent
ca. 650	Book of Durrow, earliest known illuminated manuscript
ca. 650–750	Irish canon and vernacular laws written; Irish metalworking and stone sculpture at their height; Ossory group of highcrosses

| ca. 668–750 | Gradual transition from tribal rule to established dynastic kingships |
| ca. 670–90 | Primacy of Armagh established |

From Viking Invasions to Royal Confrontations

795	Viking raids begin
841–42	Vikings found Dublin
ca. 950	Second period of Viking raids ends
975	Brian Boru, king of Munster and, from 1022, king of Ireland
1014	Battle of Clontarf (April 23); death of Brian Boru
1022–72	High kingship in abeyance
ca. 1050–1200	Late Middle Irish linguistic period; reworking of ancient sagas
1086–1119	Muirchertach O'Brien, king of Munster and de facto king of Ireland
1142	Mellifont, the first Cistercian house, founded
1152	Synod of Kells-Mellifont, an islandwide church organization, established
1166	Rory O'Connor, king of Connacht, becomes high king; Dermot MacMurough, king of Leinster, driven to England; he seeks help from King Henry II

From the Norman Invasion to the Anglo-Irish Administration

1169	Anglo-Norman invasion under Strongbow
1171	Death of MacMurrough and succession of Strongbow as lord of Munster; Henry II arrives; submission of Irish bishops and most Irish kings
ca. 1200–1600	Classical period in Irish literature
ca. 1224	Dominicans and Franciscans arrive
1235	Conquest of Connacht by Richard de Burgh completed
1264	First Irish assembly called a "parliament" meets at Casteldermot
1348	Black Death ravages east coast ports
1366	Statutes of Kilkenny (February 19)

1394–95	King Richard II's first expedition; receives submission of Irish kings
1399	Richard's second expedition
1479–1513	Gerald Mor Fitzgerald, eighth earl of Kildare, lord deputy
1494	Poynings's Law (December 1)

The Planting of Protestant Power

1541–43	Irish parliament declares Henry VIII king of Ireland; "surrender and regrant" program started
1547–53	Reign of Edward VI; Reformation in Ireland
1553–58	Reign of Queen Mary; Catholicism restored
1560	Second Reformation parliament restores Anglican Church in Ireland
1568–73	First Desmond rebellion
1569–71	Private colonization efforts in Munster and Ulster
1571	First book printed in Irish language in Dublin
1573–76	Earl of Essex campaigns in Ulster; private colonization ventures in Ulster
1592	Trinity College, first Irish college, founded
1595	Hugh O'Neill, earl of Tyrone, launches rebellion
1598	Tyrone victorious at Battle of Yellow Ford (August 14); rebellion spreads to Munster
1603	Tyrone surrenders to Mountjoy; Elizabeth I dies, and James I accedes to English throne
1607	"Flight of the Earls"
1608–10	Ulster plantations prepared and begun
1632–36	Compilation of *Annals of the Four Masters* in Donegal
1633–41	Viscount Thomas Wentworth, earl of Strafford, serves as lord deputy
1642	Scots Covenanter army arrives in Ulster (April); Owen Roe O'Neill forms a Catholic army (July); civil war begins in England (August); Catholic confederacy formed at Kilkenny (October).
1649	Execution of Charles I (January); Cromwell lays siege to Drogheda and Wexford (September–October); defeat of O'Neill (November)

1650–53	Cromwellian conquest completed
1654–55	Cromwellian plantation carried out
1660	Restoration of Charles II (May)
1665	Act of Explanation: Cromwellian settlers to surrender one-third of their lands to be given to Catholics
1685	Accession of James II; *Dublin News-letter*, first newspaper
1688	Glorious Revolution in England: William III and Mary accede to the throne
1689	James II arrives at Kinsale (March); Catholic parliament at Dublin (May–July)
1690	William III arrives and defeats forces of James II at the Boyne (July 1); James sails to France
1691	Jacobite armies defeated; Treaty of Limerick (October 3)

Ascendancy Ireland

1695	Penal laws against Catholics begin
1718	Large-scale emigration from Ulster to America begins
1719	Toleration Act for Protestant Dissenters
1720	Declaratory Act: British parliament given right to legislate for Ireland
1726	*Gulliver's Travels* by Jonathan Swift published
1728	Catholics forbidden to vote
1759	Arthur Guinness leases brewery in Dublin
1778	Relief Act grants Catholics leaseholding and inheritance rights
1782	Volunteer convention (February); Relief Acts allow Catholics to own freeholds outside parliamentary boroughs and grant educational rights (May–July); Irish parliamentary independence conceded (June)
1783	Bank of Ireland opens
1791	Wolfe Tone's *Argument on behalf of the Catholics of Ireland* (August); Society of United Irishmen founded (October)
1795	Catholic seminary at Maynooth founded (June); Orange Order created in Ulster (September)

1798   Martial law imposed (March); United Irish rising in Leinster and Ulster (May–June); capture and execution of Tone (November)

From the Act of Union to the Great Famine

1801   Union of Great Britain and Ireland starts (January 1)

1803   Robert Emmet's rising (July 23)

1822   Irish Constabulary Act sets up county police forces

1823   Catholic Association founded

1828   Daniel O'Connell elected to parliament

1829   Catholic Emancipation Act

1831   Primary education system established

1845   Potato blight first appears (September)

1847   Famine at its height; mass emigration in progress

The Drive for Independence

1858   Fenians (Irish Republican Brotherhood) established in Dublin

1859   Fenian Brotherhood founded in the United States

1866   Paul Cullen becomes the first Irish cardinal

1867   Fenian rising

1869   Disestablishment of the Church of Ireland

1873   Home Rule League established

1879   Irish National Land League founded

1880   Parnell elected chairman of Irish Parliamentary Party

1882   Irish National League replaces outlawed Land League; chief secretary and undersecretary assassinated by Invincibles in Phoenix Park, Dublin

1884   Gaelic Athetic Association established

1886   Catholic hierarchy endorses Home Rule; Government of Ireland bill (Home Rule) defeated in Commons.

1890   O'Shea names Parnell as co-respondent in divorce petition (November); Parnell repudiated by his party (December)

1893	Gaelic League founded; second Home Rule bill defeated
1898	United Irish League founded
1902	*Cathleen ni Houlihan* by W. B. Yeats
1903	Wyndham's Land Purchase Act
1907	Griffith's Sinn Féin founded
1908	Irish Transport and General Workers' Union founded
1913	Ulster Volunteer Force, Irish Citizens' Army, and Irish (National) Volunteers formed; strikes in Dublin
1914	Arms illegally imported by Ulster Volunteers (April) and Irish Volunteers (July–August); enactment and suspension of Home Rule
1916	Easter Rising: Irish Republic proclaimed (April 24); rebels surrender (April 29).
1918	Republicans win general elections (December)
1919	Dáil Éireann formed
1920	Riots in Ulster; "Bloody Sunday" in Dublin (November 21); Government of Ireland Act establishes home rule parliaments and administrations in Dublin and Belfast (December 23)
1921	Anglo-Irish peace conference followed by Anglo-Irish Treaty (December 6)

Making Modern Ireland

1922	Provisional Government under Collins formed (January); outbreak of civil war (June); Irish Free State established without Northern Ireland (December); *Ulysses* by James Joyce
1923	Irregulars surrender; Cumann na nGaedheal founded
1925	Boundary Commission disbands; partition confirmed
1926	De Valera founds Fianna Fáil
1927	O'Higgins assassinated; Fianna Fáil elected to Dáil
1930	First censorship board in Irish Free State
1932–38	Tariff war between Irish Free State and Britain
1933	United Ireland Party (Fine Gael) founded

1936	External Relations Act weakens ties with Britain
1937	Constitution of Éire replaces Irish Free State constitution
1939	IRA bombing campaign in Britain; outbreak of World War II and Éire remains neutral
1941	Height of German air raids on Belfast
1948	National Health Insurance in Northern Ireland
1949	Irish Republic inaugurated (April)
1955	Republic admitted to the United Nations
1956–62	IRA conducts border campaign
1958	Economic expansion program launched in republic (repeated in 1963–64 and 1969)
1959	De Valera elected president (June); Lemass elected Taoiseach (June)
1966	Ulster Volunteer Force founded; de Valera reelected president (June)
1967	Northern Ireland Civil Rights Association established

Two Irish Visions in Collision

1969	Democracy march from Belfast to Derry (January); explosions in Belfast (March) and first deaths in "Troubles" (July); British army sent to Northern Ireland (August); Fianna Fáil wins general elections in republic
1970	IRA splits into "Official" and "Progressive" wings (January); Ulster Defence Regiment replaces B Specials; Social Democratic and Labour Party formed in Northern Ireland
1971	Rev. Ian Paisley's Democratic Unionist Party founded; internment introduced
1972	"Bloody Sunday" (January 30); direct rule imposed in Northern Ireland (March 24); "Bloody Friday" (July 21)
1973	Republic joins the EC; tripartite Sunningdale Conference; general elections in republic, Fine Gael–Labour coalition with Cosgrave as Taoiseach elected
1974	Direct rule reimposed (May): multiple killings

1977	General elections in republic, Fianna Fáil government with Lynch as Taoiseach
1979	Terrorist violence at 10-year peak; relaxation of republic's ban on contraception
1981	Hunger striker Bobby Sands wins Fermanagh–South Tyrone by-election (March); IRA bombs British targets on European continent
1982	Fianna Fáil wins general election in republic with Haughey as Taoiseach (February); Fine Gael–Labour forms coalition government
1983	Unionists win 15 out of 17 seats in Northern Ireland parliamentary elections; All-Ireland forum fails
1984	Provisional IRA bombs Conservative Party conference in Brighton, England (October)
1985	Anglo-Irish Agreement at Hillsborough (November 15) launches massive loyalist protests
1989	General election in the republic, Haughey Taoiseach of a Fianna Fáil–PD coalition
1990	Mary Robinson elected republic's first woman president
1992	Haughey resigns as Taoiseach, succeeded by Reynolds; referendum in the republic approves Maastricht Treaty on European Union
1993	Downing Street Declaration (December 15)
1994	IRA cease-fire
1995	"Rainbow coalition" government in the republic, Bruton as Taoiseach; divorce referendum passed
1996	IRA ends cease-fire
1997	General election in the republic, Fianna Fáil–PD coalition with Bertie Ahern Taoiseach; IRA reinstates its cease-fire; Mary McAleese wins presidential election in the republic
1998	Good Friday Agreement signed (April 10) and approved in referendums; 29 killed in bomb attack in Omagh by "Real IRA" (August 16)
1999	Devolved government in Northern Ireland

Ireland in the Twenty-first Century

2000	Direct rule over Northern Ireland reimposed (February 11); devolved government restored (May 29)
2001	IRA weapons' decommissioning plan rejected by First Minister Trimble; IRA withdraws decommissioning offer; republic's population reaches 120-year high (3.84 million)
2002	Euro replaces the punt (January 1); general election in the republic, Fianna Fáil–PD coalition returned with Bertie Ahern as Taoiseach, Fine Gael loses a third of its seats (May); voters in the republic endorse Nice Treaty (October); Northern Ireland Assembly again suspended (October)
2003	Elections for a new Northern Ireland Assembly are held but it remains suspended (November)
2005	Cork named European cultural capital of the year
2006	St. Andrew's Agreement (October)
2007	Elections to a third Northern Ireland Assembly and power-sharing Northern Ireland Executive elected (March); general election in the republic, Fianna Fáil–PD-Green coalition with Bertie Ahern as Taoiseach (June)
2008	Bertie Ahern steps down as Taoiseach; replaced by Brian Cowen (May); Ian Paisley leaves government in Northern Ireland (May); Irish voters reject proposed Treaty of Lisbon (June)

Appendix 4

Irish Leaders from 1922 to 2008

Governors-General of the Irish Free State	
Name	Term
Tim Healy	1922–1928
James MacNeill	1928–1932
Domhnall Ua Buachalla	1932–1937

Presidents of the Executive Council of the Irish Free State		
Name	Term	Party
William T. Cosgrove	1922–1932	Cumann na nGaedheal
Eamon de Valera	1932–1937	Fianna Fáil

Prime Ministers (Taioseach) of Éire/Republic of Ireland, 1937–2008

Name	Entered Office	Left Office	Party
Eamon de Valera	December 29, 1937	February 18, 1948	Fianna Fáil
John A. Costello	February 18, 1948	June 13, 1951	Fine Gael
Eamon de Valera	June 13, 1951	June 2, 1954	Fianna Fáil
John A. Costello	June 2, 1954	March 20, 1957	Fine Gael
Eamon de Valera	March 20, 1957	June 23, 1959	Fianna Fáil
Sean Lemass	June 23, 1959	November 10, 1966	Fianna Fáil
Jack Lynch	November 10, 1966	March 14, 1973	Fianna Fáil
Liam Cosgrave	March 14, 1973	July 5, 1977	Fine Gael
Jack Lynch	July 5, 1977	December 11, 1979	Fianna Fáil
Charles Haughey	December 11, 1979	June 30, 1981	Fianna Fáil
Garret Fitzgerald	June 30, 1981	March 9, 1982	Fine Gael
Charles Haughey	March 9, 1982	December 14, 1982	Fianna Fáil
Garret Fitzgerald	December 14, 1982	March 10, 1987	Fine Gael
Charles Haughey	March 10, 1987	February 11, 1992	Fianna Fáil
Albert Reynolds	February 11, 1992	December 15, 1994	Fianna Fáil
John Bruton	December 15, 1994	June 26, 1997	Fine Gael
Bertie Ahern	June 26, 1997	May 6, 2008	Fianna Fáil
Brian Cowen	May 6, 2008		Fianna Fáil

Presidents of Éire/Republic of Ireland, 1938–2008

Name	Term of Office	Party
Douglas Hyde	1938–1945	no party
Sean T. O'Kelly	1945–1959	Fianna Fáil
Eamon de Valera	1959–1973	Fianna Fáil
Erskine H. Childers	1973–1974	Fianna Fáil
Cearbhall Ó Dálaigh	1974–1976	Fianna Fáil
Patrick J. Hillery	1976–1990	Fianna Fáil
Mary T. W. Robinson	1990–1997	Labour
Mary McAleese	1997–	Fianna Fáil

Prime Ministers of Northern Ireland, 1921–1972

Name	Term	Party
Sir James Craig	June 1921–November 1940	Ulster Unionist
John Miller Andrews	November 1940–May 1943	Ulster Unionist
Sir Basil Brooke (Viscount Brookeborough)	May 1943–March 1963	Ulster Unionist
Terence M. O'Neill	March 1963–May 1969	Ulster Unionist
James Chichester-Clarke	May 1969–March 1971	Ulster Unionist
Brian Faulkner	March 1971–March 1972	Ulster Unionist

Secretaries of State for Northern Ireland, 1972–2008

Name	Term	Party
William Whitelaw	March 1972–November 1973	Conservative
Francis Pym	December 1973–February 1974	Conservative
Merlyn Rees	March 1974–September 1976	Labour
Roy Mason	September 1976–May 1979	Labour
Humphrey Atkins	May 1979–September 1981	Conservative
James Prior	September 1981–September 1984	Conservative
Douglas Hurd	September 1984–September 1985	Conservative
Tom King	September 1985–July 1989	Conservative
Peter Brooke	July 1989–April 1992	Conservative
Sir Patrick Mayhew	April 1992–April 1997	Conservative
Marjorie "Mo" Mowlam	May 1997–October 1999	Labour
Peter Mandelson	October 1999–January 2001	Labour
John Reid	January 2001–October 2002	Labour
Paul Murphy	October 2002–May 2005	Labour
Peter Hain	May 2005–June 2007	Labour
Shaun Woodward	June 2007–	Labour

Ministers of the Northern Ireland Executive*

First Minister	Term	Party
David Trimble	July 1998–July 2001	Ulster Unionist
Reg Empey (acting)	July 2001–November 2001	Ulster Unionist
David Trimble	November 2001–October 2002	Ulster Unionist
Ian Paisley	May 2007– June 2008	Democratic Unionist
Peter Robinson	June 2008–	Democratic Unionist

Deputy First Minister	Term	Party
Seamus Mallon	July 1998–November 2001	Social Democrat and Labour
Mark Durkan	November 2001–October 2002	Social Democrat and Labour
Martin McGuinness	May 2007–	Sinn Féin

*The Northern Ireland Executive was suspended February 11, 2000–May 30, 2000; August 10, 2001–August 11, 2001; September 22, 2001–September 23, 2001; October 14, 2002–May 7, 2007.

Appendix 5

Bibliography

"An Act That the King of England, His Heirs and Successors Be Kings of Ireland." 33 Henry VIII, c. 1, vol. 1, *Irish Statutes* (1786), 176.

Anglo-Irish Treaty, 6 December 1921. The National Archives of Ireland, "Documents on Irish Foreign Policy Series: text of the Anglo-Irish Treaty." Available online. URL: http://www.nationalarchives.ie/topics/anglo_irish/dfaexhib2.html. Accessed September 3, 2007.

BBC. "A Short History of Ireland." Available online. URL: http://www.bbc.co.uk/northernireland/ashorthistory/Archive/intro213.shtml. Accessed November 12, 2007.

BBC News. "Northern Ireland Chronology: 2002." Available online. URL: http://www.news.bbc.co.uk/1/hi/northern_Ireland/2933949.stm. Accessed October 29, 2007.

Beresford, John. *The Correspondence of the Right Honorable John Beresford.* 2 vols. London: Woodfell and Kinder, 1854.

Brooke, Sir Basil. "Prime Minister's Message." *Belfast Telegraph*, January 24, 1949, 1.

Carey, John, ed. *Eyewitness to History*. Cambridge, Mass.: Harvard University Press, 1988.

Carty, J., ed. *Ireland from the Flight of the Earls to Grattan's Parliament (1607–1782)*. Dublin: C.J. Fallon, 1966.

Ceinton, Bill. "Remarks by the President of USA at Mackies, Belfast, 30 November 1995." Available online. URL: http//www.cain.ulst.ac.uk/events/peace/docs/pres1.htm. Accessed November 18, 2007.

Cosgrove, Art. *Late Medieval Ireland, 1370–1541*. Dublin: Helicon, 1981.

Davies, Norman. *The Isles: A History*. Oxford: Oxford University Press, 1999.

Davitt, Michael. *The Fall of Feudalism in Ireland; or, the Story of the Land League Revolution*. London: Harper and Bros., 1904.

Derry and the Boyne: A Contemporary Account of the Siege of Derry, the Battle of the Boyne, and the General Condition of Ireland in the Jacobite War. Belfast: Belfast Historical and Educational Society, 1990.

Devlin, Bernadette. *The Price of My Soul*. New York: Alfred A. Knopf, 1969.

Donnelly, James. "A Church in Crisis: The Irish Catholic Church Today." *History Ireland* 8, no. 3 (Autumn 2000): 12–27.

Downing Street Declaration. Available online. URL: http://www.c-r.org/our_work.accord.northern-ireland/downing.street.declaration.php. Accessed November 19, 2007.

Duffy, Charles Gavan. *Young Ireland: A Fragment of Irish History, 1840–50*. London: Cassell, Petter, Galpin, 1880.

Emmet, Robert. "The Speech from the Dock: Robert Emmet's Speech on the Eve of His Execution" (September 19, 1803). Available online. URL: http://www.robertemmet.org/speech.htm. Accessed December 19, 2007.

Evans, Michael. "Garrison to Be Halved as Army Winds Up Longest Operation." *The Times*, August 2, 2005, 1.

Ferriter, Diarmaid. *The Transformation of Ireland*. Woodstock, N.Y.: The Overlook Press, 2004.

Fletcher, Martin. *Silver Linings: Travels around Northern Ireland*. London: Little, Brown, 2000.

Froissart, Jean. *Froissart's Chronicles*. Edited and translated by John Joliffe. London: Harvill, 1967.

Gregory, Lady. *Lady Gregory's Journals*. Edited by Daniel J. Murphy. New York: Oxford University Press, 1978–1987.

Harkness, David. *Northern Ireland since 1920*. Dublin: Helicon, 1983.

Hastings, Max, ed. *The Oxford Book of Military Anecdotes*. New York: Oxford University Press, 1985.

"Ireland: Definition." "Economy." Available online. URL: http://www.answers.com/topic/ireland?cat=travel. Accessed November 26, 2007.

"Ireland's Economy Grew 6.7 Percent in First Half of 2007, Leading Euro Zone." *International Herald Tribune*, September 27, 2007. Available online. URL: http://www.iht.com/articles/ap/2007/09/27/business/EU-FIN-ECO-Ireland-Economy.php. Accessed October 19, 2007.

Jackson, Charles. *A Narrative of the Sufferings and Escapes of Charles Jackson, Late Resident at Wexford in Ireland*. Dublin: J. Jones, 1798.

Jeffery, Keith, and Hamilton Norway, eds. *The Sinn Féin Rebellion as They Saw It*. Dublin: Irish Academic Press, 1999.

Joyce, James. *A Portrait of the Artist as a Young Man.* Edited by S. Deane. London: Penguin, 1991.

Kilroy, James F. *The "Playboy" Riots.* Dublin: Dolmen Press, 1971.

Mangan, James Clarence. *Prose, 1840–1882.* Dublin: Irish Academic Press, 2002.

McLoughlin, Michael, ed. *Great Irish Speeches of the Twentieth Century.* Dublin: Poolbeg Press, 1996.

Melville, Herman. *Redburn: His First Voyage.* New York: Harper & Bros., 1850.

Newman, Peter R. *Companion to Irish History, 1603–1921: From the Submission of Tyrone to Partition.* New York: Facts On File, 1991.

"The Order's Fight for the Union, 1886–1921." Available online. URL: http://www.grandorange.org/uk/history/Fight_For_Union.html. Accessed November 25, 2007.

O'Toole, Fintan. *The Irish Times Book of the Century: 1900–1999.* Dublin: Gill and Macmillan, 2000.

Patrick, Saint. *Patrick in His Own Words.* Dublin: Veritas, 2000.

———. *The Works of Saint Patrick.* Translated by Ludwig Bieler. Westminster, Md.: Newman Press, 1953.

Pearse, Padraic H. *Collected Works of Padraic H. Pearse: Political Writings and Speeches.* Dublin: Maunsel and Roberts, 1922.

Redmond-Howard, Louis G. *Six Days of the Irish Republic.* 1916. Reprint, Aubane, Ireland: Aubane Historical Society, 2006.

Shaw, George Bernard. *The Matter with Ireland.* Edited by David H. Greene and Dan H. Lawrence. London: Rupert Hart-Davis, 1962.

Shaw-Lefevre, George. *Gladstone and Ireland, the Irish Policy of Parliament from 1850–1894.* London: Methuen, 1912.

Sturgis, Mark. *The Last Days of Dublin Castle: The Mark Sturgis Diaries.* Edited by Michael Hopkinson. Dublin: Irish Academic Press, 1999.

Synge, John Millington. *Collected Works.* 4 vols. Oxford: Oxford University Press, 1962–1968.

Tacitus, Cornelius. *Dialogus Agricola Germanicus/Tacitus.* Translated by W. Peterson and M. Hutton. Cambridge, Mass.: Harvard University Press, 1914.

Theroux, Paul. *The Kingdom by the Sea: A Journey around the Coast of Great Britain.* London: Hamish Hamilton, 1983.

Thomas, Colin, and Avril Thomas. *Historical Dictionary of Ireland.* Lanham, Md.: Scarecrow Press, 1997.

Tocqueville, Alexis de. *Journeys to England and Ireland.* Translated by George Lawrence and K. P. Mayert. Edited by J. P. Mayer. London:

Faber and Faber, 1958. Reprint. North Stratford, N.H.: Ayer Company Publishers, 1998.

Vaughn, W. E., and A. J. Fitzpatrick, eds. *Irish Historical Statistics: Population, 1821–1971*. Dublin: Royal Irish Academy, 1978.

World Development Indicators Database. World Bank, September 14, 2007. Atlas Methodology. Available online. URL: http://sitesources. worldbank.org/DATASTATISTICS/Resources/gnipc.pdf. Accessed November 19, 2007.

Yeats, William Butler. "Nobel Lecture, December 15, 1923: The Irish Dramatic Movement." Available online. URL: http://nobelprize.org/ nobel_prizes/literature/laureates/1923/yeats-lecture.html. Accessed November 23, 2007.

———. *Collected Poems*. London: Macmillan, 1955.

Young, Arthur. *A Tour in Ireland, with General Observations on the Present State of That Kingdom: Made in the Years 1776, 1777, and 1778 and Brought Down to the End of 1779*. London: For T. Cadell and J. Dodsley, 1780.

Appendix 6

SUGGESTED READING

General Works

Allen, Kieran. *Fianna Fáil and Irish Labour: 1926 to the Present*. London: Pluto Press, 1997.

Allen, Michael, ed. *Seamus Heaney*. New York: St. Martin's Press, 1997.

Bardon, Jonathan. *A History of Ulster*. Belfast: Blackstaff Press, 1992.

———, and Stephen Conlin. *Belfast: 1000 Years*. Belfast: Blackstaff Press, 1985.

Bartlett, Tom, and Keith Jeffery, eds. *A Military History of Ireland*. Cambridge: Cambridge University Press, 1996.

Bielenberg, Andy, ed. *The Irish Diaspora*. New York: Longman, 2000.

Boullier, Dianna. *Exploring Irish Music and Dance*. Dublin: O'Brien Press, 1998.

Boyce, David George. *Ireland, 1825–1923: From Ascendancy to Democracy*. Oxford: Blackwell, 1992.

———. *The Irish Question and British Politics, 1868–1996*. New York: St. Martin's Press, 1996.

———. *Nineteenth-Century Ireland: The Search for Stability*. Dublin: Gill and Macmillan, 1990.

Bracken, Damian, and Dagmar Ó Riain-Radel, eds. *Ireland and Europe in the Twentieth Century: Reform and Renewal*. Dublin: Four Courts Press, 2006.

Breathnach, Breandán. *Folk Music and Dances of Ireland*. Rev. ed. Dublin: Mercier Press, 1993.

Brennan, Helen. *The Story of Irish Dance*. Dingle, Ireland: Brandon, 1999.

Carlson, Julia. *Banned in Ireland: Censorship and the Irish Writer*. Athens: University of Georgia Press, 1990.

Coakley, John, and Michael Gallagher, eds. *Politics in the Republic of Ireland*. Dublin: Folens Publishers, 1993.

Cone, Polly. *Treasures of Irish Art, 1500 B.C.–1500 A.D.* New York: Metropolitan Museum of Art and Alfred A. Knopf, 1977.

Coogan, Tim Pat. *De Valera: Long Fellow, Long Shadow.* London: Hutchinson, 1993.

———. *Wherever Green Is Worn: The Story of the Irish Diaspora.* London: Hutchinson, 2000.

Connolly, Colm. *Michael Collins.* London: Weidenfeld and Nicolson, 1996.

Corbett, Tony. *Brian Friel: Decoding the Language of the Tribe.* Dublin: Liffey Press, 2002.

Corcoran, Tony. *The Goodness of Guinness: The Brewery, Its People and the City of Dublin.* Dublin: Liberties Press, 2005.

Corish, Patrick J. *The Catholic Community in the Seventeenth and Eighteenth Centuries.* Wilkinstown, Dublin: Helicon, 1981.

Cronin, Anthony. *Samuel Beckett: The Last Modernist.* London: HarperCollins, 1997.

Cronin, Mike, and Daryl Adair. *The Wearing of the Green: A History of St. Patrick's Day.* New York: Routledge, 2002.

Cullen Owens, Rosemary. *A Social History of Women in Ireland, 1870–1970.* Dublin: Gill and Macmillan, 2005.

Duggan, John P. *A History of the Irish Army.* Dublin: Gill and Macmillan, 1991.

Dungan, Myles. *Distant Drums: Irish Soldiers in Foreign Armies.* Belfast: Appletree Press, 1993.

Edwards, Ruth Dudley. *An Atlas of Irish History.* 3d ed. London: Routledge, 2005.

Ellis, Peter Berresford. *Eyewitness to Irish History.* Hoboken, N.J.: John Wiley and Sons, 2004.

English, Richard. *Armed Struggle: The History of the IRA.* London: Macmillan, 2003.

Evans, E. Estyn. *The Personality of Ireland: Habitat, Heritage and History.* Cambridge: Cambridge University Press, 1973.

Feeham, John. *Farming in Ireland: History, Heritage and Environment.* Dublin: University College Dublin, 2003.

Feeney, Brian. *Sinn Féin: A Hundred Turbulent Years.* Madison: University of Wisconsin Press, 2002.

Fitzpatrick, David. *Irish Emigration, 1801–1921.* Dublin: Economic and Social History Society of Ireland, 1984.

Flynn, Roderick, and Patrick Brereton. *Historical Dictionary of Irish Film.* Lanham, Md.: Scarecrow Press, 2007.

Foster, Robert F. *W. B. Yeats: A Life*. 2 vols. Oxford: Oxford University Press, 1997–2003.

Graham, Brian, ed. *In Search of Ireland: A Cultural Geography*. London: Routledge, 1997.

Grote, Georg. *Torn between Politics and Culture: The Gaelic League, 1893–1993*. New York: Waxmann, 1994.

Haddock-Flyn, Kevin. *A Short History of Orangeism*. Cork: Mercier Press, 2005.

Horgan, John. *Irish Media: A Critical History since 1922*. New York: Routledge, 2001.

Hourihane, Jim. *Ireland and the European Union: The First Thirty Years, 1973–2002*. Dublin: Lilliput Press, 2003.

Humphries, Tom. *Green Fields: Gaelic Sport in Ireland*. London: Weidenfeld and Nicolson, 1996.

Inglis, Tom. *Moral Monopoly: The Catholic Church in Modern Irish Society*. Dublin: Gill and Macmillan, 1987.

Jeffares, A. Norman, and Peter van de Kamp, eds. *Irish Literature: The Nineteenth Century*. 3 vols. Dublin: Irish Academic Press, 2006.

Kearney, Richard, ed. *The Irish Mind: Exploring Intellectual Traditions*. Dublin: Wolfhound Press, 1985.

Kelly, Fergus. *A Guide to Early Irish Law*. Dublin: Institute for Advanced Studies, 1988.

Kilfeather, Siobhán Marie. *Dublin: A Cultural and Literary History*. Dublin: Liffey Press, 2005.

Knowlson, James. *Damned to Fame: The Life of Samuel Beckett*. New York: Simon and Schuster, 1996.

Luddy, Maria. *Hanna Sheehy Skeffington*. Dublin: Dundalgan Press, 1995.

Lynch, Larry. *Set Dances of Ireland: Tradition and Evolution*. San Francisco: Seádna Books, 1991.

Mahon, Brid. *The Land of Milk and Honey: The Story of Traditional Irish Food and Drink*. Dublin: Poolbeg, 1991.

Mays, Michael. *Nation-States: The Culture of Irish Nationalism*. Lanham, Md.: Lexington Books, 2007.

McConville, Michael. *Ascendancy to Oblivion: The Story of the Anglo-Irish*. London: Quartet Books, 1982.

McCoole, Sineád. *No Ordinary Women: Irish Female Activists in the Revolutionary Years, 1916–1923*. Dublin: O'Brien Press, 2003.

Murphy, Colin, and Lynne Adair, eds. *Untold Stories: Protestants in the Republic of Ireland, 1922–2000*. Dublin: Liffey Press, 2002.

O'Brien, Eugene. *Seamus Heaney: Creating Irelands of the Mind*. Dublin: Liffey, 2002.

Ó Cróinin, Dáibhí. *Early Medieval Ireland, 400–1200*. London: Longman, 1995.

O'Donnell, Catherine. *Fianna Fáil, Irish Republicanism and the Northern Ireland Troubles, 1968–2005*. Dublin: Irish Academic Press, 2007.

O'Dowd, Mary. *A History of Women in Ireland, 1500–1800*. New York: Pearson Longman, 2005.

O'Flanagan, P., P. Ferguson, and K. Whelan, eds. *Rural Ireland: Modernisation and Change, 1600–1900*. Cork: Cork University Press, 1987.

Ó Gráda, Cormac. *Ireland: A New Economic History, 1780–1939*. Oxford: Clarendon Press, 1994.

———. *A Rocky Road: The Irish Economy since the 1920s*. Manchester: Manchester University Press, 1997.

O'Hart, John. *Irish Pedigrees: Or, the Origin and Stem of the Irish Nation*. Baltimore: Genealogical Publishing Company, 1976.

Pierce, David. *Irish Writing in the Twentieth Century: A Reader*. Cork: Cork University Press, 2000.

Ryan, Ray, ed. *Writing in the Irish Republic: Literature, Culture, Politics, 1949–1999*. New York: St. Martin's Press, 2000.

Smyth, Gerry. *Noisy Island: A Short History of Irish Popular Music*. Cork: Cork University Press, 2005.

Somerville-Large, Peter. *The Irish Country House: A Social History*. London: Sinclair-Stevenson, 1995.

Sweeney, Valerie. *Shannon Airport: A Unique Story of Survival*. Shannon: Self-published, 2004.

Tóibín, Colm, ed. *The Penguin Book of Irish Fiction*. New York: Viking, 2000.

Walker, Brian Mercer. *Dancing to History's Tune: History, Myth and Politics in Ireland*. Belfast: Queen's University of Belfast, 1996.

Walker, Graham. *A History of the Ulster Unionist Party: Protest, Pragmatism and Pessimism*. Manchester, U.K.: Manchester University Press, 2004.

Weldon, Niall G. *Pioneers in Flight: Aer Lingus and the Story of Flight in Ireland*. Dublin: Liffey, 2002.

White, Carolyn. *A History of Irish Fairies*. Dublin: Mercier Press, 2001.

Wichert, Sabine. *Northern Ireland since 1945*. 2d ed. New York: Longman, 1999.

Beginnings to the End of Pagan Ireland (Prehistory–431)

Di Martino, Vittorio. *Roman Ireland*. Cork: Collins, 2002.

Dooley, Ann. *Playing the Hero: Reading the Irish Saga Táin bó Cúailnge*. Toronto: University of Toronto Press, 2006.

Flanagan, Laurence. *Ancient Ireland: Life before the Celts*. Dublin: Gill and Macmillan, 1998.

Herity, Michael, and George Eogan. *Ireland in Prehistory*. London: Routledge and Keegan Paul, 1977.

Hickey, Elizabeth. *The Legend of Tara*. Dundalk, Ireland: Dundalgan Press, 1953.

MacKillop, James. *Myths and Legends of the Celts*. London: Penguin Books, 2005.

Megaw, M. Ruth. *Early Celtic Art in Britain and Ireland*. Princes Risborough, England: Shire, 2005.

Moffat, Alistair. *The Sun Kingdoms: The Story of Celtic Britain and Ireland*. London: HarperCollins, 2001.

Patterson, Nerys Thomas. *Cattle-Lords and Clansmen: The Social Structure of Early Ireland*. 2d ed. Notre Dame, Ind.: Notre Dame University Press, 1994.

Raftery, Barry. *Pagan Celtic Ireland*. London: Thames and Hudson, 1994.

Slavin, Michael. *The Ancient Books of Ireland*. Dublin: Wolfhound Press, 2005.

Woodman, Peter C. *The Mesolithic in Ireland*. Oxford: British Archaeological Reports, 1978.

Christianity Arrives and Thrives (431–795)

Cahill, Thomas. *How the Irish Saved Civilization: The Untold Story of Ireland's Heroic Role from the Fall of Rome to the Rise of Medieval Europe*. New York: Nan A. Talese/Doubleday, 1995.

Charles-Edwards, T. M. *Early Christian Ireland*. Cambridge: Cambridge University Press, 2000.

Freeman, Philip. *St. Patrick of Ireland: A Biography*. New York: Simon and Schuster, 2004.

Herbert, Máire. *Iona, Kells and Derry: The History and Hagiography of the Monastic "Familia" of Columba*. New York: Oxford University Press, 1988.

Hillgarth, J. N. *Visigothic Spain, Byzantium, and the Irish*. London: Variorum Reprints, 1985.

Jaski, Bart. *Early Irish Kingship and Succession.* Dublin: Four Courts Press, 2000.

Mytum, H. C. *The Origins of Early Christian Ireland.* New York: Routledge, 1992.

Richter, Michael. *Ireland and Her Neighbors in the Seventh Century.* Dublin: Four Courts Press, 1999.

Swift, Catherine. *Ogam Stones and the Earliest Christians.* Maynooth, Ireland: St. Patrick's College, 1997.

From Viking Invasions to Royal Confrontations (795–1169)

Clarke, Howard B., Máire Ní Mhaonaigh, and Raghnall Ó Floinn, eds. *Ireland and Scandinavia in the Early Viking Age.* Dublin: Four Courts Press, 1998.

Ellis, Peter Berresford. *Erin's Royal Blood: The Gaelic Noble Dynasties of Ireland.* Rev. ed. New York: Palgrave, 2002.

Jaski, Bart. *Early Irish Kingship and Succession.* Dublin: Four Courts Press, 2000.

Marsden, John. *The Fury of the Northern Saints, Shrines and Sea-Raiders in the Viking Age A.D. 793–878.* London: Kyle Cathie, 1993.

From the Norman Invasion to the Anglo-Irish Administration (1169–1534)

Clarke, H. B., ed. *Medieval Dublin.* 2 vols. Dublin: Irish Academic Press, 1990.

Cosgrove Art. *Late Medieval Ireland, 1370–1451.* Dublin: Helicon, 1981.

———, ed. *Medieval Ireland, 1169–1534.* Oxford: Clarendon Press, 1993.

Duffy, Seán. *Ireland in the Middle Ages.* New York: St. Martin's Press, 1997.

Ellis, Steven G. *Reform and Revival: English Government in Ireland, 1470–1524.* New York: St. Martin's Press, 1986.

Esposito, Mario. *Irish Books and Learning in Medieval Europe.* Aldershot, England: Variorum, 1990.

Ford, Alan, and John McCafferty, eds. *The Origins of Sectarianism in Early Modern Ireland.* Cambridge: Cambridge University Press, 2005.

Fram, Robin. *English Lordship in Ireland, 1318–1361.* Oxford: Clarendon Press, 1982.

Fulton, Helen, ed. *Medieval Celtic Literature and Society.* Dublin: Four Courts Press, 2005.

Furlong, Nicholas. *Diarmit, King of Leinster.* Cork: Mercier Press, 2006.

Gwynn, Aubrey. *The Irish Church in the Eleventh and Twelfth Centuries.* Dublin: Four Courts Press, 1992.

Lydon, James. *The Lordship of Ireland in the Middle Ages.* Dublin: Four Courts Press, 2003.

O'Neill, T. *Merchants and Mariners in Medieval Ireland.* Dublin: Irish Academic Press, 1987.

O'Riordan, M. *The Gaelic Mind and the Collapse of the Gaelic World.* Cork: Cork University Press, 1991.

Orpen, Goddard Henry. *Ireland under the Normans, 1169–1333.* Dublin: Four Courts Press, 2005.

Sheehy, Maurice. *When the Normans Came to Ireland.* Cork: Mercier Press, 1998.

Simms, Katherine. *From Kings to Warlords: The Changing Political Structure of Gaelic Ireland in the Later Middle Ages.* Woodbridge, England: Boydell Press, 1987.

Stalley, R. A. *The Cistercian Monasteries of Ireland.* New Haven, Conn.: Yale University Press, 1987.

The Planting of Protestant Power (1534–1691)

Brady, Ciaran. *The Chief Governors: The Rise and Fall of Reform Government in Tudor Ireland, 1536–1588.* Cambridge: Cambridge University Press, 1982.

———, and Jane Ohlmeyer, eds. *British Interventions in Early Modern Ireland.* Cambridge: Cambridge University Press, 2005.

Ellis, Steven G. *Ireland in the Age of the Tudors, 1447–1603: English Expansion and the End of Gaelic Rule.* London: Longman, 1998.

Ford, Alan, and John McCafferty, eds. *The Origins of Sectarianism in Early Modern Ireland.* Cambridge: Cambridge University Press, 2005.

Leniham, Pádraig, ed. *Conquest and Resistance: War in Seventeenth-Century Ireland.* Leiden, Netherlands: Brill, 2001.

Lennon, Colm. *Sixteenth-Century Ireland: The Incomplete Conquest.* Dublin: Gill and Macmillan, 1994.

McNally, Michael. *Battle of the Boyne 1690: The Irish Campaign for the English Crown.* Oxford: Osprey, 2005.

Quinn, David B. *Ireland & America: Their Early Associations, 1500–1640.* Liverpool: Liverpool University Press, 1991.

Ascendancy Ireland (1691–1800)

Carpenter, Andrew, ed. *Verse in English from Eighteenth-Century Ireland.* Cork: Cork University Press, 1998.

Connolly, Sean J. *Religion, Law, and Power: The Making of Protestant Ireland 1660–1760*. Oxford: Oxford University Press, 1992.

Dickson, David. *New Foundations in Ireland, 1660–1800*. 2d rev. ed. Dublin: Irish Academic Press, 2000.

Fagan, Patrick. *The Second City: Portrait of Dublin, 1700–1760*. Dublin: Branar, 1986.

Gough, H., and D. Dickson, eds. *Ireland and the French Revolution*. Dublin: Irish Academic Press, 1990.

Jeffares, A. Norman, and Peter van de Kamp, eds. *Irish Literature: The Eighteenth Century*. Dublin: Irish Academic Press, 2001.

Johnston-Liik, Edith Mary. *The History of the Irish Parliament 1691–1800: Commons, Constituencies and Statutes*. 6 vols. Belfast: Ulster Historical Foundation, 2002.

Mansergh, Danny. *Grattan's Failure: Parliamentary Opposition and the People of Ireland 1779–1800*. Dublin: Irish Academic Press, 2005.

McDowell, Robert B. *Ireland in the Age of Imperialism and Revolution, 1760–1801*. Oxford: Clarendon Press, 1979.

McMahon, Seán. *Wolfe Tone*. Cork: Mercier, 2001.

McMinn, Joseph. *Jonathan Swift: A Literary Life*. London: Macmillan, 1991.

Packenham, Thomas. *The Year of Liberty: The Irish Rebellion of 1798*. London: Orion, 1992.

Sheperd, Robert. *Ireland's Fate: The Boyne and After*. London: Aurum, 1990.

Stewart, Anthony Terence Quincey. *A Deeper Silence: The Hidden Roots of the United Irish Movement*. London: Faber and Faber, 1993.

Swords, Liam. *Protestant, Catholic and Dissenter: The Clergy and 1798*. Blackrock, Ireland: Columbia Press, 1997.

From the Act of Union to the Great Famine (1800–1849)

Connolly, Sean J. *Priests and People in Pre-Famine Ireland, 1780–1845*. Dublin: Four Courts Press, 2001.

Davis, Richard. *The Young Ireland Movement*. Dublin: Gill and Macmillan, 1987.

Donnelly, James S. *The Great Irish Potato Famine*. Stroud, England: Sutton, 2002.

Duffy, Peter. *The Killing of Major Denis Mahon: A Mystery of Old Ireland*. New York: HarperCollins, 2007.

Geoghegan, Patrick. *Robert Emmet: A Life*. Dublin: Gill and Macmillan, 2002.

Hollingworth, Brian. *Maria Edgeworth's Irish Writing: Language, History, Politics*. New York: St. Martin's Press, 1997.

Kinealy, Christine. *The Great Irish Famine: Impact, Ideology and Rebellion*. New York: Palgrave, 2002.

Laxton, Edward. *The Famine Ships: The Irish Exodus to America, 1846–51*. London: Bloomsbury, 1991.

McCartney, Donal. *The Dawning of Democracy: Ireland 1800–1870*. Dublin: Helicon, 1987.

———, ed. *The World of Daniel O'Connell*. Dublin: Mercier Press, 1980.

O'Brien, George. *The Economic History of Ireland from the Union to the Famine*. Clifton, Ireland: A. M. Kelly, 1972.

Ó Cathaoir, Brendan. *Famine Diary*. Dublin: Irish Academic Press, 1999.

O'Donnell, Ruan. *Robert Emmet and the Rising of 1803*. Dublin: Irish Academic Press, 2003.

Stewart, Bruce, ed. *Hearts and Minds: Irish Culture and Society under the Act of Union*. Buckinghamshire, England: Colin Smythe, 2002.

Whelan, Irene. *The Bible War in Ireland: The "Second Reformation" and the Polarization of Protestant and Catholic Relations 1800–1840*. Dublin: Lilliput Press, 2005.

The Drive for Independence (1849–1922)

Anderson, William Keys. *James Connolly and the Irish Left*. Dublin: Irish Academic Press, 1994.

Barry, Tom. *Guerrilla Days in Ireland: A First-hand Account of the Black and Tans War (1919–1921)*. New York: Devin-Adair, 1956.

de Búrea, Marcus. *The GAA: A History*. 2d ed. Dublin: Gill and Macmillan, 1999.

Dudley Edwards, Ruth. *Patrick Pearse: The Triumph of Failure*. Dublin: Irish Academic Press, 2006.

Finnan, Joseph P. *John Redmond and Irish Unity, 1912–1918*. Syracuse, N.Y.: Syracuse University Press, 2004.

Githens-Mazer, Jonathan. *Myths and Memories of the Easter Rising: Cultural and Political Nationalism in Ireland*. Dublin: Irish Academic Press, 2006.

Golway, Terry. *Irish Rebel: John Devoy and America's Fight for Ireland's Freedom*. New York: St. Martin's Press, 1998.

Hennessey, Thomas. *Dividing Ireland: World War I and Partition*. London: Routledge, 1998.

Hopkinson, Michael. *The Irish War of Independence*. Dublin: Gill and Macmillan, 2002.

Jeffery, Keith. *The GPO and the Easter Rising*. Dublin: Irish Academic Press, 2006.

———. *Ireland and the Great War*. Cambridge: Cambridge University Press, 2000.

Knirck, Jason K. *Imagining Ireland's Independence: The Debates over the Anglo-Irish Treaty of 1921*. Lanham, Md.: Rowman and Littlefield, 2006.

———. *Women in the Dáil: Gender, Republicanism and the Anglo-Irish Treaty*. Dublin: Irish Academic Press, 2006.

Loughlin, James. *Gladstone, Home Rule, and the Ulster Question, 1882–93*. Dublin/Atlantic Highlands, N.J.: Gill and Macmillan/Humanities Press International, 1986.

Matthews, P. J. *Revival: The Abbey Theatre, Sinn Féin, the Gaelic League and the Co-operative Movement*. Cork: Cork University Press, 2003.

Maume, Patrick. *The Long Gestation: Irish Nationalist Life 1891–1918*. Dublin: Gill and Macmillan, 1999.

Moran, Seán Farrell. *Patrick Pearse and the Politics of Redemption: The Mind of the Easter Rising, 1916*. Washington, D.C.: Catholic University of America Press, 1994.

O'Connor, Ulick. *Michael Collins and the Troubles: The Struggle for Irish Freedom, 1912–1922*. Edinburgh: Mainstream, 2001.

O'Day, Alan. *Irish Home Rule, 1867–1921*. Manchester: Manchester University Press, 1998.

Ring, Jim. *Erskine Childers*. London: John Murray, 1996.

Russell, Rees. *Nationalism and Unionism in Nineteenth-Century Ireland*. Newtownards, Ireland: Colourpoint Press, 2001.

Tóibín, Colm, ed. *Synge: A Celebration*. Dublin: Carysfort Press, 2005.

Townshend, Charles. *Easter 1916: The Irish Rebellion*. Chicago: Ivan R. Dee, 2006.

Turner, Michael. *After the Famine: Irish Agriculture, 1850–1914*. Cambridge: Cambridge University Press, 1996.

Vaughn, W. E. *Landlords and Tenants in Mid-Victorian Ireland*. Oxford: Oxford University Press, 1994.

Walsh, Donagh. *Ireland's Independence, 1880–1923*. London: Routledge, 2002.

Making Modern Ireland (1922–1969)

Allen, Trevor. *The Storm Passed By: Ireland and the Battle of the Atlantic, 1940–41*. Dublin: Irish Academic Press, 1996.

Augusteijn, Joost. *Ireland in the 1930s: New Perspectives*. Dublin: Four Courts Press, 1999.

Barton, Brian. *Northern Ireland in the Second World War*. Belfast: Ulster Historical Foundation, 1995.

Carroll, Joseph T. *Ireland in the War Years, 1939–1945*. Rev. ed. San Francisco: International Scholars Publications, 1998.

Carter, Carolle J. *The Shamrock and the Swastika: German Espionage in Ireland in World War II*. Palo Alto, Calif.: Pacific Books, 1977.

Daly, Mary E. *Industrial Development and Irish National Identity, 1922–1939*. Syracuse, N.Y.: Syracuse University Press, 1992.

Delaney, Enda. *Demography, State and Society: Irish Migration to Britain, 1921–71*. Liverpool: Liverpool University Press, 2000.

Doherty, Richard. *Irish Volunteers in the Second World War*. Dublin: Four Courts Press, 2002.

Fallon, B. *An Age of Innocence: Irish Culture 1930–1960*. Dublin: Gill and Macmillan, 1998.

Farrell, Brian. *The Founding of Dáil Éireann: Parliament and Nation Building*. Dublin: Gill and Macmillan, 1971.

Ferriter, Diarmiad. *Judging Dev: A Reassessment of the Life and Legacy of Eamon de Valera*. Dublin: Royal Irish Academy, 2007.

Fitzpatrick, D. *The Two Irelands 1912–1939*. Oxford: Oxford University Press, 1998.

Garvin, Tom. *1922: The Birth of Irish Democracy*. Dublin: Gill and Macmillan, 1996.

Girvin, Brian. *The Emergency: Neutral Ireland, 1939–45*. London: Macmillan, 2006.

Hand, G. J. *Report of the Boundary Commission, 1925*. Shannon: Irish University Press, 1969.

Harmon, Maurice. *Seán O'Faoláin*. London: Constable, 1994.

Johnson, David. *The Interwar Economy in Ireland*. Dublin: Economic and Social History of Ireland, 1985.

Keogh, Dermot. *Ireland and the Vatican: The Politics and Diplomacy of Church-State Relations, 1922–1960*. Cork: Cork University Press, 1995.

———, and Mervyn O'Driscoll, eds. *Ireland in World War II: Diplomacy and Survival*. Cork: Mercier Press, 2004.

Kerrigan, Gene. *Another Country: Growing Up in '50s Ireland*. Dublin: Gill and Macmillan, 1998.

Mulholland, Marc. *Northern Ireland at the Crossroads: Ulster Unionism in the O'Neill Years, 1960–69*. Houndsmill, Basingstoke, England: Macmillan, 2000.

O'Leary, Philip. *Gaelic Prose in the Irish Free State, 1922–1939*. University Park: Pennsylvania State University Press, 2004.

Porter, Raymond J. *Brendan Behan*. New York: Columbia University Press, 1973.

Puirséil, Niamh. *The Irish Labour Party, 1922–73*. Dublin: University College Dublin Press, 2007.

Purdue, Bob. *Politics in the Streets: The Origins of the Civil Rights Movement in Northern Ireland*. Belfast: Blackstaff Press, 1990.

Rafter, Kevin. *The Clann: The Story of Clann na Poblachta*. Dublin: Mercier Press, 1996.

Tobin, Fergal. *The Best of Decades: Ireland in the Nineteen Sixties*. Dublin: Gill and Macmillan, 1984.

Ward, Margaret, ed. *In Their Own Voice: Women and Irish Nationalism*. Dublin: Attic Press, 1995.

Whelan, Bernadette. *Ireland and the Marshall Plan, 1947–57*. Dublin: Four Courts Press, 2000.

Two Irish Visions in Collision (1969–2000)

Anderson, Don. *Fourteen May Days: The Inside Story of the Loyalist Strike of 1974*. Dublin: Gill and Macmillan, 1994.

Arnold, Bruce. *Haughey: His Life and Unlucky Deeds*. London: HarperCollins, 1993.

Bew, Paul. *The Making and Remaking of the Good Friday Agreement*. Dublin: Liffey, 2007.

———. *Northern Ireland: A Chronology of the Troubles, 1968–1999*. Dublin: Gill and Macmillan, 1999.

Bruce, Steve. *Paisley: Religion and Politics in Northern Ireland*. Oxford: Oxford University Press, 2007.

Coogan, Tim Pat. *The Troubles: Ireland's Ordeal 1966–1995 and the Search for Peace*. London: Hutchinson, 1995.

Cunningham, Michael J. *British Government Policy in Northern Ireland, 1969–2000*. Manchester: Manchester University Press, 2001.

Donnelly, James. "A Church in Crisis: The Irish Catholic Church Today." *History Ireland* 8, no. 3 (Autumn 2000): 12–27.

Ferguson, Harry. "The Paedophile Priest: A Deconstruction." *Studies* 84, no. 335 (Autumn 1995): 247–257.

Grant, Patrick. *Breaking Enmities: Religion, Literature, and Culture in Northern Ireland, 1967–97*. New York: St. Martin's Press, 1999.

Hesketh, Tom. *The Second Partitioning of Ireland? The Abortion Referendum of 1983*. Dun Laoghaire, Ireland: Brandsma Books, 1990.

Holland, Jack. *The American Connection: U.S. Guns, Money, and Influence in Northern Ireland.* New York: Viking, 1987.

Hopper, Keith. *Flann O'Brien: A Portrait of the Artist as a Young Postmodernist.* Cork: Cork University Press, 1995.

Horgan, John. *Mary Robinson: An Independent Voice.* Dublin: O'Brien Press, 1997.

Hughes, Eamonn, ed. *Culture and Politics in Northern Ireland, 1960–90.* Milton Keyes, England: Open University Press, 1991.

Keena, Colm. *Gerry Adams, a Biography.* Dublin: Mercier Press, 1990.

Kenny, Anthony. *The Road to Hillsborough: The Shaping of the Anglo-Irish Agreement.* New York: Pergamon, 1996.

Kirkland, Richard. *Literature and Culture in Northern Ireland since 1965: Moments of Danger.* London: Longman, 1996.

McElroy, Gerard. *The Catholic Church and the Northern Ireland Crisis, 1968–86.* Dublin: Gill and Macmillan, 1991.

McKittrick, David, Seamus Kelters, Brian Ferry, and Chris Thornton. *Lost Lives: The Stories of the Men, Women, and Children Who Died as a Result of the Northern Ireland Troubles.* Edinburgh and London: Mainstream Publishing, 1999.

Mikami, Hiroko, Minako Okamura, and Naoko Yogi. *Ireland on Stage: Beckett and After.* Dublin: Carysford Press, 2007.

Morrissey, Michael. *Northern Ireland: The Thatcher Years.* London: Zed Books, 1990.

Murray, Gerard. *John Hume and the SDLP: Impact and Survival in Northern Ireland.* Dublin: Irish Academic Press, 1998.

O'Brien, Justin. *The Modern Prince: Charles J. Haughey and the Quest for Power.* Dublin: Merlin, 2002.

O'Brynes, Stephen. *Hiding behind a Face: Fine Gael under FitzGerald.* Dublin: Gill and Macmillan, 1986.

O'Hearn, Denis. *Nothing but an Unfinished Story: Bobby Sands, the Irish Hunger Striker Who Ignited a Generation.* New York: Nation Books, 2006.

O'Mahony, T. P. *Jack Lynch: A Biography.* Dublin: Blackwater Press, 1991.

Owen, Arwel Ellis. *The Anglo-Irish Agreement: First Three Years.* Cardiff: University of Wales Press, 1994.

Rudiger, Imhof. *The Modern Irish Novel: Irish Novelists after 1945.* Dublin: Wolfhound Press, 2002.

Smyth, Sam. *Riverdance: The Story.* London: Andre Deutsch, 1996.

Taylor, Peter. *Provos: The IRA and Sinn Féin.* London: Bloomsbury, 1997.

Ireland in the Twentieth-first Century: The Pain-Filled Past Recedes at Last?

Adams, Gerry. *A Farther Shore: Ireland's Long Road to Peace*. New York: Random House, 2003.

Brady, Eoin, ed. *The Quiet Quarter: Anthology of New Irish Writing*. Dublin: New Island, 2004.

Craig, Patricia. *The Ulster Anthology*. Belfast: Blackstaff Press, 2006.

Downing, John. *Most Skilful, Most Devious, Most Cunning: A Political Biography of Bertie Ahern*. Dublin: Blackwater Press, 2004.

Holmes, Michael, ed. *Ireland and the European Union: Nice, Enlargement and the Future of Europe*. Manchester: Manchester University Press, 2005.

Kerr, Michael. *Transforming Unionism: David Trimble and the 2005 General Election*. Dublin: Irish Academic Press, 2006.

Kirbe, Peadar, Luke Gibbons, and Michael Cronin. *Reinventing Ireland: Culture, Society and the Global Economy*. London: Pluto Press, 2002.

Kuhling, Carmen. *Cosmopolitan Ireland: Globalisation and Quality of Life*. London: Pluto Press, 2007.

Lennon, Brian. *After the Ceasefires: Catholics and the Future of Northern Ireland*. Blackrock, Ireland: Columba Press, 1995.

Mackey, James P., and Enda McDonagh, eds. *Religion and Politics in Ireland: At the Turn of the Millennium*. Blackrock, Ireland: Columba Press, 2003.

MacSharry, Ray. *The Making of the Celtic Tiger: The Inside Story of Ireland's Boom Economy*. Cork: Mercier, 2000.

McCloskey, James. *Voices Silenced: Has Irish a Future?* Dublin: Cois Life Teoranta, 2001.

Millar, Frank. *David Trimble: The Price of Peace*. Dublin: Liffey Press, 2004.

Morrissey, Mike. *Northern Ireland after the Good Friday Agreement: Victims, Grievance, and Blame*. London: Pluto Press, 2002.

O'Connell, Michael. *Changed Utterly: Ireland and the New Irish Psyche*. Dublin: Liffey Press, 2001.

Peillon, Michael, ed. *Place and Non-place: The Reconfiguration of Ireland*. Dublin: Institute of Public Administration, 2004.

Smyth, Lisa. *Abortion and Nation: The Politics of Reproduction in Contemporary Ireland*. Aldershot, England: Ashgate, 2005.

Whelan, Patrick. *Cross-Departmental Challenges: A Whole-of-Government Approach for the Twenty-first Century*. Dublin: Institute of Public Administration, 2003.

INDEX

Note: **Boldface** page numbers indicate primary discussion of a topic. Page numbers in *italic* indicate illustrations. The letters *c* and *m* indicate chronology and maps, respectively.